The Children's Literature Lover's BOOK OF LISTS

JOANNA SULLIVAN

Bernice Golden, Editor

JOSSEY-BASS
A Wiley Imprint
www.josseybass.com

Published by Jossey-Bass
A Wiley Imprint
989 Market Street, San Francisco, CA 94103-1741 www.josseybass.com

Our editors have made every effort to ensure that the Web sites used in this book were accurate and current when it went to press. We recognize, however, that electronic media are ever-changing; therefore, we advise that you preview this information before sharing it with others.

Jossey-Bass books and products are available through most bookstores. To contact Jossey-Bass directly, call our Customer Care Department within the U.S. at (800) 956-7739, outside the U.S. at (317) 572-3993 or fax (317) 572-4002.

Jossey-Bass also publishes its books in a variety of electronic formats. Some content that appears in print may not be available in electronic books.

Library of Congress Cataloging-in-Publication Data

Sullivan, Joanna.
The children's literature lover's book of lists / Joanna Sullivan ; Bernice Golden, editor.—1st ed.
p. cm.
Includes bibliographical references.
ISBN 0-7879-6595-2 (pbk.)
1. Children's literature—Bibliography. 2. Children—Books and reading—United States—Bibliography. 3. Best books—United States. 4. Children's literature—Computer network resources. I. Golden, Bernice. II. Title.
Z1037.S895 2004
011.62—dc22

2003023185

Printed in the United States of America
FIRST EDITION
PB Printing 10 9 8 7 6 5 4 3

This book is for my teacher
of children's literature,
Dr. Helen Huus,
and
for all the migrant children
I've worked with
who love owning their own book.

Acknowledgments

First, I am most grateful to my editor, Bernice Golden, who initiated the idea for this book and guided me along the way. Without her hands-on involvement, list contributions, and encouragement, this book would not have been possible.

I would also like to thank M. Jerry Weiss, my longtime friend and colleague, who graciously gave his time and professional expertise to develop several lists and who enlightened me many years ago, when I was director of the Fairleigh Dickinson Reading Clinic in New Jersey, to expand my skills-only approach to include quality literature in the teaching of reading.

Louise Stearns, outstanding professor of children's literature at Southern Illinois University, generously contributed lists for this text at all grade levels. Linda Orvell, librarian at Harris Stowe College in St. Louis, also contributed to these lists, and thanks to many other contributors.

I also want to express my appreciation to Debby Kyritz, Children's Librarian at the Oradell (New Jersey) Public Library, not only for creating the series lists, but also for her keen eye in reviewing, checking, and modifying every list in the book.

I am grateful as well to Amy Sears, Head of Children's Services at the Teaneck (New Jersey) Public Library, who took time out of a busy schedule, which included her duties on the 2003 Newbery Committee, to assist in reviewing the lists, Diane Turso, Development Editor, and Tracy Antonevich and Brandi Pinnell for typing the lists.

In researching this book of lists, librarians from the Shawnee (Southern Illinois) Library system in Carterville, Illinois—including Ellen Poppet and her staff—were also very helpful and resourceful.

This book would not have been possible without the help of numerous libraries and professional organizations such as the American Library Association, the International Reading Association, the National Council of Teachers of English, the Children's Book Council, the New York Public Library, and the Monroe County (Indiana) Public Library; they very generously gave permission to use many of their recommended lists.

Other extremely valuable resources for checking book titles and providing descriptions of current books to add to the lists included Novelist, many bookstore Web sites such as www.Amazon.com, www.Barnesandnoble.com, and www.Powells.com as well as several publishers' Web sites on the Internet and print sources listed at the back of this book, such as *A to Zoo* edited by Carolyn Lima and *Best Books for Children* edited by John T. Gillespie.

For these and many other children's literature lovers who helped along the way, I would like to say thank you.

About the Author

Joanna Sullivan received her doctorate in Education from Lehigh University in Bethlehem, Pennsylvania, and recently completed a Master's degree in Conflict Resolution at Lesley University in Cambridge, Massachusetts. Presently, Dr. Sullivan is director of the Family Literacy Program for Migrant Workers affiliated with Southern Illinois University in Carbondale. She also teaches graduate courses in education, conflict resolution, and reading at Webster University in St. Louis. She is the author of 45 articles in reading, children's literature, and language arts, including articles related to conflict resolution. Dr. Sullivan has taught reading, children's literature, and language arts at Pennsylvania State University and Florida Atlantic University, and was director of the Reading Clinic at Fairleigh Dickinson University in Teaneck, New Jersey.

About This Resource

This unique resource can guide anyone interested in selecting quality children's literature from a wide variety of genres for preschoolers through grade 6. At your fingertips and under one convenient cover, it provides numerous lists of books organized by grade level, theme, and curriculum area for easy access. This book will help simplify your search through the myriad Internet home pages, teacher resources, and publications that are available today to children's literature lovers.

Whether you are using a basal reading program, a literature-based program, or a leveled reading program with your children, this all-inclusive resource is useful for extending and enriching the reading and language arts curriculum. It offers useful lists of favorite authors and illustrators, award-winning books, and books by grade level for preschoolers through grade 6. (Those book titles with an asterisk have been highly recommended by a teacher, parent, or child.) It also includes teacher and student resources, including lists of up-to-date Web sites.

A major strength of *The Children's Literature Lover's Book of Lists* is its flexibility and ease of use. It is not meant to be read in one sitting from cover to cover. Rather, it is designed to be savored in small chunks in order to gather ideas for books on different topics to use with students of various grade levels and ability levels. Each list is easily reproducible to distribute to parents, grandparents, students, and librarians as suggestions for leisure reading, reading instruction, independent reading, summer reading, reading clubs, and book reports.

This book appeals to the children's literature lover in all of us. We've attempted to select the best and most popular titles, while at the same time providing enough of an array to appeal to a broad spectrum of children's interests and to meet the needs of children reading at various levels.

It is important to remember that grade-level suggestions are neither exclusive nor rigid. We used several criteria for determining grade level. These included suggestions from teachers and librarians, publishers' recommendations, leveling suggestions from professional organizations such as the International Reading Association, standard readability formulas such as Lexile levels, state-recommended reading lists, and our own evaluation of various books' levels of difficulty and interest levels.

State curriculum standards were used to create the categories of lists and to select themes for book lists. Although standards from twelve states were reviewed, those from three states—New Jersey, Illinois, and California—were used as the basis for theme selection. These states' requirements best reflect what is required by most states. Because states mandate that various genres of quality literature be read both for enjoyment and for learning reading, mathematics, and science, this book will be especially useful.

Since teachers need to know their students' strengths and weaknesses as well as their interests, it is important to become familiar with as much children's literature as possible in order to be able to provide as rich a literacy opportunity as possible for each student. Since there is a wide range of reading levels within grades, it is wise for teachers to look beyond the grade levels when selecting books. It is for this process of selection that *The Children's Literature Lover's Book of Lists* will be a valuable resource for you.

Section One: Books for Pre-K through Grade 1

The lists in this section are divided into five categories: Favorites, Emergent Readers, Story and Picture Books, Content Area Books, and Poetry and Language. Lists include favorite classics; authors and illustrators; read-alouds; ABC books; board books; concept books; wordless picture books; predictable books; animal stories, folktales and fairy tales; books to teach social studies, science, and math, as well as books about art, music, and dance and sports; and rhymes, riddles, and poetry.

Section Two: Books for Grades 2 and 3

These lists reflect children's changing interests and the expansion of themes based upon curriculum standards. There are a growing number of series books at this level on relationships, multicultural themes, and biographies of historical figures, sports heroes, and other famous personalities. The lists include appropriate titles in the content areas, as well as lists of all-time favorites; realistic fiction; variants of the Cinderella story; books to teach content areas; poetry; and reference books.

Section Three: Books for Grades 4 Through 6

In these upper elementary grades, chapter books are more widely read and the content areas are emphasized. Biographies, historical fiction, poetry, science fiction, legends, and novels of realistic fiction on social topics are especially appealing at these grade levels. In sixth grade, students begin to look at where they fit into their family, their social circle and community, and the wider world.

Section Four: Children's Book Awards and Recommended Literature

This section includes ten lists of award-winning books, including the *Newbery Medal Winners and Honor Books*, *Caldecott Winners and Honor Books*, and the *Coretta Scott King Winners and Honor Books*. Also included are recommended lists including *Children's Choices*, *Teachers' Choices*, *ALA Notables*, *New York Public Library 100 Favorite Children's Books*, and lists of all-time favorites.

Section Five: Children's Literature Web Sites and Teacher References

This section includes lists of recommended children's literature Web sites and teacher resources.

Historical Outline of Children's Literature

A brief look at the early years of children's literature shows that books published for children did not always keep their needs or interests in mind. The literature has always been and still is, however, a clear reflection of a society's values and its expectations of children during the various time periods.

Prehistory–14th century Children learned the religious beliefs, values, and legends of their family and culture through storytelling. Tales were told around the fire by an elder, or by a wandering musician or storyteller.Thus began what we think of today as classical legends and epics, traditional mythology, and folklore.To some, we can attribute an early written version (for example, Homer); to others, we have no name for the individual who first applied quill or stylus to parchment.

15th century Gutenberg began mass production of books in the mid-1450s. Caxton established a printing press in England, and the first books for children emerged. Called "hornbooks" (printed sheets with the text mounted on a paddle-shaped piece of wood and covered with translucent cow horn), these books were meant to teach children the alphabet or daily prayers.

16th century The first attempt at creating cheap, sturdy books for children began. "Chapbooks" (poorly printed and bound between wooden boards) were hawked by traveling peddlers, or "chapmen." Most stories were based on ballads, traditional folktales, and religious stories. They were popular in both England and America.

17th century Puritan influences put morality and religious teachings above all else. Now, the traditional folktales about giants, fairies, and witches were considered inappropriate and corrupting for children. Consequently, the writing of books solely for instruction in religious and moral development began, the most famous being *The Pilgrim's Progress*. Later in the century, due to the teachings of philosopher John Locke, children's healthy mental and physical development became important. Society no longer viewed children as small adults. Charles Perrault began to collect stories such as "Puss in Boots" and "Sleeping Beauty" from French oral tradition.

18th century	Adventure stories, such as Robert Louis Stevenson's *Robinson Crusoe* and Jonathan Swift's *Gulliver's Travels* appeared. Children read *Gulliver's Travels* for its adventure, while adults read it for its daring political and social satire. John Newbery began publishing children's books in earnest.
19th century	In Germany, Jacob and Wilhelm Grimm began collecting and writing down folktales including "The Frog Prince," "Hansel and Gretel," and "Little Red Riding Hood." Hans Christian Andersen wrote "The Ugly Duckling," "The Little Mermaid," and "The Red Shoes." At this time, Randolph Caldecott and his contemporaries revolutionized the illustration of children's books, replacing crude woodcuts with elaborate color and pen-and-ink drawings showing action and vitality not seen before in children's books. After a brief return to moral instruction similar to that of the 17th century, a lighter side returned with the fantasies of Lewis Carroll (*Alice in Wonderland*) and Edward Lear (*A Book of Nonsense*). Adventure again became popular with Robert Louis Stevenson's *Treasure Island* and *Kidnapped*, Howard Pyle's *The Merry Adventures of Robin Hood*, and Jules Verne's *Twenty Thousand Leagues Under the Sea* and *Around the World in Eighty Days*. Realistic fiction emerged in the United States with Mark Twain's *Tom Sawyer* and *Adventures of Huckleberry Finn*, Anna Sewell's *Black Beauty*, and Louisa May Alcott's *Little Women*.
20th century	The style of children's books shows more variety with the increasing popularity of mysteries, science fiction, western stories, and modern realistic fiction that grow from the highly popular but heavily frowned upon dime-novel adventure genre. Great literature abounds for children.

Source: Adapted from: Norton, Donna E. *Through the Eyes of a Child: An Introduction to Children's Literature*, fifth edition. New York: Merrill/Macmillan, 1999.

Contents

Section Four: Children's Book Awards and Recommended Literature 213

CHLDREN'S BOOK AWARDS

RECOMMENDED LITERATURE

Section Five: Children's Literature Web Sites and Teacher Resources 337

SECTION ONE

Books for Pre-K Through Grade 1

1.1 Classics and All-Time Favorites

Children submerged in a rich literary environment become better readers and writers as they grow. Younger children enjoy these favorites as read-alouds; older children enjoy hearing them over and over until they begin to read the books independently.

Amelia Bedelia (series) by Peggy Parish
Are You My Mother? by P. D. Eastman
Arthur (series) by Marc Brown
Barnyard Dance! by Sandra Boynton
Blueberries for Sal by Robert McClosky
Brown Bear, Brown Bear, What Do You See? by Bill Martin Jr.
Caps for Sale by Esphyr Slobodkina
Chicka Chicka Boom Boom by Bill Martin Jr. and John Archambault
Cloudy With a Chance of Meatballs by Judi Barrett
Corduroy (series) by Don Freeman
Curious George (series) by H. A. Rey
Eloise (series) by Hilary Knight
Fables by Arnold Lobel
Frances (series) by Russell Hoban
Frog and Toad (series) by Arnold Lobel
George and Martha by James Marshall
Goodnight Moon by Margaret Wise Brown
Green Eggs and Ham by Dr. Seuss
Happy Birthday Moon by Frank Asch
If You Give a Mouse a Cookie (series) by Laura J. Numeroff
The Little Engine That Could by Watty Piper
Lyle, Lyle, Crocodile by Bernard Waber
Madeline (series) by Ludwig Bemelmans
Make Way for Ducklings by Robert McCloskey
Mike Mulligan and His Steam Shovel by Virginia Lee Burton
Millions of Cats by Wanda Gag
Mr. Brown Can Moo! Can You? by Dr. Seuss
Mufaro's Beautiful Daughters: An African Tale by John Steptoe
The Napping House by Audrey Wood
The Polar Express by Chris Van Allsburg
The Runaway Bunny by Margaret Wise Brown
The Snowy Day by Ezra Jack Keats
The Story About Ping by Marjorie Flack
The Story of Babar, the Little Elephant (series) by Jean de Brunhoff
The Story of Ferdinand by Munro Leaf
The Tale of Peter Rabbit by Beatrix Potter
Three Tales of My Father's Dragon by Ruth Stiles Gannett
Tikki Tikki Tembo by Arlene Mosel
The Velveteen Rabbit by Margery Williams Bianco
The Very Hungry Caterpillar by Eric Carle
Where the Wild Things Are by Maurice Sendak
Winnie-the-Pooh by A. A. Milne

1.2 Read-Aloud Favorites

Read-aloud favorites are written to capture the rhythm of the language. They create a tone and mood that stir young listeners; yet they are believable, with defining characters and a moving but simple plot. The books described below are among those that have stood the course of time as read-aloud favorites. (*Note:* Those books with an asterisk have been highly recommended by a teacher, parent, or child.)

Aardema, Verna. Illustrated by Petra Mathers
Borreguita and the Coyote
The little lamb outwits the coyote in this Mexican folktale.

Asch, Frank
Just Like Daddy
Little Bear loves to imitate his daddy.

Brett, Jan
*The Mitten**
A young boy drops his mitten and many animals crawl inside.

Brown, Marc
Arthur Meets the President
Arthur's essay wins the prize; now he has to read it in front of the President!

Bunting, Eve. Illustrated by Jan Brett
The Mother's Day Mice
Three little mice go looking for Mother's Day gifts. The smallest one brings home a song he heard a human sing.

Cannon, Janell
*Stellaluna**
A baby bat is separated from his mother and adopted by a family of birds.

dePaola, Tomie
*Strega Nona**
Strega Nona has a magic pasta pot. What happens when the pot overflows?

Flack, Marjorie
Angus and the Ducks
Angus is a curious Scottie who escapes from his house.

Fleming, Denise
*In the Tall, Tall Grass**
A child's-eye view of the creatures that live in the tall, tall grass.

Freeman, Don
*Corduroy**
Corduroy is a teddy bear who wants to be loved.

Heine, Helme
The Most Wonderful Egg in the World
A king must decide which of three hens laid the most beautiful egg.

Hoban, Russell. Illustrated by Lillian Hoban
Bread and Jam for Frances
Frances will only eat bread and jam. What will her parents do?

Howe, James. Illustrated by Lillian Hoban
The Day the Teacher Went Bananas
A popular teacher turns out to be a gorilla.

Johnson, Crockett
*Harold and the Purple Crayon**
Harold goes for an adventurous walk in the moonlight with his purple crayon.

Keats, Ezra Jack
Peter's Chair
Peter is not pleased that his old baby furniture has been repainted pink for his baby sister.

Kellogg, Steven
The Island of the Skog
A group of mice sail away to a remote island and make friends with the inhabitants there.

Kimmel, Eric. Illustrated by Janet Stevens
Anansi and the Moss-Covered Rock
When Anansi the spider tries to trick the other animals, Bush Deer decides to teach him a lesson.

Kraus, Robert
Whose Mouse Are You?

1.2 *continued*

Little Mouse is trying to figure out how he fits into his family.

Lee, Jeanne M.
Silent Lotus
Long ago in Kampuchea, a baby girl was born who could not hear or speak—but how she could dance!

Lionni, Leo
Swimmy
A little fish discovers a way to protect his friends from being eaten by bigger fish.

Martin, Bill, Jr. and John Archambault. Illustrated by Lois Ehlert
*Chicka Chicka Boom Boom**
Come along and join the alphabet as it attempts to climb a coconut tree!

McCloskey, Robert
Make Way for Ducklings
Mr. and Mrs. Mallard manage to raise their family in the middle of Boston.

McGovern, Ann. Illustrated by Winslow Pinney Pels
Stone Soup
When a little old lady claims she has no food to give him, a hungry young man proceeds to make soup with a stone and water.

Mercer, Mayer
There's a Nightmare in My Closet
Sometimes nightmares aren't so bad as they first appear, as the heroine of this story quickly discovers.

Rosen, Michael. Illustrated by Helen Oxenbury
*We're Going on a Bear Hunt**
Brave bear hunters travel through grass, a river, mud, and other obstacles before the inevitable encounter with the bear forces their retreat. (Ideal for acting out.)

Sendak, Maurice
Where the Wild Things Are
A naughty little boy, sent to bed without his supper, sails to the land of the wild things where he becomes their king.

Slobodkina, Esphyr
Caps for Sale
A band of mischievous monkeys steals every one of a peddler's caps while he takes a nap under a tree.

Steig, William
Brave Irene
A little girl battles a fierce snowstorm in order to deliver the duchess's ball gown.

Thayer, Jane. Illustrated by Lisa McCue
The Popcorn Dragon
Though his hot breath is the envy of all the other animals, a young dragon learns that showing off does not make friends.

Turkle, Brinton
Thy Friend, Obadiah
Obadiah is a six-year-old Quaker who lives in Colonial Nantucket.

Van Allsburg, Chris
The Polar Express
A magical train ride on Christmas Eve takes a boy to the North Pole to receive a special gift from Santa Claus.

Viorst, Judith
Alexander and the Terrible, Horrible, No Good, Very Bad Day
Alexander is experiencing one of the worst days of his life, but his mother just says, "Some days are like that!"

Waber, Bernand
Ira Sleeps Over
Ira is hesitant to take his teddy bear on his first sleep over.

Wood, Audrey
The Napping House
In this cumulative tale, a wakeful flea atop a number of sleepy creatures causes a commotion with just one bite.

Source: List 1.2 was compiled by Dr. Louise Stearns, Professor of Children's Literature at Southern Illinois University.

1.3 Favorite Author Series†

Introducing a favorite series is one way to "hook" children into reading. When reading fiction, children become familiar with the characters and await the next book to find out what has happened to their new "friends." When reading nonfiction, children feel more comfortable because the format of the books remains consistent and predictable.

PRESCHOOL

Popular read-alouds by the following authors have delighted children at the preschool level for years.

Frank Asch Little Bear is a lovable character trying to make sense of his world. Bear is especially enchanted by the moon, which is reflected in *Moonbear*, *Moondance*, *Moonbear's Shadow*, *Mooncake*, and the all-time favorite, *Happy Birthday Moon*. The sweet, simple illustrations by the author perfectly match the text.

Tana Hoban Hoban's photographs—some in color, some in black and white—illustrate familiar objects and animals as well as simple concepts including colors, shapes, and size. The pages are uncluttered with few or no words.

Shirley Hughes Young children can easily relate to the actions depicted in the pictures, such as *Hiding*, *Bouncing*, *Giving*, and *Chatting*. The realistic, charming illustrations depicting simple concepts make these books ideal for toddlers who are curious about their world.

Jan Ormerod This author's simple books portray everyday events in a toddler's life. The light, soothing illustrations feature activities all children can relate to, such as *Reading*, *Sleeping*, and *Making Friends*. Also, check out *Mom's Home*, *Dad's Back*, and *This Little Nose (has a bad cold!)*. These small-sized books are just right for little hands.

Helen Oxenbury The thirteen *Tom and Pippo* books tell about a young boy's everyday adventures with his toy monkey as they go out for a walk, meet a dog, or go shopping. In Oxenbury's seven "Out-and-About" books, children who have outgrown board books are introduced to new experiences: *The Birthday Party*, *The Checkup*, *The Dance Class*, *Eating Out*, *The Car Trip*, *The First Day at School*, and visiting *Grandma and Grandpa*. These small books feature few words per page. The humorous illustrations are perfectly geared to toddlers.

Richard Scarry For years children have enjoyed the bright busy books of animals going about their daily—and very human—lives. Huckle Cat, Lowly Worm, Mr. Frumble, and Tinder and Tanker are some of Scarry's familiar and much-loved characters. While some of his books deal with the activities of Busytown, others are concept books such as *Short and Tall* and *On the Farm*.

Nancy Tafuri This author's strength is her beautiful illustrations, especially of animals. The large, colorful pictures are readily recognizable. There are few or no words on the page. Children can travel to the farm, the jungle, or the forest in books titled *Jungle Walk*, *Follow Me*, *Do Not Disturb*, *Early Morning in the Barn*, and *Spots, Feathers, and Curly Tails*.

†For an excellent listing of individual titles in favorite author series, go to www.monroe.lib.in.us/childrens/serieslist.html.

1.3 *continued*

Shigeo Watanabe The little bear in these 13-page picture books deals with situations that will be familiar to young listeners, such as waiting for dad, getting dressed, and eating. Each story teaches some quality, such as perseverance, goal setting, and right and wrong ways to get dressed. There are just a few words and happy full-color pictures.

K THROUGH GRADE 1+

The following series focus on a single character or groups of characters.

Amelia Bedelia (*originally written by Peggy Parish, taken over by her nephew Herman Parish*) This silly, good-hearted girl takes everything said to her as literally as one can imagine. Young children ages 5–8 love the silly situations she gets herself into. These 40- to 60-page books work either as independent reading or a rousing time of read-aloud.

Angelina Ballerina (*by Katharine Holabird, illustrated by Helen Craig*) These thirteen gentle picture books show how a plucky little mouse deals with friends, family, and her love of ballet. The illustrations are exuberant and the characters are charming. For children ages 5–8.

Arthur (*by Lillian Hoban*) The often-worried chimp and his wise little sister Violet take beginning readers into their family. Charmingly written and illustrated, they are old-fashioned yet timeless. Part of the "I Can Read Book, Series 2" by HarperCollins, the books are in the 64-page range for children in grades 1–3.

Arthur (*by Marc Brown*) The always-thinking aardvark navigates the bewildering world of family, friends, and school. Little sister D.W., parents, teachers, and a host of multi-specied classmates portray Arthur's problems in a funny and sympathetic way in more than twenty-five books. Arthur is a favorite of children at the pre-K level through grade 2.

Babar (*by Jean and Laurent de Brunhoff*) For over 50 years, the elephant king, his friends, and family have been charming young readers ages 4–8. There are over twenty books, with Jean's son, Laurent, continuing the series.

Berenstain Bears (*by Stan and Jan Berenstain*) Life's lessons are taught through a family of bears: silly Papa, wise Mama, and rambunctious cubs. All sorts of social situations encountered in families—such as lying, a new baby-sitter, a new baby sister, the "gimmes," and making the team—are dealt with. This series has over thirty picture books for ages 4–7. Check out the authors' Web site at www.berenstainbears.com.

Clifford the Big Red Dog (*by Norman Bridwell*) Owned by a young girl named Emily Elizabeth, huge Clifford tries to do the right thing but doesn't always succeed. Young children can relate to his mishaps, and feel assured that everything will turn out all right. There are bright full-color illustrations and one, two, or three sentences on a page. Clifford is featured in over a dozen adventures and is a big hit with children ages 4–8.

Curious George (*originally written by H. A. Rey, later books are adapted by Houghton Mifflin from animated films*) The picture books about the curious, mischievous little monkey and his friend, "the man with the yellow hat," have been delighting children ages 4–7 for over 50 years. The original series had seven books. In the more than twenty that have been added in the familiar style, George has adventures at the parade, with a dump truck, making pancakes, and with puppies.

1.3 *continued*

Dr. Seuss Beginner Books (*by Dr. Seuss*) Rollicking rhymes and whimsical pictures make these beloved books perfect for beginning readers. Some of the titles include *The Cat in the Hat*, *Green Eggs and Ham*, and *Fox in Socks*. The 62-page books have few words on the page, but lots of smiles!

Everett Anderson (*by Lucille Clifton*) These sensitive books tell the story of a six-year-old African-American boy who lives in the city with his mother and confronts serious issues of daily living: death, a new neighbor, friendship, his mother's new boyfriend, and child abuse of a friend. Told in story rhyme.

George and Martha (*by James Marshall*) Two hippos work through misunderstandings, silly jokes, and hurt feelings to remain "the best of friends." The author of these delightful picture books has charmed children ages 5–8 with his silly pictures and sly hippo adventures for years.

Henry and Mudge (*by Cynthia Rylant, illustrated by Sucie Stevenson*) Beginning readers can enjoy the adventures of Henry and his best friend—the rambunctious, but well-meaning dog, Mudge. Childish, full-color illustrations that wander all over the page complement the short stories about family, friends, and other pets. In the 40-page range, there are over twenty books in the series for ages 5–7 and 6–8. Visit www.HenryandMudge.com.

Junie B. Jones (*by Barbara Park, illustrated by Denise Brunkus*) The irrepressible kindergartener (a first grader in later books) is a favorite of both boys and girls for her humorous antics. The nineteen books are laugh-out-loud funny. Kids who start the series read them all, anxiously awaiting the newest. The books are in the 70- to 80-page range and appeal to 6- to 8-year-olds.

Lionel (*by Stephen Krensky, illustrated by Suzanne Natti*) The 7-year-old boy is faced with many of the same problems faced by his 6- to 8-year-old readers. There's lively dialogue and lovely full-color illustrations that young readers should enjoy. The seven books in the series are 40 to 60 pages.

Little Bear (*by Else Holmelund Minarik, illustrated by Maurice Sendak*) Written and illustrated in a style reminiscent of the turn-of-the-century illustrators, these pleasant easy readers for pre-K through grade 3 are written as early chapter books. Sendak is always worth looking at, and Minarik has a gift for gentle humor and understanding the way young children think and react.

Madeline (*by Ludwig Bemelmans*) The smallest, but bravest orpheline, Madeline is just as popular with 3- to 8-year-old girls today as she was when she first debuted in the 1930s. The rhyming text, charming drawings of Paris, and the plucky heroine make these works timeless. The six original works have spawned movies, play sets, and toys.

Morris (*by Bernard Wiseman*) The goofy moose and his exasperated, short-tempered friend Boris the Bear will have kids ages 4–6 or 5–8 howling at the silly plays on words, misunderstandings, and cartoon-like illustrations. The seven readers are in the 40- to 60-page range.

1.3 *continued*

Nate the Great (*by Marjorie Weinman Sharmat with Mitchell Sharmat, Craig Sharmat, and Rosalind Weinman; illustrated by Marc Simont*) The pancake-loving detective and his dog Sludge have successfully solved over twenty cases. These 48-page books for readers ages 6–9 are one of the few easy-reader series with a first-person narrator.

Strega Nona (*by Tomie dePaola*) Grandma Witch, her bumbling assistant Anthony, and the baker's daughter, Bambolana, are real favorites. The 32-page picture books for ages 4–8 are enhanced by full-color, cartoonish illustrations and peppered with Italian words and expressions. Various publishers put out the eight books in the series, which include a "biography" of Grandma Witch and Big Anthony.

Turtle and Snake (*by Kate Spohn*) The simple vocabulary, frequent repetition, and silly, colorful pictures make these five books a hit with beginning readers. The 32-page books are for children ages 5–8.

Source: List 1.3 was compiled by Debby Kyritz, Children's Librarian at Oradell (New Jersey) Public Library, with input from Linda Orvell, Librarian at Harris Stowe College, St. Louis, MO.

1.4 Favorite Publisher Series

There are numerous publisher series that are available on multiple levels enabling readers to transition comfortably from a lower reading level to a higher level. Some publisher series spotlight favorite stories by popular authors; others feature nonfiction on topics ranging from animals, the five senses, or biographies. Ordering catalogs from these publishers is the best way to learn about the array of series that is available for children of all levels in your classroom.

I Can Read Books (*HarperCollins*) This over 200-book series was inaugurated with Minarik's *Little Bear*. The books include poetry, mysteries, humor, and historical fiction written by such authors as Arnold Lobel, Sid Hoff, Betsy Byars, and Lillian Hoban. The books are from 32 to 62 pages depending on the level. "I Can Read Chapter Books" are for the independent reader.

Bank Street Ready to Read (*Bantam Books*) The fifty-three books in the series target 4- to 8-year-olds. There are three levels: 1 (blue)—getting ready to read, 2 (red)—reading together, and 3 (yellow)—I can read it myself. The 32- to 64-page books are chosen by the Bank Street College of Education. The different types of stories include animals, bible stories, and bedtime stories. The full-color illustrations are done in a variety of styles that complement the different subjects.

Bob Books (*Scholastic*) Children ages 4–8 enjoy the unique format of these boxed sets of little books with stories and pictures to make learning alphabet sounds enjoyable. There are three levels: Level A (12 or 16 pages) focuses on the alphabet, 3-letter words, and short vowels; Level B (16 or 24 pages) has longer words, short vowels, and consonant blends; and Level C (16 or 24 pages) has words with long vowel sounds and consonant blends. Written by Bobby Lynn Maslen, there are two sets at each level.

Cat in the Hat Beginner Books (*Random House*) The blend of simple words and pictures that began with *The Cat in the Hat* continue in these delightful rhyming books. Authors Theo LeSieg, Dr. Seuss, and P. D. Eastman encourage children in these great read-alouds.

DK Readers (*Dorling Kindersley*) There are over sixty-five Level One and Level Two books of 32 pages each for children from preschool age through grade 2 or 3. All books have the stunning photographs for which the publisher is known. Level One includes books on "A Day in the Life of . . ." a builder, a doctor, a musician, a firefighter, and so on. This level also has books on the weather, dinosaurs, trucks, cats, and puppies. Level Two titles include *Castle Under Attack*, *Slinky, Scaly Snakes*, *Horse Show*, *Survivors*, and *Firefighter!*

Get Ready, Get Set, Read (*Forest House*) There are over thirty-five books in this series designed for first readers. The 18-page stories have limited sight vocabulary and introduce a "word family" (for example, "at," "ike"). Word lists, of both types of words, are included.

Hello Reader! (*Scholastic*) Over 300 fiction and nonfiction titles of 32, 40, or 48 pages each are written on four levels ranging from the emergent reader through grade 4. The series include *Hello Science Readers!* and *Hello Math Readers!* at each level, as well as favorites by Norman Bridwell, David M. McPhail, and Peggy Parish. Many titles are available in Spanish.

Ladders (*World Book*) The 30-page oversized books in this series for ages 3–6 are jam-packed with facts, full-color illustrations and photographs, vocabulary, words to know, puzzles, a true-or-false quiz with page references, a story about the book's theme, an index, and a look-and-find

1.4 *continued*

page of pictures that were discussed in the book. The pages are bright and visually appealing. The eight titles include *Tough Trucks*, *On the Move*, *Wild Animals*, *My Body*, and *Rain Forest Animals*.

Let's-Read-and-Find-Out Science Books (*HarperCollins*) The 32-page Stage 1 books are easily understood introductions to science with just enough information in them so that beginning readers aren't overwhelmed. Lots of good illustrations enhance the simple text. Franklin M. Branley, one of the authors, has written books on black holes, comets, magnets, and sunshine. Other authors include Millicent Selsam, Melvin Berger, and Aliki who cover subjects including sleep, parts of the body, recycling, and animals. Stage 2 is for grades 2–4.

Life Cycle of a . . . (*Heinemann*) The eleven titles in this series for children ages 5–7 take a look at the life cycles of familiar plants and animals such as an apple, a dog, a pumpkin, and a butterfly. The 32-page books, written by Angela Royston, have full-color photographs, a picture summary of the life cycle, a glossary of key terms, and illustrated timelines.

Machines at Work (*Child's World*) Truck books are always popular with young boys. These big, colorful books have simple text and full- or half-page photographs on each 2-page spread. The books detail the uses of the trucks and have an "up close" spread with clearly labeled parts. A glossary is included. Books on "big machines" include *Diggers, Dump Trucks, and Fork Lifts*; those on "rescue machines" include *Fire Trucks and Ambulances*; "transportation machines" include *Cars, Trains, and Airplanes*. There are also books about *Snowplows*, *Cranes*, and *Tow Trucks*.

Pets (*Heinemann*) These beautifully photographed 24-page books include the history, care, and selection of the pet. The books are endorsed by the ASPCA and appeal to children ages 5–8. Animals in the series include rabbits, cats, dogs, hamsters, and goldfish.

A Picture Book of . . . (*Holiday House*) David A. Adler's twenty introductory 32-page biographies are fully illustrated and accessible in interest and reading levels ranging from grades 2–5. Subjects include Martin Luther King Jr., Benjamin Franklin, Harriet Tubman, Helen Keller, Davy Crockett, Anne Frank, and Christopher Columbus. Adler is also the author of the popular Cam Jansen Mystery series for ages 7–10.

Read and Learn (*Heinemann*) These primary-level science resources feature clear vocabulary, facts, and full-color photographs. Different subject sets within the series are: 24-page Ooey-gooey animals, musty-crusty animals, the colors we eat, plants, candle time, and circus for 4- to 6-year-olds; and 32-page materials and plants for 5- to 7-year-olds.

Real Kid Readers (*Millbrook Press*) The three levels in this series feature full-page photographs of "real kids" in real-life situations with family and friends. Level 1 is for pre-K–1 (ages 4–6) and Level 2 is geared to K–2; both sets are in the 30-page range. Level 3 has 40–44 pages and is for grades 1–3.

Rookie Read-About Science (*Children's Press/Scholastic*) With this new series of 32 pages each, the natural world comes alive for young readers ages 4–7. Striking, full-color photos and just the right amount of text spotlight such topics as *Solid, Liquid, or Gas? The Sun's Family of Planets*, *The Earth Is Mostly Ocean*, and *Inside an Ant Colony*.

Rookie Reader (*Children's Press/Scholastic*) Rookie Readers teach concepts such as categorizing and collecting, addition, city birds, and sharing through simple stories or verse. Level A (16 books,

1.4 *continued*

24 pages) is for emergent readers and has one or two lines of text and much repetition on each page. Level B (63 books, 32 pages) is for early fluent readers in grades 1–2; these books have longer sentences, some repetition, and two or three lines of text. Level C (38 books) is for fluent readers in grades 1–2.

Sand Castle (*Abdo*) These 24-page nonfiction books are available in three levels for beginning readers. Level 1 is for pre-K–K with five or fewer words per page; Level 2 for K–1 has five to ten words per page; Level 3 for grades 1–2 has ten to fifteen words on a page. The "Write On!" set has books on punctuation and parts of a sentence. "See it. Say it. Hear it." describes long vowels. Books have a glossary and word list. Check out sandcastle@abdopub.com.

Scholastic First Biographies (*Scholastic*) Young readers learn about the important figures who shaped our country's history in this "Let's Read About . . ." series featuring Christopher Columbus, George Washington, Abraham Lincoln, and Martin Luther King Jr. Some titles are available in Spanish.

Tasty Treats (*Rourke Press*) Elaine Landau has written a 6-book set for grades K–2 about some of our favorite foods. The 24-page books have full-page color photos and include an index, glossary, "for further reading" section, and recipes. Treats covered are chocolate, pretzels, ice cream, pizza, chewing gum, and pizza.

Viking Easy to Read (*Viking*) The series has full-color illustrations and three levels of reading competency. Level 1 is "just getting started" with simple sentences and lots of repetition for ages 4–7; Level 2 is "beginning to read" with more words and longer sentences for ages 5–8; and Level 3 is "reading alone" with lively, fast-paced text for ages 6–9.

Welcome Books (*Children's Press*) This emergent-reader, nonfiction series has controlled vocabulary, easy sentences, and full-color photographs that are clearly linked to the text. Sets within this series include *celebrations*, which are about kids' favorite holidays; *city shapes*, where kids find familiar shapes in unusual settings; *communities* from all over the world; and *hide and seek* where kids look for camouflaged animals.

Windows on Literacy (*National Geographic*) This leveled set of nonfiction readers boasts the beautiful photographs for which the publisher is known. For preschoolers, *Step Up to Windows* includes wordless books, word books, and simple-sentence books. Books for emergent readers focus on a single familiar concept or topics such as: *Making Raisins*, *My Bed is Soft*, *Wood*, and *The Little Panda*. Text in first-grade readers have more variety and complexity; titles include *Hairy Harry*, *Popcorn and Candy*, *On the Moon*, and *Mud, Mud, Mud.* Later levels are for grades 2–3; topics include technology (*What's My Job*, *Tunnels*, *Going Fishing*), geography (*People Live Here*, *The Park*, *River Life*), history/culture (*In My Bag*, *Class Teddy*, *In My Family*), and economy/government (*New Clothes*, *Class Rules*, *Ice Cream for You*).

Source: List 1.4 was compiled by Debby Kyritz, Children's Librarian at Oradell (New Jersey) Public Library.

1.5 Alphabet Books

Alphabet books, along with Mother Goose rhymes, were among the first books for children. Today, there are alphabet books that are appropriate for all age groups. Alphabet books for young children usually depict simple objects, animals, or concepts that promote an awareness of letter/sound relationships. The illustrations in alphabet books for older children may depict multiple hidden pictures that begin with a letter or they may provide information on nature, culture, geography, and history. Children may enjoy creating their own alphabet books.

Object ABC's

My First ABC, Jane Bunting
Helen Oxenbury's ABC's of Things, Helen Oxenbury
A, Apple Pie, Kate Greenaway
A, B, See!, Tana Hoban
It Begins with an A, Stephanie Calmenson
On Market Street, Arnold and Anita Lobel
The ABC of Cars, Trucks and Machines, Adelaide Holl
The Alphabet Boat, George Mendoza
The Airplane Alphabet Book, Jerry Palotta
The Boat Alphabet Book, Jerry Palotta
Tomorrow's Alphabet, George Shannon

Regional ABC's

Hey Look at Me! A City ABC, Alexander Grant
A Is for Appalachia: The Alphabet Book of Appalachian Heritage, Linda Hager Pack
A Is for Asia, Cynthia Chin-Lee
Prairie Primer: A to Z, Caroline Stutson
A Prairie Alphabet, Yvette Moore
Antler, Bear, Canoe: A Northwoods Alphabet Year, Betsy Bowen
Alphabet City, Stephen Johnson
Arctic Alphabet: Exploring the North from A to Z, Wayne Lynch
A Northern Alphabet, Ted Harrison
The Jungle ABC, Micael Roberts
L Is for the Last Frontier (Discover America State by State), Carol Crane
L Is for Lincoln: An Illinois Alphabet, Kathy-Jo Wargin
A Farmer's Alphabet, Mary Azarian
A Prairie Alphabet, Jo Bannatyne-Cugnet
Pedro, His Perro, and the Alphabet Sombrero, Lynn Rowe Reed
As I Was Crossing Boston Common, Norma Farber
A Mountain Alphabet, Margaret Ruurs and Andrew Kiss
The Desert Alphabet, Jerry Palotta
The Folks in the Valley: A Pennsylvania Dutch ABC, Jim Aylesworth

Rhythmic ABC's

Chicka Chicka Boom Boom, Bill Martin Jr. and John Archambault
From Acorn to Zoo and Everything in Between, Satoshi Kitamura

Silly ABC's

Antics!, An Alphabetical Anthology (words with "ant"), Catherine Hepworth
The Alphabet from Z to A with Much Confusion on the Way, Judith Viorst
The Z Was Zapped: The Alphabet Theatre Proudly Presents the Z . . .: A Play in 26 Acts, Chris Van Allsburg
A Riddle-iculous Rid-alphabet Book, Ann Bishop
Dr. Seuss's ABC, Dr. Seuss
The Monster Book of ABC Sounds, Alan Snow
Crazy ABC, Judy Hindley
Chuck Murphy's Alphabet Magic, Chuck Murphy
Magic Monsters Act the Alphabet, Jane Bek Moncure
Circus ABC, Sue Dreamer
An Edward Lear Alphabet, Vladimir Radunsky
Dog's ABC: A Silly Story About the Alphabet, Emma Dodd

1.5 ***continued***

The Sea ABC's

Under the Sea from A to Z, Anne Doubilet
The Ocean Alphabet Book, Jerry Palotta
The Underwater Alphabet Book, Jerry Palotta
The Freshwater Alphabet Book, Jerry Palotta
Into the A, B, Sea, Deborah Lee Rose

Food ABC's

Eating the Alphabet: Fruits and Vegetables from A to Z, Lois Ehlert
Applebet, Clyde Watson
Apricot ABC, Miska Miles
What Pete Ate from A to Z, Maira Kalman
The Spice Alphabet Book: Herbs, Spices, and Other Natural Flavors, Jerry Palotta

Nature ABC's

ABC Book of Flowers for Young Gardeners, Joann Stoker
Alison's Zinnia, Anita Lobel
All in the Woodland Early: An ABC Book, Jane Yolen
The Flower Alphabet Book, Jerry Palotta
ABC Cedar: An Alphabet of Trees, George Ella Lyon
ABC in the Woods, Barbara Leonard Gibson
Wildflower ABC: An Alphabet of Potato Prints, Diana Pomeroy
Zoo Flakes: ABC, Will C. Howell

Animal, Insect, and Reptile ABC's

A Guinea Pig ABC, Kate Duke
ABC de Babar, Jean de Brunhoff
ABC Dogs, Kathy Darling
ABC Fun: Applebee Cat's Activity Alphabet, David Pelham
ABC T-Rex, Bernard Most
Alligators All Around: An Alphabet, Maurice Sendak
Alphabears: An ABC Book, Kathleen Hague
Alphabeasts: A Hide-and-Seek Alphabet Book, Durga Bernhard
Alphabet Under Construction, Denise Fleming
Amazon ABC, Kathy Darling
An Alphabet of Dinosaurs, Peter Dodson
Alphabet Zoo: A Pop-up ABC, Lynette Ruschak
Animal Action ABCs, Karen Pandell
Animal Alphabet, Gill Davies
Animalia, Graeme Base
Ape in a Cape: An Alphabet of Odd Animals, Fritz Eichenberg
Arf! Beg! Catch! Dogs from A to Z, Henry Horenstein
Aster Aardvark's Animal Adventures, Steven Kellogg
Aye-ayes, Bears, and Condors: An ABC of Endangered Animals, Neecy Twinem
Babar's ABC, Laurent De Brunhoff
Black and White Rabbit's ABC, Alan Baker
Clifford's ABC, Norman Bridwell
I Love My Anteater with an A, Dahlov Ipcar
Insectlopedia: Poems and Paintings, Douglas Florian
Maisy's ABC, Lucy Cousins
Old Black Fly, Jim Aylesworth
Paddington's ABC, Michael Bond
Pigs from A to Z, Arthur Geisert
The A to Z Beastly Jamboree, Robert Bender
The ABC Bunny, Wanda Gag
The Berenstains' B Book, Stan and Jan Berenstain
The Bird Alphabet Book, Jerry Palotta
The Butterfly Alphabet Book, Brian Cassie
The Frog Alphabet Book, Jerry Palotta
The Furry Alphabet Book, Jerry Palotta
The Icky Bug Alphabet Book, Jerry Palotta
The Little Cats ABC Book, Martin Leman
The Yucky Reptile Alphabet Book, Jerry Palotta
The Wild Animals of Africa ABC, Hope Ryden
Where Is Everybody? An Animal Alphabet, Eve Merriam
The Wildlife A-B-C: A Nature Alphabet Book, Jan Thornhill
Winnie-the-Pooh's ABC, E. H. Shepard

1.5 *continued*

Adventure ABC's

The ABC Mystery, Doug Cushman
Alphaboat, Michael Chesworth
ABC Pirate Adventure, Ida Delage
*Harold's ABC**, Crocket Johnson
*Anno's Alphabet: An Adventure in Imagination**, Mitsumasa Anno
*Astronaut to Zodiac**, Roger Ressmeyer

A Child's ABC

A, My Name Is Alice, Jane Bayer and Steven Kellogg
Baby's ABC, Bettina Paterson
Annie's ABC, Annie Owen
My First Board ABC, Jane Bunting
Alphabet Parade, Seymour Chwast
From Anne to Zach, Mary Jane Martin
Peter Piper's Alphabet: Peter Piper's Practical Principles of Plain and Perfect Pronunciation, Marcia Brown

Action and Sports ABC's

Baseball ABC, Florence Cassen Mayers
Alphabatics, Suse MacDonald
NBA Action from A to Z, James Preller
Alphabestiary: Animal Poems A to Z, Jane Yolen (editor)
Look Once, Look Twice, Janet Marshall
Firefighter's A–Z, Chris L. Demarest

Multicultural ABC's

A Is for Allah, Yusuf Islam
Ashanti to Zulu: African Traditions, Margaret Musgrove
A Caribou Alphabet, Mary Beth Owens
A Peaceable Kingdom: The Shaker Abecedarius, Alice & Martin Provensen (illustrator)
A Is for Africa, Ifeoma Onyefulu
Cajun Alphabet, James Rice
My First Arabic Alphabet Book, Siddiqua Juma
Navajo ABC: A Diné Alphabet Book, Luci Tapahonso
A Jewish Holiday ABC, Malka Drucker
K Is for Kwanzaa: A Kwanzaa Alphabet Book, Juwanda G. Ford
Afro-bets ABC Book, Cheryl Willis
Turtle Island ABC: A Gathering of Native American Symbols, Gerald Hausman
*Many Nations: An Alphabet of Native America**, Joseph Bruchac
Play Mas'! A Carnival ABC, Dirk McLean

Bilingual ABC's

From Albatross to Zoo: An Alphabet Book in Five Languages, Patricia Borlenghi
Jambo Means Hello: Swahili Alphabet Book, Muriel Feelings
Turtle Island ABC: A Gathering of Native American Symbols, Gerald Hausman

Fantasy ABC

Elfabet: An ABC of Elves, Jane Yolen
Miss Spider's ABC, David Kirk

ABC Games and Puzzles

ABCDiscovery! An Alphabet Book of Picture Puzzles, Izhar Cohen
Have You Ever Seen . . . ? An ABC Book, Beau Gardner
What's Inside?: The Alphabet Book, Satoshi Kitamura
My Little ABC Board Book, Jane Bunting
Tomorrow's Alphabet, George Shannon
My Pop-up Surprise ABC, Robert Crowther

Holiday ABC's

Not Enough Beds! A Christmas Alphabet Book, Lisa Bullard
ABC Christmas, Ida DeLage
ABC Easter Bunny, Ida DeLage
ABC Halloween Witch, Ida DeLage
ABC Santa Claus, Ida DeLage

1.5 *continued*

A Merry-Mouse Christmas A B C, Priscilla Hillman
K Is for Kwanzaa, Juwanda G. Ford
My Hanukkah Alphabet, Claudia Kunin
Chanukah A–Z, Smadar Shir Sidi
A Jewish Holiday ABC, Malka Drucker
The Christmas Alphabet,* Robert Sabuda
Z Is for Zombies, Merrily Kutner
Alligator Arrived with Apples: A Potluck Alphabet Feast, Crescent Dragonwagon
Trick or Treat, It's Halloween, Linda Lowery

Sign Language ABC

Handsigns: A Sign Language Alphabet, Kathleen Fain
Handtalk: An ABC of Finger Spelling & Sign Language, Remy Charlip, Mary Beth and George Ancona

Artistic ABC's

The ABC Exhibit, Leonard Everett Fisher
*The Graphic Alphabet**, David Pelletier

1.6 Board Books

The practicality of board books for preschoolers is apparent. These books can withstand a young child's rough treatment. As shown below, board books cover a wide spectrum of topics. Concept board books are particularly instructive for children between the ages of 3 and 5.

Alphabet Board Books

Miss Spider's ABC, David Kirk
A to Z, Sandra Boynton
A, You're Adorable, Buddy Kaye
Baseball A-B-C, James Buckley
A.B.C. An Amazing Alphabet Book, Dr. Seuss
The Alphabet Book, P. D. Eastman
Barney's Alphabet Soup, Mary Ann Dudko
My Little ABC Board Book (My First Board Books series), Jane Bunting

African American Board Books

Mama, Do You Love Me?, Barbara M. Joosse
My Aunt Came Back, Pat Cummings

Animal Board Books

Baby Beluga, Raffi
Barney's Baby Farm Animals, Guy Davis
Brown Bear, Brown Bear, What Do You See?, Bill Martin Jr.
Dinosaur Roar, Paul and Henrietta Stickland
Good Night, Gorilla, Peggy Rothmann
Have You Seen My Cat?, Eric Carle
Maisy's Favorite Animals, Lucy Cousins
Mama Mama, Jean Marzollo
Miss Spider's New Car, David Kirk
Moo, Baa, La La La, Sandra Boynton
Papa Papa, Jean Marzollo
Peek-A-Moo, Bernard Most
Touch and Feel Jungle Animals, DK Publishing
Tumble Bumble, Felicia Bond

Concept Board Books

Apples Up on Top, Theo LeSieg
The Berenstain Bears He Bear She Bear, Stan Berenstain
P. B. Bear Board Book: Colors, Lee Davis
Corduroy's Day: A Counting Board Book, Don Freeman
Go, Dog, Go: P. D. Eastman's Book of Things to Do, P. D. Eastman
Hand, Hand, Fingers, Thumb, Al Perkins
How a Baby Grows, Nola Buck
In & Out, Up & Down, Michael Smolling
Mr. Brown Can Moo! Can You? Dr. Seuss's Book of Wonderful Noises, Dr. Suess
My Many Colored Days, Dr. Seuss
The Shape of Me and Other Stuff: Dr. Suess's Surprising Word Book, Dr. Seuss

Flap Board Books

Good Friends, Lisa Ann Marsoli
The Perfect Picnic Spot, Lisa Ann Marsoli
A Walk in the Woods, Lisa Ann Marsoli
Who Hid the Honey, Lisa Ann Marsoli
Lift a Rock, Christopher Santoro
The Foot Book, Dr. Seuss
Maisy's Season: A Big Flap Book, Lucy Cousins

Pop-up Board Books

Thomas in the Snow, Rev. W. Awdry
Trouble on the Train, Rev. W. Awdry
Bob's Busy Day, Mary Man-Kong

Science Board Book

My First Body Board Book, Helen Melville (editor)

Song Board Books

My First Songs, Jane Manning
My First Nursery Rhymes, Bruce Whatley (illustrator)
Miss Mary Mack, Mary Hoberman
Daisy Says, "If You're Happy and You Know It," Jane Simmons
Hokey Pokey (Wee Sing series), Pamela Conn Beal

1.6 *continued*

Texture Board Books

Pat the Bunny, Dorothy Kunhardt
The Real Mother Goose Touch and Feel, Scholastic
Touch and Feel Wild Animals (Touch and Feel series), DK Publishing

Transportation Board Books

Richard Scarry's Cars and Trucks From A to Z, Richard Scarry
Corduroy on the Go, Lisa McCue
The Wheels on the Bus, Raffi
School Bus Board Book, Donald Crews
Planes, Byron Barton

Vocabulary Board Books

Ernie & Bert Can . . . Can You, Michael Smolling
Maisy's Favorite Clothes, Lucy Cousins
Maisy's Favorite Toys, Lucy Cousins
Wake Up and Goodnight, Charlotte Zolotow

1.7 Concept Books

PRESCHOOL

Preschoolers are very active, so the ideal books for them invite participation, song, and movement. Recently graduating from cloth books and board books, numerous concept books are available to help preschoolers bounce into reading through finger plays, rhyming, singing, and clapping.

Animals

Brown Bear, Brown Bear, What Do You See?, Bill Martin Jr.
Polar Bear, Polar Bear, What Do You Hear?, Bill Martin Jr.
Have You Seen My Cat?, Eric Carle
Have You Seen My Duckling?, Nancy Tafuri
The Very Busy Spider, Eric Carle

Everyday Experiences

Can't You Sleep, Little Bear?, Martin Waddell
Changes, Changes, Pat Hutchins
Goodnight Moon, Margaret Wise Brown
How Do I Put It On? Getting Dressed, Shigeo Watanabe
Jesse Bear, What Will You Wear?, Nancy Carlstrom
Look! Look! Look, Tana Hoban
Of Colors and Things, Tana Hoban
Red Is a Dragon: A Book of Colors, Rosanne Thong

Finger Plays

Finger Rhymes, Marc Tolon Brown
Hand Rhymes, Marc Tolon Brown
Itsy Bitsy Spider, Iza Trapani
Let's Do Finger Plays, Marion Grayson

Letters

(See List 1.5, Alphabet Books)
Black and White Rabbit's A B C, Alan Baker
Eating the Alphabet, Lois Ehlert
On Market Street, Arnold and Anita Lobel

Numbers and Counting

Butterfly Ball: A Counting Rhyme, Jane Yolen
A Cake All for Me!, Karen M. Beil
Count and See, Tana Hoban
Hippos Go Berserk!, Sandra Boynton
Mouse Count, Ellen Stoll Walsh
My First Counting Book, Lillian Moore
1, 2, 3 to the Zoo, Eric Carle
Ten Black Dots, Donald Crews
Ten Go Tango, Arthur Dorros
Ten, Nine, Eight, Molly Bang
Ten Rosy Roses, Eve Merriam
12 Ways to Get to 11, Eve Merriam
Uno Dos Tres; One, Two, Three, Pat Mora
The Very Hungry Caterpillar, Eric Carle
Who's Counting?, Nancy Tafuri

Nursery Rhymes

Here Comes Mother Goose, Iona Opie (editor)
Mother Goose: Seventy-seven Verses, Tasha Tudor
The Random House Book of Mother Goose, selected by Arnold Lobel
Tomie dePaola's Mother Goose, Tomie dePaola

Participation Books

Clap Hands, Helen Oxenbury
Here Are My Hands, Bill Martin Jr. and John Archambault
Mary Had a Little Lamb, Sara Josepha Hale
Old MacDonald Had a Farm, with pictures by Holly Berry
Over in the Meadow: A Counting-out Rhyme, Olive A. Wadsworth
Pat the Bunny, Dorothy Kunhardt
Pat-A-Cake, Moira Kemp
Peek-A-Boo, Janet and Allan Ahlberg
Peek-A-Moo, Marie Torres Cimarusti
Where's Spot, Eric Hill

1.7 ***continued***

K THROUGH GRADE 1

The following books can be used with children ages 5–7 to reinforce concepts introduced earlier. The topics of these math and science concept books include directions, shapes, opposites, light and color, bubbles, shadows, numbers, patterns, and classifying.

Bubbles, Shadows, Reflection

Soap Bubble Magic, Seymour Simon
The Bubble Factory, Tomie dePaola
Bear's Shadow, Frank Asch
My Shadow, R. Stevenson

Classifying

Bread, Bread, Bread, Ann Morris
Close, closer, closest, Shelley Rotner and Richard Olivo
Hats, Hats, Hats, Ann Morris
How Many Snails?, Paul Giganti Jr.
More Than One, Miriam Schlein
No Dodos: A Counting Book of Endangered Animals, Amanda Wallwork
Shoes, Shoes, Shoes, Ann Morris
Sorting All Sorts of Socks, Betsy Franco
Ten Little Rabbits, Virginia Grossman

Counting and Problem Solving

Anno's Counting Book, Mitsumasa Anno
Counting Cranes, Mary Beth Owens
Fish Eyes: A Book You Can Count On, Lois Ehlert
The Icky Bug Counting Book, Jerry Palotta
1 Hunter, Pat Hutchins
One Tortoise, Ten Wallabies: A Wildlife Counting Book, Jakki Wood
Ten Terrible Dinosaurs, Paul Stickland

Directions, Shapes, Opposites

Big and Small: Animal Opposites, Rod Theodorou
Chuck Murphy's Black Cat, White Cat, Chuck Murphy
Hand, Hand, Fingers, Thumb, Al Perkins
In & Out, Up & Down, Michael Smollin (illustrator)
Olivia's Opposites, Ian Falconer
Opposites (Slide 'N' Seek), Chuck Murphy
Rolie Polie Shapes, William Joyce
Sea Shapes, Suse MacDonald
Ten Apples Up on Top, Dr. Seuss
The Shape of Me and Other Stuff, Dr. Seuss
What Is Round?, Rebecca Kai Dotlich

Light and Color

The Color Box, Dayle Ann Dodds
Color Color Color Color, Ruth Heller
Color Dance, Ann Jonas
Color Everywhere, Tana Hoban
Colors (Slide 'N' Seek), Chuck Murphy
Is it Red? Is it Yellow? Is it Blue? An Adventure in Color, Tana Hoban
Mouse Paint, Ellen Stoll Walsh
My Crayons Talk, Patricia Hubbard
My Many Colored Days, Dr. Seuss
Seven Blind Mice, Ed Young

Senses and Sounds

The Berenstain Bears He Bear She Bear, Stan Berenstain
Go, Dog, Go, P. D. Eastman
How a Baby Grows, Nola Buck
Is it Rough? Is it Smooth? Is it Shiny?, Tana Hoban
Mr. Brown Can Moo! Can You?, Dr. Seuss
The Very Quiet Cricket, Eric Carle

1.8 Flap Books

The interaction that occurs through flap books is important for preschoolers. The books listed below not only hold children's attention as they guess what's under the flap, but also teach them to make predictions.

An Adventure with Billy Bunny, Maurice Pledger
Animal Train, Jane Yolen
Ants in Your Pants, Sue Heap
Big Blue Engine, Ken Wilson-Max
Big Silver Space Shuttle, Ken Wilson-Max
Big Yellow Taxi, Ken Wilson-Max
Cat in a Flap, Shoo Rayner
Catch Up, Little Cheetah!, Michele Coxon
Chicken Licken: A Wickedly Funny Flap Book, Jonathan Allen
Dinosaur's Binkit, Sandra Boynton
Everyone Hide from Wibbly Pig (A Lift-the-Flap Book), Nick Inkpen
Good Friends, Lisa Ann Marsoli
Grandmas Are for Giving Tickles, Harriet Ziefert
The Great Pet Sale, Nick Inkpen
Is There a Monster in the House?: Sesame Street, R. U. Scary
I've Lost My Yellow Zebra, Angela Brooksbank
Kipper's Sunny Day, Nick Inkpen
Lift a Rock, Find a Bug, Christopher Santoro
My Cat Tuna, Lynn Reiser
My Mommy and Me: A Lift-the-Flap Story, Laura Traser
Peekaboo Friends, Lucy Su
The Perfect Picnic Spot, Lisa Ann Marsoli
Pooh's Birthday Surprise, Lift the Flap: Learn and Grow, Kathleen W. Zoehfeld
Rotten Ralph's Thanksgiving Wish, Jack Gantos
Spot, Eric Hill
Super Silly Riddles!, Keith Falkner
Ten Scary Monsters, R. U. Scary
There's a Monster in My House, Jenny Tyler
Wake Up, Ginger, Ant Parker
A Walk in the Woods, Lisa Ann Marsoli
What's for Dinner, Ann Garrett
Who Hid the Honey, Lisa Ann Marsoli
Who's in My Bed?, Helen Piers

1.9 Pop-up Books

At one time pop-up books were mostly for entertainment; however, today there are numerous informational books in this increasingly popular format. Some of these three-dimensional books stimulate curious readers with hands-on activities involving mirrors, inset texts, and pull-outs that are guaranteed to surprise and amaze with each turn of the page. The list below includes titles for ages 4–8 and 9–12.†

Amazing Monkeys (National Geographic Action Book), Robert Hynes and Judith E. Rinard
The Amazing Pop-Up Flexible Body, David Hawcock
The Amazing Pop-Up Geography Book, Kate Petty and Jennie Maizels
The Amazing Pop-Up Grammar Book, Jennie Maizels
The Amazing Pop-Up Music Book, Kate Petty and Jennie Maizels
The Amazing Pop-Up Pull-Out Mummy Book, David Hawcock
The Amazing Pop-Up Pull-Out Space Shuttle, David Hawcock
The Amazing Pull-Out Pop-Up Body in a Book, David Hawcock
Animal Acrobats (National Geographic Pop-up Book), Robert Cremins
Animal Homes (National Geographic Pop-up Book), Alice Jablonsky
Animal Homes (National Geographic Action Book), Jeffrey Terreson and Alice Jablonsky
Animals Showing Off (National Geographic Action Book), Tony Chen
Art of Science: A Pop-Up Adventure in Art, Jay Young
Color Surprises, Chuck Murphy
Cookie Count: A Tasty Pop-Up, Robert Sabuda
Explore a Tropical Forest (National Geographic Action Book), Barbara Gibson and Donald J. Crump
Hide & Seek (National Geographic Action Book), Toni Eugene
Kwanzaa Celebration, Nancy Williams and Robert Sabuda
Little Red Riding Hood, Marjorie Priceman
The Moon Book: A Lunar Pop-Up Celebration, Arlene Seymour
The Movable Mother Goose, Robert Sabuda
The Night Before Christmas, Robert Sabuda
The Paper Dragon, Marguerite W. Davol and Robert Sabuda
Pop-Up Book of Nightmares, Gary Greenberg
Secret Treasures (National Geographic Action Book), Catherine Howell and John Buxton
The 12 Days of Christmas: A Pop-up Celebration, Robert Sabuda
Undersea Treasures (National Geographic Action Book), Peter M. Fiore
The Wheels on the Bus, Paul Zelinsky
Who Will You Meet in Scary Street? Nine Pop-Up Nightmares, Christine Tagg
Witch Zelda's Birthday Cake: A Wild and Wicked Pop-Up, Pull-the-Tab Book, Eva Tatcheva
The Wonderful Wizard of Oz, Robert Sabuda
Young Naturalist Pop-up Handbook: Beetles, Robert Sabuda and Matthew Reinhart
Young Naturalist Pop-up Handbook: Butterflies, Robert Sabuda and Matthew Reinhart

†Canadian author and illustrator Joan Irvine describes how to make original pop-up books at www.makersgallery.com/joanirvine. Ms. Irvine is the author of *How to Make Pop-Ups*, published by William Morrow (1988).

1.10 Predictable Books

"Predictable books make use of rhyme, repetition of words, phrases, sentences and refrains, and such patterns as cumulative structure, repeated scenes, familiar cultural sequences, interlocking structure and turn-around plots. These stories invite children to make predictions or guesses about words, phrases, sentences, events and characters that could come next in the story."

—Mary Jett-Simpson in *Reading Resource Book* (Atlanta: Humanics Limited, 1986)

There are eight kinds of predictable books:

1. *Chain or Circular Story:* The plot is interlinked so that the ending leads back to the beginning.
2. *Cumulative Story:* Each time a new event occurs, all previous events in the story are repeated.
3. *Familiar Sequence:* The sequence is organized by recognizable themes, such as days of the week or numbers.
4. *Pattern Story:* Scenes are repeated with some variation.
5. *Question and Answer:* The same or similar questions are repeated throughout the story.
6. *Repetition of Phrase:* The word order in a phrase or sentence is repeated.
7. *Rhyme:* Rhyming words, refrains, or patterns are used throughout the book.
8. *Songbooks:* Familiar songs with predictable elements, such as repetitive phrases.

Chain or Circular Story

(Beginning and ending of story is interlinked.)

Aardema, Verna. *Why Mosquitoes Buzz in People's Ears*
Elkins, Benjamin. *Why the Sun Was Late*
Janovitz, Marilyn. *Look out, Bird!*
Numeroff, Laura J. *If You Give a Moose a Muffin*
Numeroff, Laura J. *If You Give a Mouse a Cookie*

Cumulative

(Events are repeated throughout the story.)

Arnold, K. *Knock, Knock, Teremok!*
Bishop, Gavin. *Chicken Licken*
Brisson, Pat. *Benny's Pennies*
Burningham, John. *Mr. Gumpy's Outing*
Capucilli, Alyssa Satin. *Inside a Barn in the Country*
Carle, Eric. *Today Is Monday*
Chandra, Deborah. *Miss Mabel's Table*
Cole, Henry. *Jack's Garden*
Cole, Joanna. *It's Too Noisy*
Duff, Maggie. *Rum Pum Pum*
Dunbar, Joyce. *Seven Sillies*
Dunphy, Madeleine. *Here Is the Southwestern Desert*
Dunphy, Madeleine. *Here Is the Tropical Rain Forest*
Galdone, Paul. *Little Tuppen: An Old Tale*
Galdone, Paul. *The Old Woman and Her Pig*
Hutchins, Pat. *Little Pink Pig*
Lobel, Arnold. *The Rose in My Garden*
MacDonald, Elizabeth. *Mike's Kite*
McLeish, Kenneth. *Chicken Licken*
Neitzel, S. *The Bag I'm Taking to Grandma's*
Ormerod, Jan. *The Story of Chicken Licken*
Oxenbury, Helen. *It's My Birthday*
Pizer, Abigail. *It's a Perfect Day*
Polacco, Patricia. *In Enzo's Splendid Gardens*

1.10 *continued*

Sloat, Teri. *The Thing That Bothered Farmer Brown*
Tolstoy, Alexei. *The Great Big Enormous Turnip*
Waddell, Martin. *The Pig in the Pond*
West, Colin. *"Buzz, Buzz, Buzz," Went Bumblebee*
West, Colin. *Have You Seen the Crocodile?*
West, Colin. *"I Don't Care!" Said the Bear*
West, Colin. *"Not Me," Said the Monkey*
Zernach, Harve. *The Judge*

Familiar Sequence (days of week, months of year, etc.)

Carle, Eric. *Today Is Monday*
Kraus, Robert. *Come Out and Play, Little Mouse*
Sendak, Maurice. *Chicken Soup With Rice*
Shiefman, Vicky. *Sunday Potatoes, Monday Potatoes*
Ward, Cindy. *Cookie's Week*

Familiar Sequence (numbers)

Bucknall, Caroline. *One Bear All Alone*
Wood, Jakki. *Moo, Moo, Brown Cow*

Pattern Story

(Scenes are repeated with variations.)

Banks, Kate. *Peter and the Talking Shoes*
Banks, Kate. *Spider, Spider*
Bender, Robert. *A Most Unusual Lunch*
Brown, Margaret Wise. *The Runaway Bunny*
De Regniers, Beatrice Schenk. *Going for a Walk*
Domanska, Janina. *Little Red Hen*
Dunbar, Joyce. *Four Fierce Kittens*
Dunbar, Joyce. *Seven Sillies*
Gag, Wanda. *Millions of Cats*
Galdone, Paul. *The Gingerbread Boy*
Galdone, Paul. *Little Red Hen*
Galdone, Paul. *The Three Bears*
Galdone, Paul. *The Three Billy Goats Gruff*
Hutchins, Pat. *Little Pink Pig*
Jennings, Sharon. *Jeremiah and Mrs. Ming*
Kalan, Robert. *Stop, Thief!*
Krauss, Ruth. *The Carrot Seed*
Maris, Ron. *Are You There Bear?*
Maris, Ron. *I Wish I Could Fly*
McNaughton, C. *Suddenly!*
Nodset, Joan L. *Who Took the Farmer's Hat?*
Patron, Susan. *Dark Cloud Strong Breeze*
Wing, Natasha. *Hippity Hop, Frog on Top*
Zemach, Margot. *The Little Red Hen*

Question and Answer

Coxe, Molly. *Whose Footprints?*
Greeley, Valerie. *Where's My Share?*
Guy, Ginger Foglesong. *Black Crow, Black Crow*
Janovitz, Marilyn. *Is it Time?*
Kraus, Robert. *Whose Mouse Are You?*
Martin, Bill, Jr. *Brown Bear, Brown Bear, What Do You See?*

Repetition of Phrase

Alborough, Jez. *Watch Out! Big Bro's Coming!*
Archambault, John & Bill Martin Jr. *A Beautiful Feast for a Big King Cat*
Brown, Margaret Wise. *The Important Book*
Brown, Margaret Wise. *Goodnight Moon*
Brown, Ruth. *A Dark, Dark Tale*
Butler, Dorothy. *A Happy Tale*
Carle, Eric. *Do You Want to Be My Friend?*
Carle, Eric. *Have You Seen My Cat?*
Coxe, Molly. *Whose Footprints?*
Date, Penny. *Ten Out of Bed*
Day, David. *King of the Woods*
De Regniers, Beatrice Schenk. *Going for a Walk*
De Regniers, Beatrice Schenk. *How Joe the Bear and Sam the Mouse Got Together*
Dunbar, Joyce. *Four Fierce Kittens*
Gordon, Jeffrie Ross. *Two Badd Babies*
Greeley, Valerie. *Where's My Share?*
Grindley, Sally. *Knock, Knock! Who's There?*
Guarino, Deborah. *Is Your Mama a Llama?*
Guy, Ginger Foglesong. *Black Crow, Black Crow*

1.10 *continued*

Harnsa, Bobbie. *Dirty Larry*
Hayes, Sarah. *This Is the Bear and the Picnic Lunch*
Hennessy, B. G. *Jake Baked the Cake*
Hoberman, Mary Ann. *A House Is a House for Me*
Hutchins, Pat. *Little Pink Pig*
Kahn, Joan. *You Can't Catch Me*
Kalan, Robert. *Stop, Thief!*
King, Bob. *Sitting on the Farm*
Knowles, Tizzie. *No, Barnaby*
Kraus, Robert. *Come Out and Play, Little Mouse*
Kraus, Robert. *Where Are You Going, Little Mouse?*
Krauss, Ruth. *Big and Little*
Lindbergh, Reeve. *There's a COW in the Road!*
Lockwood, Primrose and Clara Vulliarny. *Cat Boy!*
MacDonald, Elizabeth. *Mike's Kite*
Martin, Bill, Jr. *Brown Bear, Brown Bear, What Do You See?*
McGilvray, Richard. *Don't Climb Out of the Window Tonight*
Masurel, Claire & Marie H. Henry. *Good Night!*
Masurel, Claire. *No, No, Titus!*
Most, Bernard. *If the Dinosaurs Came Back*
Pizer, Abigail. *It's a Perfect Day*
Pryor, Ainslie. *The Baby Blue Cat Who Said No*
Rathmann, Peggy. *Good Night, Gorilla*
Rogers, Paul & Emma. *What's Wrong, Tom?*
Sawicki, Nonna Jean. *The Little Red House*
Sendak, Maurice. *Chicken Soup With Rice*
Serfozo, Mary. *Who Said Red?*
Shannon, George. *Dance Away*
Shannon, George. *The Piney Woods Peddler*
Shieftman, Vicky. *Sunday Potatoes, Monday Potatoes*
Sloat, Teri. *The Thing That Bothered Farmer Brown*
Tafuri, Nancy. *Have You Seen My Duckling?*
Van Laan, Nancy. *A Mouse in My House*
Van Laan, Nancy. *Possum Come A-Knockin'*
Waddell, Martin. *Sailor Bear*
Watanbe, Shigeo. *How Do I Put It On?*
West, Colin. *"Buzz, Buzz, Buzz," Went Bumblebee*
West, Colin. *Have You Seen the Crocodile?*
West, Colin. *"Hello, Great Big Bullfrog!"*
West, Colin. *I Bought My Love a Tabby Cat*
West, Colin. *"I Don't Care!" Said the Bear*
West, Colin. *"Not Me," Said the Monkey*
Wing, Natasha. *Hippity Hop, Frog on Top*
Wolkstein, Diane. *Step by Step*
Wong, O. *From My Window*
Wood, Audrey. *Silly Sally*
Wood, Jakki. *Moo, Moo, Brown Cow*
Wylie, Joanne & David. *A Big Fish Story*
Wylie, Joanne & David. *A More or Less Fish Story*
Zamorano, Ana. *Let's Eat!*

Rhyme

Ackerman, Karen. *This Old House*
Adlerman, Daniel. *Africa Calling: Nighttime Failing*
Archambault, John & Bill Martin Jr. *A Beautiful Feast for a Big King Cat*
Brooke, Leslie. *Johnny Crow's Garden*
Capucilli, Alyssa Satin. *Inside a Barn in the Country*
Carlstrom, Nancy White. *Rise and Shine*
Chandra, Deborah. *Miss Mabel's Table*
Dunbar, Joyce. *Four Fierce Kittens*
Fleming, Denise. *Barnyard Banter*
Florian, Douglas. *A Beach Day*
Florian, Douglas. *A Summer Day*
Florian, Douglas. *A Winter Day*
Gag, Wanda. *The ABC Bunny*
Guarino, Deborah. *Is Your Mama a Llama?*
Hayes, Sarah. *This Is the Bear and the Picnic Lunch*
Hennessy, B. G. *Jake Baked the Cake*
Hoberman, Mary Ann. *A House Is a House for Me*
Janovitz, Marilyn. *Is it Time?*
Jaques, F. *There Once Was a Puffin*
Leuck, L. *Sun Is Falling, Night Is Calling*

1.10 *continued*

Levine, Abby. *You Push, I Ride*
Lindbergh, Reeve. *There's a COW in the Road!*
Mandel, Peter. *Red Cat, White Cat*
Marzollo, J. *Sun Song*
Patron, Susan. *Dark Cloud Strong Breeze*
Pomerantz, Charlotte. *Flap Your Wings and Try*
Punnett, Dick. *Our Brat Cat*
Robinson, M. *The Zoo at Night*
Samton, Sheila White. *Beside the Bay*
Shaw, Nancy. *Sheep in a Shop*
Shaw, Nancy. *Sheep on a Ship*
Siebert, Diane. *Train Song*
Sloat, Teri. *The Thing That Bothered Farmer Brown*
Stickland, Paul. *One Bear, One Dog*
Wahl, J. *Cats and Robbers*
Weiss, Nicki. *Sun Sand Sea Sail*
Wellington, M. *Night House Bright House*
West, Colin. *I Bought My Love a Tabby Cat*
Winthrop, Elizabeth. *Shoes*
Wood, Audrey. *Silly Sally*
Zemach, Harve. *The Judge*

Songbook

Emberley, Barbara. *One Wide River to Cross*
Hoffman, Hilde. *The Green Grass Grows All Around*
Keats, Ezra Jack. *Over in the Meadow*
King, Bob. *Sitting on the Farm*
Langstaff, John M. *Over in the Meadow*
Langstaff, John M. *Soldier, Soldier, Won't You Marry Me?*
Turner, Gwenda. *Over on the Farm*
Zuromskis, Diane. *The Farmer in the Dell*

Source: List 1.10 was compiled by Virginia Richey, Children's Department Manager, Monroe County (Indiana) Public Library. There are over thirty outstanding children's literature booklists on the Monroe County Public Library Children's Department Web site at www.monroe.lib.in.us/childrens/children_booklists.html. Used with permission.

1.11 Sound Awareness Books

Auditory discrimination, one of the basic reading skills, is introduced through sound awareness books. These books use words with the same initial sounds as well as rhyming words to reinforce the concept of letter/sound relationships. Many of the books are best shared as read-alouds.

VOWEL SOUND AWARENESS BOOKS

Short A

Anno, Mitsumasa. *Anno's Alphabet: An Adventure in Imagination*
Anno, Mitsumasa. *Anno's Counting Book*
Asch, Frank. *Just Like Daddy*
Balian, Lorna. *Amelia's Nine Lives*
Barrett, Judi. *Animals Should Definitely Not Act Like People*
Barrett, Judi. *Animals Should Definitely Not Wear Clothing*
Cameron, Polly. *"I Can't," Said the Ant*
Carratello, Patty. *My Cap*
Flack, Marjorie. *Angus and the Cat*
Flack, Marjorie. *Ask Mr. Bear*
Fox, Mem. *Arabella the Smallest Girl in the World*
Gag, Wanda. *Millions of Cats*
Gibbons, Gail. *The Seasons of Arnold's Apple Tree*
Griffith, Helen. *Alex and the Cat*
Guilfoile, Elizabeth. *Nobody Listens to Andrew*
Kent, Jack. *The Fat Cat*
Most, Bernard. *There's an Ant in Anthony*
Nodset, Joan L. *Who Took the Farmer's Hat?*
Orbach, Ruth. *Apple Pigs*
Robins, Joan. *Addie Meets Max*
Schmidt, Karen L. *The Gingerbread Man*
Seeger, Pete. *Abiyoyo*
Seuss, Dr. *The Cat in the Hat*

Long A

Aardema, Verna. *Bringing the Rain to Kapiti Plain*
Bang, Molly. *The Paper Crane*
Burton, Virginia Lee. *Katy and the Big Snow*
Carratello, Patty. *Skate, Kate, Skate!*
Henkes, Kevin. *Sheila Rae, the Brave*
Hines, Anna G. *Taste the Raindrops*
Howard, Elizabeth. *The Train to Lulu's*
McPhail, David. *The Train*

Long and Short A

Aliki. *Jack and Jake*
Slobodkina, Esphyr. *Caps for Sale*

Short E

Carratello, Patty. *Brett, My Pet*
Demi. *The Empty Pot*
dePaola, Tomie. *Little Grunt & the Big Egg*
Galdone, Paul. *The Little Red Hen*
Kraus, Robert. *The Happy Egg*
McPhail, David. *Emma's Pet*
Ness, Evaline. *Yeck Eck*
Parkes, Brenda. *The Enormous Watermelon*
Shecter, Ben. *Hester the Jester*
Tsuchiya, Yukio. *Faithful Elephants*
Wing, Henry Ritchet. *Ten Pennies for Candy*
Wood, Audrey. *Elbert's Bad Word*

Long E

Archambault, John. *Counting Sheep*
dePaola, Tomie. *Mice Squeak, We Speak*
Galdone, Paul. *Little Bo-Peep*
Gordon, Jeffie R. *Six Sleepy Sheep*
Hughes, Shirley. *An Evening at Alfte's*
Keller, Holly. *Ten Sleepy Sheep*
Martin, Bill, Jr., *Brown Bear, Brown Bear, What Do You See?*
Oppenheim, Joanne. *Have You Seen Trees?*
Peet, Bill. *The Kweeks of Kookatumdee*
Shaw, Nancy. *Sheep in a Jeep*
Shaw, Nancy. *Sheep on a Ship*
Wellington, Monica. *The Sheep Follow*

1.11 *continued*

Long and Short E

Keller, Holly. *The Sleepy Sheep*
Soule, Jean Conder. *Never Tease a Weasel*

Short I

Anno, Mitsumasa. *In Shadowland*
Brown, Marc. *The Important Book*
Brown, Ruth. *If At First You Do Not See*
Carratello, Patty. *Will Bill?*
Hoban, Tana. *Is It Red? Is It Yellow? Is It Blue?*
Hoban, Tana. *Is It Rough? Is It Smooth? Is It Shiny?*
Hutchins, Pat. *Titch*
Keats, Ezra Jack. *Whistle for Willie*
Lionni, Leo. *Inch by Inch*
Lionni, Leo. *It's Mine*
Lionni, Leo. *Swimmy*
Lobel, Arnold. *Small Pig*
Maccarone, Grace. *Itchy, Itchy Chicken Pox*
McPhail, David. *Fix-It*

Long I

Berenstain, Stan & Jan. *The Bike Lesson*
Carlson, Nancy. *I Like Me*
Carratello, Patty. *Mice on Ice*
Cole, Sheila. *When the Tide Is Low*
Hazen, Barbara S. *Tight Times*
Kirk, David. *Miss Spider* (series)
Steig, William. *Brave Irene*
Waber, Bernard. *Ira Sleeps Over*

Short O

Benchley, Nathaniel. *Oscar Otter*
Carratello, Patty. *Dot's Pot*
Crews, Donald. *Ten Black Dots*
Emberley, Barbara. *Drummer Hoff*
Hawkins, Cohn & Jacqui. *Tog the Dog*
McKissack, Patricia C. *Flossie and the Fox*
Peppe, Rodney. *Odd One Out*
Seuss, Dr. *Fox in Socks*
Seuss, Dr. *Hop on Pop*

Long O

Cole, Brock. *The Giant's Toe*
dePaola, Tomie. *Joe and the Snow*
Gerstein, Mordicai. *Roll Over!*
Johnston, Tony. *The Adventures of Mole and Troll*
Tresselt, Alvin R. *White Snow, Bright Snow*
Wadsworth, Olive A. *Over in the Meadow*

Short U

Abolafia, Yossi. *My Three Uncles*
Anno, Mitsumasa. *Upside-Downers*
Carratello, Patty. *My Truck and My Pup*
Euvremer, Teryl. *The Sun's Up*
Feczko, Kathy. *Umbrella Parade*
Gibbons, Gail. *Sun Up, Sun Down*
Marshall, James. *The Cut-Ups* (series)
Monsell, Mary E. *Underwear*
Pinkwater, Daniel. *Roger's Umbrella*
Prelutsky, Jack. *The Baby Uggs Are Hatching*
Ryder, Joanne. *Under the Moon*
Thorne, Jenny. *My Uncle*
Udry, Janice Mae. *Thump and Plunk*
Yashima, Taro. *Umbrella*
Yolen, Jane. *Sleeping Ugly*

Long U

Carratello, Patty. *Duke the Blue Mule*
Coville, Bruce & Katherine. *Sarah's Unicorn*
Segal, Lore. *Tell Me a Trudy*

1.11 ***continued***

CONSONANT AWARENESS: B BOOK LIST

Allen, Pamela. *Bertie and the Bear*
Ancona, George. *It's a Baby!*
Barton, Byron. *Boats*
Barton, Byron. *Buzz, Buzz, Buzz*
Berenstain, Stan & Jan. *The B Book*
Brown, Marc. *Benji's Blanket*
Brown, Marc. *Big Red Barn*
Cohen, Miriam. *Best Friends*
dePaola, Tomie. *Big Anthony and the Magic Ring*
Freeman, Donald. *Beady Bear*
Gans, Roma. *Bird Talk*
Gibbons, Gail. *Boat Book*
Martin, Bill, Jr. *Brown Bear, Brown Bear, What Do You See?*
Rice, Eve. *Benny Bakes a Cake*
Yektai, Niki. *Bears in Pairs*

Bl Book List

Burningham, John. *The Blanket*
Cooney, Nancy. *The Blanket That Had to Go*
Crews, Donald. *Ten Black Dots*
dePaola, Tomie. *Legend of Bluebonnet*
James, Simon. *Dear Mr. Blueberry*
Kraus, Robert. *Leo the Late Bloomer*
Kraus, Robert. *Mert the Blurt*
Macaulay, David. *Black and White*
MacDonald, Amy. *Rachel Fister's Blister*

Br Book List

Bishop, Claire H. *The Five Chinese Brothers*
De Regniers, Beatrice. *May I Bring a Friend?*
Dunrea, Oliver. *Fergus and Bridey*
Hoban, Russell. *Bread and Jam for Frances*
Mein, Elonore. *Brave Daniel*
Machotka, Hana. *Breathtaking Noses*
Margolis, Richard. *Secrets of a Small Brother*
Martin, Bill, Jr. *Brown Bear, Brown Bear, What Do You See?*
Steig, William. *Brave Irene*

C BOOK LIST

Carle, Eric. *Have You Seen My Cat?*
Freeman, Don. *A Pocket for Corduroy*
Gag, Wanda. *Millions of Cats*
Gray, William R. *Camping Adventures*
Krauss, Ruth. *The Carrot Seed*
Lionni, Leo. *A Color of His Own*
McMillan, Bruck. *Counting Wildflowers*
Oxenbury, Helen. *The Car Trip*
Robart, Rose. *The Cake That Mack Ate*
Seuss, Dr. *The Cat in the Hat*
Simon, Norma. *Cats Do, Dogs Don't*
Slobodkina, Esphyr. *Caps for Sale*

Ch Book List

Ginsburg, Mirra. *The Chick & the Duckling*
Ginsburg, Mirra. *The Chinese Mirror*
Heller, Ruth. *Chickens Aren't the Only Ones*
Hutchins, Pat. *Changes, Changes*
Keats, Ezra Jack. *Peter's Chair*
Little, Lessie. *Children of Long Ago*
Luton, Mildred. *Little Chicks' Mothers & All Others*
Martin, Bill, Jr. & Archambault, John. *Chicka Chicka Boom Boom*
Pomerantz, Charlotte. *The Chalk Doll*
Ryder, Joanne. *Chipmunk Song*
Sendak, Maurice. *Chicken Soup With Rice*
Weiss, Nicki. *Chuckie*
Williams, Vera B. *A Chair for My Mother*

Cl Book List

Bridwell, Norman. *Clifford* (series)
dePaola, Tomie. *Charlie Needs a Cloak*
dePaola, Tomie. *The Cloud Book*
Greene, Carol. *Hi, Clouds*
Hutchins, Pat. *Clocks & More Clocks*
Mayer, Mercer. *There's a Nightmare in My Closet*
Miller, Edna. *Mousekin's Close Call*
Oxenbury, Helen. *Clap Hands*

1.11 ***continued***

Cr Book List

Bang, Molly. *The Paper Chase*
Carle, Eric. *The Very Quiet Cricket*
Caudill, Rebecca. *A Pocketful of Cricket*
Devlin, Wende & Harry. *Cranberry Thanksgiving*
Isadora, Rachel. *At the Crossroads*
Jorgensen, Gail. *Crocodile Beat*
Lionni, Leo. *Six Crows*
McDonald, Megan. *Is This a House for Hermit Crab?*
West, Colin. *Have you Seen the Crocodile?*
Yashima, Taro. *Crow Boy*

D BOOK LIST

Aliki. *Digging Up Dinosaurs*
Cohen, Miriam. *Jim's Dog Muffins*
Freedman, Sally. *Devin's New Bed*
Freeman, Don. *Dandelion*
Gibbons, Gail. *Dinosaurs, Dragonflies, & Diamonds*
Hankin, Rebecca. *I Can Be a Doctor*
Hoban, Tana. *Dig, Drill, Dump, Fill*
Hoff, Sid. *Danny and the Dinosaur*
Hughes, Shirley. *Dogger*
Hutchins, Pat. *The Doorbell Rang*
McCloskey, Robert. *Make Way for Ducklings*
Simon, Norma. *Cats Do, Dogs Don't*
Steig, William. *Dr. Desoto*
Wildsmith, Brian. *Daisy*
Zion, Gene. *Harry the Dirty Dog*

Dr Book List

dePaola,Tomie. *The Knight & the Dragon*
Emberley, Ed. *Drummer Hoff*
Gannett, Ruth S. *My Father's Dragon*
James, Betsy. *The Dream Stair*
Kent, Jack. *There's No Such Thing as a Dragon*
Stevenson, James. *The Dreadful Day*
Surat, Michele M. *Angel Child, Dragon Child*
Wildsmith, Brian. *My Dream*

F BOOK LIST

Brown, Margaret Wise. *Four Fur Feet*
Cohen, Miriam. *First Grade Takes a Test*
Cohen, Miriam. *Starring First Grade*
Coxe, Molly. *Whose Footprints*
Elkin, Benjamin. *Six Foolish Fishermen*
De Regniers, Beatrice Schenk. *Catch a Little Fox: Variations on a Folk Rhyme*
Fox, Mem. *Hattie and the Fox*
Hutchins, Pat. *Don't Forget the Bacon!*
Hutchins, Pat. *Follow That Bus!*
Ipcar, Dahlov Zorach. *The Biggest Fish in the Sea*
Lionni, Leo. *Fish Is Fish*
McPhail, David. *Farm Morning*
Palmer, Helen. *A Fish Out of Water*
Peet, Bill. *Farewell to Shady Glade*
Pfister, Marcus. *The Rainbow Fish*
Seuss, Dr. *One Fish, Two Fish*

Fl Book List

Bunting, Eve. *Fly Away Home*
Eastman, Philip D. *Flap Your Wings*
Gelman, Rita G. *Why Can't I Fly?*
Heller, Ruth. *The Reason for a Flower*
McKissack Patricia C. *Flossie and the Fox*
Peet, Bill. *Merle the High Flying Squirrel*
Pomerantz, Charlotte. *Flap Your Wings and Try*

Fr Book List

Aliki. *We Are Best Friends*
Anglund, Joan W. *A Friend Is Someone Who Likes You*
Carle, Eric. *Do You Want to Be My Friend?*
Cohen, Miriam. *Will I Have a Friend?*
Cohen, Miriam. *Best Friends*

1.11 *continued*

Crews, Donald. *Freight Train*
Delton, Judy. *Two Good Friends*
De Regniers, Beatrice. *May I Bring a Friend?*
Gross, Janet & Harster, Jerome. *It Didn't Frighten Me*
Heide, Florence Parry & VanClief, Sylvia Worth. *That's What Friends Are For*
Heine, Helme. *Friends*
Hoban, Russell. *Bread and Jam for Frances*
Lionni, Leo. *Frederick*
Lobel, Arnold. *Frog and Toad* (series)
McNaughton, Colin. *Making Friends With Frankenstein*
Oxenbury, Helen. *Friends*

G BOOK LIST

Hard G Book List

Baylor, Byrd. *Guess Who My Favorite Person Is?*
Burningham, John. *Mr. Gumpy's Motor Car*
Cohen, Miriam. *No Good in Art*
Delaney, Antoinette. *The Gunnywolf*
Delton, Judy. *Two Good Friends*
Douglas, Barbara. *Good as New!*
Miller, Edna. *Mousekin's Golden House*
Rice, Eve. *Goodnight, Goodnight*
Seuss, Dr. *I Am Not Going to Get Up Today!*
Showers, Paul. *Where Does the Garbage Go?*

Soft G Book List

Arno, Enrico. *The Gingerbread Man*
Berger, Melvin. *Germs Make Me Sick*
Galdone, Paul. *The Gingerbread Boy*
Joyce, William. *George Shrinks*
Keller, Holly. *Geraldine's Blanket*
Lord, John V. *The Giant Jelly Sandwich*
Marshall, James. *George & Martha One Fine Day*

Gl Book List

Peet, Bill. *Farewell to Shady Glade*

Gr Book List

Berger, Barbara H. *Grandfather Twilight*
Buckley, Helen E. *Grandfather and I*
Buckely, Helen E. *Grandmother and I*
Buckley, Richard. *The Greedy Python*
Carle, Eric. *The Grouchy Ladybug*
dePaola, Tomie. *Little Grunt & the Big Egg*
Ehlert, Lois. *Growing Vegetable Soup*
Hoffman, Henrich. *The Green Grass Grows All Around*
Hutchins, Pat. *You'll Soon Grow Into Them, Titch*
Krauss, Ruth. *Growing Story*
Spier, Peter. *Gobble, Growl, Grunt*

H BOOK LIST

Aliki. *My Hands*
Anno, Mitsumasa. *Anno's Hat Tricks*
Burton, Virginia Lee. *The Little House*
Calhoun, Mary. *Hot Air Henry*
Carle, Eric. *A House for Hermit Crab*
Galdone, Paul. *Henny Penny*
Fox, Mem. *Hattie and the Fox*
Hoberman, Mary Ann. *A House Is a House for Me*
Hurd, Edith. *Hurry, Hurry*
Morris, Ann. *Hats, Hats, Hats*
Morris, Ann. *Houses and Homes*
Seuss, Dr. *Hop on Pop*
Stow, Jenny. *The House That Jack Built*
Wood, Audrey. *Heckedy Peg*
Ziefert, Harriet. *Hurry Up, Jessie*
Zion, Gene. *Harry the Dirty Dog*

1.11 ***continued***

J BOOK LIST

Ahlberg, Janet & Allan. *The Jolly Postman*
Aliki. *Jack and Jake*
Arnold, Tedd. *No Jumping on the Bed*
Coleridge, Sara. *January Brings the Snow*
Degen, Bruce. *Jamberry*
Galdone, Paul. *Jack and the Beanstalk*
Kalan, Robert. *Jump, Frog, Jump*
Keats, Ezra Jack. *Jenny's Hat*
Lord, John V. *The Giant Jam Sandwich*
Mayer, Mercer. *Just Grandpa and Me*
Walsh, Ellen S. *Hop Jump*

K BOOK LIST

Bridwell, Norman. *Kangaroo Stew*
dePaola, Tomie. *The Kids' Cat Book*
Fox, Mem. *Koala Lou*
Heller, Ruth. *Kites Sail High*
Holl, Adelaide. *One Kitten for Kim*
Keats, Ezra Jack. *Kitten for a Day*
Patterson, Francine. *Koko's Kitten*
Payne, Emmy. *Katy No-Pocket*
Selsam, Millicent E. *How Kittens Grow*
Yashima, Taro. *Momo's Kitten*

L BOOK LIST

Giff, Patricia R. *Lazy Lions, Lucky Lambs*
Guarino, Deborah. *Is Your Mama a Llama?*
Cohen, Miriam. *Liar, Liar, Pants on Fire*
Keats, Ezra Jack. *A Letter to Amy*
Kraus, Robert. *Leo the Late Bloomer*
Lionni, Leo. *Little Blue and Little Yellow*
Lobel, Arnold. *Lucille*
Piper, Watty. *The Little Engine That Could*
Rice, Eve. *Oh, Lewis*
Rockwell, Anne. *I Like the Library*
Showers, Paul. *The Listening Walk*
Waber, Bernard. *Loveable Lyle*
Waber, Bernard. *Lyle, Lyle, Crocodile*

M BOOK LIST

Asch, Frank. *Mooncake*
Barrett, Judi. *Cloudy With a Chance of Meatballs*
Bemelmans, Ludwig. *Madeline* (series)
Bonsall, Crosby. *Mine's the Best*
Branley, Franklyn. *Mickey's Magnet*
Brown, Margaret Wise. *Goodnight Moon*
Cohen, Miriam. *Jim's Dog Muffins*
Duncan, Lois. *Birthday Moon*
Eastman, Philip D. *Are You My Mother?*
Hines, Anna. *Come to the Meadow*
Holl, Adelaide. *Moon Mouse*
Langley, Andrew. *The Moon*
Lionni, Leo. *It's Mine!*
Numeroff, Laura J. *If You Give a Moose a Muffin*
Simon, Norma. *I Was So Mad!*
Yolen, Jane. *Owl Moon*

1.11 ***continued***

N BOOK LIST

Brown, Margaret Wise. *Noisy Book*
Brown, Margaret Wise. *The Summer Noisy Book*
Brown, Margaret Wise. *The Winter Noisy Book*
Geraghty, Paul. *Stop that Noise!*
Guilfoile, Elizabeth. *Nobody Listens to Andrew*
Hughes, Shirley. *Noisy*
Kuskin, Karla. *All Sizes of Noise*
Mayer, Mercer. *There's a Nightmare in My Closet*
McGovern, Ann. *Too Much Noise*
Rylant, Cynthia. *Night in the Country*
Wood, Audrey. *The Napping House*

P BOOK LIST

Ahlberg, Janet & Allan. *The Jolly Postman*
Andersen, Hans Christian. *The Princess and the Pea*
Behrens, June. *I Can Be a Pilot*
Bond, Michael. *Paddington* (series)
Carle, Eric. *Pancakes, Pancakes*
dePaola, Tomie. *The Popcorn Book*
Ets, Marie H. *Play With Me*
Freeman, Don. *A Pocket for Corduroy*
Goodall, John S. *Paddy's New Hat*
Keats, Ezra Jack. *Peter's Chair*
Leedy, Loreen. *Pingo the Plaid Panda*
Matthias, Catherine. *I Can Be a Police Officer*
Pizer, Abigail. *It's a Perfect Day*
Titherington, Jeanne. *Pumpkin, Pumpkin*
Van Allsburg, Chris. *The Polar Express*
Wood, Audrey. *Little Penguin's Tale*

Pl Book List

Carle, Eric. *Papa, Please Get the Moon for Me*
Leedy, Loreen. *Pingo the Plaid Panda*
Titherington, Jeanne. *A Place for Ben*

Pr Book List

Calmenson, Stephanie. *The Principal's New Clothes*
Campbell, Rod. *My Presents*
dePaola, Tomie. *The Prince of the Dolomites*
Grifalconi, Ann. *Osa's Pride*
Munsch, Robert. *The Paper Bag Princess*
Rey, Margaret. *Pretzel*
Rylant, Cynthia. *Birthday Presents*
Scieszka, Jon. *The Frog Prince Continued*

Q BOOK LIST

Brown, Margaret Wise. *The Quiet Noisy Book*
Carle, Eric. *The Very Quiet Cricket*
Causley, Charles. *"Quack" Said the Billy Goat*
Flournoy, Valerie. *The Patchwork Quilt*
Johnston, Tony. *The Quilt Story*
Jonas, Ann. *The Quilt*
Wood, Audrey. *Quick as a Cricket*
Zolotow, Charlotte. *The Quarreling Book*

1.11 ***continued***

R BOOK UST

Alborough, Jez. *Running Bear*
Brown, Margaret Wise. *The Runaway Bunny*
Ehlert, Lois. *Planting a Rainbow*
Gregory, Valiska. *Riddle Soup*
Hyman, Trina. *Little Red Riding Hood*
Hutchins, Pat. *Rosie's Walk*
Le Tord, Bijou. *Rabbit Seeds*
McLean, Anne. *The Bus Ride*
McLerran, Alice. *Roxaboxen*
Peek, Merle. *Roll Over! A Counting Book*
Pfister, Marcus. *The Rainbow Fish*
Stinson, Kathy. *Red Is Best*
Tafuri, Nancy. *Rabbit's Morning*

S BOOK LIST

Crews, Donald. *School Bus*
Gibbons, Gail. *The Seasons of Arnold's Apple Tree*
Gregory, Valiska. *Riddle Soup*
Hoban, Lillian. *Silly Tilly & the Easter Bunny*
Hoberman, Mary Ann. *The Seven Silly Eaters*
Le Tord, Bijou. *Rabbit Seeds*
Lionni, Leo. *Six Crows*
Lionni, Leo. *Swimmy*
McGovern, Ann. *Stone Soup*
Morgan, Allan. *Sadie and the Snowman*
Selsam, Millicent E. *Seeds and More Seeds*
Steig, William. *Sylvester and the Magic Pebble*
Ziefert, Harriet. *Sarah's Questions*
Zolotow, Charlotte. *Something Is Going to Happen*

Sh Book List

Asch, Frank. *Bear's Shadow*
Burton, Virginia Lee. *Mike Mulligan and His Steam Shovel*
Hoban, Tana. *Shapes, Shapes, Shapes*
Kline, Suzy. *SHHHH!*
Parkes, Brenda. *Who's in the Shed*
Peet, Bill. *Farewell to Shady Glade*
Shaw, Nancy. *Sheep in a Jeep*
Shaw, Nancy. *Sheep on a Ship*
Tompert, Ann. *Nothing Sticks Like a Shadow*
Wells, Rosemary. *Shy Charles*

Shr Book List

Joyce, William. *George Shrinks*
Steig, William. *Shrek*

Sk Book List

Cohen, Miriam. *The Real-Skin Rubber Monster Mask*
Gibbons, Gail. *Up Goes the Skyscraper*
Hines, Anna. *Sky All Around*
Kellogg, Steven. *The Island of Skog*
Rose, Gerrald. *The Tiger Skin Rug*

Sl Book List

Dabcovich, Lydia. *Sleepy Bear*
Miller, Eve. *Mousekin's Woodland Sleepers*
Seuss, Dr. *The Sleep Book*
Waber, Bernard. *Ira Sleeps Over*
Yolen, Jane. *Sleeping Ugly*
Zolotow, Charlotte. *Sleepy Book*

Sm Book List

Cutting, Brian & Jillian. *A Small World*
Fox, Mem. *Arabella the Smallest Girl in the World*
Lobel, Arnold. *Small Pig*
Margolis, Richard. *Secrets of a Small Brother*

Sn Book List

Briggs, Raymond. *The Snowman*
Brown, Ruth. *The Big Sneeze*
Coleridge, Sara. *January Brings the Snow*
Giganti, Paul. *How Many Snails?*
Goffstein, M. B. *Our Snowman*
Keats, Ezra Jack. *The Snowy Day*
Lobe, Mira. *The Snowman Who Went for a Walk*

1.11 ***continued***

McCully, Emily A. *First Snow*
Morgan, Allan. *Sadie and the Snowman*
Munsch, Robert. *Thomas's Snowsuit*
Rockwell, Anne & Harlow. *The First Snowfall*
Ryder, Joanne. *Snail's Spell*
Tresselt, Alvin. *White Snow, Bright Snow*

Sp Book List

Arkhurst, Joyce. *The Adventures of Spider*
Arkhurst, Joyce. *More Adventures of Spider*
Carle, Eric. *The Very Busy Spider*
Carter, Jill & Ling, Judy. *Spiders in Space*
Clifton, Lucille. *The Boy Who Didn't Believe in Spring*
Gelman, Rita. *More Spaghetti I Say*
Kirk, David. *Miss Spider's Tea Party*
Margolis, Richard. *Big Bear, Spare That Tree*
Moncure, Jane B. *Spring Is Here*
Raskin, Ellen. *Spectacles*
Rockwell, Anne. *First Comes Spring*
Shaw, Charles G. *It Looked Like Spilt Milk*

St Book List

Burton, Virginia Lee. *Mike Mulligan and His Steam Shovel*
Cohen, Miriam. *Starring First Grade*
Fisher, Leonard. *Storm at the Jetty*
McClintock, Mike. *Stop That Ball*
Stolz, Mary. *Storm in the Night*
Tompert, Ann. *Nothing Sticks Like a Shadow*

Str Book List

Bruchac, Joseph. *First Strawberries: A Cherokee Story*
dePaola, Tomie. *Strega Nona* (series)
Ginsburg, Mirra. *Across the Stream*
Lobel, Arnold & Anita. *On Market Street*
Politi, Leo. *Pedro, the Angel of Olvera Street*
Van Allsburg, Chris. *The Stranger*
Williams, Vera & Williams, Jennifer. *Stringbean's Trip to the Shining Sea*

Sw Book List

Adams, Pam. *There Was an Old Lady Who Swallowed a Fly*
Lionni, Leo. *Swimmy*
Mayer, Mercer. *Liza Lou and the Yeller Belly Swamp*
Politi, Leo. *Song of the Swallows*
Tejima, Keizaburo. *Swan Sky*

T BOOK LIST

Baker, Alan. *Two Tiny Mice*
Bang, Molly. *Ten, Nine, Eight*
Bennett, Jill. *Teeny Tiny*
Brett, Jan. *Town Mouse, Country Mouse*
Carle, Eric. *The Tiny Seed*
Cohen, Miriam. *First Grade Takes a Test*
Crews, Donald. *Ten Black Dots*
Gretz, Susanna. *Teddy Bears 1 to 10*
Hutchins, Pat. *Titch*
Kellogg, Steven. *The Mysterious Tadpole*
Kennedy, Jimmy. *The Teddy Bears' Picnic*
Lester, Helen. *Tacky the Penguin*
Mosel, Arlene. *Tikki Tikki Tembo*
Pomerantz, Charlotte. *How Many Trucks Can a Tow Truck Tow?*
Potter, Beatrix. *The Tale of Peter Rabbit* (series)
Preston, Edna M. *The Temper Tantrum Book*
Sadler, Marilyn. *Alistair's Time Machine*
Seuling, Barbara. *The Teeny Tiny Woman*
Weiss, Leatie. *My Teacher Sleeps in School*
Zolotow, Charlotte. *A Tiger Called Thomas*

Th Book List

Browne, Anthony. *Things I Like*
Hayes, Sarah. *This Is the Bear*
Koontz, Robin. *This Old Man: The Counting Song*
Peet, Bill. *No Such Things*
Perkins, Al. *Hand, Hand, Fingers, Thumb*
Polacco, Patricia. *Thank You Mr. Falker*
Polacco, Patricia. *Thunder Cake*
Rockwell, Anne. *Things That Go*

1.11 *continued*

Rylant, Cynthia. *This Year's Garden*
Seuss, Dr. *Thidwick the Big-hearted Moose*
Slepian, Jan & Siedler, Ann. *The Hungry Thing*
Tashjian, Virginia A. *Juba This and Juba That*
Terban, Marvin. *I Think I Thought, and Other Tricky Verbs*

Thr Book List

Appleby, Ellen (illustrator). *Three Billy-Goats Gruff*
Battaglia, Aurelius (illustrator). *The Three Little Pigs*
Brustlein, Daniel. *One, Two, Three, Going to Sea*
Cauley, Lorinda. *Goldilocks & the Three Bears*
Child, Lydia Maria. *Over the River and Through the Woods*
Emberley, Rebecca. *Three Cool Kids*
Galdone, Paul. *The Three Bears*
Galdone, Paul. *The Three Billy Goats Gruff*
Galdone, Paul. *The Three Little Pigs*
Hooks, William H. *The Three Little Pigs*
Ivimey, John W. *Three Blind Mice*
Parkes, Brenda. *The Three Little Pigs*
Trivizas, Eugene. *The Three Little Wolves and the Big Bad Pig*

Tr Book List

Gackenbach, Dick. *Mighty Tree*
Howard, Elizabeth F. *The Train to Lulu's*
Isadora, Rachel. *Ben's Trumpet*
Jonas, Ann. *Round Trip*
Keats, Ezra Jack. *The Trip*
Lobel, Arnold. *A Treeful of Pigs*
Margolis, Richard. *Big Bear, Spare That Tree*
Martin, Bill, Jr. *The Ghost-Eye Tree*
McCord, David. *Every Time I Climb a Tree*
McPhail, David. *The Train*
Miller, Eve. *Mousekin Takes a Trip*
Oxenbury, Helen. *The Car Trip*
Petrie, Catherine. *Joshua James Likes Trucks*
Pomerantz, Charlotte. *How Many Trucks Can a Tow Truck Tow?*
Ross, Pat & Joel. *Your First Airplane Trip*
Scieszka, Jon. *The True Story of the Three Little Pigs*
Siebert, Diane. *Truck Song*
Udry, Janice May. *A Tree Is Nice*
Wood, Leslie. *Tom and His Tractor*

V BOOK LIST

Andrews, Jan. *The Very Last First Time*
Bunting, Eve. *The Valentine Bears*
Carle, Eric. *The Very Busy Spider*
Carle, Eric. *The Very Hungry Caterpillar*
Cohen, Miriam. *Bee My Valentine!*
Ehlert, Lois. *Growing Vegetable Soup*
Viorst, Judith. *Alexander & the Terrible, Horrible, No Good, Very Bad Day*
Williams, Margery. *The Velveteen Rabbit*

W BOOK LIST

Aliki. *We Are Best Friends*
Brown, Margaret Wise. *The Winter Noisy Book*
Carle, Eric. *Rooster's Off to See the World*
Carrick, Carol. *Old Mother Witch*
Cohen, Miriam. *Will I Have a Friend?*
Cowley, Joy. *Mrs. Wishy-Washy*
Cristini, Ermanno & Puricelli, Luigi. *In the Woods*
Ets, Marie H. *Gilberto & the Wind*
Howe, James. *I Wish I Were a Butterfly*
Hutchins, Pat. *Rosie's Walk*
Hutchins, Pat. *The Wind Blew*
Kantrowitz, Mildred. *Willy Bear*
Keats, Ezra Jack. *Whistle for Willie*
McMillan, Bruce. *Counting Wildflowers*
Miller, Eve. *Mousekin's Woodland Sleepers*

1.11 *continued*

Parkes, Brenda. *The Enormous Watermelon*
Peet, Bill. *Wump World*
Sendak, Maurice. *Where the Wild Things Are*
Showers, Paul. *The Listening Walk*
Zolotow, Charlotte. *William's Doll*

Wh Book List

Cohen, Miriam. *So What?*
Cohen, Miriam. *When Will I Read?*
Gackenbach, Dick. *What's Claude Doing?*
Gelman, Rita G. *Why Can't I Fly?*
Gerson, Mary-Joan. *Why the Sky Is Far Away*
Godkin, Celia. *What About Ladybugs*
Hill, Eric. *Where's Spot?*
Jonas, Ann. *Where Can It Be?*
Keats, Ezra Jack. *Whistle for Willie*
Kovalski, Maryann. *The Wheels on the Bus*
Kraus, Robert. *Whose Mouse Are You?*
Parkes, Brenda. *Who's in the Shed?*
Peet, Bill. *Whingdingdilly*
Rockwell, Anne & Harlow. *When I Go Visiting*
Rossetti, Christina. *What Is Pink?*
Sendak, Maurice. *Where the Wild Things Are*
Simon, Norma. *Where Does My Cat Sleep?*
Yabuuchi, Masayuki. *Whose Baby?*
Yoshi. *Who's Hiding Here?*
Zolotow, Charlotte. *When the Wind Stops*

X BOOK LIST

Carter, David. *How Many Bugs in a Box?*
Fox, Mem. *Hattie and the Fox*
Hall, Donald. *Ox-Cart Man*

Y BOOK LIST

Ehlert, Lois. *Red Leaf, Yellow Leaf*
Félix, Monique. *Yum Yum I'll Be My Own Cook*
Grey, Judith. *Yummy, Yummy*
Hoban, Tana. *Is It Red? Is It Yellow? Is It Blue?*
Johnston, Tony. *Yonder*
Lionni, Leo. *A Busy Year*
Lionni, Leo. *Little Blue and Little Yellow*
Mayer, Mercer. *Liza Lou and the Yeller Belly Swamp*
Provensen, Alice & Martin. *The Year at Maple Hill Farm*
Ross, Pat & Joel. *Your First Airplane Trip*
Wolff, Ashley. *A Year of Beasts*
Wolff, Ashley. *A Year of Birds*

Z BOOK LIST

Barton, Byron. *Buzz Buzz Buzz*
Bridges, William. *The Bronx Zoo Book of Wild Animals*
Earle, Ann. *Zipping, Zapping, Zooming Bats*
Ehlert, Lois. *Color Zoo*
Gibbons, Gail. *Zoo*
Hoban, Tana. *A Children's Zoo*
Lopshire, Robert. *Put Me in the Zoo*
McDermott, Gerald. *Zomo the Rabbit*
Peet, Bill. *Zella, Zack, & Zodiac*
Pulver, Robin. *Mrs. Toggle's Zipper*
Seuss, Dr. *If I Ran the Zoo*
Van Allsburg, Chris. *The Wreck of the Zephyr*
Van Allsburg, Chris. *The Z Was Zapped*

Source: List 1.11 is adapted from *Hands-On Phonics Activities for Elementary Children* by Karen Stangl, published by Prentice Hall Direct, Paramus, NJ (2000).

1.12 Wordless Picture Books

"Reading" books without pictures helps children as young as 3 or 4 years of age to develop oral literacy skills. Children love making up their own stories to accompany the pictures. Including wordless picture books in your library is an ideal and fun way to help children develop vocabulary and a keen sense of story. Some books in the list below will be enjoyed by older readers.

Mitsumasa Anno, *Anno's Counting Book*
Mitsumasa Anno, *Anno's Journey*
Mitsumasa Anno, *Topsy-Turvies: Pictures to Stretch the Imagination*
Jeannie Baker, *Window*
Molly Bang, *The Grey Lady and the Strawberry Snatcher*
Istavan Banyai, *R.E.M Rapid Eye Movement*
Istavan Banyai, *Zoom*
Raymond Briggs, *The Snowman*
Dick Bruna, *Another Story to Tell*
Kathleen Bullock, *The Rabbits Are Coming*
Eric Carle, *Do You Want to Be My Friend?*
Peter Collington, *The Angel and the Soldier Boy*
Alexandra Day, *Carl Goes Shopping*
Alexandra Day, *Good Dog Carl*
Tomie dePaola, *Pancakes for Breakfast*
Henrik Drescher, *The Yellow Umbrella*
John Goodall, *Paddy Under Water*
John Goodall, *Story of a Main Street*
John Goodall, *The Story of the Seashore*
Martin Handford, *Where's Waldo?*
Tana Hoban, *I Read Signs*
Tana Hoban, *Is It Red? Is It Yellow? Is It Blue?*
Pat Hutchins, *Changes, Changes*
Pat Hutchins, *Rosie's Walk*
Steve Jenkins, *Looking Down*
Ezra Jack Keats, *Skates!*
Lisa Maizlish, *The Ring*
Lisa Maizlish, *A Boy, a Dog and a Frog*
Mercer Mayer, *Frog Goes to Dinner*
Mercer Mayer, *Frog, Where Are You?*
Mercer & Marianna Mayer, *A Boy, a Dog, a Frog, and a Friend*
Mercer & Marianna Mayer, *One Frog Too Many*
Emily Arnold McCully, *Picnic*
Emily Arnold McCully, *School*
Dav Pilkey, *The Paperboy*
Peter Spier, *Noah's Ark*
Hanne Turk, *Happy Birthday, Max*
Chris Van Allsburg, *The Mysteries of Harris Burdick*
Lynd Ward, *The Silver Pony*
David Wiesner, *Free Fall*
David Wiesner, *Tuesday*

1.13 Picture Books

The picture book is a relatively new genre in the field of children's literature. Today the picture book illustrator is sensitive to a child's response to color, line, shape, expression, and vitality expressed through illustrations. In concept books, ABC books, and other works of nonfiction, the pictures can be used to enhance the subject under study. In fiction picture books, the story is told through the text and the pictures together and cannot be told through the text itself. Below is a list of recommended picture books.†

Eric Carle

*The Very Hungry Caterpillar**
The Very Quiet Cricket
Does a Kangaroo Have a Mother, Too?
The Grouchy Ladybug
The Very Busy Spider
The Very Lonely Firefly

Joan Holub

Boo Who?
Happy Monster Day!
Light the Candles: A Hanukkah Lift-the-Flap Book
The Spooky Sleepover

William Joyce

Dinosaur Bob and His Adventures with the Family Lazardo
Santa Calls
Rolie Polie Olie (series)
The Leaf Men and the Brave Good Bugs

Steven Kellogg

Johnny Appleseed
Paul Bunyan, A Tall Tale
Pecos Bill, A Tall Tale
Mike Fink: A Tall Tale

David Kirk

Miss Spider's New Car
Miss Spider's Tea Party
Miss Spider's Wedding

Justine Korman

Stinky Socks
I Love You, Grumpy Bunny
The Grumpy Bunny's Field Trip
The Grumpy Bunny's Spooky Night
At the Auto Repair Center

Leo Lionni

Inch by Inch
Swimmy
A Color of His Own
Frederick
Fish Is Fish
Cornelius: A Fable

Jean Marzollo

I Spy: A Book of Picture Riddles
I Spy Fantasy: A Book of Picture Riddles

Raffi

Baby Beluga
Five Little Ducks
One Light, One Sun
Wheels on the Bus: Raffi Songs to Read

Maurice Sendak

*Where the Wild Things Are**
Alligators All Around: An Alphabet
Chicken Soup With Rice: A Book of Months
In the Night Kitchen
One Was Johnny: A Counting Book

Chris Van Allsburg

The Polar Express
Two Bad Ants
Jumanji
The Garden of Abdul Gasazi

†Also see List 4.16 "The New York Public Library's 100 Picture Books Everyone Should Know."

1.13 *continued*

Rosemary Wells

McDuff and the Baby
McDuff Goes to School
Max's Dragon Shirt
Max Cleans Up
Felix Feels Better
Max's Bedtime
Bunny Party
Edward Unready for School
McDuff's New Friend
Yoko's Paper Cranes
Night Sounds, Morning Colors
Yoko
Read to Your Bunny
Timothy Goes to School
Noisy Nora

David Wiesner

Sector 7
Tuesday
Free Fall
Hurricane
June 29, 1999

Hans Wilhelm

A Cool Kid—Like Me!
Don't Cut My Hair!
Let's Be Friends Again!
Oh, What a Mess
Schnitzel Is Lost

Vera B. Williams

"More More More!" Said the Baby: 3 Love Stories
A Chair for My Mother
Cherries and Cherry Pits
Lucky Song
Music, Music for Everyone
Something Special for Me
Stringbean's Trip to the Shining Sea
Three Days on a River in a Red Canoe

Audrey Wood

Oh My Baby Bear!
The Napping House
Little Penguin's Tale
Heckedy Peg
Silly Sally
Scaredy Cats
The Tickleoctopus
Sweet Dream Pie
A Book for Honey Bear

Additional Picture Books

Chicken Sunday, Patricia Polacco
Kermit the Hermit, Bill Peet
Pamela Camel, Bill Peet
The House on East 88th Street, Bernard Waber
Anno's Journey, Mitsumasa Anno
Animals Should Definitely Not Wear Clothing, Judi Barrett
Aunt Harriet's Underground Railroad in the Sky, Faith Ringgold
Bear Shadow, Frank Asch
Amelia's Show-and-Tell Fiesta, Mimi Chapra
Bringing the Rain to Kapiti Plain: A Nandi Tale, Verna Aardema
Run, Jump, Whiz, Splash, Vera Rosenberry
Mr. Gumpy's Outing, John Burningham
*In the Tall, Tall Grass**, Denise Fleming
Secret Place, Eve Bunting
*Make Way for Ducklings**, Robert McCloskey
The Salamander Room, Anne Mazer
Flower Garden, Eve Bunting
Tadpoles, Betsy James
Cloudy with a Chance of Meatballs, Judi Barrett
Dinner at Aunt Connie's House, Faith Ringgold
Harry by the Sea, Gene Zion
Harry the Dirty Dog, Gene Zion
Little Gorilla, Ruth Bornstein
The Little Wizard, Jody Bergsma
Lottie's New Beach Towel, Petra Mathers
Jonathan and His Mommy, Irene Smalls-Hector
The Button Box, Margarette S. Reid

1.13 *continued*

Bein' With You This Way, W. Nikola-Lisa
How Many, How Many, How Many, Rick Walton
10 Minutes Till Bedtime, Peggy Rathmann
The Shape of Things, Dayle Ann Dodds
Taking a Walk: A Book in Two Languages—Caminando: un libro en dow lenguas, Rebecca Emberley
Where Are You Going, Manyoni?, Catherine Stock
Just a Little Bit, Ann Tompert
No Jumping on the Bed!, Tedd Arnold
No More Water in the Tub!, Tedd Arnold
No Roses for Harry, Gene Zion
Parts, Tedd Arnold
*Roxaboxen**, Alice McLerran, illustrated by Barbara Cooney
Abuela, Arthur Dorros, illustrated by Elisa Kleven
*Corduroy**, Don Freeman
Down the Road, Alice Schertle, illustrated by E. B. Lewis
Tacky the Penguin, Helen Lester, illustrated by Lynn Munsinger
Sheila Rae, the Brave, Kevin Henkes
Max Found Two Sticks, Brian Pinkney
Stellaluna, Jannell Cannon
The Five Chinese Brothers, Clair Huchet Bishop & Kurt Wiese
*The Doorbell Rang**, Pat Hutchins
Who Sank the Boat?, Pamela Allen
Albert's Alphabet, Leslie Tryon
Sleeping Bunny, Emily Snomell Keller
Home Lovely, Lynne Rae Perkins
Where's Spot?, Eric Hill
*Goodnight Moon**, Margaret Wise Brown
Sam Who Never Forgets, Eve Rice
*I Went Walking**, Sue Williams, illustrated by Julie Vivas
*Caps for Sale: A Tale of a Peddler, Some Monkeys, and Their Monkey Business**, Esphyr Slobodkina
Zebra: Striped Whale with a Polka Dot Tail, Shari F. Donahue

1.14 Animal Stories

All young children enjoy animals stories. In some animal stories the characters act and behave so much like people that, if it were not for the illustrations, as in *Bread and Jam for Frances* by Russell Hoban, readers would think the characters were human! In others, such as *Ice Bear and Little Fox* by Jonathan London or *Giraffe Trouble* by Jean Craighead George, the animals live in their natural, realistic settings and retain their way of life but think and speak like people.

A Million Fish . . . More or Less, Patricia McKissack
Albert, Donna Jo Napoli
The Animal Mall, Cooper Edens
Arthur (series), Marc Brown
Babar (series), Jean de Brunhoff
Barnyard Tracks, Dee Dee Duffy
Benjamin's Balloon: Story and Pictures, Alan Baker
Big Bear Ball, Joanne Ryder
Bill and Pete to the Rescue, Tomie DePaola
The Brave Ones, Tony Kerins
Bread and Jam for Frances, Russell Hoban
Can't You Sleep, Little Bear?, Martin Waddell
Circus Caps for Sale, Esphyr Slobodkina
Cock-a-Doodle Dudley, Bill Peet
Come Along Daisy, Jane Simmons
Come to My Party, Judith Benet Richardson
Curious George (series), H. A. Rey
The Dumb Bunnies Go to the Zoo (series), Sue Denim
Ebb and Flo and the Baby Seal, Jane Simmons
Elmer, David McKee
Farmer Duck, Martin Waddell
Farmer Will, Jane Cowen-Fletcher
Find the Piglet, Stephen Cartwright
Flossie and the Fox, Patricia C. McKissack
Froggy Gets Dressed (series), Jonathan London
Giraffe Trouble, Jean Craighead George
Good Night, Gorilla, Peggy Rathmann
Hey, Pipsqueak!, Kate and Jim McMullan
How the Reindeer Saved Santa, Carolyn Haywood
Ice Bear and Little Fox, Jonathan London
Jungle Jamboree, Kimberley Knutson
Last Night at the Zoo, Michael Garland
Leo the Late Bloomer, Robert Kraus
Little Louie the Baby Bloomer, Robert Kraus
Little Pink Pig, Pat Hutchins
Look Out, Bird!, Marilyn Janovitz
Lost Moose, Jan Slepian
Monkey Trouble, John A. Rowe
Olivia Saves the Circus, Ian Falconer
One Rainy Night, Doris Gove
Petunia, Roger Duvoisin
Plunk's Dreams, Helen V. Griffith
Rats on the Range and Other Stories, James Marshall
Slim and Jim, Richard Egielski
Someday, Diane Paterson
The Stolen Egg, Sue Vyner
That's Good! That's Bad!, Margery Cuyler
The Emperor Lays an Egg, Brenda Z. Guiberson
The Great Race, David McPhail
The Littlest Wolf, Larry Dane Brimner
The Most Amazing Dinosaur, James Stevenson
The Park in the Dark, Martin Waddell
The Pig Is in the Pantry, the Cat Is on the Shelf, Shirley Mozelle
Rainbow Fish, Marcus Pfister
The Secret Path, Nick Butterworth,
The Stray Dog, Marc Simon
The Story of Ferdinand, Munro Leaf
This Little Chick, John Lawrence
Three at Sea, Timothy Bush
The Trek, Ann Jonas
When Moose Was Young, Jim Latimer
Where Are You Going, Little Mouse?, Robert Kraus
Where's Bear?, Hilary McKay
Will's Mammoth, Rafe Martin
Wipe Your Feet!, Daniel Lehan
You and Me, Little Bear, Martin Waddell
You Can't Catch Me!, Annabel Collis

1.15 Folktale and Fairy-Tale Read-Alouds

Folktales were born out of the oral tradition and contain the common elements of ogres, witches or giants, supernatural helpers such as fairies or elves, magic and marvels, tasks and quests. There are cumulative tales (*Henny Penny*), animal tales (*The Bremen Town Musicians*), tales of magic and wonder (*Cinderella*), porquoi or "why" tales (*Why Mosquitoes Buzz in People's Ears*), and realistic tales (*Dick Whittington and His Cat*). Folktales cut across cultures and time. Here is a list of several modern retellings appropriate for reading aloud to children of all ages.

African

The Adventure of Spider: A West African Folktale, Joyce Cooper Arkhurst
Anansi and the Magic Stick, Eric A. Kimmel
Anansi Does the Impossible: An Ashanti Tale, Verna Aardema
Anansi the Spider: A Tale from the Ashanti, Gerald McDermott
Anansi's Feast, Tololwa Mollel
Fly Eagle Fly: An African Fable, Christopher Gregowski and Nikki Daly
Mufaro's Beautiful Daughters: An African Tale, John Steptoe
The Ox of the Wonderful Horns: And Other African Folktales, Ashley Bryan
Rabbit Makes a Monkey of Lion, Verna Aardema
A Story, A Story: An African Tale, Gail Haley
Why Mosquitoes Buzz in People's Ears, Verna Aardema
Zomo the Rabbit, Gerald McDermott

Asian

Brother's Rabbit (Cambodia), Minfong Ho
The Dragon Prince: A Chinese Beauty and the Beast Tale, Laurence Yep
The Emperor and the Kite, Jane Yolen
The Greatest Treasure, Demi
The Jade Stone, Caryn Yacowitz
Kites: Magic Wishes That Fly Up to the Sky, Demi
Little Inchkin: A Tale of Old Japan, Fiona French
Lon Po Po: A Red Riding Hood Story From China, Ed Young
The Lost House: A Chinese Folktale, Ed Young
The Monkey and the Crocodile (India), Paul Galdone
The Paper Crane, Molly Bang
The Rooster's Antlers: A Story of the Chinese Zodiac, Eric A. Kimmel
The Runaway Rice Cake, Ying Chang Compestine
Stonecutter: A Japanese Folktale, Gerald McDermott
Sun Girl and the Moon Boy: A Korean Tale, Yangsook Choi
Tikki Tikki Tembo, Arlene Mosel
The Weaving of a Dream, Marilee Heyer

English

Dick Whittington and His Cat, Marcia Brown
Henny Penny, Paul Galdone

1.15 *continued*

Jack and the Beanstalk, Steven Kellogg
Lazy Jack, Vivian French
The Three Little Pigs, James Marshall

French

Beauty and the Beast, Carol Heyer
Beauty and the Beast, Marianna Mayer
Cinderella, Paul Galdone
Fairytale Favorites in Story and Song, Jim Weiss
The Little Juggler, Barbara Cooney
Puss in Boots, Paul Galdone
Three Sacks of Truth: A Story from France, Eric A. Kimmel
The Turtle and the Two Ducks: Animal Fables Retold from La Fontaine, Patricia Plante

German (Jacob and Wilhelm Grimm)

The Bremen Town Musicians, Ilse Plume
Cinderella, Nonny Hogrogian
The Elves and the Shoemaker, Lucy Crane
The Fisherman and his Wife, Rosemary Wells
Frog Goes to Dinner, Mercer Mayer
The Frog Prince, Cindy McKay
Froggie Went A-Courting, Marjorie Priceman
The Goose Girl: A Story From the Brothers Grimm, Eric A. Kimmel
Hansel and Gretel, Anthony Browne
Little Red Riding Hood, Paul Galdone
Little Red Riding Hood, Trina Schart Hyman
Rumpelstiltskin, Paul Galdone
The Sleeping Beauty, Trina Schart Hyman
Snow White and Rose Red, Bernadette Watts

Greek

Aesop's Tales, Russell Ash
The Gods and Godesses of Olympus, Aliki
The Hare and the Tortoise, Carol Jones
The Lion and the Mouse, Carol Jones
King Midas and the Golden Touch, Charlotte Craft
Town Mouse, Country Mouse, Carol Jones

Hispanic

Borreguita and the Coyote: A Tale from Ayutla, Mexico, Verna Aardema
The Bossy Gallito (a Cuban Tale), Lucia M. Gonzalez

1.15 *continued*

Cuckoo/Cucu (A Mayan Tale), Lois Ehlert
Jabuti the Tortoise (Amazon), Gerald McDermott
Las Nanas de Aguelita—Grandmother's Nursery Rhymes, Nelly Palacio Jaramillo
The Little Red Ant and the Great Big Crumb (American Southwest), Shirley Climo
Mediopollito: Half-Chicken, Alma Flor Ada
Moon Rope: A Peruvian Tale, Lois Ehlert
The Tale of Rabbit and Coyote (Mexico), Tony Johnston
The Tree That Rains: The Flood Myth of the Huichol Indians of Mexico, Emery Bernard
Viborita De Cascabel/Baby Rattlesnake, Te Ata

Jewish

Bone Button Borscht, Aubrey Davis
Hershel and the Hanukkah Goblins, Eric A. Kimmel
It Could Always Be Worse, Margot Zemach
Something from Nothing, Phoebe Gilman
Such a Noise! A Jewish Folktale, Aliana Brodman, reteller
Yettele's Feathers, Joan Rothenberg

Middle Eastern

A Is for Allah, Yusef Islan
The Legend of the Persian Carpet, Tomie dePaola
The Tale of Aladdin and the Wonderful Lamp, Eric A. Kimmel

Native American

A Boy Called Slow: The True Story of Sitting Bull, Joseph Bruchac
Fire Race: A Karuk Coyote Tale of How Fire Came to the People, Jonathan London
The First Strawberries, A Cherokee Folktale, Joseph Bruchac
Gift Horse: A Lakota Story, S. D. Nelson
The Legend of the Indian Paintbrush, Tomie dePaola
Mama Do You Love Me? (Inuit), Barbara M. Joosse
The Mud Pony: A Traditional Skidi Pawnee Tale, Caron L. Cohen
Rainbow Crow: A Lenape Tale, Nancy Van Laan
The Story of Jumping Mouse, John Steptoe
The Story of the Milky Way: A Cherokee Tale, Joseph Bruchac
Ten Little Rabbits, Virginia Grossman
Thirteen Moons on Turtle's Back: A Native American Year of Moons, Joseph Bruchac

Scandinavian

Boots and his Brothers: A Norwegian Tale, Eric A. Kimmel
The Three Billy Goats Gruff, Paul Galdone
Thumbelina (A Hans Christian Andersen Tale), Amy Ehrlich

1.16 Books to Teach Math

Below are only a few of the many fiction and nonfiction books available for exploring mathematics concepts with children in grades K–1. For more information, you may wish to look at *The Wonderful World of Mathematics: A Critically Annotated List of Children's Books in Mathematics*, published by the National Council of Teachers of Math (1998).

The 100th Day Worries, Margery Cuyler (COLLECTING)
Action Math Series: Shapes, Games, Measure, Patterns, Ivan Bulloch
Anno's Counting Book, Mitsumasa Anno
Bat Jamboree, Kathi Appelt (MULTIPLES OF THREE)
Color Zoo, Lois Ehlert (SHAPES AND PATTERNS)
Counting on Frank, Rod Clement (MEASUREMENT)
Eating Fractions, Bruce Macmillan
Ed Emberley's Picture Pie: A Circle Drawing Book, Ed Emberley (SHAPES)
Eight Hands Round: A Patchwork Alphabet, Ann Whitford Paul (PATTERNS)
512 Ants on Sullivan Street (series), Carol Losi
Fraction Action, Loreen Leedy
Fraction Fun, David Adler (MONEY)
G Is for Googol: A Math Alphabet Book, David M. Schwartz
Gater Pie, Louise Mathews (DIVISION)
A Giraffe and a Half, Shel Silverstein (MEASUREMENT)
Hello Reader: Math (series published by Scholastic)
How Big Is a Foot?, Rolf Myller (MEASUREMENT)
How Many Stars in the Sky?, Lenny Hort
How Much Is Million, David M. Schwartz
If You Hopped Like a Frog, David M. Schwartz (RATIOS AND PROPORTION)
If You Made a Million, David M. Schwartz
Just a Little Bit, Ann Tompert (MEASUREMENT)
The King's Chessboard, David Birch
The Lotus Seed, Sherry Garland (MULTIPLICATION)
Mathstart Series, Stuart J. Murphy (PROBABILITY, ESTIMATION)
Max's Dragon Shirt, Rosemary Wells (MONEY)
Me and the Measure of Things, Joan Sweeney
Me Counting Time: From Seconds to Centuries, Joan Sweeney
Measuring Penny, Laureen Leedy
A Million Fish . . . or More, Patricia McKissack (ESTIMATION)
Miss Bindergarten Celebrates the 100th Day of Kindergarten, Josie Slate (COLLECTING)
Miss Rumphius, Barbara Cooney (MULTIPLICATION)
Mission Addition, Laureen Leedy
More Than One, Miriam Klein (SETS)
Nine O-clock Lullaby, Marilyn Singer (TIME)
One Grain of Rice: A Mathematical Folktale, Demi (MULTIPLICATION)
One Guinea Pig Is Not Enough, Kate Duke (ADDITION)
One Hundred Hungry Ants, Elinor Pinczes (DIVISION)

1.16 *continued*

Pigs Will Be Pigs (series), Amy Axelrod (BASIC OPERATIONS)
Pigs Will Be Pigs: Fun With Math and Money, Amy Axelrod
The Relatives Came, Cynthia Rylant (BASIC OPERATIONS)
Remainder of One, Elinor Pinczes (REMAINDER)
Splash, Ann Jonas (ADDITION AND SUBTRACTION)
Subtraction Action, Laureen Leedy
Twelve Snails to One Lizard, Susan Hightower (MEASUREMENT)
Twenty Is Too Many, Kate Duke (SUBTRACTION)
2 × 2 Boo!, Laureen Leedy (MULTIPLICATION)
A Village of Round and Square Houses, Ann Grifalcone (SHAPES)

1.17 Books to Teach Science

Most children in pre-K–grade 1 come to school with some knowledge of scientific principles. There are many science picture books with excellent photographs and illustrations that extend what they already know. Central concepts at this early level include books about how animals survive in different habitats, the beauty of sea creatures and mammals, as well as elements of the earth, weather, and ecology. The list of books below will help you address the important science topics at the pre-K–1 level.

ANIMAL HABITATS†

Understanding ways animals meet their needs is a central purpose of animal habitat books. These books explain that where animals live and what they eat determines why some animals have fur and why reptiles have hard protective coverings.

Animal Homes, Alice Jablonsky & Jeffrey Terreson
The Armadillo From Amarillo, Lynn Cherry
At the Frog Pond, Tilde Michels
Bear in the Forest, Michelle Cartledge
Elephants in the Jungle, Michelle Cartledge
Guess Where I Live, Anni Axworthy
Hide and Seek, Toni Eugene
*A House Is a House for Me**, Mary Ann Hoberman
In the Woods: Who's Been Here?, Lindsay George
*Nuts to You**, Lois Ehlert
Raccoon on His Own, Jim Arnosky
Squirrels, Brian Wildsmith

ECOLOGY

Ecology seeps into much of children's modern fiction. For example, *The Great Kapok Tree* is a story about how animals of the rainforest plead with the woodcutter to preserve the Kapok tree. An appreciation of our earth and how we can preserve our natural resources has grown more important as the world becomes globally connected politically, economically, and technologically. The following books serve to inform children of ways they can contribute to preserving the world around us.

A Clearing in the Forest, Carol Carrick
A First Look at Rocks, Millicent E. Selsam & Joyce Hunt
A View From the Air: Charles Lindbergh's Earth and Sky, Reeve Lindbergh
The Air We Breathe!, Enid Bloome
And Still the Turtle Watched,* Sheila MacGill Callahan
Animals in Danger, Benjamin Kalman
Be a Friend to Trees, Patricia Lauber
The Blue Spruce, Mario Cuomo

†For an excellent list of books about nature, go to www.booksaboutnature.com. Also see National Geographic's Action Book series.

1.17 *continued*

The Earth and I, Frank Asch
Earthquakes, Franklyn M. Branley
Everybody Needs a Rock, Byrd Baylor
Forest Fire!, Mary Ann Fraser
Forest, Ron Hirschi
Grandfather Twilight, Barbara Berger
The Great Kapok Tree, Lynne Cherry
Here in Space, David Milgrim
Here Is the Coral Reef, Madeleine Dunphy
I Took a Walk,* Henry Cole
It's My Earth Too: How Can I Help the Earth Stay Alive?, Kathleen Krull
Mother Earth, Nancy Luenn
My River, Shari Halpern
Old Turtle, Douglass Wood
On My Beach There Are Many Pebbles, Leo Lionni
Puddles and Ponds: Living Things in Watery Places, Phyllis S. Busch
Timmy Green's Blue Lake, Donna Bergman
Were You a Wild Duck, Where Would You Go?, George Mendoza
When the Earth Wakes, Ani Rucki
World Water Watch, Michelle Koch

FOOD

Understanding the wide variety of fruits and vegetables available to us is a part of the science curriculum in the early grades. Numerous books that teach scientific concepts about foods are included in the list below along with such humorous and entertaining books as *Tops and Bottoms*—the story of how a lazy bear loses out.

Animals Eating, Jane Burton
Baby's Food, Lynn Breeze
A Book of Fruit, Barbara Hirsch Lember
Bread and Jam for Frances, Russell Hoban
Bread, Bread, Bread, Ann Morris
Cat's Cake, Richard Fowler
Dinnertime, Claire Henley
Eating Out, Helen Oxenbury
*Eating the Alphabet: Fruits and Vegetables from A to Z**, Lois Ehlert
*Everybody Bakes Bread**, Norah Dooley
*Everybody Cooks Rice**, Norah Dooley
Food, Jan Pienkowski
Food, Sara Lynn
From Lemon to Lemonade, Ali Mitgutsch
Growing Vegetable Soup, Lois Ehlert
Hedgehog Bakes a Cake, Maryann MacDonald
How Are You Peeling?, Saxton Freymann

1.17 *continued*

Jake Baked the Cake, B. G. Hennessy
Little Chick's Breakfast, Mary DeBall Kwitz
Lunch, Denise Fleming
Lunch With Milly, Jeanne Modesitt
Maisy Makes Gingerbread, Lucy Cousins
Milk, Donald Carrick
Mmm, Cookies!, Robert N. Munsch
Molly and the Strawberry Day, Pamela T. Conrad
My Very First Book of Food, Eric Carle
Oliver's Fruit Salad, Vivian French
Oliver's Vegetables, Vivian French
Pancakes for Breakfast, Tomie dePaola
Pancakes, Pancakes, Eric Carle
Pop! Goes the Turnip, Harold Berson
Spot Bakes a Cake, Eric Hill
Sun Bread, Elisa Kleven
Teddy Bears' Picnic Cookbook, Abigail Darling
The Enormous Potato, Aubrey Davis
The Giant Carrot, Jan Peck
The Lunch Box Surprise, Grace Maccarone
The Orange Book, Richard McGuire
The Pancake, Anita Lobel
The Popcorn Book, Tomie dePaola
The Roly Poly Cookie, Sara Murphey
The Seed the Squirrel Dropped, Haris Petie
The Ugly Vegetables, Grace Lin
The World's Biggest Birthday Cake, Carol Greene
Time to Eat, Margaret Miller
We're Making Breakfast for Mother, Shirley Neitzel
What's on My Plate, Ruth Belov Gross
When Batistine Made Bread, Treska Lindsey
Who Eats What?: Food Chains and Food Webs, Patricia Lauber

INSECTS

Children of all ages are curious about how insects live, eat, and survive. There are numerous lavishly illustrated picture books that delight their curious minds. These books examine the beauty and unique habits of bugs. One of the most popular is *The Very Hungry Caterpillar*.

Be Nice to Spiders, Margaret Bloy Graham
Bees, Wasps, and Ants, George S. Fichter
Bugs and Beasties ABC, Cheryl Nathan
Bumble Bee, Margaret Wise Brown
Bumblebee, Bumblebee, Do You Know Me?: A Garden Guessing Game, Anne Rockwell
Butterfly House, Eve Bunting

1.17 *continued*

Caterpillar, Caterpillar, Vivian French
Creepy, Crawly Caterpillars, Margery Facklam
Creepy, Crawly Creatures (National Geographic Action Book), Warren Cutler
Find the Hidden Insect, Joanna Cole
Grasshopper on the Road, Arnold Lobel
Half-a-Ball-of-Kenki: An Ashanti Tale Retold, Verna Aardema
I Like Butterflies, Gladys Conklin
In the Tall, Tall Grass, Denise Fleming
Inch by Inch, Leo Lionni
Little Miss Spider at Sunny Patch School, David Kirk
Old Black Fly, Jim Aylesworth
Some Bugs Glow in the Dark, Claire Llewellyn
Spider, Spider, Kate Banks
Spinning Spiders, Ruth Berman
The Best Bug Parade, Stuart J. Murphy
The Creepy Crawly Book, Bobbi Katz
The Grouchy Ladybug, Eric Carle
The Little Squeegy Bug, Bill Martin Jr. & Michael Sampson
The Very Busy Spider, Eric Carle
The Very Hungry Caterpillar, Eric Carle
Two Bad Ants, Chris Van Allsburg
Who's in Rabbit's House?, Verna Aardema
Why Mosquitoes Buzz in People's Ears: A West African Tale, Verna Aardema

PLANTS

Information about plants that grow in different environments is central to the science curriculum for early learners. The books listed below are humorous and adventurous as well as informative. Children learn about seasonal and regional plants, planting, how seeds grow, and harvesting.

*A Tree Is a Plant**, Clyde Robert Bulla
All About Seeds, Susan Kuchala
And a Sunflower Grew, Aileen Lucia Fisher
Bean and Plant, Christine Back
Cactus Hotel, Brenda Z. Guiberson
Cactus in the Desert, Phyllis S. Busch
Clementina's Cactus, Ezra Jack Keats
*Corn Is Maize**, Aliki
Evolution, Joanna Cole
Fran's Flower, Lisa Bruce
Hard Scrabble Harvest, Dahlov Ipcar
It's Pumpkin Time!, Zoe Hall
Jack's Garden, Henry Cole
Miss Rumphius, Barbara Cooney
Mrs. McGinty and the Bizarre Plant, Gavin Bishop

1.17 *continued*

Plants That Never Ever Bloom, Ruth Heller
Rabbit Garden, Miska Miles
Some Plants Have Funny Names, Diana Harding Cross
The Enormous Potato, Aubrey Davis
The Magic Beans, Margaret Hillert
The Tiny Seed, Eric Carle
Watermelon Day, Kathi Appelt
What Is a Plant?, Gene Darby
Your First Garden Book, Marc Tolon Brown

SEA LIFE

Sea life—particularly whales, sharks, and dolphins—has always intrigued youngsters, Some stories take children on adventures under the sea while others stimulate thinking and are helpful for creating displays and murals of sea life. Children learn such facts as what fish eat and how they reproduce through a number of these delightful books.

A First Look at Sharks, Millicent E. Selsam & Joyce Hunt
A Fish Hatches, Joanna Cole & Jerome Wexler
A Swim Through the Sea, Kristen Joy Pratt
Big Al, Andrew Clement
Blue Sea, Robert Kalan
Clark the Toothless Shark, Corinne Mellor
Find Demi's Sea Creatures: An Animal Game Book, Demi
Fish Eyes, Lois Ehlert
Fish Is Fish, Leo Lionni
The Biggest Fish in the Sea, Dahlov Ipcar
The Fish, Dick Bruna
The Salmon, Paula Z. Hogan
What Is a Fish, Gene Darby
What Is a Fish?, David Eastman
What's It Like to Be a Fish?, Wendy Pfeffer
Which One Is Whitney?, James Stevenson

SEASONS

Numerous books on spring, summer, fall, and winter answer questions that children ask and weave animal adventure into information about the seasons.

A Busy Year, Leo Lionni
A Child's Book of Seasons, Satomi Ichikawa
Around the Seasons: Poems, Eleanor Farjeon
Around the Year, Tasha Tudor
Bear's Busy Year: A Book About Seasons, Marcia Leonard
Big Goof and Little Goof, Joanna & Philip Cole
Calico Cat's Year, Donald Charles

1.17 *continued*

Changing Seasons, Rose Greydanus
Discover the Seasons, Diane Iverson
Everett Anderson's Year, Lucille Clifton
Farming, Gail Gibbons
Four Stories for Four Seasons, Tomie dePaola
Here Comes Spring, and Summer and Fall and Winter, Mary Murphy
How Does the Wind Walk?, Nancy White Carlstrom
In My Garden, Charlotte Zolotow
Jemima Remembers, Crescent Dragonwagon
My Book of the Seasons, Stephanie Calmenson
Night Sounds, Morning Colors, Rosemary Wells
Ring Out, Wild Bells: Poems About Holidays and Seasons, Lee Bennett Hopkins
The Seasons of Arnold's Apple Tree, Gail Gibbons
Seasons on the Farm, Jane Miller
Seasons, John Burningham
Seasons, Stephen Oliver
Songs of Praise, Kathleen Krull
Spring Is, Janina Domanska
The House of Four Seasons, Roger Antoine Duvoisin
The Little Island, Margaret Wise Brown
The Reasons for Seasons, Gail Gibbons
The Seasons, Debbie MacKinnon
The Turning of the Year, Bill Martin Jr.
What Comes in Spring?, Barbara Sawadge Horton

Spring

Easter Buds Are Springing: Poems for Easter, Lee Bennett Hopkins
Hi, Mister Robin, Alvin R. Tresselt
I Love Spring!, Steven Kroll
Spring Is, Janina Domanska
Spring Is Here, Lois Lenski
Spring Story, Jill Barklem
Spring, Ron Hirschi
The First Robin, Robert Kraus
Wake up, Groundhog!, Carol L. Cohen
What Comes in Spring?, Barbara Sawadge Horton

Summer

Heat Wave at Mud Flat, James Stevenson
Hotter than a Hot Dog, Stephanie Calmenson
Sea, Salt, and Air, Miriam Bat-Ami
The Summer Noisy Book, Margaret Wise Brown
The Swimming Hole, Jerrold Beim
Those Summers, Aliki

1.17 *continued*

Fall

Autumn, Colin McNaughton
Autumn Harvest, Alvin R. Tresselt
Autumn Leaves, Ken Robbins
Digger, The Story of a Mole in the Fall, Tessa Potter
In November, Cynthia Rylant
When Autumn Comes, Robert Maass
Why Do Leaves Change Color?, Betsy Maestro

Winter

Animals in Winter, Henrietta Bancroft
In a Meadow, Two Hares Hide, Jennifer Bartoli
Katy and the Big Snow: Story and Pictures, Virginia Lee Burton
The Winter Hedgehog, Ann Cartwright
Winter, Ann Blades

STARS, SPACE, AND PLANETS

Space themes at the pre K–1 level are generally written to entertain, although they introduce children to the concepts of space, stars, and planets. Most books listed below are humorous adventures, such as *Space Bunnies* and *Cosmo and the Robot.*

Moon

Good Morning, Good Night, Ivan Gantschev
I See the Moon, Kathi Appelt
I Want to See the Moon, Louis Baum
Look at the Moon, May Garelick
The Moonlit Journey, Peter O'Donnel
Moon Rope: A Peruvian Folk Tale, Lois Ehlert
Owl Moon, Jane Yolen
Possum's Harvest Moon, Anne Hunter
What's the Full Moon Full Of?, Shulamith Levy Oppenheim
See the Moon, Robert Kraus
So That's How the Moon Changes Shape!, Allan Fowler
The Moon Is Following Me, Philip Heckman
The Moon Seems to Change, Franklyn M. Branley
The Truth About the Moon, Clayton Bess
To See the Moon, Ethel Bacon

1.17 *continued*

Space

Astronaut Piggy Wiggy, Christyan Fox
Astro Bunnies, Christine Loomis
Cosmo and the Robot, J. Brian Pinkney
Dmitri the Astronaut, Jon Agee
Dogs in Space, Nancy Coffelt
Hugo and the Spacedog, Lee Lorenz
I Want to Be an Astronaut, Byron Barton
I Wonder Why Stars Twinkle, Carole Stott
Journey to the Moon, Erich Fuchs
The Magic Rocket, Steven Kroll
Planet Monster, Heather Maisner
Richie's Rocket, Joan Anderson
Seeing Stars, Sharleen Collicott
A Space Story, Karla Kuskin
Tom and Pippo See the Moon, Helen Oxenbury

WEATHER

There are numerous nonfiction and fiction books about weather—a topic that is especially interesting to children because they see the weather change from day to day. Nonfiction weather books, such as *Why Does It Thunder and Lightning?* and *First Snow, Magic Show*, introduce children to the wonders of nature. In fictional books such as *A Letter to Amy* and *The Snowy Day*, children can relate to the fun and complications caused by stormy weather. Fiction can be used as a springboard to motivate children to learn more about the weather.

Rain

A Letter to Amy, Ezra Jack Keats
Cloudy With a Chance of Meatballs, Judi Barrett
Good-bye Thunderstorm, Dorothy Marino
Listen to the Rain, Bill Martin Jr. & John Archambault
*Noah's Ark**, Jerry Pinkney
Rain, Robert Kalan
Rain, Peter Spier
Sam Panda and Thunder Dragon, Chris Conover
Splish, Splash!, Marcia Leonard
The Little Girl and the Rain, Milena Lukesova
The Puddle, David M. McPhail
The Rain Puddle, Adelaide Holl
The Rain, Michael Laser
What Does the Rain Play?, Nancy White Carlstrom
When It Rains, Mary DeBall Kwitz
When the Rain Stops, Sheila Cole
Will It Rain?, Holly Keller

1.17 *continued*

Snow

Amy Loves the Snow, Julia Hoban
Blizzard at the Zoo, Robert Bahr
BRRR!, James Stevenson
First Snow, Emily Arnold McCully
First Snow, Magic Show, John Cech
I Like Winter, Lois Lenski
In the Flaky Frosty Morning, Karla Kuskin
In the Snow, a Pull-the-Tab and Lift-the-Flap Book, Kate Burns & Dawn Apperly
Katy and the Big Snow, Virginia Lee Burton
Sleepy Bear, Lydia Dabcovich
Snowballs, Lois Ehlert
Snip, Snip . . . Snow!, Nancy Poydar
Snow on Bear's Nose: A Story of a Japanese Moon Bear Cub, Jennifer Bartoli
Snowie Rolie, William Joyce
The Happy Day, Ruth Krauss
The Snow, John Burningham
The Snowy Day, Ezra Jack Keats
The Winter Bear, Ruth Craft
Time to Sleep, Denise Fleming
What Can You Do in the Snow?, Anna Grossnickle Hines
When it Starts to Snow, Phillis Gershator
Whose Footprints?, Molly Coxe

Storms

Gilberto and the Wind, Marie Hall Ets
Hurricane, David Wiesner
The Story of Lightning and Thunder, Ashley Bryan
Thunder Cake, Patricia Polacco
Why Does It Thunder and Lightning?, Chris Arvetis
The Wind Blew, Pat Hutchins

1.18 Books to Teach Social Studies

This list will help you identify books that will not only broaden children's knowledge of their environment, but also help them live more effectively in a social world. The books are organized around the themes of getting along with friends and family, understanding the roles of community workers, comparing and contrasting how people live in different geographic regions, and recognizing the accomplishments of famous Americans.

COMMUNITIES AND COMMUNITY WORKERS

It is important for children to know the types of workers within the community in which they live. They need to understand the roles of firefighters, postal workers, and police officers. Books about the community also touch upon such places as the playground, the grocery store, and the neighborhood. Colorful illustrations and humor attract young readers to these informative stories.

A Trip to the Firehouse, Wendy Cheyette Lewison
A Visit to the Sesame Street Firehouse: Featuring Jim Henson's Sesame Street Muppets, Dan Elliott
A Visit to the Sesame Street Hospital: Featuring Jim Henson's Sesame Street Muppets, Deborah Hautzig
Arthur's Neighborhood, Marc Brown
Building a House, Byron Barton
Clifford Gets a Job, Norman Bridwell
Clifford the Firehouse Dog, Norman Bridwell
Clifford to the Rescue, Norman Bridwell
Clifford Visits the Hospital, Norman Bridwell
Clifford's First Snow Day, Norman Bridwell
Clifford's Pals, Norman Bridwell
Clifford's Family, Norman Bridwell
Corduroy's Busy Street, Don Freeman
Corduroy Goes to School, Don Freeman
Curious George at the Fire Station, Margaret & Alan J. Shalleck
Curious George Goes to School, Margaret & Alan J. Shalleck
Curious George in the Big City, Margaret & H. A. Rey
Fire Fighters, Norma Simon
Fire Fighters, Paulette Bourgeois
Garbage Collectors, Paulette Bourgeois
Good-bye, Curtis, Kevin Henkes
Guess Who?, Margaret Miller
I Want to Be a Firefighter, Daniel Lieberman
I Want to Be a Police Officer, Daniel Lieberman
Jonathan Goes to the Grocery Store, Susan K. Baggette
Look, Michael Grejniec
Maisy Goes to School, Lucy Cousins
Maisy Goes to the Playground, Lucy Cousins
Maxi, the Hero, Debra & Sal Barracca
My Very Own Jewish Community, Judyth Saypol Groner
*New York's Bravest**, Mary Pope Osborne
Night on Neighborhood Street, Eloise Greenfield

1.18 *continued*

On My Street, Eve Merriam
Police Officers, Paulette Bourgeois
Postal Workers, Paulette Bourgeois
Prairie Town, Bonnie Geisert
The Adventures of Taxi Dog, Debra & Sal Barracca
The Fire Cat, Esther Averill
The Green Truck Garden Giveaway: A Neighborhood Story and Almanac, Jacqueline Briggs Martin
*The Magic School Bus at the Waterworks**, Joanna Cole
The Playground, Debbie Bailey
Trashy Town, Andrea Zimmerman & David Clemesha
Yard Sale, Mitra Modarressi
Your Best Friend, Kat, Pat Brisson

CONFLICTS

Conflicts create natural tension in stories, drawing readers to the characters and the ways they resolve a situation. In the early grades, conflicts are clearly defined and have specific outcomes as in *All By Myself* and *I Was So Mad*. Conflicts for children at this level include teasing, not sharing, a new baby, and separation anxiety, such as when Sophie, in *When Sophie Gets Angry, Really, Really Angry*, has a conflict with her little sister over a toy and has the habit of leaving home to cool off. In the upper grades, a series of conflicts are woven throughout the story. In order to be successful, the conflict must be resolved to the satisfaction of the reader.

All By Myself, Mercer Mayer
The Boy Who Couldn't Roar, Grace Berquist
Feelings, Aliki
Furlie Cat, Berniece Freschet
Goggles, Ezra Jack Keats
I Just Forgot, Mercer Mayer
I Was So Mad, Mercer Mayer
Just a Bully, Gina & Mercer Mayer
Just a Rainy Day, Mercer Mayer
Just Go to Bed, Mercer Mayer
Just Go to the Dentist, Mercer Mayer
Just My Friend and Me, Mercer Mayer
Katie, Kit and Cousin Tom, Tomie dePaola
Me Too!, Mercer Mayer
Mr. and Mrs. Pig's Evening Out, Mary Rayner
No, David!, David Shannon
Rotten Ralph, Jack Gantos
Rough, Tough, Rowdy: A Bank Street Book About Values, William H. Hooks
The Shrinking of Treehorn, Florence Parry Heide
What a Bad Dream, Mercer Mayer
When Sophie Gets Angry, Really, Really Angry, Molly Bang
Where the Wild Things Are, Maurice Sendak

1.18 *continued*

FAMILY

Family love, problems with siblings, as well as a search for the perfect family are among the themes in the books below.

ABC A Family Alphabet Book, Bobbie Combs
Dumpling Soup, Jama Kim Rattigan
Families Are Different, Nina Pellegrini
The Grandpa Days, Joan W. Blos
Hattie and the Wild Waves: A Story from Brooklyn, Barbara Cooney
On the Day I Was Born, Deborah M. Newton
1-2-3 A Family Counting Book, Bobbie Combs
Prairie Willow, Maxine Trottier
Somebody's New Pajamas, Isaac Jackson
Something Special for Me, Vera Williams
*Song and Dance Man**, Karen Ackerman
*This Is the Way We Eat Our Lunch: A Book About Children Around the World**, Edith Baer
What's in Aunt Mary's Room?, Elizabeth Fitzgerald Howard
Who's in a Family?, Robert Skutch
You're Just What I Need, Ruth Krauss & Julia Noonan

FOREIGN LANDS AND CULTURES

Stories set in other countries and cultures combine details about how people live with an engaging story line. Nonfiction books, however, such as *People* and *Celebrating Chinese New Year*, present information that children can use to make comparisons. (See List 1.15, Folktales and Fairy-Tale Read-Alouds.)

Ahoy There, Little Polar Bear, Hans de Beer
Annika's Secret Wish, Beverly Lewis
Babar and His Children, Jean de Brunhoff
Babar the King, Jean de Brunhoff
Big Anthony and the Magic Ring, Tomie dePaola
Bringing the Rain to Kapiti Plain: A Nandi Tale, Verna Aardema
Celebrating Chinese New Year, Diane Hoyt-Goldsmith
Chidi Only Likes Blue: An African Book of Colors, Ifeoma Onyefulu
Cocoa Ice, Diana Karter Applebaum
Kofi and His Magic, Maya Angelou
The Littlest Matryoshka, Corrine Demas Bliss
Market, Ted Lewin
People, Peter Spier
Strega Nona, Tomie dePaola
Strega Nona: Her Story, Tomie dePaola
Strega Nona's Magic Lessons, Tomie dePaola
The Five Chinese Brothers, Claire Huchet Bishop
The Story about Ping, Marjorie Flack

1.18 *continued*

The Story of Babar, Jean de Brunhoff
The Story of Little Babaji, Helen Bannerman
*The Tomten**, Astrid Lindgren
The Travels of Babar, Jean de Brunhoff
Village of Round and Square Houses, Ann Grifalconi
Why Mosquitoes Buzz in People's Ears: A West African Tale, Verna Aardema

FRIENDS AND SHARING

Stories of friendship begin very early. Developmental theorists report that most preschoolers do not share with others until they are aware of others' needs. Problems with friendship are often portrayed through animal fantasy as in the books *Jessica* and *Little Bear's Friend.*

Amanda Pig and Her Big Brother Oliver, Jean Van Leeuwen
Amanda Pig on Her Own, Jean Van Leeuwan
Angelo, David Macaulay
Arthur's First Sleepover, Marc Tolon Brown
Best Friends, Steven Kellogg
Best Friends for Frances, Russell Hoban
Richard Scarry's Busy, Busy Town, Richard Scarry
Carl Goes Shopping, Alexandra Day
Carl Goes to Daycare, Alexandra Day
Carl's Afternoon in the Park, Alexandra Day
Chester's Way, Kevin Henkes
*Clever Sticks**, Bernard Ashley
Do You Want to Be My Friend?, Eric Carle
Everett Anderson's Friend, Lucille Clifton
Friends, Helme Heine
Friends, Rachel Isadora
Friends, Helen Oxenbury
Frog and Toad Are Friends, Arnold Lobel
George and Martha 'Round and 'Round, James Marshall
Ira's Sleepover, Bernard Waber
Jessica, Kevin Henkes
Little Bear's Friend, Else Holmelund Minarik
Matthew and Tilly, Rebecca C. Jones
May I Bring a Friend?, Beatrice Schenk de Regniers
Me and Neesie, Eloise Greenfield
My Best Friend, Pat Hutchins
Overnight at Mary Bloom's, Aliki
Spot Sleeps Over, Eric Hill
Together!, George Ella Lyon
What Do People Do All Day?, Jean Van Leeuwan
What Is Your Language?, Debra Leventhal
*Yo! Yes?**, Chris Raschka

1.18 ***continued***

HISTORICAL BIOGRAPHY

The following books will introduce children to the fascinating lives of several people from U.S. history.

Let's Read About . . . Christopher Columbus, Kimberly Weinberger
Let's Read About . . . George Washington, Kimberly Weinberger
Let's Read About . . . Martin Luther King, Jr., Courtney Baker
A Picture Book of Christopher Columbus, David A. Adler
A Picture Book of George Washington, David A. Adler

PATRIOTISM

The United States has many patriotic symbols, such as the flag, the Liberty Bell, Uncle Sam, and the Statue of Liberty. Introduce children in the early elementary grades to these and other patriotic symbols through the following books. Many of these books are read-alouds.

America, A Patriotic Primer, Lynne V. Cheney
America the Beautiful, Kathleen Lee Bates
America's Top Ten National Monuments, Tanya Lee Stone
By the Dawn's Early Light: The Story of the Star Spangled Banner, Steven Kroll
The Flag We Love, Pam Muñoz Ryan
The Fourth of July Story, Alice Dalgliesh
If I Were President, Catherine Stier
Many Nations: An Alphabet of Native America (IRA Teacher's Choice), Joseph Bruchac
Oh Beautiful for Spacious Skies, Katherine Lee Bates
Red, White and Blue: The Story of the American Flag, John Herman
The Scrambled States of America, Laurie Keller
The Star Spangled Banner, Francis Scott Key, Peter Spier (illustrator)
The Story of America's Birthday, Patricia Pingrey
The Wall (Vietnam Veterans Memorial), Eve Bunting

REGIONAL FICTION AND NONFICTION

Nonfiction, as well as stories with settings in various geographic regions, introduce children to what it has been like for plants, animals, and people to live in climates different from their own. Through well-illustrated picture books, for example, children learn to compare the prairies of the United States with the cold arctic regions, or the woodlands and the deserts of the southwest with the mountain regions.

America: My Land, Your Land, Our Land, W. Nikola-Lisa
Antarctica, Helen Cowcher
Appalachia: The Voices of Sleeping Birds, Cynthia Rylant
Between Earth and Sky: Legends of Native American Sacred Places, Joseph Bruchac
Beyond the Ridge, Paul Goble
Coyote: A Trickster Tale from the American Southwest, Gerald McDermott
Dandelions, Eve Bunting

1.18 *continued*

The Desert Is Theirs, Byrd Baylor
Desert Voices, Byrd Baylor
Dream Wolf, Paul Goble
The Igloo, Charlotte Yue
Iktomi (series), Paul Goble
The Little Red Lighthouse and the Great Gray Bridge, Hildegarde Hoyt Swift
Living in the Arctic, Allan Fowler
Living in the Mountains, Allan Fowler
Living on the Plains, Allan Fowler
My Arctic 1,2,3, Michael Arvaarluk Kusugak & Vladyana Krykorka
My Little Island, Frane Lessac
North America (Rookie Read About Geography), Allan Fowler
North Pole, South Pole: Journeys to the Ends of the Earth, Bertrand Imbert
Northern Lullaby, Nancy White Carlstrom
Northwoods Cradle Song: From a Menominee Lullaby, Douglas Wood
Penguins, Gail Gibbons
Polar Bears and Other Arctic Animals, Melissa Kim
Raven: A Trickster Tale from the Pacific Northwest, Gerald McDermott

TRANSPORTATION

The books listed below are extremely popular among the very youngest children, whose curiosity leads them to learn more about how boats, trains, and other vehicles work. In addition, many of these books take children on trips to different geographic regions.

Boats

Boats, Anne F. Rockwell
Boats Afloat, Shelley Rotner
Daisy's Taxi, Ruth Young
My Red Rowboat, Dana Meachen Rau
Row Your Boat, Anthony Lishak
Tugboats, Robert Maass

Buses

Bus Stop Bop, Robin Kingsland
Bus Stop, Bus Go, Daniel Kirk
Bus Stops, Taro Gomi
Maisy Drives the Bus, Lucy Cousins
School Bus, Donald Crews
This Is the Way We Go to School, Edith Baer
Wheels Go Round, W. Nikola-Lisa

Planes

Airport, Byron Barton
The Big Book of Real Airplanes, Gina Ingoglia
First Flight, David McPhail
First Words: Cars, Boats, and Planes, Ed Emberley
Planes, Anne F. Rockwell
This Is an Airport, Richard Bagwell

Tractors

Drive Your Tractor, Anna Nilsen
If I Drove a Tractor, Miriam Young
Let's Look at Tractors, Graham Rickard
Parsnip and the Runaway Tractor, Sue Porter
Little Red Tractor Books, Elizabeth Laird
The Rusty Trusty Tractor, Joy Cowley
Tractor Mac, Billy Steers

1.18 *continued*

Trains

All Aboard!, James Stevenson
All Aboard the Whistle-Stop Train, June Doolittle
Barney's Book of Trains, Linda Cress Dowdy
*The Caboose Who Got Loose**, Bill Peet
Casey Jones, Allan Drummond
Christina Katerina and the Great Bear Train, Patricia Lee Gauch
*Clickety Clack**, Robert Spence III
*Choo Choo: The Story of a Little Engine Who Ran Away**, Virginia Lee Burton
*Chugga-Chugga, Choo-Choo**, Kevin Lewis
Engine, Engine, Number Nine, Stephanie Calmenson
Freight Train, Donald Crews
Here Comes the Train, Charlotte Voake
*Hey! Get Off Our Train**, John Burmingham
I Like Trains, Catherine Wooley
Inside the Freight Train, Donald Crews
It's Funny Where Ben's Train Takes Him, Robert Burleigh
Paddy Goes Traveling, John S. Goodall
Richard Scarry's Hop Aboard! Here We Go!, Richard Scarry
Shortcut, Donald Crews
Teddy Bears Take the Train, Susanna Gretz
The Christmas Train, Ivan Gantschev
The Freight Train Book, Jack Pierce
*The Little Engine That Could**, Watty Piper
The Polar Express, Chris Van Allsburg
The Train Ride, June Crebbin
The Train That Rode on Water, June Doolittle
*Time Train**, Paul Fleischman
Tracks, David Galef
Train, Charles A. Temple
Train Song, Diane Siebert
Trains, Anne F. Rockwell
Trains, Jon Richards
Trains, Ray Broekel
*Two Little Trains**, Margaret Wise Brown
Underground Train, Mary Quattlebaum

Trucks

Big Rigs, Hope Irvin Marston
Cars and Trucks and Other Vehicles, created by Gallimard Jeunesse & Claude Delafosse
Dazzling Diggers, Tony Mitton
Five Trucks, Brian Floca
Isaac the Ice Cream Truck, Scott Santoro
Seymour Simon's Book of Trucks, Seymour Simon
Trash Trucks, Daniel Kirk
Truck, Donald Crews
The Truck Book, Harry McNaught
Trucks, Trucks, Trucks, Peter Sis

1.19 Multicultural Books

Multicultural books reflect the diversity of the community and the classroom. They develop in children an appreciation for the uniqueness of a particular culture through an awareness of its traditions, experiences, and values without stereotyping or generalizing. Exposing children in grades pre-K–1 to multicultural literature gives them the opportunity to become aware of the values, traditions, and experiences of their own cultures.

African American

Amazing Grace, Mary Hoffman
Aunt Flossy's Hat, Elizabeth F. Howard
The Best Time of Day, Valerie Flournoy
Black White, Just Right!, Marguerite W. Davol
Boundless Grace, Mary Hoffman
*Cornrows**, Camille Yarbrough
Daddy Calls Me, Angela Johnson
Faraway Drums, Virginia L. Kroll
Nappy Hair, Carolivia Herron
Martin's Big Words: The Life of Martin Luther King, Jr., Doreen Rappaport
*Mirandy and Brother Wind**, Patricia McKissack
Patchwork Quilt, Valerie Flournoy
*Peter's Chair**, Ezra Jack Keats
Rosa Parks (Wonder Books), Robert B. Noyed
Shades of Black: A Celebration of Our Children, Sandra L. Pinkney
Shipwreck Saturday, Bill Cosby
Smoky Night, Eve Bunting
Stevie, John Steptoe
Ten Nine Eight, Molly Bang
When I Am Old With You, Angela Johnson

African Culture

Count Your Way Through Africa, Jim Haskins
It Takes a Village, Jane Cowen-Fletcher
Not So Fast, Songalolo (A South African Story), Nikki Daly
Jambo Means Hello, A Swahili Alphabet, Muriel L. Feelings
Moja Means One: Swahili Counting Book, Muriel L. Feelings
Swahili Counting Book, Tom Feelings
Village of Round and Square Houses, Ann Grifalconi
Zamani Goes to Market, Muriel L. Feelings
A Zulu Family, Nancy Durrell McKenna

Appalachian

Night in the Country, Cynthia Rylant
No Star Nights, Anna Egan Smucker
Until the Cows Come Home, Patricia Mills

1.19 *continued*

When the Relatives Came, Cynthia Rylant
*When I Was Young in the Mountains**, Cynthia Rylant

Asian American

Angel Child, Dragon Child, Michele M. Sarat
Ashok by Any Other Name (India), Sandra S. Yamate
Celebrating Chinese New Year, Diane Hoyt-Goldsmith
Cleversticks, Bernard Ashley
The Dancing Dragon, Marcia K. Vaughn
Halmoni and the Picnic, Sook Nyul Choi
How My Parents Learned to Eat (Japanese), Ina Friedman
Lion Dancer, Ernie Wan's Chinese New Year, Kate Waters
The Next Year (Chinese New Year), Janet S. Wong
Our Home Is the Sea, Riki Levinson
Sam and the Lucky Money, Karen Chinn
Yumi and Halmoni's Trip, Sook Nyul Choi

Asian Culture

At the Beach, Voun Lee
Ba Nam (Vietnamese), Jeanne M. Lee
*Boy of the Three-Year Nap**, Diane Snyder
Count Your Way Through China, Jim Haskins
Count Your Way Through Japan, Jim Haskins
The Dream Eater (A Japanese Story), Christian Garrison
The Magic Fan (Japanese), Keith Baker
Take a Trip to Indonesia, Keith Lye

Australia

Koalas and Kangaroos: Strange Animals of Australia, Toni Eugene
One Woolly Wombat, Rod Trinca and Kerry Argent
Possum Magic, Mem Fox

Caribbean

The Calypso Alphabet, John Agard
A Coconut Kind of Day, Lynn Joseph

European Culture

A Drop of Honey (Armenian), Djemma Bider
Pig and Bear (Czech), Vit Horejs
My Uncle Nikkos (Greek), Judy Delton
Tony's Bread: An Italian Tale, Tomie dePaola
Count Your Way Through Italy (1–10), Jim Haskins
*The Red Balloon** (French), Albert Lamorisse

1.19 *continued*

Erik Has a Squirrel (Swedish), Hans Petersen (Christine Hyatt, translater)
Lotta's Bike (Swedish), Astrid Lindgren
Lotta on Troublemaker Street (Swedish), Astrid Lindgren
Mirabelle (Swedish), Astrid Lindgren
Fu Dog (English/Chinese), Rumer Godden

Hispanic

A Birthday Basket for Tia, Pat Mora
Abuela, Arthur Dorros
Arroz Con Leche (Popular Songs and Rhymes), Lulu Delacre
Big Bushy Mustache, Gary Soto
Big Enough, Ofelia Dumas Lachtman
Calor, Juanita Alba
Chato and the Party Animals, Gary Soto
Family, Diane Gonzales Bertrand
Grandma Fina and Her Wonderful Umbrellas, Benjamin Alire Saenz
Home at Last, Susan Middleton Elya
In My Family, Carmen Lomas-Garza
La Mariposa, Simó Silva
Say Hola to Spanish at the Circus, Susan M. Elya
Eight Animals on the Town, Susan M. Elya
The Most Beautiful Place in the World (A Guatemala Picture Story), Ann Cameron
The Tamale Quilt, Jane Tenorio-Coscarelli
Carlos and the Squash Plant (bilingual), Jan Romero Stevens
Ten Little Fingers and Other Play Rhymes and Action Songs from Mexico, Jose-Luis Orozco
Saturday Sancocho, Leyla Torres
The Bakery Lady, Pat Mora
In Rosa's Mexico, Campbell Geeslin
Sip, Slurp, Soup, Soup, Caldo, Caldo, Caldo, Diane Gonzalez Bertrand
Hello Amigos!, Tricia Brown
Gathering the Sun: An Alphabet Book in Spanish and English, Alma Flor Ada
New Shoes for Sylvia, Johanna Hurwitz
Carlos Digs to China (series), Jan Romero Stevens
Hairs: Pelitos, Sandra Cisneros
Juan Bobo (series), Marisa Montes

Jewish

We Remember the Holocaust, David A. Adler
The Jewish Children's Bible, Sheryl Parenefu
A Treasury of Jewish Stories, Adele Geras
Sweet Words to God, A Child's Book of Jewish Prayers, Arnold M. Goodman
A Child's Garden of Torah: A Read-Aloud Bedtime Bible, Joell Grishaver
The Borrowed Hanukkah Latkes, Linda Glaser

1.19 *continued*

Dance, Sing, Remember: A Celebration of Jewish Holidays, Leslie Kimmelman
The Friday Nights of Nana, Amy Hest
Just Right: The Story of a Jewish Home, Ellen Emerman
The Keeping Quilt, Patricia Polacco
My Brother's Bar Mitzvah, Janet Gallant
My Sister's Wedding, Richard Rosenblum
My Two Grandmothers, Effin Older
Shabbat, Miriam Nerlove
Shabbat Box, Lesley Simpson

Middle Eastern

Nadia the Willful (about a young Arab girl), Sue Alexander
Joshua's Dream (caring for the environment in Israel), Sheila Segal
Alina: A Russian Girl Comes to Israel (a picture story), Mira Meir
Count Your Way Through the Arab World, Jim Haskins

Native American

Dancing with the Indians, Angela S. Medearis
Turtle Island ABC: A Gathering of Native American Symbols, Gerald Hausmman
Iktomi and the Ducks: A Plains Indian Story, Paul Goble
How Thunder and Lightning Came to Be, Beatrice O. Harrell
Knots on a Counting Rope, Bill Martin Jr. and John Archambault
Coyote: A Trickster Tale from the American Southwest, Gerald McDermott
Rabbit and the Moon, Douglas Wood
Sky Dog, Jane Yolen
Native Americans (Starting Point History Series), Gallimard Jeunesse
Annie and the Old One, Miska Miles
Less Than Half, More Than Whole, Kathleen Lacapa
*Mama, Do You Love Me?** (Inuit), Barbara Josse
On Mother's Lap (Inuit), Ann Herbert Scott
Runaway Mittens, Jean Rogers
Skysisters, Jan Bourdeau Waboose
Where Did You Get Your Moccasins?, Bernelda Wheeler
Jingle Dancer, Cynthia Leitich Smith

1.20 Books About Feelings and Conflicts

Feelings and social conflicts are central themes of many stories throughout grades K and 1. They are important because they mirror everyday conflicts among children. Encouraging positive behavior requires a variety of interventions, including classroom rules and modeling. The following books can be used effectively to discuss specific problems.

Life with One Parent, Jim Boulden
Dear Bear, Joanna Harrison
It's Mine!, Alice Garcia de Lynam
Harry and the Terrible Whatzit, Dick Gackenbach
Off to School, Baby Duck, Amy Hest
Go Away Dark Night, Liz Curtis Higgs
Noel the Coward, Robert Kraus
Leo the Late Bloomer, Robert Kraus
Moonbear's Dream, Frank Asch
Roger Takes Charge, Susanna Gretz
I Won't Be Afraid, Joan Hanson
Go Away, Bad Dreams!, Susan Hill
Scaredy Dog, Stephen H. Lemberg
We Are Monsters, Mary Packard
Wemberly Worried, Kevin Henkes
I Was So Mad, Karen Erickson
There's a Nighmare in My Closet, Mercer Mayer
Go Away, Big Green Monster!, Ed Emberley
Little Tiger's Big Surprise, Julie Sykes
Hannah's Temper, Celia Berridge
The Wee Little Woman, Byron Barton
Be Boy Buzz, Bell Hooks
Look Out! He's Behind You, Tony Bradman
Benjamin Rabbit and the Stranger Danger, Irene Keller
Nappy Hair, Carolivia Herron
My Rotten-Headed Older Brother, Patricia Polara
Big Sister, Little Sister, Charlotte Zolotow
Sisters, David McPhail
Matthew and Tilly, Rebecca C. Jones
Alexander and the Terrible, Horrible, No Good, Very Bad Day, Judith Viorst (available in Spanish)
Alexander, Who's Not (Do You Hear Me? I Mean It!) Going to Move, Judith Viorst
Absolutely Positively Alexander (The Complete Stories), Judith Viorst
I Like Me!, Nancy L. Carlson
Chrysanthemum, Kevin Henkes
I'm Terrific, Marjorie Weinman Sharmat

1.21 Books About Holidays and Traditions

Both national and religious holidays are represented in this list. These books can be read aloud and discussed. Sharing holiday books is an ideal way to help children develop an appreciation for the diverse traditions and celebrations of all people in their community and around the world. (Also see List 2.16.)

David Adler, *Chanukah in Chelm*
George Ancona, *Pablo Remembers: The Fiesta of the Day of the Dead*
Bonny Becker, *The Christmas Crocodile*
June Behrens, *Gung Hay Fat Choy*
Emery Bernhard, *Happy New Year!*
Jan Brett, *Christmas Trolls*
Jan Brett, *Who's That Knocking on Christmas Eve?*
Tricia Brown, *Chinese New Year*
Ray Buckley, *The Give Away: A Christmas Story*
Eve Bunting, *One Candle* (Hanukkah)
David A. Carter, *Chanukah Bugs: A Pop-up Celebration*
David A. Carter, *Easter Bugs: A Springtime Pop-up*
Eric Carle, *Dream Snow*
Deborah Newton Chocolate, *My First Kwanzaa Book*
Demi, *Happy New Year! Kung-His-Fa-T's Ai*
Tomie dePaola, *The Legend of the Poinsettia*
Tomie dePaola, *Merry Christmas, Strega Nona*
Tomie dePaola, *An Early American Christmas*
Tomie dePaola, *The Night of Las Posadas*
Wende Devlin, *Cranberry Easter*
Arlene Erlbach, *Happy New Year, Everywhere!*
Marie Hall Ets, *Nine Days to Christmas* (Mexico)
Cathy Goldberg Fishman, *On Rosh Hashanah and Yom Kippur*
Juwanda Ford, *K Is for Kwanzaa*
Mem Fox, *Wombat Divine* (Australia)
Priscilla Friedrich, *The Easter Bunny That Overslept*
Christina Mia Gardeski, *Diwali* (Hindu) (Rookie Read-About Holidays)
Suhaib Hamid Ghazi, *Ramadan*
Gail Gibbons, *Easter*
Rachna Gilmore, *Lights for Gita* (Diwali)
Barbara Goldin, *A Mountain of Blintzes* (Shavuot)
Barbara Goldin, *While the Candles Burn; Eight Stories for Hanukkah*
Christina Goodings, *Bartimouse and the Easter Egg*
Wilma Willis Gore, *Independence Day*
Amy Hest, *The Friday Nights of Nana* (Jewish Sabbath)
Dubose Heyward, *The Country Bunny and the Little Gold Shoes*
E. Hoffmann, *Nutcracker*
Diane Hoyt-Goldsmith, *Celebrating Kwanzaa*
Diane Hoyt-Goldsmith, *Celebrating Chinese New Year*
Trina Schart Hyman, *How Six Found Christmas*
Tony Johnston, *Day of the Dead*
Barbara Joosse, *A Houseful of Christmas*
William Joyce, *Snowie Rolie*
Eric Kimmel, *Hershel and the Hanukkah Goblins*
Eric Kimmel, *When Mindy Saved Hanukkah*
Cynthia Fitterer Klingel, *The Fourth of July*
Alfred J. Kolatch, *Let's Celebrate Our Jewish Holidays!*
Camille Kress, *Purim!*
Virginia Kroll, *A Carp for Kimiko*
Nancy Luenn, *Celebrations of Light*
Nancy Luenn, *A Gift for Abuellita*
Dianne M. Macmillan, *Japanese Children's Day and the Obon Festival*
Dianne M. Macmillan, *Mexican Independence Day and Cinco de Mayo*
Dianne M. Macmillan, *Ramadan and Id al-Fitr*
Dianne M. Macmillan, *Tet: Vietnamese New Year*
Fran Manushkin, *The Matzah that Papa Brought Home*

1.21 *continued*

Colleen Monroe, *A Wish to Be a Christmas Tree*
Robin Nelson, *Independence Day*
Leslea Newman, *Runaway Dreidel!*
Jeffery O'Hare, *Hanukkah: Festival of Lights*
Meenal Atul Pandya, *Here Comes Diwali: The Festival of Lights*
Betty Paraskevas, *Nibbles O'Hare* (Easter)
Betty Paraskevas, *On the Day the Tall Ships Sailed* (4th of July)
Andrea Davis Pinkney, *Mim's Christmas Jam*
Mark Podwal, *The Menorah Story*
Patricia Polacco, *Uncle Vova's Tree*
Jack Prelutsky, *It's Christmas*
Mary Quattlebaum, *The Shine Man: A Christmas Story*
Ronne Randall, *The Hanukkah Mice*
Michael J. Rosen, *Chanukah Lights Everywhere*
Michael J. Rosen, *Elijah's Angel: A Story for Chanukah and Christmas*
Cynthia Rylant, *Christmas in the Country*
Robert Sabuda, *The Christmas Alphabet*
Robert Sabuda, *The Night Before Christmas*
Alison Samuels, *Christmas Soul: African American Holiday Stories*
Luis San Vicente, *Festival of the Bones: El Festival de las Calaveras*
Richard Scarry, *The Night Before the Night Before Christmas*
Maxine Schur, *The Peddler's Gift* (Hanukkah)
Otto Seibold, *Olive, the Other Reindeer*
Dr. Seuss, *How the Grinch Stole Christmas*
Emily Sper, *Hanukkah: A Counting Book in English, Hebrew, and Yiddish*
Kay Thompson, *Eloise at Christmastime*
Sandy Turner, *Silent Night*
Chris Van Allsburg, *The Polar Express*
Marcia K. Vaughn, *The Dancing Dragon*
Kate Waters, *Lion Dancer: Ernie Wan's Chinese New Year*
Rosemary Wells, *Max's Chocolate Chicken*
Rosemary Wells, *Morris's Disappearing Bag*
Hans Wilhelm, *Bunny Trouble*
Janet S. Wong, *Apple Pie 4th of July*
Janet S. Wong, *This Next New Year*
Arthur Yorinks, *The Flying Latke* (Chanukah)
Harriet Ziefert, *Hats Off for the Fourth of July!*
Johnny Zucker, *Apples and Honey: A Rosh Hashanah Story*
Johnny Zucker, *Eight Candles for Lighting: A Chanukah Story*

1.22 Books About Music, Dance, and Art

Music and dance cannot be separated at the preschool and primary levels. Children use their bodies to express their feelings as they clap to the rhythm of the music. They also learn to work together as they dance and sing collectively. The delightful and sometimes humorous stories below introduce children to various forms of dance.

Art is another expressive form. Books listed below on this topic are informative and fun. Many are read-aloud books, introducing children to galleries and museums.

Music and Song

Yankee Doodle, Edward Bangs
Dem Bones, Bob Barner
Berlioz the Bear, Jan Brett
Billy Boy, Richard Chase
Down by the Bay, Raffi
Little White Duck, Walt Whippo
The Bear Who Loved Puccini, Arnold Sundgaard
The Philharmonic Gets Dressed, Karla Kuskin
Pet of the Met, Don Freeman
Crash! Bang! Boom!, Peter Spier
Ben's Trumpet, Rachel Isadora
Fireside Songbook of Birds and Beasts, Jane Yolen (editor)
She'll Be Comin' Round the Mountain, Tom Birdseye
Jane Yolen's Songs of Summer, Jane Yolen (editor)
Jane Yolen's Mother Goose Songbook, Jane Yolen (editor)
Good Night, Good Night, Sandra Boynton
The Teddy Bears Picnic, Jimmy Kennedy
Play Rhymes, Marc Tolon Brown
Caribbean Carnival: Songs of the West Indies, Irving Burgie (compiler)
Today Is Monday, Eric Carle
Dancing, Denys Cazet
Over the River and Through the Wood, Lydia Maria Child
Six Little Ducks, Chris Conover
We All Sing With the Same Voice, J. Philip Miller
What a Wonderful World, George Weiss

Dance

Angelina Ballerina, Katharine Holabird
Ballerina Flying, Alexa Brandenberg
Barn Dance, Bill Martin Jr. & John Archambault
Bill and the Google-Eyed Goblins, Alice Schertle
The Dancing Class, Helen Oxenbury
Harriet's Recital, Nancy Carlson
Nina, Nina, Star Ballerina (African American), Jane O'Connor
Mirandy and Brother Wind (Native American), Pat McKissack
Buffalo Dance (Hispanic), Nancy Van Laan
Boogie Bones, Elizabeth Loredo
Dance, Annie, Dawn Friedman
Mama Does the Mambo, Katherine Leiner
Sophie and Lou, Petra Mathers
Ragtime Tumpie (Josephine Baker), Alan Schroeder
Boy! Can He Dance!, Eileen Spinelli
Marie in the Fourth Position, The Story of Degas' "Little Dancer," Amy Littlesugar
Dance Me a Story: Twelve Tales from the Classic Ballets, Jane Rosenberg
Hen Lake, Mary Jane Auch
Bravo, Tanya, Patricia Gauch
Opening Night, Rachel Isadora
How Can You Dance?, Rick Walton

Art

A Bird or Two: A Story About Henri Matisse, Bijou LeTord
A Blue Butterfly: A Story About Claude Monet, Bijou LeTord

1.22 *continued*

Camille and the Sunflowers: A Story About Vincent Van Gogh, Laurence Anholt
Degas and the Little Dancer: A Story About Edgar Degas, Laurence Anholt
Family Pictures, Carmen Lomas Garza
Frida, Jeanette Winter
Katie Meets the Impressionists, James Mayhew
Katie and the Mona Lisa, James Mayhew
Katie and the Sunflowers, James Mayhew
Linnea in Monet's Garden, Christina Bjork
Michelangelo, Diane Stanley
Once Upon A Lily Pad: Froggy Love in Monet's Garden, Joan Sweeney
Picasso and the Girl With the Ponytail: A Story About Pablo Picasso, Laurence Anholt
You Can't Take a Balloon into the Metropolitan Museum, Jacqueline Preiss Weitzman
You Can't Take a Balloon into the National Gallery, Jacqueline Preiss Weitzman

1.23 Sports Books

Some of these appealing read-aloud books for preschoolers and primary-grade children use animal characters who engage in all types of sports. The tricks and antics of these animals, who do many things that humans can't do, appeal to children. Since children at this age are just becoming involved in sports, they find these books informative and fun as they learn new sports concepts.

Baseball

Baseball Mouse, Sid Hoff
Game Day, Cari Meister
Mouse Practice, Emily Arnold McCully
My Baseball Book, Gail Gibbons
Nate the Great and the Stolen Base, Marjorie Sharmat
Playing Right Field, Willy Welch
Slugger Sal's Slump, Sid Hoff
Who Tossed that Bat?, Leonard Kessler

Bicycling

D. W. Rides Again!, Marc Brown
The New Bike, Marie Vinje
Bear on a Bike, Stella Blackstone
Franklin Rides a Bike, Paulette Bourgeois
Bicycle Race, Donald Crews
Kit and Kat, Tomie dePaola
You Can Do It, Rabbit, Paul Dowling
Annie Flies the Birthday Bike, Crescent Dragonwagon
Angelina's Birthday Surprise, Katherine Holabird
Shawn's Red Bike, Petronella Breinburg
Little Duck's Bicycle Ride, Dorothy Stott
Lulu on Her Bike, Susanne Strub

Football

Louanne Pig in Making the Team, Nancy L. Carlson
The Dallas Titans Get Ready for Bed, Karla Kuskin
Snail Saves the Day, John Stadler

Gymnastics

D. W. Flips!, Marc Tolon Brown
A Very Young Gymnast, Jill Kremetz

Ice-Skating

Elephants on Ice, Anna DiVito
Mr. Pig and Sonny Too, Lillian Hoban
Angelina Ice Skates, Katherine Holabird
Dog Boy Cap Skate, Nicki Weiss
Elfantina's Dream, X. J. Kennedy

Skiing

Do Teddy Bears Ski?, Rick Sanger
Ski Pup, Don Freeman
A Very Young Skier, Jill Krementz

Sledding

A Perfect Day for It, Jan Fearnly
Let's Go Sledding, Steve Metzger
Balto and the Great Race, Elizabeth Cody Kimmel
Running with the Big Dogs, Lori Yanuchi
The Story of a Boy Named Will, Who Went Sledding Down the Hill, Daniil Kharms

Soccer

Willy the Wizard, Anthony Browne
Dylan's Day Out, Peter Catalanotto
Froggy Plays Soccer, Jonathan London

Swimming

Michael and the Sea, Allison Coles
Maisy Goes Swimming, Lucy Cousins
The Chick and the Duckling, Mirra Ginsburg
Otter Swims, Derek Hall
The Littlest Duckling, Gail Herman
Swimming Lessons, Betsy Jay
Froggy Learns to Swim, Jonathan London
Elephants Swim, Linda Capus Riley
Tony's First Dive, Leonard Shortall
Hooray for Pig!, Carla Stevens
Lulu Goes Swimming, Susanne Strub
The Pig in the Pond, Martin Waddell
Edward in Deep Water, Rosemary Wells

1.24 Mother Goose and Nursery Rhymes

Repetition, rhythm, and rhyme are important links between children's own language and the language of the printed word. Hundreds of beautifully illustrated books of nursery and Mother Goose rhymes are available for young children today. Below is a sample of only a few that are sure to stimulate, delight, and even instruct.

Collections of Mother Goose Rhymes

Tomie dePaola's Mother Goose, Tomie dePaola
This illustrated collection of over 200 Mother Goose nursery rhymes is filled with fresh life and brilliant full-color paintings.

Here Comes Mother Goose, edited by Iona Opie, illustrated by Rosemary Wells
Written by a world-renowned folklorist, this collection of favorite and lesser-known nursery rhymes will surely be a classic.

Random House Book of Mother Goose, Arnold Lobel (reissued as *The Arnold Lobel Book of Mother Goose*)
This illustrated collection includes well-known rhymes as well as those that are less familiar.

Marguerite de Angeli's Book of Nursery and Mother Goose Rhymes, edited by Marguerite de Angeli
De Angeli's warm illustrations are generously spread throughout these fanciful pages.

My Very First Mother Goose, Iona Wells, illustrated by Rosemary Wells
This book has great pictures of some favorite characters like Humpty Dumpty, Jack and Jill, and Little Boy Blue.

Chinese Mother Goose Rhymes, edited by Robert Wyndam, illustrated by Ed Young
This enchanting collection of poems, lullabies, counting rhymes, and songs from the Chinese tradition is beautifully illustrated.

The Alaska Mother Goose (Last Wilderness Adventure), Shelly Gill
This is a humorous collection of nursery rhymes with a northern flair that focuses on animals and how they behave.

Nursery Rhyme Tales

Children will enjoy the following individual retellings of nursery rhymes in picture book format.

The House That Jack Built by Sims Taback
Old Mother Hubbard by James Marshall
The Three Little Kittens by Paul Galdone

1.25 Rhyming Books

The books below are recommended for their rich use of melodious language, rhythm, and rhyming patterns. Ideally, they should be read aloud in order for children to hear the engaging rhythms. Many of the books also lend themselves to dramatization, which develops oral language skills and encourages retelling the story events in sequence.

Ants in Your Pants, Sue Heap
Before I Go to Sleep, Thomas Hood
Out and About, Shirley Hughes
The Boy Who Wouldn't Go to Bed, Helen Cooper
Bug in a Rug, Sue Heap
A Cake for Herbie, Petra Mathers
Chicka Chicka Boom Boom, Bill Martin Jr. & John Archambault
The Christmas Tree Tangle, Margaret Mahy
Cocoa Ice, Diana Karter Applebaum
Crow Moon, Worm Moon, James Skofield
The Drowsy Hours: Poems for Bedtime, selected by Susan Pearson
Duck in the Truck, Jez Alborough
Fix It Duck, Jez Alborough
A Hug Goes Around, Laura Krauss Melmed
I Am the Dog, I Am the Cat, Donald Hall
I Love You as Much . . . , Laura Krauss Melmed
I'm Not Going to Chase the Cat Today, Jessica Harper
Jump! The Adventures of Brer Rabbit, Joel Chandler Harris
Mama Had a Dancing Heart, Libby Moore Gray
Moishe's Miracle, Laura Krauss Melmed
Mrs. McNosh and the Great Big Squash, Sarah Weeks
Mrs. McNosh Hangs Up Her Wash, Sarah Weeks
Oh My Gosh, Mrs. McNosh!, Sarah Weeks
One Fish, Two Fish, Red Fish, Blue Fish, Dr. Seuss
One Lonely Seahorse, Saxton Freymann
Over in the Meadow: An Old Nursery Counting Rhyme, Paul Galdone
The Owl Who Became the Moon, Jonathon London
Peekaboo Friends!, Lucy Su
The Rainbabies, Laura Krauss Melmed
Rainbow Fish and the Sea Monster's Cave, Marcus Pfister
Sea Elf, Joanne Ryder
Turtle Bay, Savious Pirotta
Turtle, Turtle, Watch Out!, April Pulley Sayre
The Very Noisy Night, Diana Hendry
Was It a Good Trade?, Beatrice Schenk de Regniers
We Played Marbles, Tres Seymour
What a Wonderful Day to Be a Cow, Carolyn Lesser
Where Do You Sleep, Little One?, Patricia Hooper
Whiffle Squeek, Caron Lee Cohen
White Is the Moon, Valerie Greeley
Who Is the World For?, Tom Pow

1.26 Poetry

As with nursery rhymes and Mother Goose rhymes, language development is enriched by the new words and phrases that children encounter in poetry. The list below offers many selections to help you introduce children to the wonderful world of poetry.

Animal Crackers, Jane Dyer
Beneath a Blue Umbrella, Jack Prelutsky, illustrated by Garth Williams
Come Sunday, Nikki Grimes, illustrated by Michael Bryant
Crowning Glory: hair a gift wrapped ribboned curled tied, Joyce Carol Thomas, illustrated by Brenda Jaysmith
*Dinosaur Dances**, Jane Yolen, illustrated by Bruce Degen
Every Time I Climb a Tree, David McCord, illustrated by Marc Simont
*Festivals**, Myra Cohn Livingston, illustrated by Leonard Everett Fisher
A Fine Fat Pig, Mary Ann Hoberman, illustrated by Malcah Zeldis
*The Gingham Dog and the Calico Cat**, Eugene Field, illustrated by Janet Street
Give Yourself to the Rain: Poems for the Very Young, Margaret Wise Brown
The House of a Mouse, Aileen Fisher, illustrated by Joan Sandin
I Can Draw a Weeposaur and other Dinosaurs, Eloise Greenfield, illustrated by Jan Spivey Gilchrist
*I'll Be You and You Be Me**, Ruth Krauss, illustrated by Maurice Sendak
I Never Did That Before, Lilian Moore, illustrated by Lillian Hoban
*It's Raining Pigs and Noodles**, Jack Prelutsky, illustrated by James Stevenson
Lemonade Sun and Other Summer Fun, Rebecca Kai Dotlich, illustrated by Jan Spivey Gilchrist
Let's Count Raindrops, Fumi Kosaka
Lizards, Frogs, and Polliwogs, Douglas Florian
Love to Mama, edited by Pat Mora, illustrated by Paula S. Barragan
Messages to Ground Zero: Children Respond to September 11, 2001, compiled by Shelley Harwayne
*Monster Goose**, Judy Sierra, illustrated by Jack E. Davis
*Ook the Book**, Lisa Rovetch, illustrated by Shannon McNeill
Outside the Lines: Poetry at Play, Brad Burg, illustrated by Rebecca Gibbon
Pocketful of Nonsense, James Marshall
A Poke in the I: A Collection of Concrete Poems, edited by Paul Janeczko, illustrated by Chris Raschka
Raining Cats and Dogs, Jane Yolen, illustrated by Janet Street
Sun Dance Water Dance, Jonathan London, illustrated by Greg Couch
Ride a Purple Pelican, Jack Prelutsky, illustrated by Garth Williams
Rumpus of Rhymes: A Book of Noisy Poems, Bobbi Katz, illustrated by Susan Estelle Kwas
*Seasons: A Book of Poems**, Charlotte Zolotow (An I Can Read Book), illustrated by Erik Blegvad
*Shoe Magic**, Nikki Grimes, illustrated by Terry Widener
Sing a Song of Popcorn: Every Child's Book of Poems, selected by Beatrice Schenk de Regniers, illustrated by Marcia Brown
Sky scrape/City scape: Poems of City Life, selected by Jane Yolen, illustrated by Ken Condon
*Some from the Moon Some from the Sun: Poems and Songs for Everyone**, Margot Zemach
Spring: A Haiku Story, George Shannon, illustrated by Malcah Zeldis

1.26 *continued*

*Summersaults: Poems and Paintings**, Douglas Florian
Talking Like the Rain, X. J. Kennedy, illustrated by Jane Dyer
*Timothy Tunny Swallowed a Bunny**, Bill Grossman, illustrated by Kevin Hawkes
The Way I Feel Sometimes, Beatrice Schenk de Regniers
There Was an Old Lady Who Swallowed a Fly, Simms Taback
*This Big Sky**, Pat Mora, illustrated by Steve Jenkins
This Place I Know: Poems of Comfort, Georgia Heard
The Three Bears Holiday Rhyme Book, Jane Yolen, illustrated by Jane Dyer
*The Three Bears Rhyme Book**, Jane Yolen, illustrated by Jane Dyer
Walking the Bridge of Your Nose: Wordplay Poems, selected by Michael Rosen, illustrated by Cloe Cheese
*When the Moon Is Full: A Lunar Year**, Penny Pollock, illustrated by Mary Azarian
*Wool Gathering: A Sheep Family Reunion**, Lisa Wheeler
Zoo Doings: Animal Poems, Jack Prelutsky, illustrated by Paul O. Zelinsky
Some of the Days of Everett Anderson, Lucille Clifton, illustrated by Ann Grifalconi
The Little Dog Laughed and Other Nursery Rhymes, Lucy Cousins
Jamberry, Bruce Degan
Tomi dePaola's Favorite Nursery Tales, Tomie dePaola
Animal Crackers, Jane Dyer
Wynken, Blynken, and Nod, Eugene Field, illustrated by Barbara Cooney
Pumpkin Eye, Denise Fleming
Little Dog Poems, Kristine O'Connell George
Mary Had a Little Lamb, Sarah Hale
Pretend You're a Cat, Jean Marzollo, illustrated by Jerry Pinkney

1.27 Jokes, Riddles, and Trick Books

Jokes and riddles touch upon different themes: insects, animals, fish, mummies, and space. In addition to their humor, they are cleverly illustrated. For example, the illustrations in *Monika Beisner's Book of Riddles* provide answers to questions in the text.

Bumblebee, Bumblebee Do You Know Me?: A Garden Guessing Game, Anne Rockwell
Clifford's Riddles, Norman Bridwell
I Can Fly, What Am I?, Alain Crozon
I Can Roll, What Am I?, Alain Crozon
I Spy (series), Jean Marzollo
It Looked Like Spilt Milk, Charles Green Shaw
Little Critters Joke Book, Mercer Mayer
Monika Beisner's Book of Riddles, Monika Beisner
One Riddle, One Answer, Lauren Thompson
What Am I?, Alain Crozon
What in the World?, Eve Merriam
What Time Is It?, Sheila Keenan
Who Am I?, Alain Crozon
Give a Dog a Bone: Stories, Poems, Jokes about Dogs, compiled by Joanna Cole & Stephanie Calmenson
What Am I?, Margaret Hillert
Q Is for Duck, Mary Elting
Summer Camp Crack-ups: and Lots s'more Knock-Knock Jokes to Write Home About, Katy Hall & Lisa Eisenberg
Back-to-School Belly Busters, Katy Hall & Lisa Eisenberg
Creepy Riddles, Katy Hall & Lisa Eisenberg
Geese Find the Missing Piece, Marco Maestro
Giggle Fit: Goofy Riddles, Joseph Rosenbloom
Giggle Fit: Nutty Jokes, Matt Rissinger & Philip Yates
Giggle Fit: Silly Knock-Knocks, Joseph Rosenbloom
Goofy Riddles, Joseph Rosenbloom
What Do You Hear When Cows Sing? And Other Silly Riddles, Marco Maestro
Peephole Riddles, Margaret Anastas
Pig Giggles and Rabbit Rhymes: Book of Animal Riddles, Mike Downs
Riddles and More Riddles, Bennett Cert
Super Silly Riddles, Keith Faulkner

SECTION TWO

Books for Grades 2 and 3

2.1 Classics and All-Time Favorites

The list below includes titles of long-time favorites and classics on a range of grade levels from easy grade 2 to advanced grade 3. Those titles with two asterisks (**) indicate an advanced grade 3 reading level and, in some cases, a grade 4 level. Children this age also enjoy hearing classics for older children read aloud, such as *Tom Sawyer* by Mark Twain and *Alice in Wonderland* by Lewis Carroll.

*The Adventures of Danny Meadow Mouse***, by Thornton W. Burgess
The Adventures of Pippy Longstocking (Series)**, by Astrid Lindgren
*The Adventures of Poor Mrs. Quack***, by Thornton W. Burgess
Amelia Bedelia (Series), by Peggy Parish
*Blacky the Crow***, by Thornton W. Burgess
Blueberries for Sal, by Robert McCloskey
*The Boxcar Children***, by Gertrude Chandler Warner
*The Chalk Box Kid***, by Clyde Robert Bulla
*Charlotte's Web***, by E. B. White
*Classic Poems to Read Aloud***, by James R. Berry
Eloise (Series), by Kay Thompson
Frog and Toad Are Friends, by Arnold Lobel
The Giving Tree, by Shel Silverstein
*The Hundred Dresses***, by Eleanor Estes
Jumanji, by Chris Van Allsburg
*Little House on the Prairie*** (Series), by Laura Ingalls Wilder
Madeline (Series), by Ludwig Bemelmans
Make Way for Ducklings, by Robert McCloskey
Mrs. Piggle Wiggle's Farm (Series), by Betty MacDonald
Officer Buckle and Gloria, by Peggy Rathmann
Owl Moon, by Jane Yolen
A Giraffe-and-a Half (poetry), by Shel Silverstein
Ramona (Series)**, by Beverly Cleary
*Sarah, Plain and Tall***, by Patricia MacLachlan
The Story of Babar, the Little Elephant (Series), by Jean de Brunhoff
Sylvester and the Magic Pebble, by William Steig
Town Mouse, Country Mouse, by Jan Brett
The Velveteen Rabbit, by Margery Williams

2.2 Favorite Chapter Books

The plots are rather simple in picture books. There is one main problem or conflict and a series of events take place in order to resolve it. In second grade, children begin reading chapter books, with plots that are more complex. Even though a central question binds the events together, the theme of the story can be revealed through one or more subplots, such as conflict between friends or within the main character.

Ada, A. *My Name Is Maria Isabel.* Immigrant Maria Isabel wants to fit in at school, and a writing assignment called "My Greatest Wish" gives her that opportunity.

Adams, L. *Alice and the Boa Constrictor.* After learning in science class that boa constrictors make wonderful pets, Alice begins saving her money.

Adler, D. *"Cam Jansen"* series. A fifth-grade sleuth uses her photographic memory to solve crimes.

Ahlberg, J. *Jeremiah in the Dark Woods.* A young boy sets out to find the thief of his grandmother's strawberry tarts and meets some unusual characters during his search.

Alexander, S. *Lila on the Landing.* Lila creates imaginative activities on the landing of her apartment building.

Apablasa, B. *"Rhymin' Simon"* mystery series. A rhyme-making sleuth and his friends solve crimes.

Auch, M. *Angel and Me and the Bayside Bombers.* Can *any* soccer team beat the Bayside Bombers? Watch out for the Bomber Busters!

Baker, B. *N-O Spells No!* During the events of one weekend, Walter and his sister, Annie, come to appreciate each other.

Berends, P. *The Case of the Elevator Duck.* An 11-year-old detective sets out on an adventure after finding a duck in the elevator of his apartment building.

Brimner, L. *Cory Coleman, Grade 2.* Cory is planning his seventh birthday party, when his mother tells him he has to invite everyone—even the class bully!

Broome, E. *Tangles.* Sophie takes money from a neighbor's wallet to buy a kitten. The "tangles" are her emotions.

Brown, M. *Sneakers.* Follow the escapades of a very curious cat.

Bulla, C. *The Chalk Box Kid.* Gregory's house does not have room for a garden, but he still is able to create a surprising and unusual one. (See also this author's *White Bird*, among others.)

Buller, J. *No Tooth, No Quarter!* A boy must accompany an unlucky tooth fairy to her queen so he can explain that he mislaid his tooth.

Bunting, E. *The Big Cheese.* The purchase of an enormous cheese results in greatly enriched lives for two old women.

Byars, B. *Beans on the Roof.* Each member of the Bean family tries to write a "roof" poem in order to win a contest.

Byars, B. *The Seven Treasure Hunts.* Two boys make up a series of treasure hunts for each other, with disastrous and hilarious results.

Cameron, A. *"Julian"* series. Stories about a little boy with a big imagination.

Castaneda, O. *Abuela's Weave.* A Guatemalan girl and her grandmother grow close as they make weavings and travel to market to sell them.

Cazet, D. *Saturday.* Barney the dog spends busy days with his grandparents. (See also *Sunday.*)

Chang, H. *Elaine and the Flying Frog.* Elaine feels like an outcast after moving to a small town, until she shares a science project with a girl strongly interested in frogs.

2.2 *continued*

Charbonnet, G. *Snakes Are Nothing to Sneeze At.* Although he's not furry and her best friend thinks he's yucky, Annabel loves her new pet snake.

Chew, R. *Second-hand Magic.* Two children mend a discarded kite—which turns out to be magic!

Choi, S. *Halmoni and the Picnic.* A Korean-American girl's third-grade class helps her newly arrived grandmother adapt to life in the United States.

Christian, M. *"Sebastian (Super Sleuth)"* series. Follow the exploits of the world's greatest dog detective. (See also this author's *"Determined Detectives"* series.)

Christiansen, C. B. *Sycamore Street.* Angel and Chloe avoid obnoxious Rupert. Then Angel goes on vacation. Who will Chloe play with?

Christopher, M. *The Dog That Pitched a No-Hitter.* Mike's telepathic dog, Harry, helps the team. (This author has written three other books about this amazing dog, as well as many other early chapter books with a sports theme.)

Christopher, M. *Zero's Slider.* Zero discovers that he can throw a slider when there's a bandage on his injured thumb.

Clarke, J. *Teddy B. Zoot.* A kindhearted teddy bear journeys to his owner's elementary school in the middle of the night to retrieve her math assignment.

Cleary, B. *"Ramona"* series. (See also the many other titles by this author.)

Clifford, E. *"Flatfoot Fox"* series. Flatfoot has been called "the world's greatest detective." He just happens to be a fox!

Cone, M. *"Mishmash"* series. Mishmash, a precocious dog, and his owner, Pete, share experiences in their neighborhood and school.

Conford, E. *"Jenny Archer"* series. Nine-year-old Jenny has a big imagination. She makes her own adventures!

Cresswell, H. *Almost Good-bye.* Gumball Gumford wishes on a magic lamp to be invisible. Now the lamp is lost. Is it "good-bye Gumball"?

Cuyler, M. *Weird Wolf.* Harry Walpole is turning into a werewolf! Can he break the curse—without a silver bullet?

Delton, J. *"Pee Wee Scouts"* series. A series about a group of scouts and their larger-than-life experiences.

Dicks, T. *"Adventures of Goliath"* series. Goliath is a small puppy who grows and grows and grows. He's the source of many problems, and lots of fun!

Duffey, B. *How to Be Cool in the Third Grade.* Robby decides that the only way to get through third grade is to be "cool."

Duggan, A. *Violet's Finest Hour.* Two young cats use a magic cape to stop a gang of bank robbers.

Duncan, L. *Wonder Kid Meets the Evil Lunch Snatcher.* Terrorized by a bully, Brian and a fellow comic-book fan devise a plan involving a new superhero named Wonder Kid.

Dutton, S. *Tales of Belva Jean Copenhagen.* Belva Jean shares stories of her classmates, neighbors, and family.

Etra, J. *Aliens for Breakfast.* Finding an intergalactic special agent in his cereal box, Richard joins in a fight to save Earth from aliens, one of whom is masquerading as his classmate. (See also *Aliens for Lunch* by this author.)

Feder, P. *Did You Lose the Car Again?* When Daddy forgets where the car is parked near their apartment, two sisters have exciting exploits while joining the search.

2.2 *continued*

Galbraith, K. *"Roommates"* series. A new baby is on the way, so now two sisters have to share a room.

Giff, P. *"Kids of the Polk Street School"* series. Go through the year in Ms. Rooney's class. (See also the author's other transitional series: *"New Kids at the Polk Street School," "Polka Dot Private Eye,"* and *"Lincoln Lions Band."*)

Gilson, J. *You Cheat!* Nathan bribes his brother into going fishing, then wishes he hadn't.

Gondosch, L. *Brutus the Wonder Poodle.* How will Ryan's poodle puppy ever win a pet contest against Tony's boxer? (See also this author's *The Monsters of Marble Avenue.*)

Greene, C. *The Jenny Summer.* Robin discovers the pleasure of having a best friend when Jenny moves in next door.

Greenwood, P. *What About My Goldfish?* Jamie worries about moving to a new city, but, with the help of his pets, he adjusts to his new home.

Gross, V. *The Day It Rained Forever.* Based on the Johnstown flood event, a dam bursts, releasing a wall of water 125 feet high.

Hall, L. *The Mystery of Pony Hollow Panda.* When her pony disappears from the pet parade, Sarah follows clues to unravel the mystery. (See also this author's other age-appropriate animal stories.)

Harvey, J. *Great-Uncle Dracula.* Emily's life takes a strange turn when she moves to Transylvania USA with an odd relative.

Haywood, C. *"Betsy"* series. Life among friends at school and the neighborhood, with a nostalgic feel. (See also this author's *"Eddie"* series.)

Herman, C. *Max Malone and the Great Cereal Rip-off.* Tired of feeling cheated by cereal box prizes, Max decides to fight back.

Herman, C. *Millie Cooper, 3B.* Millie copes with school and other problems in creative and funny ways.

Hesse, K. *Sable.* Tate is happy when a stray dog appears, but Sable causes trouble with the neighbors and has to go.

Hiser, C. *Scoop Snoops.* The exciting life of fourth graders working on the school newspaper.

Hooks, W. *Pioneer Cat.* A pioneer girl smuggles a cat aboard her wagon train. How long can she keep it a secret?

Howard, E. *The Cellar.* Though her brothers tease her about not being big enough to do farm jobs, Faith proves herself brave enough to go to the dark cellar for apples.

Howe, J. *"Pinky and Rex"* series. Pinky's a boy, Rex is a girl, and these are the stories of their special friendship.

Hurwitz, J. *"Ali Baba Bernstein"* series. When David Bernstein was eight years old, he changed his name to Ali Baba. Then mysterious things began to happen. (Other series by the author are *"Aldo"* and *"Russell."*)

Impey, R. *Desperate for a Dog.* Two sisters really want a dog. Their parents really don't. Can this situation be worked out?

Johnson, L. *A Week with Zeke & Zach.* The exploits of wild and weird twins who can't stay out of trouble.

King-Smith, D. *Sophie's Snail.* Four-year-old Sophie dreams of being a farmer.

Kleitsch, C. *It Happened at Pickle Lake.* Rachel would rather be vacationing in Florida than camping, until . . . .

2.2 *continued*

Kline, S. *"Herbie Jones"* series. How do you turn simple things into major mix-ups? Just leave it to Herbie Jones. (See also the author's *"Horrible Harry"* series.)

Landon, L. *"Meg Mackintosh"* series. Readers are challenged to put clues together and solve a mystery before Meg does.

Lawlor, L. *How to Survive Third Grade*. Can a "loser" become a winner? Ernest attempts to make a difficult adjustment.

LeGuin, U. *Catwings*. Four kittens with wings fly from city slums in search of a safe home. (See also *Catwings Return*.)

Leverich, K. *"Best Enemies"* series. Felicity complicates Priscilla's life both in and out of school.

Leverich, K. *Hilary and the Troublemakers*. Strange creatures get Hilary into trouble. Can she turn the tables on them?

Levy, E. *"Something Queer"* series. Strange things happen when Jill and Gwen get together.

MacLachlan, P. *Sarah, Plain and Tall*. Newbery-Award winner about a unique early settler family.

Marshall, J. *Rats on the Roof: and Other Stories*. Seven hilarious animal stories in one book. (See also *Rats on the Range*.)

Marzollo, J. *Red Ribbon Rosie*. Rosie is tired of being second in school races. Is it worth cheating to win a blue ribbon?

O'Connor, J. *The Ghost in Tent 19*. A mysterious ghost leads the four boys of Tent 19 on the trail of buried pirate treasure.

Osborne, M. *"Magic Tree House"* series. Jack and Annie travel through history, to prehistoric, ancient, and other times.

Park, B. *"Junie B. Jones"* series. Junie herself tells about life as a kindergartener.

Park, M. *Harvey and Rosie . . . and Ralph*. A magic spell turns Harvey's dog into a girl who helps pull his soccer team out of its slump.

Peterson, J. *"Littles"* series. The Littles are a tiny family who live in the walls of the house of the Bigg family. (Currently, most titles are available only in paperback.)

Peterson, P. J. *I Hate Camping*. Dan dreads a camping trip with his mom's boyfriend, Mike, and Mike's two kids. Can they ever become friends?

Peterson, P. J. *The Sub*. Two friends switch seats to fool a substitute teacher and find it isn't easy being someone else.

Pfeffer, S. *The Riddle Streak*. Her older brother always wins at everything, so Amy decides to be best at telling riddles.

Porte, B. *Taxicab Tales*. Daddy entertains his loving family with stories about the colorful passengers he picks up in his taxi.

Regan, D. *The Curse of the Trouble Dolls*. Guatemalan trouble dolls are said to make troubles go away, but Angie's friends get mad when the magic doesn't work for them.

Sachar, L. *"Marvin Redpost"* series. The adventures and misadventures of an imaginative nine-year-old.

Sachs, B. *The Boy Who Ate Dog Biscuits*. All Billy wants is a dog of his own, but he gets a baby sister instead.

Scieszka, J. *"Time Warp Trio"* series. Funny time-travel fantasies that take the reader to pirate ships, the Wild West, medieval England, and prehistoric times.

Sharmat, M. *"Genghis Khan"* series. Fred enters his mean-looking but sweet dog in a contest that could lead to fame and fortune.

2.2 *continued*

Skurzynski, G. *The Minstrel in the Tower*. A brother and sister travel the French countryside in the year 1195.

Smith, J. "*Adam Joshua*" series. A series of episodes about the life of a young boy.

Warner, G. "*Boxcar Children*" series. The adventures of four self-sufficient brothers and sisters.

Weiss, E. *The Adventures of Ratman*. He was a mild-mannered 8-year-old . . . until he put on his fuzzy brown suit!

Whelan, G. *Silver*. Can the runt of the litter win the dogsled championship?

Source: List 2.2 was compiled by Mary D'Eliso of Monroe Public Library Children's Services, Monroe, Indiana. This and other lists can be found at www.monroe.lib.in.us/childrens/children_booklist.html. Printed with permission.

2.3 Favorite Author Series

If your goal is to interest and draw children into the world of reading, then you must tip your hat to the creators of series books. These books are not only good for children, they are also a lot of fun. In some series, stories have continuing characters and reappearing issues. Other series simply follow the same course of action with different characters. Occasionally, minor characters appear from earlier stories to tie the action together.

A–Z Mysteries (*by Ron Roy*) These fast-paced collectible mysteries for beginning chapter book readers feature one title for each letter of the alphabet, such as *The Absent Author*, *The Missing Mummy*, and *The Quicksand Question*. There is another new series from the same author called "Capital Mysteries" about two 9-year-old kids who live in Washington, D.C., and go to all the neat places like the White House, the Smithsonian Institute, and the Air and Space Museum. Both series are published by Random House. (ages 7–9)

Amber Brown (*by Paula Danziger*) These eight books follow Amber through third and fourth grade as she struggles with the problems brought on by her parents' divorce. Told in the first person, the humorous true-life dialogue and realistic relationships between friends, teachers, and family will engage young readers. Amber is a sympathetic character, if somewhat bemused by life. In the 80- to 100-page range, these books, published by Putnam, include whimsical black-and-white sketches that add to the reader's enjoyment. (ages 7–9)

Arthur Chapter Books (*by Marc Brown*) The whole gang—Francine, the Brain, DW, and, of course, the lovable aardvark—is here. The 57- to 61-page books have nine or ten short chapters and full-page black-and-white sketches. Published by Little, Brown, these books explore the friendships and relationships in greater depth than in the picture books with more complex plots and more details. Children will enjoy the realistic dialogue. (ages 6–8)

Bailey School Kids (*by Debbie Dadey and Marcia Thornton Jones*) Scholastic publishes these 75-page popular books about Bailey City where some pretty weird grown-ups work! Titles in this 47-book series include *Frankenstein Doesn't Plant Petunias* and *Zombies Don't Play Soccer*. (ages 7–10)

Boxcar Children (*by Gertrude Chandler Warner*) The original "Boxcar Children" book was a non-mystery written in the 1930s by this author about the Alden family of orphaned children trying to make their way on their own. They have many adventures, eventually finding a loving grandfather when they were expecting a cold and hateful man. The original is the best, but it is followed by fun, interesting, little mysteries geared to happy endings appropriate for this age group, just entering chapter books and easily discouraged by more elaborate stories. There are over 70 books in the series published by Albert Whitman. (ages 8–9)

Cam Jansen (*by David A. Adler, illustrated by Suzanna Natti*) Fifth-grader Jennifer's photographic memory is so amazing that people call her "Camera," or "Cam" for short. She and her friends solve mysteries in over 20 action-packed books. The black-and-white illustrations add to the enjoyment of these 50-page books published by Viking. (ages 7–10)

Captain Underpants (*by Dav Pilkey*) George and Harold, a couple of wise guys, hypnotize their principal into becoming the super hero Captain Underpants. The five books in this series tell their comic-book exploits as they fight the talking toilets, incredibly naughty cafeteria ladies, and, of course, Professor Poopypants! Boys love these books for their irreverent humor, snappy dialogue, and funny, cartoon illustrations. Each 134-page book is published by Scholastic. (ages 7–10)

2.3 *continued*

Cobble Street Cousins (*by Cynthia Rylant, illustrated by Wendy Anderson Halperin*) This gentle series of six books is about three 9-year-old cousins who live with their Aunt Lily. The 55-page books include pencil sketches that give them an old-fashioned air. These are Simon and Schuster Books for Young Readers. (ages 7–10)

Danger Guys (*by Tony Abbott, illustrated by Joanne Scribner*) Noodle and Zeke can't help it—they just find danger anywhere! The six 70- to 80-page Harper/Trophy books have short chapters jam-packed with mad scientists, artifact thieves, and a sea captain's ghost. The dialogue is witty and the black-and-white illustrations add to the humor. (ages 7–9)

Encyclopedia Brown (*by Walter Sobol*) Children enjoy watching the 10-year-old son of the police chief solve the cases that stump his father. The "super sleuth in sneakers" single-handedly keeps Idaville's crimes under control. Several short cases are given, and the reader has a chance to look at the clues and attempt to solve them. The answers are given at the end of the book. These are a great introduction to mysteries. The 23 books are published by Delacorte. (ages 7–10)

Here Come the Brownies (*by Marcia Leonard and Jane O'Connor, illustrated by Laurie Struck Long*) The girls in this multicultural second-grade troop learn about cooperation and friendship. Grosset publishes the 12 books in association with the Girl Scouts of America. There is a Brownie activity at the end of each book. (ages 6–9)

Jenny Archer (*by Ellen Conford, illustrated by Diane Palmisciano*) Jenny's lively imagination makes these eight books fun to read. The humorous situations include writing a book, being in a TV commercial, and entering a photography contest. The books are in the 56- to 61-page range and are published by Little, Brown. (ages 7–9)

Jigsaw Jones (*by James Preller*) Scholastic publishes these first-person detective stories about private eye Theodore "Jigsaw" Jones. The 18 books are in the 70- to 80-page range with eleven to twelve short chapters. Each book is about a single case that Jigsaw and his best friend Mila Yeh have to solve. The illustrations add to the humor. (ages 7–10)

Julian (*by Ann Cameron*) These five books are first-person narratives by a 7-year-old African-American boy. He's a dreamer and a storyteller, but his stories sometimes get him, his best friend Gloria, and his little brother Huey into some big trouble. The 62-page short chapter books are Random House Stepping Stone books. (ages 7–9)

Kids of Polk Street School (*by Patricia Reilly Giff*) The kids in Ms. Rooney's second-grade class are sympathetic, normal kids dealing with problems of friendship, jealousy, insecurity, and classroom relationships in realistic and entertaining simple chapter books. The fifteen 80-page books of nine to ten chapters work well for 6- to 9-year-olds. There are also some longer special books.

Magic School Bus (*by Joanna Cole, illustrated by Bruce Degen*) What kid wouldn't want a teacher like Ms. Frizzle who takes her class on trips from inside the human body to outer space! The cartoon-like illustrations are clever, and the science concepts go down painlessly. Scholastic has a winner in this scientific series of 45 titles. They have expanded on the concept, with other authors writing chapter-book versions. (ages 7–9)

2.3 *continued*

The Magic Treehouse (*by Mary Pope Osborne*) These 25 unique adventures give children in the elementary grades a taste of history, anthropology, and culture as they try to survive in mysterious surroundings. The Random House Stepping Stone books are hugely popular with both boys and girls. (ages 8–11)

Marvin Redpost (*by Louis Sachar*) Poor Marvin . . . Why do crazy things always happen to this third-grade boy? He's sure the new kid in class is an alien from outer space; pet-sitting for his teacher brings unforeseen problems; and he's convinced he's the missing prince of Shampoon! These eight funny 70- to 80-page books are Random House Stepping Stones. (ages 7–10)

Meg Mackintosh (*by Lucinda Landon*) The eight mysteries in this series challenge the reader to "solve-it-yourself." Meg finds a stolen treasure map, a missing baseball signed by Babe Ruth, and solves the theft of a rare book from the library. Both the text and line drawings in the 48-page books provide key clues that help young detectives solve the case.

Pee Wee Scouts (*by Judy Delton*) There are over 40 books in this Dell Young Yearling series. The 80-page books are a humorous look at a lively coed troop of 7-year-olds. The funny dialogue and black-and-white sketches make Troop 23 very inviting. (ages 6–9)

Picture the Past (*by Sally Senzell Isaacs*) Heinemann publishes a 12-book series that looks at American communities of the past, such as a colonial town, a Hopi village, Ellis Island, and a Dust Bowl community. Each 32-page book includes informative sidebar information, illustrations and photographs, a glossary, and an index. There are also recipes and a very useful time line. (ages 5–8)

Pony Pals (*by Jeanne Betancourt*) Anna, Lulu, and Pam are good friends who work together to take care of their ponies. The 36 books published by Scholastic are 70 to 80 pages with detailed pencil sketches. They are for horse-loving girls not yet ready for the more advanced series. (ages 7–10)

Something Queer (*by Elizabeth Levy, illustrated by Mordicai Gerstein*) The cartoon-like illustrations perfectly complement these entertaining mysteries solved by Jill and Gwen, with the help (or hindrance) of Gwen's dog, Fletcher. The girls are funny, but they always solve the case. The 12 books are 42 pages each. (ages 7–10)

Time Warp Trio (*by Jon Scieszka, illustrated by Lane Smith*) These tongue-in-cheek books follow Fred, Joe, and Sam as they travel in time thanks to the magical, but uncontrollable *Book*. The fast action and snappy dialogue make these Viking books fun to read; the historical details add a little painless learning. (ages 7–11)

The Zack Files (*by Dan Greenburg*) The 26 books in this series cleverly spoof the horror genre as a 10-year-old boy has to cope with everything from clones to aliens to Great-Grandpa being reincarnated as a dog. The books, published by Grosset, are approximately 50 pages long and are illustrated with full-page, black-and-white cartoons. (ages 8–10)

Source: List 2.3 was compiled by Debby Kyritz, Children's Librarian, Oradell (New Jersey) Public Library, with input from Linda Orvell, Librarian at Harris Stowe College, St. Louis, MO.

2.4 Favorite Publisher Series

There are many popular series available from publishers for children in grades 2 and 3. All series are developed with appropriate print size, page format, and design to address the needs of readers at various beginning reading levels. Ordering catalogs from these publishers is the best way to find out which series are most appropriate for the children in your classroom.

DK/Eyewitness Readers (*Dorling Kindersley*) Levels 3 and 4 of this series are geared toward grades 2–3 and grades 2–4, respectively. Level 3 has more informational boxes and complex sentence structure than the lower levels. Titles include *Invaders from Outer Space*, *Spies*, *Troy Aikman*, and *Plants Bite Back*. Level 4 books have rich, challenging vocabulary, longer sentences, and informational sidebars. They include *Horse Heroes*, *Micro Monsters*, *Creating the X-Men*, and *Extreme Machines*. Most of the books are 48 pages, and all have black-and-white and color photographs, illustrations, and a glossary. (ages 7–9)

History Opens Windows (*Heinemann*) The lives and culture of ten key civilizations are featured in these 32-page books. There are colorful photographs, original source materials, maps, and diagrams. Included are the Maya, Ancient Greeks, the Middle Ages, and the Ancient Chinese civilizations. (ages 7–9)

Hyperion Chapters (*Hyperion*) The more than 20 books in this series are divided into second grade, second/third grade, and third grade. The books are in the 47- to 63-page range and are delineated by print size, chapter length, and complexity. Some authors in the series include Dick King-Smith, Suzanne Williams, and Steven Kroll.

I Didn't Know that . . . and other amazing facts (*Copper Beech Books, an imprint of Millbrook Press*) The 14 books in this 32-page series have full-color pictures, true-and-false questions with their answers, search-and-finds, projects, glossaries, and indexes. Titles include *I Didn't Know that Spiders Have Tusks*, *People Chase Twisters*, and *Some Boats Have Wings*. (ages 6–8)

Look What Came from . . . (*Franklin Watts/Scholastic*) These 32-page books tell us what "cool stuff" comes from other countries, including animals, fashions, toys, customs, inventions, games/sports, and food. The 12 books include recipes or crafts, glossaries, indexes, "to find out more" with books, organizations and Web sites, and what doesn't come from the country. By focusing on what each specific country has contributed to the world, the series provides a unique twist on the usual country books. (ages 7–10)

My America (*Scholastic*) This exciting series of award-winning historical fiction features a diary format. Written as journals by distinguished writers in the genre, characters are featured through multiple books, their observations and points of view growing and changing as they encounter the real events in our American past. Titles include *Elizabeth's Jamestown Colony Adventure*, *Hope's Revolutionary War Diary*, *Corey's Underground Railroad Diary*, *Virginia's Civil War Diary*, and *Meg's Prairie Diary*. (ages 7–9)

Ready for Chapters (*Aladdin/Simon and Schuster*) There are more than 15 books written by a variety of favorite authors of approximately 50–76 pages each in this series, including true stories, historical fiction, fantasy, Nancy Drew notebooks, Jake Drake, the Cobble Street Cousins, and Pinkwater's werewolf club. (ages 6–9)

Rookie Read About . . . (*Children's Press/Scholastic*) This series of 32-page books each includes Rookie Read-About Geography, Rookie Read-About Holidays, and Rookie Read-About Science. The geography series includes *Living in a Desert*, *Living in the Arctic*, *Living Near a River*, and *Living Near the Sea*. Science titles include *Recycle That!*, *Solid, Liquid, or Gas?* and *North, South, East, West*. Ideal for building fluency. (ages 6–7)

Scholastic If You . . . (*Scholastic*) This series of 17 books takes your students on trips into the past while teaching basic concepts. In popular question-and-answer format, readers find out what life was really like during various times in our history. Titles include *If You Sailed on the Mayflower in 1620*, *If You Lived at the Time of the American Revolution*, and *If You Lived at the Time of Martin Luther King*. (ages 9–12)

Scholastic Question and Answer (*Melvin and Gilda Berger*) These 48-page books answer many of the questions children have about science. The books have hundreds of facts, brightly colored illustrations, and indexes. Titles include *Why Don't Haircuts Hurt?*, *How Do Flies Walk Upside Down?*, and *Can Snakes Crawl Backwards?* (ages 7–12)

Trophy Chapter Books (*Harper Trophy*) Each book is approximately 75 pages with large-sized print. Included are folktales, Jean Craighead George's "One Day in the . . ." ecological series, Little House chapter books about the Rose and Caroline years, Clyde Robert Bulla's historical fiction, and Susan Saunders's Black Cat club books. (ages 8–10)

World Book Animals of the World (*World Book*) These 64-page books ask and answer questions about animals with each page of text facing a full-page photograph. Physical characteristics, behavior, and differences between species are covered. There are fun facts, indexes, glossaries, and animals' classifications. There are three sets of ten books with titles such as *Ants and Other Social Insects*, *Rattlers and Other Snakes*, *Spiders and Other Arachnids*, and *Beavers and Other Rodents*. (ages 7–9)

Source: List 2.4 was compiled by Debby Kyritz, Children's Librarian, Oradell (New Jersey) Public Library, with input from Linda Orvell, Librarian at Harris Stowe College, St. Louis, MO.

2.5 Realistic Fiction

Many realistic stories created for early elementary grades portray the typical experiences of children their own age and reflect the same desires and fears, as well as their hopes and dreams. Realistic stories can extend children's horizons and show that there is more than one way to solve a problem or view their world. In all cases, the characters are believable, and readers can easily identify with them.

Amelia (Series), Mariss Moss
The Show and Tell War, Janice Lee Smith
The Kid in the Red Jacket, Barbara Park
Gila Monsters Meet You at the Airport, Marjorie Weinman Sharmat
Herbie Jones and the Monster Ball, Suzy Kline
Mama One, Mama Two, Patricia MacLachlan
The Hundred Penny Box, Sharon Bell Mathis
Russell and Elisa, Johanna Hurwitz
The One in the Middle Is the Green Kangaroo, Judy Blume
Muggie Maggie, Beverly Cleary
Mitch and Amy, Beverly Cleary
No Dogs Allowed, Jane Cutler
The 18th Emergency, Betsy Byars
Stay Away from Simon, Carol Carrick
Thank you, Mr. Falker, Patricia Polacco
My Mama Had a Dancing Heart, Libba Moore Gray
A Game of Catch, Helen Cresswell
Almost Starring Skinny Bones, Barbara Park
Amelia's Flying Machine, Barbara Shook Hazen
Nana Upstairs and Nana Downstairs, Tomie dePaola
How Does It Feel to Be Old?, Norma Farber
Mustard, Charlotte Graeber
Arthur the Kid, Alan Coren
Beezus and Ramona, Beverly Cleary
Annie Bananie (Series), Leah Komaiko
*Jake Drake** (Series), Andrew Clements
Horrible Harry (Series), Suzy Kline
Arthur for the Very First Time, Patricia MacLachlan
Ox-Cart Man, Donald Hall
Benny, Barbara Cohen
Chester, Mary Francis Shura
Daniel's Duck, Clyde Robert Bulla
Eunice (the Egg Salad) Gottlieb, Tricia Springstubb
The Fourth Grade Wizards, Barthe DeClements
Ginger Pye, Eleanor Estes
Grandaddy's Place, Helen V. Griffith
Harald and the Great Stag, Donald Carrick
Henry and Mudge (Series), Cynthia Rylant
Joel and the Great Merlini, Eloise Jarvis McGraw
Lily and Miss Liberty, Carla Stevens
My Daddy Was a Soldier, Deborah Kogan Ray
My Dog and the Birthday Mystery, David Adler
Gloria's Way, Ann Cameron
Stories Julian Tells, Ann Cameron
Judy Moody (Series), Megan McDonald
The Gardener, Sarah Stewart
Poppy and the Outdoor Cat, Dorothy Haas
Ramona and Her Father, Beverly Cleary
Ramona Quimby, Age 8, Beverly Cleary
Raymond's Best Summer, Jean Rogers
School Can Wait, Tessa Dahl
Some Friend!, Carol Carrick
The Five Little Peppers and How They Grew, Margaret Sidney
The Grandma Mix-Up, Emily Arnold McCully
The Magic Moth, Virginia Lee
The Missing Tooth, Joanna Cole
The Singing Hill, Meindert DeJong
The Library, Sarah Stewart
New Neighbors for Nora (Riverside Kids Series), Johanna Hurwitz
Miss Alaineus: A Vocabulary Disaster, Debra Frasier
Zero Grandparents (Jackson Friends Books), Michelle Edwards
Gus and Granapa (Series), Claudia Mills
JoJo & Winnie, Marilyn Sachs

2.5 *continued*

Best Enemies Again, Kathleen Leverich
Dakota Dugout, Ann Turner
The Bracelet, Yoshiko Uchida
Wagon Wheels, Barbara Brenner
A Birthday for Blue, Kerry Raines Lydon
Anna, Grandpa, and the Big Storm, Carla Stevens
Best Friends, Steven Kellogg
Chester's Way, Kevin Henkes
Everett Anderson's Friend, Lucille Clifton
Jessica, Kevin Henkes
Matthew and Tilly, Rebecca Jones
Me and Neesie, Eloise Greenfield
Messy Bessey and the Birthday Overnight, Patricia C. McKissack
My Best Friend, Pat Hutchins
Overnight at Mary Bloom's, Aliki
Yo! Yes!, Chris Raschka
*The Hundred Dresses**, Eleanor Estes
Miss Rumphius, Barbara Cooney
Rufus M, Eleanor Estes
Raising Yoder's Barn, Jane Yolen
*Ira Sleeps Over**, Bernard Waber
Pinky and Rex (Series), James Howe
Yoko and Friends (Series), Rosemary Wells
Your Best Friend Kate, Pat Brisson
Third Grade Is Terrible, Barbara Baker
Maxie, Rosie and Earl—Partners in Crime, Barbara Park
Pink and Say, Patricia Polacco

2.6 Animal Stories

Animal stories remain popular among second and third graders. Reality turns to fantasy in some of the stories when a child's drawings come to life as in *Andy's Wild Animal Adventure* by Gerda Scheidl and when a child wanders into the jungle and dragons appear as in *Komodo* by Peter Sis. The butler has to solve the mystery when the animal family goes on a picnic in *Picnic with Piggins* by Jane Yolen, and readers learn a bit of ecology when Ronnie, a red-eyed tree frog, consults the Great Wise Toad in his effort to save the rain forest in *Journey of the Red-Eyed Tree Frog* by Martin and Janis Jordan.

Mo to the Rescue, Mary Pope Osborne
A Million Fish . . . More or Less, Pat McKissack
Andy's Wild Animal Adventure, Gerda Marie Scheidl
Berta: A Remarkable Dog, Celia Barker Lottridge
Bright Lights, Little Gerbil (The Weebie Zone Series), Stephanie Spinner
Cock-a-Doodle Dudley, Bill Peet
Dingoes at Dinnertime (Magic Treehouse Series), Mary Pope Osborne
Edward in the Jungle, David McPhail
Elliot's Emergency, Andrea Beck
The Story of Ferdinand, Munro Leaf
Flatfoot Fox and the Case of the Missing Eye, Eth Clifford
Freddy and the Perilous Adventure, Walter R. Brooks
Pauline, Georg Hallensleben
The Grizzly Sisters, Cathy Bellows
Ice Bear and Little Fox, Jonathan London
Journey of the Red-Eyed Tree Frog, Martin and Janis Jordan
Jungle Jamboree, Kimberley Knutson
Komodo!, Peter Sis
Last Night at the Zoo, Michael Garland
Little Pink Pig, Pat Hutchins
Look to the North: A Wolf Pup Diary, Jean Craighead George
My Grandma Lived in Gooligulch, Graeme Base
Never Trust a Squirrel!, Patrick Cooper
Night Ride, Michel Gay
Nora's Stars, Satomi Ichikawa
Officer Buckle and Gloria, Peggy Rathmann
Picnic With Piggins (Piggins Series), Jane Yolen
Piggy's Pancake Parlor, David McPhail
Plunk's Dreams, Helen V. Griffith
Pony Parade (Animal Ark Pets), Ben M. Baglio
Rats on the Range and Other Stories, James Marshall
Rhino Romp, Jean Craighead George
The Stray Dog: From a True Story by Reiko Sassa, Marc Simont
Someday, Diane Paterson
The Animal Mall, Cooper Edens
The Dumb Bunnies Go to the Zoo, Sue Denim
The Great Race, David McPhail
The Great Summer Camp Catastrophe, Jean Van Leeuwen
The Secret Path, Nick Butterworth
The Trek, Ann Jonas
Throw-Away Pets (Pet Patrol Series), Betsy Duffey
Thumbelina, adapted by Jane Falloon
Tigers at Twilight (Magic Tree House Series), Mary Pope Osborne
Trouble at Christmas, Russell Johnson
The Water Hole, Graeme Base
Will's Mammoth, Rafe Martin
Wipe Your Feet!, Daniel Lehan
You Can't Catch Me!, Annabel Collis

2.7 Folktale and Fairy-Tale Read-Alouds

Fairy tales, folktales, tall tales, and fables are ideal for introducing second and third graders to world cultures. Children enjoy the tales' adventures, and can see the heroes and villains clearly defined. When reading tales from various countries, ask children to think about how the story tells what is important to the people, such as family, the land, or helping others in order to survive. (See List 1.15, Folktale and Fairy-Tale Read-Alouds.)

African and African-American Tales

Why Mosquitoes Buzz in People's Ears	Verna Aardema
Bringing the Rain to Kapiti Plain: A Nandi tale	Verna Aardema
How the Ostrich Got Its Long Neck: A Tale from the Akumba of Kenya	Verna Aardema
Misoso: Once Upon a Time Tales from Africa	Verna Aardema
Sungura and Leopard: A Swahili Trickster Tale	Barbara Knutson
Ananse's Feast: An Ashanti Tale	Tololwa M. Mollel
Mufaro's Beautiful Daughters: An African Tale	John Steptoe
Uncle Remus: The Complete Tales	Julius Lester
Jackal's Flying Lesson: A Khoikhoi Tale	Verna Aardema
A Ring of Tricksters: Animal Tales from America, the West Indies, and Africa	Virginia Hamilton
Blanchette et les Sept Petits Cajuns: A Cajun Snow White	Sheila Herbert-Collins

American Tall Tales and Legends

Paul Bunyan: A Tall Tale	Steven Kellogg
Pecos Bill: A Tall Tale	Steven Kellogg
Mike Fink: A Tall Tale	Steven Kellogg
Sally Ann Thunder, Ann Whirlwind Crockett	Steven Kellogg
The True Tale of Johnny Appleseed	Margaret Hodges
The Bunyans	Audrey Wood
John Henry	Julius Lester
Tailypo: A Newfangled Tall Tale	Angela Shelf Medearis

Asian Tales

Children of the Dragon: Selected Tales from Vietnam	Sherry Garland
China's Bravest Girl: The Legend of Hua Mu Lan	Charlie Chin
Chinese Mother Goose Rhymes	Robert Wyndham
Little Plum	Ed Young
Monkey King Wreaks Havoc in Heaven	Debby Chen
Oranges on Golden Mountain	Elizabeth Partridge
The Dragon Prince (Beauty and the Beast)	Laurence Yep
The Dragon's Pearl	Julie Lawson
The Enchanted Tapestry: A Chinese Folktale	Robert SanSouci
The Magic Tapestry: A Chinese Folktale	Demi
The Making of the Monkey King	Robert Kraus

2.7 *continued*

The Mouse Bride: A Chinese Folktale	Monica Chang
Two of Everything: A Chinese Folktale	Lily Toy Hong
White Tiger, Blue Serpent	Grace Tseng
Why Rat Comes First: A Story of the Chinese Zodiac	Clara Yen
Why Snails Have Shells: Minority and Han Folktales from China	Carolyn Han
The Weaving of a Dream: A Chinese Folktale	Marilee Heyer
Older Brother, Younger Brother: A Korean Folktale	Nina Jaffe
Legend of the Milky Way	Jeanne M. Lee
Mysterious Tales of Japan	Martin Rafe
Magic Spring: A Korean Folktale	Nami Rhee
Three Strong Women: A Tall Tale from Japan	Claus Stamm
Lon Po Po: A Red Riding Hood Story from China	Ed Young
The Crane Wife	Odds Bodkin
The Sun Girl and the Moon Boy	Yangsook Choi
The Stonecutter: A Japanese Folk Tale	Gerald McDermott
Brave Little Parrot (Jataka/India)	Rafe Martin
The Funny Little Woman	Arlene Mosel
The Boy Who Drew Cats: A Japanese Folktale	Arthur Levine
Grandpa's Town	Takaaki Nomura
Toad Is the Uncle of Heaven: A Vietnamese Folktale	Jeanne M. Lee

Hispanic Tales†

The Tree That Rains: The Flood Myth of Huichol Indians of Mexico	Emily Bernhard
The Flame of Peace: A Tale of the Aztecs	Deborah Nourse Lattimore
Spirit Child: A Story of the Nativity	John Bierhorst
Doctor Coyote: A Native American Aesop's Fables	John Bierhorst
Princess Florecita and the Iron Shoes: A Spanish Fairy Tale	John Warren Stewig
The Bossy Gallito/El Gallo de Bodas: A Traditional Cuban Folktale	Lucia M. Gonzaléz
The Race of Toad and Deer	Pat Mora
The Golden Flower: A Taino Myth from Puerto Rico	Nina Jaffe

Jewish Tales

Chanukah in Chelm	David A. Adler
The Jar of Fools: Eight Hanukkah Stories from Chelm	Eric A. Kimmel
Raisel's Riddle	Erica Silverman
Folktales of Joha, Jewish Trickster	Matilda Koen-Sarango
Mazel and Shlimazel, or the Milk of the Lioness	Isaac Bashevis Singer
Zlatah the Goat: And Other Stories	Isaac Bashevis Singer
My Grandmother's Stories: A Collection of Jewish Folk Tales	Adèle Geras
While Standing on One Foot: Puzzle Stories and Wisdom Tales from the Jewish Tradition	Nina Jaffe & Steve Zeitlin

†For an excellent introduction to Hispanic children's literature and culture, see Donna Norton's *Through the Eyes of a Child*, pages 651–653.

2.7 *continued*

Native American Tales

Ma'ii and Cousin Horned Toad: A Traditional Navajo Story	Shonto Begay
The Woman Who Fell from the Sky: The Iroquois Story of Creation	John Bierhorst
How the Sea Began: A Taino Myth	George Crespo
The Girl Who Loved Wild Horses	Paul Goble
The Blizzard's Robe	Robert Sabuda
Coyote: A Trickster Tale from the American Southwest	Gerald McDermott
The Boy Who Lived With the Seals	Rafe Martin
Keepers of the Earth: Native American Stories and Environmental Activities for Children	Michael J. Caduto & Joseph Bruchac
Keepers of the Animals: Native American Stories and Wildlife Activities for Children	Michael J. Caduto & Joseph Bruchac
People of Corn: A Mayan Story	Mary-Joan Gersen
Iktomi and the Buzzard: A Plains Indian Story	Paul Goble
Coyote and the Fire Stick: A Pacific Northwest Indian Tale	Barbara Diamond Goldin
How Thunder and Lightning Came to Be: A Choctaw Legend	Beatrice Orcutt Harrell
Follow the Stars: A Native American Woodlands Tale	Kristina Rodanas
The Precious Gift: A Navaho Creation Myth	Ellen B. Jackson
Native American Legends (series)	Terri Cohlene

Traditional Tales and Fables

Aesop's Fables, Jerry Pinkney
Doctor Coyote: A Native American Aesop's Fables, John Bierhorst
The Town Mouse and the Country Mouse: An Aesop Fable, Bernadette Watts
The Lion and the Mouse: An Aesop Fable, Bernadette Watts
A Sip of Aesop, Jane Yolen
To Swim in Our Own Pond: Ta Ve Ta Tam Ao Ta, A Book of Vietnamese Proverbs, Ngoc Dung Tran (compiler)
Twelve Tales from Aesop, retold and illustrated by Eric Carle
A Frog Prince, Alix Berenzy
Beauty and the Beast, retold by Mary Pope Osborne
Cinderella, retold by Amy Ehrlich
Cinderella, adapted and illustrated by Nonny Hogrogian, retold from The Brothers Grimm
Cinderella, Paul Galdone
Cinderella, or, The Little Glass Slipper, a free translation from the French of Charles Perrault with pictures by Marcia Brown (Caldecott medal winner)
Froggie Went A-Courting, Marjorie Priceman
Hansel and Gretel by the Brothers Grimm, illustrated by Anthony Browne
Hansel and Gretel by Jacob Grimm, adapted with pictures by Susan Jeffers
Little Red Riding Hood by The Brothers Grimm, retold by Trina Schart Hyman
Little Red Riding Hood, adapted from the retelling by The Brothers Grimm by Paul Galdone
Puss in Boots, Paul Galdone
Rapunzel from The Brothers Grimm, retold by Barbara Rogasky

2.7 *continued*

Rapunzel: A Fairy Tale by Jacob and Wilhelm Grimm, translated by Anthea Bell
Rumpelstiltskin, retold and illustrated by Paul Galdone
Rumpelstiltskin, retold and illustrated from the German of The Brothers Grimm by Paul Zelinsky
Sleeping Beauty and Other Favorite Fairy Tales, chosen and translated by Angela Carter
Snow White and Rose Red by Jacob and Wilhelm Grimm, retold and illustrated by Bernadette Watts
Snow White from the Fairy Tale by The Brothers Grimm, adapted and illustrated by Bernadette Watts
The Bremen Town Musicians: A Grimms Fairy Tale, retold and illustrated by Donna Diamond
The Dragon and the Unicorn, Lynne Cherry
The Elves and the Shoemaker, retold by Marcia Leonard
The Elves and the Shoemaker by Jacob and Wilhelm Grimm, retold and illustrated by Bernadette Watts
The Fisherman and His Wife by The Brothers Grimm, retold by Samantha Easton
The Fisherman and His Wife: A Brand New Version, Rosemary Wells
The Frog Prince, Paul Galdone, adapted from the retelling by The Brothers Grimm, translated by Lucy Crane
The Golden Bird and Other Fairy Tales of The Brothers Grimm, translated by Randall Jarrell
The Golden Goose, Susan Saunders
The Goose Girl: A Story from The Brothers Grimm, retold by Eric A. Kimmel
The Little Juggler, adapted from an old French legend and illustrated by Barbara Cooney

2.8 Cinderella Variants from Around the World

According to Iona and Peter Opie in *The Classic Fairy Tales* (Oxford University Press, 1974), the Cinderella story is at least 1,000 years old. There are approximately 700 Cinderella variants from cultures around the world. Here is a list of several that have been retold in colorful picture books format. (Also see List 2.9, Fractured Fairy Tales.)

Abadeha: The Philippine Cinderella, Myrna J. De La Paz, illustrated by Youshang Tang
Angkat: The Cambodian Cinderella, Jewell Reinhart Coburn, illustrated by Edmund Flotte
Anklet for a Princess: A Cinderella Story from India, Lila Mehta, illustrated by Youshan Tang
Baba Yaga and Vasilisa the Brave, Marianna Mayer, illustrated by K. Y. Craft
Billy Beg and His Bull: An Irish Tale, Ellin Greene
Cendrillon: A Cajun Cinderella, Sheila Hebert Collins, illustrated by Patrick Soper
Chinye: A West African Folk Tale, Obi Onyefulu, illustrated by Evie Safarewicz
Cinderella, or The Little Glass Slipper, Charles Perrault, illustrated by Marcia Brown
Domitila: A Cinderella Tale from the Mexican Tradition, Jewell Reinhart Coburn, illustrated by Connie McLennan
The Egyptian Cinderella, Shirley Climo
Fair, Brown and Trembling: An Irish Cinderella Story, Jude Daly
The Gift of the Crocodile: A Cinderella Story (Indonesia), Judy Sierra, illustrated by Reynold Ruffins
The Golden Sandal: A Middle Eastern Cinderella Story, Rebecca Hickox, illustrated by Will Hillenbrand
The Golden Slipper: A Vietnamese Legend, Darrell H. Y. Lun, illustrated by Makeko Nagano
The Irish Cinderlad, Shirley Climo, illustrated by Loretta Krupinski
Jouanah: A Hmong Cinderella, Jewell Reinhart Coburn & Tzexa Cherta Lee, illustrated by Anne Sibley O'Brien
The Korean Cinderella, Shirley Climo, illustrated by Ruth Heller
Little Gold Star: A Spanish American Cinderella Tale, Robert D. SanSouci, illustrated by Sergio Martinez
Mufaro's Beautiful Daughters: An African Folktale (Zimbabwe), John Steptoe
Naya, the Inuit Cinderella, Brittany Marceau-Chenkie, illustrated by Shelley Brookes
The Persian Cinderella, Shirley Climo, illustrated by Robert Florczak
Raisel's Riddle (Poland), Erica Silverman, illustrated by Susan Gaber
The Rough-Face Girl (Algonquin), Rafe Martin, illustrated by David Shannon
Smoky Mountain Rose: An Appalachian Cinderella, A. Schroeder, illustrated by C. Cendrillon Perrault
Sootface: An Ojibwa Cinderella Story, Robert D. SanSouci, illustrated by Daniel SanSouci
The Talking Eggs: A Folktale from the American South, Robert D. SanSouci, illustrated by Jerry Pinkney
Tam Cam: The Vietnamese Cinderella Story, Nguiyen Nhuan
Tam's Slipper: A Story From Vietnam, Janet Palazzo-Craig
Tattercoats, Margaret Greaves, illustrated by Margaret Chamberlain
The Turkey Girl: A Zuni Cinderella, Penny Pollock, illustrated by Ed Young
Vasilisa the Beautiful, translated from the Russian by Thomas Whitney, illustrated by Nonny Hogrogian
The Way Meat Loves Salt: A Cinderella Tale from the Jewish Tradition, Nina Jaffe, illustrated by Louise August
Yeh-Shen: A Cinderella Story from China, Ai-Ling Louie, illustrated by Ed Young

2.9 Fractured Fairy Tales

Fractured fairy tales provide a unique twist on well-known fairy-tale themes. Whether they present wacky takeoffs, irreverent retellings, or different settings or points of view, they are always humorous and enjoyed by all ages.

Ziggy Piggy and the Three Little Pigs, Frank Asch
The Three Little Pigs, Steven Kellogg
The Three Pigs, David Wiesner
The Three Little Hawaiian Pigs and the Magic Shark, Donivee M. Laird, illustrated by Carol Jossem
Wait! No Paint, Bruce Whatley
The Stinky Cheese Man and Other Fairly Stupid Tales, Jon Scieszka, illustrated by Lane Smith
The True Story of the Three Little Pigs by A. Wolf, Jon Scieszka, illustrated by Lane Smith
The Three Little Wolves and the Big Bad Pig, Eugene Trivizas, illustrated by Helen Oxenbury
Cinder Edna, Ellen Jackson, illustrated by Kevin O'Malley
Prince Cinders, Babette Cole
Cinder-Elly, Frances Minters, illustrated by G. Brian Karas
Cinderella Bigfoot (Happily Ever Laughter Series), Mike Thaler, illustrated by Jared Lee
Smokey Mountain Rose: An Appalachian Cinderella, Alan Schroeder, illustrated by Charles Cendrillon
Cinderella, William Wegman (retold with photos of costumed Weimaraners)
Bubba the Cowboy Prince: A Fractured Texas Tale, Helen Ketteman
Cindy Ellen: A Wild Western Cinderella, Susan Lowell
Dusty Locks and the Three Bears, Susan Lowell
Little Red Cowboy Hat, Susan Lowell
Bootmaker and the Elves, Susan Lowell

2.10 Books to Teach Math

Many of the books listed below link math and literature in the form of games and puzzles. Others subtly weave math into story form. Problem solving and basic arithmetic skills are presented in lively, colorful formats that appeal to children, particularly those who are turned off by traditional math instruction.

Teachers will find original ways of letting children problem-solve while enjoying a story at the same time. These books can also give teachers numerous ideas for presenting math concepts in game form.

Betcha!, S. D. Schindler
Dinosaur Deals, Kevin O'Malley
Divide and Ride, George Ulrich
Game Time, Cynthia Jabar
Jump, Kangaroo, Jump, Kevin O'Malley
Lemonade for Sale, Tricia Tusa
On Beyond a Million, David Schwartz, illustrated by Paul Meisel
Penny Pot, Lynn Cravath
Ready, Set, Hop, Jon Buller
Room for Ripley, Sylvie Wickstrom
Shark Swimathon, Lynn Cravath
Too Many Kangaroo Things to Do, Kevin O'Malley
The Go-Around Dollar (MONEY), Barbara Johnson Adams
Anno's Mysterious Multiplying Jar (PROBLEM SOLVING), Anno Mitsumasa
Anno's Magic Seeds, (PRE-ALGEBRA PATTERNS), Anno Mitsumasa
Math in the Bath (and other places too!), Sara Atherlay
What Comes in 2's, 3's and 4's? (CLASSIFYING AND COUNTING), Suzanne Aker
Pigs in a Blanket (TIME, PROBLEM SOLVING), Amy Axelrod
Raps and Rhymes in Maths, Ann and Johnny Baker
Ten, Nine Eight (COUNTING, MULTICULTURAL), Molly Bang
The Biggest Pumpkin Ever (MEASUREMENT, PROBLEM SOLVING), Steven Kroll
Fish Eyes: A Book You Can Count On (COUNTING WHOLE NUMBERS), Lois Ehlert
Growing Vegetable Soup (MEASUREMENT), Lois Ehlert
Ten Apples Up on Top (COUNTING), Theo. LeSieg
Fraction Fun, David A. Adler, illustrated by Nancy Tobin
Mission Addition, Loreen Leedy
The 512 Ants on Sullivan Street, Carol Al Losi
The Mystery of the Sunken Treasure (I Love Math series), Sara Mark
The Amazing Book of Shapes (BEGINNING GEOMETRY), Lydia Sharman
Rectangles (GEOMETRY), David L. Steinecker
The Story of Time and Clocks, Anita Ganeri
Get Up and Go (Math Start series), Stuart J. Murphy
Keeping Time: From the Beginning into the 21st Century, Franklyn M. Branley

2.11 Books to Teach Science

Books of fiction and nonfiction provide a rich supplement to the science curriculum in grades 2 and 3†. The books listed below can appeal to children in different ways. They combine story form with scientific facts. They teach children to appreciate animal and insect life, as well as the need to protect our natural resources. They explore storms and weather. This list of books will help you teach and reinforce important science topics.

ANIMALS AND REPTILES

The following books introduce children to animal habitats, what animals eat, and why animals are important.

Fritz and the Beautiful Horses, Jan Brett
Danger on the African Grassland, Elizabeth Sackett
The Desert Is Theirs, Byrd Baylor
Dinosaur Named Sue, Fay Robinson
Usborne Book of Animal Facts, Anita Ganeri
Biggest, Strongest, Fastest, Steve Jenkins
Animal Sharpshooters, Anthony Fredericks
Footprints in the Sand, Cynthia Benjamin
A Whale Is Not a Fish and Other Animal Mix-Ups, Melvin Berger
Monkeys Are a Lot like Us, Allan Fowler
Animals Protecting Us (Animals That Help Us), Robert Snedden
Horns and Antlers (Rookie Read-About-Science Series), Allan Fowler
It Could Still be Endangered (Rookie Read-About Science), Allan Fowler
Is This a House for Hermit Crab?, Megan McDonald
*An Extraordinary Life: The Story of the Monarch Butterfly**, Leonard Pringle
Desert Voices, Byrd Baylor
The Magic School Bus in the Time of the Dinosaurs, Joanna Cole
Tyrannosaurus, William Lindsay
Dinosaur Encyclopedia, David Lambert
Moose Tracks, Mary Casanova
Dog to the Rescue, Seventeen True Tales of Dog Heroism, Jeannette Sanderson
Gorillas, Seymour Simon
Polar Bears, Gail Gibbons
Can Snakes Crawl Backward?: Questions and Answers About Reptiles (Scholastic Question and Answer), Melvin and Gilda Berger
Do Bears Sleep All Winter?: Questions and Answers About Bears (Scholastic Question and Answer), Melvin and Gilda Berger
Ten True Animal Rescues, Jeanne Betancourt
Dinosaurs (Worldwise), Scott Steedman

†For a list of outstanding nonfiction for children, see List 4.5, "Orbis Pictus Awards."

2.11 *continued*

THE BODY

Brain (Body Books), Anna Sandeman
The Magic School Bus Inside the Human Body, Joanna Cole
The Magic School Bus Explores the Senses, Joanna Cole
Magic Monsters Learn About Health, Jane Belk Mancure
So That's How I Was Born, Dr. Robert Brooks
How Do I Know It's Yucky? and Other Questions About the Senses (BodyWise), Sharon Cromwell

COMPUTERS

The use of computers and the Internet is becoming increasingly widespread in schools and homes. The following books will help children become computer literate.

It Could Still Be a Robot (Rookie Read-About-Science series), Allan Fowler
The Internet for Kids, Carnan Kazunas and Tom Kazunas
Personal Computers, Carnan Kazunas and Tom Kazunas
Mousetracks: A Kid's Computer Idea Book, Peggy L. Steinhauser
Get Ready for Robots!, Patricia Lauber
Computers, Paul G. Zomberg

EARTH

An appreciation of Earth and how we can preserve our natural resources have grown more important as the world becomes globally connected. What can children do to help preserve the Earth? The following books inform children how garbage is processed, the effects of oil spills on wildlife, and the importance of keeping things green. Books introduce children to many areas of the world, including rainforests, the Florida everglades, swamps, and rivers.

Ecology

Around the Pond: Who's Been Here?, Lindsay Barrett George
Amazon Boy, Ted Lewin
Beneath Your Feet, Seymour Simon
Can We Save Them?: Endangered Species of North America, David Dobson
A Clearing in the Forest, Carol and Donald Carrick
Deep in a Rainforest, Gwen Pascoe
Dinosaurs to the Rescue: A Guide to Protecting Our Planet, Laurie Krasney Brown and Marc Brown
Earth, Alfred Leutscher
Earth and Sky, Mona Dayton
Everglades, Jean Craighead George
For the Love of Our Earth, P. K. Hallinan
Forest, Ron Hirschi

2.11 *continued*

Forest Fire!, Mary Ann Fraser
Garbage, Robert Maass
Here Is the Coral Reef, Madeleine Dunphy
How Green Are You?, David Bellamy
How Mountains Are Made (Let's-Read-and-Find-Out Science), Kathleen Weidner Zoehfield
If I Built a Village, Kazue Mizumura
In the Woods: Who's Been Here?, Lindsay Barrett George
It's My Earth Too: How I Can Help the Earth Stay Alive, Kathleen Krull
Keeper of the Swamp, Ann Garrett
Mother Earth, Nancy Luenn
Oil Spill! (Let's-Read-and-Find-Out Science), Melvin Berger
One World, Michael Foreman
Our World Is Earth, Sylvia Engdahl
Poor Fish, Heide Helene Beisert
Rabbit Garden, Miska Miles
Secret Places, D. J. Arneson
Someday a Tree, Eve Bunting
Squirrel Park, Lisa Campbell Ernst
The Berenstain Bears Don't Pollute Anymore, Stan Berenstain
The Desert Is Theirs, Byrd Baylor
The Forgotten Forest, Laurence Anholt
The Great Kapok Tree, Lynne Cherry
The Great Trash Bash, Loreen Leedy
The Jungle Is My Home, Laura Fischetto
The Land of Gray Wolf, Thomas Locker
The Living Earth, Eleonore Schmid
The Magic School Bus Inside the Earth, Joanna Cole
The River and the Rain, Bijou Le Tord
The Salamander Room, Anne Mazer
The Seal and the Slick, Don Freeman
The Story of Rosy Dock, Jeannie Baker
This Is Our Earth, Laura Lee Benson
A Walk in the Desert, Caroline Arnold
A Walk in the Woods, Caroline Arnold
A Walk on the Great Barrier Reef, Caroline Arnold
A Walk Up the Mountain, Caroline Arnold
Were You a Wild Duck, Where Would You Go?, George Mendoza
What About Ladybugs?, Celia Godkin
When the Rivers Go Home, Ted Lewin
Where the Forest Meets the Sea Window, Jeannie Baker
Wilson's World, Edith Thacher Hurd
World Water Watch, Michelle Koch
World, World, What Can I Do?, Barbara Shook Hazen

2.11 *continued*

Rocks, Soil, and Fossils

Rock collecting is a favorite pastime among many youngsters who find beauty in the colorful minerals. Children can go rock and fossil hunting, using books by Byrd Baylor as a guide.

If You Find a Rock, Peggy Christian
The Magic School Bus Inside the Earth, Joanna Cole
Let's Go Rock Collecting, Roma Gans
Rocks in My Pockets, Marc Harshman
If You Are a Hunter of Fossils, Byrd Baylor
Everybody Needs a Rock, Byrd Baylor
Limestone Caves, Roy Gallant
Taking Root (Rookie Read-About-Science series), Allan Fowler

Plants and Seeds

The following books introduce children to plants, fruits, and flowers found in different parts of the world. They explain how a cactus holds water, how fruits and vegetables evolve from buds or bulbs, and the names of special types of trees. Plants are easy to grow in the classroom, so have children watch seeds grow, systematically measuring their growth and observing the birth of leaves and flowers.

Watermelon Day, Kathi Appelt
Bean and Plant, Christine Back
*Garden**, Robert Maass
Patterns of Nature, Jeffrey J. W. Baker
Mrs. McGinty and the Bizarre Plant: Story and Pictures, Gavin Bishop
A Tree Is a Plant, Clyde Robert Bulla
Cactus in the Desert (Let's-Read-and-Find-Out Science), Phyllis S. Busch
Some Plants Have Funny Names, Diana Harding Cross
What Is a Plant?, Gene Darby
The Enormous Turnip, Kathy Parkinson
And a Sunflower Grew, Aileen Lucia Fisher
Cactus Hotel, Brenda Z. Guiberson
It's Pumpkin Time!, Zoe Hall
Plants That Never Ever Bloom, Ruth Heller
Dinosaur Tree, Douglas Henderson
Hard Scrabble Harvest, Dahlov Ipcar
Jody's Beans, Malachy Doyle
A Seed, a Flower, a Minute, an Hour, Joan W. Blos
From Seed to Plant, Gail Gibbons
The Magic School Bus Plants Seeds: A Book About How Living Things Grow, Patricia Relf
The Butterfly Seeds, Mary Watson
A Handful of Seeds, Monica Hughes
How a Seed Grows, Helen J. Jordan

2.11 *continued*

FISH AND SEA MAMMALS

The following books answer such questions as "Where are certain types of fish found?" "How much of the Earth is covered with water?" "What do we find in the coral reef?" and "Is a dolphin a fish?" Children will want to keep reading these fascinating books.

The Fish from Japan, Elizabeth K. Cooper
The Care and Feeding of Fish, Sarajo Frieden
Shrimps, Judy Hawes
Ocean, Ron Hirschi
Down in the Sea, L. Patricia Kite
A Carp for Kimiko, Virginia L. Kroll
Families of the Deep Blue Sea (Saltwater Secrets), Kenneth Mallory
The Ultimate Ocean Book: A Unique Introduction to the Amazing World Under Water in Fabulous Full-Color Pop-ups, Maria Mudd-Ruth
At Home in the Coral Reef, Katherine Muzik
Here Is the Coral Reef, Madeleine Dunphy
Nature Hide and Seek Oceans, John Norris Wood
Hungry, Hungry Sharks (Step into Reading), Joanna Cole
Sharks in Action, Tenner Ottley Gay
Sharks, Gail Gibbons
The Great White Man-Eating Shark, Margaret Mahy
Great White Shark, Ruler of the Sea, Kathleen Weidner Zoehfield
The Magic School Bus on the Ocean Floor, Joanna Cole
Three at Sea, Timothy Bush
An Octopus Is Amazing, Patricia Lauber
Is a Dolphin a Fish?: Questions and Answers About Dolphins, Melvin and Gilda Berger

FOODS

Food is a favorite subject of children—and the following books will certainly help to whet their reading appetite!

Audubon Cat, Mary Calhoun
Avocado Baby, John Burningham
The Berenstain Bears and Too Much Junk Food, Stan and Jan Berenstain
Big Moon Tortilla, Joy Cowley
Bone Button Borscht, Aubrey Davis
Bread, Bread, Bread, Ann Morris
Button Soup, Doris Orgel
Chocolatina, Erik Kraft
Cucumber Soup, Vickie Leigh Krudwig
Dinner at the Panda Palace, Stephanie Calmenson
The Duchess Bakes a Cake, Virginia Kahl
Dumpling Soup, Jama Kim Rattigan
Extra Cheese, Please!: Mozzarella's Journey From Cow to Pizza, Cris Peterson

2.11 *continued*

Fifty Million Sausages, Roger Benedictus
The Fine Round Cake, Arnica Esterl
Good Enough to Eat: A Kid's Guide to Food and Nutrition, Lizzy Rockwell
Grandpa's Too Good Garden, James Stevenson
Hot Fudge, James Howe
How Nanita Learned to Make Flan, Campbell Geeslin
The Hunt for Food, Anita Ganeri
I, Crocodile, Fred Marcellino
In Enzo's Splendid Gardens, Patricia Polacco
Joshua and the Big Bad Blue Crabs, Mark Childress
Just Right Stew, Karen English
Leela and the Watermelon, Marilyn Hirsh
Lentil Soup, Joe Lasker
Lunch With Aunt Augusto, Emma Chichester Clark
The Matzah That Papa Brought Home, Fran Manushkin
Matzo Ball Moon, Leslea Newman
Mean Soup, Betsy Everitt
The Milk Makers, Gail Gibbons
The Missing Maple Syrup Sap Mystery: Or How Maple Syrup is Made, Gail Gibbons
Moon Soup, Lisa Desimini
Oliver's Fruit Salad, Vivian French
Olson's Meat Pies, Peter Zachary Cohen
One Potato: A Counting Book of Potato Prints, Diana Pomeroy
Pancake Pie, Sven Nordqvist
Pasta Factory, Hana Machotka
Pease Porridge Hot: A Mother Goose Cookbook, Lorinda Bryan Cauley
The Perfect Pancake, Virginia Kahl
The Pizza Book, Stephen Krensky
Possum Stew, Doug Cushman
Purple Delicious Blackberry Jam, Lisa Westberg Peters
Sheldon's Lunch, Bruce Lemerise
The Spaghetti Tree, Jan Fontaine
Still-Life Stew, Helena Clare Pittman
Stone Soup, Marcia Brown
Sweet Dream Pie, Audrey Wood
Sweet Strawberries, Phyllis Reynolds Naylor
This Is the Bread I Baked for Ned, Crescent Dragonwagon
To Market, to Market, Anne Miranda
Tops and Bottoms, Janet Stevenson
Turnip Soup, Christopher A. Myers
Unbeatable Bread, Lyn Littlefield Hoopes
What's on the Menu, Bobbe S. Goldstein
Where's My Share?, Valerie Greeley

2.11 *continued*

INSECTS AND SPIDERS

Children of all ages are curious about insects. These books examine the beauty and destructiveness of bugs as well as how bugs help us. Discussions of bugs and children's experiences with them is one way of introducing these books to children. After reading such books as *The Life Cycle of Spiders* or *When it Comes to Bugs*, children can collect pictures of bugs and make art collages.

The Best Book of Bugs, Claire Llewellyn
Fireflies!, Julie Brinckloe
What About Ladybugs?, Celia Godkin
The Life Cycle of a Spider, Jill Bailey
One Hungry Spider, Jeannie Baker
Spiders, Lillian Bason
When It Comes to Bugs: Poems, Aileen Fisher
Spiders Are Not Insects, Allan Fowler
Spider Watching, Vivian French
All Upon a Stone, Jean Craighead George
Spiders, Gail Gibbons
Spectacular Spiders, Linda Glaser
Never Say Ugh to a Bug, Norma Farber
Bugs!, David Greenberg
Flit, Flutter, Fly!: Poems About Bugs and Other Crawly Creatures, Lee Bennett Hopkins
Bugs, Nancy Winslow Parker
Monster Bugs, Lucille Recht Penner
Where Do They Go? Insects in Winter, Millicent E. Selsam
*ANTics! An Alphabetical Anthology**, Catherine Hepworth
Bees and Wasps, Henry Pluckrose (editor)
From Caterpillar to Butterfly, Deborah Heiligman
The Butterfly, Paula Z. Hogan
The Caterpillar and the Polliwog, Jack Kent
The Butterfly Collector, Naomi Lewis
The Butterfly, Patricia Polacco
Spider Jane, Jane Yolen
John J. Plenty and Fiddler Dan: A New Fable About the Grasshopper and the Ant, John Ciardi
The Magic School Bus Inside a Beehive, Joanna Cole and Bruce Degen
I Wish I Were a Butterfly, James Howe and Ed Young
Fireflies (Early Bird Nature Books), Sally M. Walker

2.11 *continued*

PHYSICS

Children in grades 2 and 3 observe and experience numerous science themes within their environment, including energy and motion, light, and magnetism. The following books will help teach children about the science that surrounds them every day.

Energy and Motion

The Science Book of Energy, Neil Ardley
The Science Book of Motion, Neil Ardley
Energy, Jack Challoner
Why Doesn't the Earth Fall Up? And Other Not Such Dumb Questions About Motion, Vicki Cobb

Matter: Solids, Liquids, and Gases

Solid, Liquid, or Gas (It's Science Series), Sally Hewitt
Solid, Liquid, or Gas (Rookie Read-About-Science Series), Fay Robinson
What Is the World Made Of? All About Solids, Liquids, and Gases (Let's Read-and-Find-Out Science), Kathleen Weidner Zoehfeld
The Magic School Bus Meets the Rot Squad: A Book About Decomposition, Joanna Cole and Bruce Degen
Where Do the Puddles Go? (Rookie Read-About-Science Series), Fay Robinson and Allan Fowler
Tell Me Why Planes Have Wings, Shirley Willis
From Metal to Music, Wendy Davis
From Wax to Crayon, Michael H. Forman
How Is a Crayon Made?, Oz Charles
From Plant to Blue Jeans: A Photo Essay, Arthur John L'Hommedieu

Light

Day Light, Night Light: Where Light Comes From, Franklyn Branley
Lasers, Nina Morgan
The Science Book of Color: The Harcourt Brace Science Series, Neil Ardley
Science of the Light Bulb, Neville Evans

Magnetism and Electricity

Playing with Magnets (Science for Fun), Gary Gibson
What Magnets Can Do (Rookie Read-About-Science Series), Allan Fowler
What Makes a Magnet?, Franklyn Branley
Discovering Electricity, Rae Baines
The Science Book of Magnets, Neil Ardley
The Magic School Bus and the Electric Field Trip, Joanna Cole
Experiments with Magnets (True Book), Salvatore Tocci

2.11 *continued*

Solar Energy

Energy from the Sun (Rookie Reader), Allan Fowler

SCIENCE PROJECTS

Making Things Float and Sink, Gary Gibson
Pushing and Pulling, Gary Gibson
Electricity, Simon de Pinna
Everything Kids Science Experiment Book: Boil Ice, Float Water, Measure Gravity—Challenge the World Around You!, Tom Mark Robinson
Janice Van Cleave's Science Around the Year, Janice Van Cleave
Bangs and Twangs: Science Fun with Sound, Vicki Cobb

SEASONS

Fiction, nonfiction, and poetry are among the books about seasons. *Seasons* explains what happens in different regions during the change of seasons. From a scientific viewpoint, books such as *Around the Seasons: Poems* and *The Reasons for Seasons* examine the reasons for changing seasons. Through these books children can examine how climate in different parts of the world affect the seasons and determine how people live.

Seasons, John Burmingham
How Does the Wind Walk?, Nancy White Carlstrom
Calico Cat's Year, Donald Charles
Everett Anderson's Year, Lucille Clifton
Jemima Remembers, Crescent Dragonwagon
The House of Four Seasons, Roger Antoine Duvoisin
Around the Seasons: Poems, Eleanor Farjeon
Prairie Town, Bonnie Geisert
Dear Rebecca, Winter Is Here, Jean Craighead George
Farming, Gail Gibbons
The Reasons for Seasons, Gail Gibbons
Changing Seasons, Rose Greydanus
A Child's Book of Seasons, Satomi Ichikawa
Discover the Seasons, Diane Iverson
The Seasons, Debbie MacKinnon
The Turning of the Year, Bill Martin Jr.
Snoopy's Facts and Fun Book About Seasons, Charles M. Schulz
Ring of Earth: A Child's Book of Seasons, Jane Yolen
In My Garden, Charlotte Zolotow

Spring

Spring Story, Jill Barklem
Wake up, Groundhog!, Carol L. Cohen

2.11 *continued*

Spring, Ron Hirschi
Easter Buds Are Springing, Lee Bennett Hopkins
I Love Spring!, Steven Kroll
It's Groundhog Day, Steven Kroll
Hi, Mister Robin, Alvin R. Tresselt
Lionel in the Spring, Stephen Krensky
Spring Across America, Seymour Simon

Summer

Sea, Salt, and Air, Miriam Bat-Ami
The Swimming Hole, Jerrold Beim
Heat Wave at Mud Flat, James Stevenson
Canoe Days, Gary Paulsen
Those Summers, Aliki
Summer Fun, Carolyn Haywood

Fall

Why Do Leaves Change Color?, Betsy Maestro
Digger, the Story of a Mole in the Fall, Tessa Potter
Autumn Leaves, Ken Robbins
Henry Explores the Mountains, Mark Taylor
Autumn Harvest, Alvin R. Tresselt
The Stranger, Chris Van Allsburg

Winter

Fang, the Story of a Fox in Winter, Tessa Potter
Animals in Winter, Henrietta Bancroft
In a Meadow, Two Hares Hide, Jennifer Bartoli
When Winter Comes, Russell Freedman
Brave Janet Reachfar, Jane Duncan
Ralph's Frozen Tale, Elise Primavera
Keep Looking! Where Do They Go? Insects in Winter, Millicent E. Selsam

SPACE

Children are fascinated by space. The following books will "launch" many projects, such as looking for constellations and recording them, building model spaceships, and collecting facts on astronauts. Many of these books include photos of the moon and stars that will lead to exploring the moon's surface and how the moon affects Earth.

General

Find the Constellation, H. A. Rey
Easy-to-Make Spaceships That Really Fly, Mary Blocksma

2.11 *continued*

Floating in Space, Franklyn M. Branley
Is There Life in Outer Space?, Franklyn M. Branley
Journey into a Black Hole, Franklyn M. Branley
The Planets in Our Solar System, Franklyn M. Branley
The Magic School Bus Lost in the Solar System, Joanna Cole, illustrated by Bruce Degen
The Best Book of Spaceships, Ian Graham
Astronauts Work in Space, Carol Greene
Explorers on the Moon (Adventures of Tintin), Herge
My Place in Space, Robin Hirst
Blast Off!: Poems About Space, Lee Bennett Hopkins
Space Exploration, Brian Jones
You're Aboard Spaceship Earth!, Patricia Lauber
Space Case, Edward Marshall
Alistair in Outer Space, Marilyn Sadler
Jimmy Zangwow's Out-of-This-World Moon Pie Adventures, Tony DiTerlizzi
Moon Ball, Jane Yolen
A Trip to Mars, Ruth Young
First on the Moon: What it Was Like When Man Landed on the Moon (I Was There), Barbara Hehner
Space Station: Accident on Mir (DK Reader), Angela Royston
Space Shuttle (Take it apart!), Chris Oxlade
Space Vehicles, Anne Rockwell and David Brion
You Can Jump Higher on the Moon and Other Amazing Facts About Space Exploration (I Didn't Know That), Kate Petty
Voyager: An Adventure to the Edge of the Solar System, Sally Ride and Tam O'Shaughnessy
Space Probes to the Planets, Fay Robinson
Project Apollo, Diane M. Sipiera and Paul P. Sipiera
Project Mercury, Diane M. Sipiera and Paul P. Sipiera

Airplanes

Ships of the Air, Lynn Curlee
Up and Away! Taking a Flight, Meredith Davis
Flight: Fliers and Flying Machines, David Jefferis
High in the Sky (SuperSmarts), Steve Parker

Moon

The Moon Book, Gail Gibbons
Journey to the Moon, Erich Fuchs
Abel's Moon, Shirley Hughes
When I Go to the Moon, Claudia Louise Lewis
What the Moon Is Like (Let's Read and Find Out Science), Franklyn Mansfield Branley
Moonwalk: The First Trip to the Moon (Step Into Reading), Judy Donnelly

2.11 *continued*

WEATHER

Weather affects everyone and everything—from how children should dress in the morning to how plants, animals, and insects survive. The following books will help children learn about weather, while having fun at the same time.

Many of these books describe how storms are formed and ways they affect the environment.

General

What Will the Weather Be?, Lynda DeWitt
Weather Forecasting, Gail Gibbons
Weather Words and What They Mean, Gail Gibbons
Weather, Andrew Haslam and Barbara Taylor

Storms

The Day the Hurricane Happened, Lonzo Anderson
Twister, Darlene Beard
The Magic School Bus Inside a Hurricane, Joanna Cole, illustrated by Bruce Degen
Flash, Crash, Rumble and Roll, Franklyn M. Branley
Tornado Alert, Franklyn M. Branley
Storm Chasers: Tracking Twisters, Gail Herman
The Big Storm, Bruce Hiscock
Hurricanes, Peter Murray
Floods, Peter Murray
Lightning, Peter Murray
Tornadoes, Peter Murray
Twisters!, Lucille R. Penner
Lightning, Seymour Simon
Storms, Seymour Simon

Snow

Snow Day, Moira Fain
Snow Bear, Jean Craighead George
The Last Snow of Winter, Tony Johnston
Snow Day!, Barbara M. Joosse
In the Flaky Frosty Morning, Karla Kuskin
The Snowstorm, Selina Chonz
Plants in Winter, Joanna Cole
The Mice Came in Early This Year, Eleanor Lapp

Rain

Singing Down the Rain, Joy Cowley
Rainy Day Together, Crescent Dragonwagon
Cloudy With a Chance of Meatballs, Judi Barrett

2.11 *continued*

A Wet Monday, Dorothy Edwards
Rainy Day Magic, Marie-Louise Gay
The Good Rain, Alice E. Goudy
Come on, Rain, Karen Hesse
Taste the Raindrops, Anna Grossnickle Hines
What Can You Do in the Rain?, Anna Grossnickle Hines
The Rain Puddle, Adelaide Holl
When It Rains, Mary DeBall Kwitz
The Rain, Michael Laser
The Little Girl and the Rain, Milena Lukesova
Listen to the Rain, Bill Martin
That Sky, That Rain, Carolyn Otto
Rainy Morning, Daniel Manus Pinkwater
What Makes It Rain? The Story of a Raindrop, Keith Brandt

2.12 Books to Teach Social Studies

The books in this list are an ideal supplement to the social studies curriculum. At grades 2 and 3, children begin to learn about the land regions of the United States: the rivers, mountains, grasslands, and deserts; the historical events in U.S. history, and the famous and courageous people who helped to build our country. Their studies focus on the diverse people who make up our multicultural population as well as the lives and culture of the people who live in countries outside the United States.

COUNTRIES AROUND THE WORLD

Myths, legends, poems, religious stories, adventure, and realistic fiction have their settings in countries thoughout the world. Children at the second- and third-grade levels are introduced to other countries, their people, and customs. Teachers can use these books to have children examine the ways of life in various countries and discuss how they are similar and different from life in the United States.

Diversity

Bein' With You This Way, W. Nikola-Lisa
Wake Up World: A Day in the Life of Children Around the World, Beatrice Hollyer
It's Okay to Be Different, Todd Parr
Children Just like Me, Barnabas and Anabel Kindersley
People, Peter Spier
Sidewalk Games Around the World, Arlene Erlbach
Families Are Different, Nina Pellegrini
Whoever You Are, Mem Fox

Canada

The Squaring-Off Party, Jonathan London
What's the Most Beautiful Thing You Know About Horses?, Richard Van Camp
The Biggest Bear, Lynn Ward
Nic of the Woods, Lynn Ward
The First Red Maple Leaf, Ludmila Zeman
The Very Last First Time, Jan Andrew
Flying Free (My America), Sharon Dennis Wyeth

Caribbean Islands

Island in the Sun, Harry Belafonte
Jethro and the Jumbie, Susan Cooper
Sweet, Sweet Fig Banana, Phillis Gershator
Under the Sunday Tree: Poems, Eloise Greenfield
Caribbean Canvas, Frane Lessac
My Little Island, Frane Lessac
Sense Suspense: A Guessing Game for the Senses, Bruce McMillan
Coconut Kind of Day: Island Poems, Lynn Joseph
Jasmine's Parlor Day, Lynn Joseph

2.12 *continued*

Costa Rica

Fernando's Gift, Douglas Keister

Denmark

Mr. Jensen and Cat, Lenore Blegvad
The Magic Pot, Patricia Coombs
The Talking Pot: A Danish Folktale, Virginia Haviland

Egypt

Mummies Made in Egypt, Aliki
Temple Cat, Andrew Clements
The Egyptian Cinderella, Shirley Climo
Croco'nile, Roy Gerrard
The Last Camel, Earle Goodenow
The Monster that Grew Small: An Egyptian Folktale, retold by Joan Grant

England

Anno's Britain, Mitsumasa Anno
Lucy Brown and Mr. Grimes, Edward Ardizzone
The Mousehole Cat, Antonia Barber
Madeline in London, Ludwig Bemelmans
Borka, John Burningham
Harald and the Great Stag, Donald Carrick
The House Where Jack Lives, Margaret Crompton
Dick Whittington, retold by Kathleen Lines
Dick Whittington and His Cat, Marcia Brown
Gilly and the Wicharoo, Glenn Dines
Take a Trip to England, Chris Fairclough
The Guard Mouse, Don Freeman
Matilda Jane, Jean Gerrard
The Story of a Castle, John S. Goodall
The Story of a Farm, John S. Goodall
The Witch's Cat, Margaret Greaves

France

Three Sacks of Truth: A Story from France, Eric A. Kimmel
Cows Are Going to Paris, David K. Kirby
Mirette on the High Wire, Emily Arnold McCully
Here Begins the Tale of the Marvellous Blue Mouse, Christopher Manson
I, Crocodile, Fred Marcellino
Maude and Claude Go Abroad, Susan Meddaugh
Henri Mouse, the Juggler, George Mendoza

2.12 *continued*

The Giraffe that Walked to Paris, Nancy Milton
Burgoo Stew, Susan Patron
The Butterfly, Patricia Polacco
Bonjour, Lonnie, Faith Ringgold
The Wolf Who Had a Wonderful Dream: A French Folktale, retold and illustrated by Anne F. Rockwell
That Extraordinary Pig of Paris, Roni Schotter
Colette and the Princess, Louis Slobodkin
Anatole (series), Eve Titus
Madeline (series), Ludwig Bemelmans

Germany

The Pied Piper of Hamelin, Barbara Bartos-Höppner
The Rabbit Catcher and Other Fairy Tales, Ludwig Bechstein
The Elves and the Shoemaker, Paul Galdone
Iron John, Eric A. Kimmel

Greece

My Uncle Nikos, Judy Delton
The Flying Horse, Jane B. Mason
Pegasus, Marianna Mayer
*I Have an Olive Tree**, Eve Bunting
Yanni's Rubbish, Shulamith Levey Oppenheim

Guatemala

The Most Beautiful Place in the World, Ann Cameron

Ireland

Katie's Wish, Barbara Shook Hazen
Grace the Pirate, Kathryn Lasky
O'Sullivan's Stew: A Tale Cooked Up in Ireland, Hudson Talbott
Market Day, Eve Bunting
Clancy's Coat, Eve Bunting
Saint Patrick and the Peddler, Margaret Hodges
The Last Snake in Ireland, Shelia MacGill-Callahan
St. Patrick's Day, Elizabeth O'Donnell
A Child's Treasury of Irish Rhymes, compiled by Alice Taylor
What Do You Feed Your Donkey On? Rhymes from a Belfast Childhood, collected by Colette O'Hare
Jamie O'Rourke and the Big Potato, Tomie dePaola

2.12 *continued*

Italy

Anno's Italy, Mitsumasa Anno
Five Secrets in a Box, Catherine Brighton
Felice, Marcia Brown
The Goose and the Golden Coins, Lorinda Bryan Cauley
Gabriella's Song, Candace Fleming
Pome and Peel: A Venetian Tale, Amy Ehrlich
A Boy Named Giotto, Paolo Guarnieri
The Music Box: The Story of Cristofori, Suzanne Guy
Count Your Way Through Italy, Jim Haskins
Count Silvernose: A Story from Italy, Eric A. Kimmel
Looking for Daniela, Steven Kroll
A Tale of Two Rats, Claude Lager
Jo-Jo the Melon Donkey, Michael Morpurgo
Romulus and Remus, Anne F. Rockwell
The Wonderful Eggs of Furicchia: A Picture Story from Italy, Anne F. Rockwell

Jamaica

Music in the Family, Donna Renee Carter
Anansi, Brian Gleeson
The Tangerine Tree, Regina Hanson

Russia and Russian Americans

Mimmy and Sophie, Miriam Cohen
Babushka's Doll, Patricia Polacco
*Molly's Pilgrim**, Barbara Cohen

CULTURES

At grades 2 and 3, children begin to become aware of the diverse cultural groups that make up the United States. As children read about different cultures, they compare the traditions, values, beliefs, and ways of life of these cultures with their own. (Also see "Multicultural Books," List 2.13.)

African American

Biography, folklore, and realistic fiction are among books about African Americans and the African culture. These books provide information that may not be found in traditional texts, such as the story of an African-American cowboy (*Bill Pickett* by Andrea Davis Pinkney). Teachers will find that the colorful illustrations are instructional and can be used to have students examine and compare settings in different regions or countries. Students can also use biographies to research contributions of famous African Americans. (Also see List 2.14.)

2.12 *continued*

A Band of Angels, Deborah Hopkinson
Mirandy and Brother Wind, Patricia C. McKissack
Ashanti to Zulu: African Traditions, Margaret Musgrove
My Little Island, Frane Lessac
Stories Julian Tells, Ann Cameron
Grandma Lois Remembers: An African-American Family Story (What Was It Like, Grandma?), Ann Morris
White Socks Only, Evelyn Coleman
Chicken Sunday, Patricia Polacco
Aunt Harriet's Underground Railroad in the Sky, Faith Ringgold
Bill Pickett: Rodeo Ridin' Cowboy, Andrea Davis Pinkney
Booker T. Washington, Alan Schroeder
Dear Benjamin Banneker, Andrea Davis Pinkney
Duke Ellington: The Piano Prince and His Orchestra, Andrea Davis Pinkney
Five Brave Explorers (Great Black Heroes series), Wade Hudson
Malcolm X: A Fire Burning Brightly, Walter Dean Myers
Martin Luther King, Jr., Jacqueline Woodson
Martin's Big Words: The Life of Martin Luther King, Jr., Doreen Rappaport
Mary McLeod Bethune, Eloise Greenfield
Meet Martin Luther King, Jr. (A Step-up Book), James de Kay
A Picture Book of Harriet Tubman, David A. Adler
A Picture Book of Jackie Robinson, David A. Adler
A Picture Book of Jessie Owens, David A. Adler
A Picture Book of Martin Luther King, Jr., David A. Adler
A Picture Book of Rosa Parks, David A. Adler
A Picture Book of Sojourner Truth, David A. Adler
Ragtime Tumpie, Alan Schroeder
Talking About Bessie: The Story of Aviator Bessie Coleman, Nikki Grimes
A Weed Is a Flower: The Life of George Washington Carver, Aliki
When Marian Sang, Pam Munoz Ryan
Young Frederick Douglass: Freedom Fighter, Andrew Woods

Amish

The close community ties of the Amish people, who live and dress as though in an earlier century, are reflected throughout the stories listed below.

An Amish Wedding, Richard Ammon
*An Amish Year**, Richard Ammon
Babysitting for Benjamin, Valiska Gregory
Just Like Mama, Beverly Lewis
Just Plain Fancy, Patricia Polacco
Reuben and the Quilt, Merle Good
Selina and the Bear Paw Quilt, Barbara Claasen Smucker
Raising Yoder's Barn, Jane Yolen
*Yonie Wondernose**, Marguerite de Angeli

2.12 *continued*

Asian

There are numerous books about the Asian countries and people for the early elementary grades. Fairy tales, folklore, and realistic fiction offer a comprehensive picture of the lives of children and adults from Japanese, Chinese, Indonesian, and other Asian lands.

Chinese and Chinese American

China's Bravest Girl: The Legend of Hua Mu Lan, Charlie Chin
Chinatown, William Low
Meeting Half Way, Sandra J. Fox
The Chinese New Year Mystery, Carolyn Keene
The Dragon New Year: A Chinese Legend, Dave Bouchard
Panda, Judy Allen
Tiger, Judy Allen
Chin Yu Min and the Ginger Cat, Jennifer Armstrong
A Song of Stars: An Asian Legend, Tom Birdseye
Chen Ping and His Magic Axe, Demi
*Dim Sun for Everyone**, Grace Lin
Grandma Lai Goon Remembers: A Chinese-American Family Story (What Was It Like, Grandma?), Ann Morris
The Happy Funeral, Eve Bunting
Dragon Parade: A Chinese New Year's Story, Steven A. Chin
Sam and the Lucky Money, Karen Chinn
*Chang's Paper Pony**, Eleanor Coerr
Our Baby's from China: An Adoption Story, Nancy D'Antonio
Celebrating Chinese New Year, Diane Hoyt-Goldsmith
The Ugly Vegetables, Grace Lin
Mommy Far, Mommy Near: An Adoption Story, Carol Antoinette Peacock
The Magic Leaf, Winifred Morris
Journey of Meng: A Chinese Legend, Doreen Rappaport
Moon Blossom and the Golden Penny, Louis Slobodkin
Big Bird in China, Jon Stone
Fish in the Air: Story and Pictures, Kurt Wiese
Everyone Knows What a Dragon Looks Like, Jay Williams
*Big Jimmy's Kum Kau Chinese Take Out**, Ted Lewin

Japanese

Tree of Cranes, Allen Say
The Bicycle Man, Allen Say
Momo's Kitten, Mitsu Yashima
I Live in Tokyo, Mari Takabayashi
How My Parents Learned to Eat, Ina R. Friedman
The Bracelet, Yoshiko Uchida
So Far from the Sea, Eve Bunting

2.12 *continued*

Tea With Milk, Allen Say
Tokyo Friends, Betty Reynolds

Korean

An American Face, Jan M. Czech
Dear Juno, Soyung Pak
Goodbye 382 Shin Dang Dong, Frances and Ginger Park
Korean Cinderella, Shirley Climo
The Name Jar, Yangsook Choi
The Royal Bee, Frances and Ginger Park
Sori's Harvest Mook Day: A Story of Korea, Uk-Bae Lee
We Adopted You, Benjamin Koo, Mirra Ginsburg
Where on Earth Is My Bagel?, Frances Park

Vietnamese

Angel Child, Dragon Child, Michele Maria Surat
Dia's Story Cloth: The Hmong People's Journey of Freedom, Dia Cha
The Lotus Seed, Sherry Garland
My Father's Boat, Sherry Garland
The Walking Stick, Maxine Trottier

Hispanic

The Hispanic culture is characterized by extended family ties and cultural rituals. For example, Christmas, or Samana Santa, is celebrated for a week rather than a day as in the European/American Christian tradition. It is fun to have children read books about Hispanic culture and compare the traditions of their own culture with those of others.

Abuelito Eats with His Fingers, Janice Levy
Angelita, Wendy Ann Kesselman
Bad Boy, Good Boy, Marie Hall Ets
A Birthday Basket for Tia, Pat Mora
*Calling the Doves**, Juan Felipe Herrera
Emilio's Summer Day, Miriam A. Bourne
Friday Night Is Papa Night, Ruth A. Sonneborn
Going Home, Eve Bunting
*Graciela: A Mexican-American Child Tells Her Story**, Joe Molnar
Grandma Francisca Remembers: A Hispanic-American Family Story (What Was It Like, Grandma?), Ann Morris
A Gift for Tia Rosa, Karen T. Taha
Nine Days to Christmas, Marie Hall Ets
Pablo and Pimienta, Ruth M. Covault
Pedro, the Angel of Olvera Street, Leo Politi
*Song of the Swallows**, Leo Politi
Tell Me Please! What's That?, Ruth M. Jaynes

2.12 *continued*

Tonio's Cat, Mary Calhoun
Vejigantes Masquerage, Lulu Delacre

Jewish

Religious holidays, family life, and folklore are included among the stories listed below. These books lead to discussing the meanings of Rosh Hashanah, Passover, and Yom Kippur, and explore the stories associated with each holiday.

It's Too Noisy!, Joanna Cole
*Chicken Soup by Heart**, Esther Hershenhorn
Grandma Esther Remembers: A Jewish-American Family Story (What Was It Like, Grandma?), Ann Morris
*The Keeping Quilt**, Patricia Polacco
Many Adventures of Minnie, Jan S. Hart
Northern Lights: A Hanukah Story, Diana Cohen Conway
My Grandpa Died Today, Joan Fassler
A Mountain of Blintzes, Barbara Diamond Goldin
My First Hanukkah Book, Aileen Lucia Fisher
On Passover, Cathy Fishman
On Rosh Hashanah and Yom Kippur, Cathy Fishman
Honi and His Magic Circle, Phillis Gershator
The Fable of the Fig Tree, Michael Gross
The Chanukah Tree, Eric A. Kimmel
The Magic Dreidels, Eric A. Kimmel
Hershel and the Hanukkah Goblins, Eric A. Kimmel
Matzo Ball Moon, Leslea Newman
Latkes and Applesauce: A Hanukkah Story, Fran Manushkin
*Joseph Had a Little Overcoat**, Simms Taback
Joseph Who Loved the Sabbath, Marilyn Hirsh
Jerusalem, Shining Still, Karla Kuskin
*Strudel Stories**, Joanne Rocklin

Native American

Earth Daughter Alicia of Acoma Pueblo, George Ancona
Grandma Maxine Remembers: A Native American Family Story (What Was It Like, Grandma?), Ann Morris
The Goat in the Rug, Charles Blood and Martin Link
Cheyenne Again, Eve Bunting
Keepers of the Animals: Native American Stories and Wildlife Activities for Children, Michael Caduto and Joseph Bruchac
Keepers of the Earth: Native American Stories and Environmental Activities for Children, Michael Caduto and Joseph Bruchac
When the Rain Sings: Poems by Young Native Americans, edited by Lee Francis
The Good Luck Cat, Joy Harjo

2.12 *continued*

Thunder Bear and Ko: The Buffalo Nation and Nambe Pueblo, Susan Hazen-Hammond
Apache Rodeo, Diane Hoyt-Goldsmith
Buffalo Days, Diane Hoyt-Goldsmith
Cherokee Summer, Diane Hoyt-Goldsmith
Pueblo Boy: Growing Up in Two Worlds, Marcia Keegan
Pueblo Girls: Growing Up in Two Worlds, Marcia Keegan
Totem Pole, Diane Hoyt-Goldsmith
A Rainbow at Night: The World in Words and Pictures by Navajo Children, Bruce Hucko
Pow Wow, George Ancona
Lakota Hoop Dancer, Jacqueline Left Hand Bull and Suzanne Haldane
This Land Is My Land, George Littlechild
Everglades: Buffalo Tiger and the River of Grass, Peter Lourie
Houses of Adobe (Native Dwellings series), Bonnie Shemie
Jingle Dancer, Cynthia Leitich Smith
Giving Thanks: A Native American Good Morning Message, Jake Swamp
Children of Clay: A Family of Potters, Rina Swentzell
Ininatig's Gift of Sugar/Traditional Native Sugarmaking, Laura Waterman Wittstock
Brother Eagle, Sister Sky: A Message from Chief Seattle, Susan Jeffers
Gift of the Sacred Dog, Paul Goble
The Girl Who Loved Wild Horses, Paul Goble
Rainbow Crow, Nancy Van Laan
Knots on a Counting Rope, Bill Martin Jr. and John Archambault

REGIONAL BOOKS

The outstanding photos and illustrations in many of the books listed below are as important as instructional tools as the text itself. Also, children are challenged by the riddles about mountains in *Summit Up* and enjoy such books as *When I Was Young in the Mountains* that weave facts into exciting adventure stories.

Continental U.S.

The Alphabet Atlas, Arthur Yorinks
Appalachian Spring, Cynthia Rylant
America's Top 10 Rivers, Jenny E. Tesar
From Path to Highway: The Story of the Boston Post Road, Gail Gibbons
The Great Kapok Tree, Lynn Cherry
Hands-on Rocky Mountains: Art Activities About Anasazi, American Indians, Settlers, Trappers and Cowboys, Yvonne Y. Merrill
Heartland, Diane Siebert
Hey, Al, Arthur Yorinks
Hills and Mountains (Step-by-Step Geography), Sabrina Crewe
Living in a . . . (Rookie Read-About-Geography Series)
Marshes and Swamps, Gail Gibbons
Minn of the Mississippi, Holling C. Holling

2.12 *continued*

Mountains, Seymour Simon
Owl Moon, Jane Yolen
Sierra, Diane Siebert
Rio Grande: From the Rocky Mountains to the Gulf of Mexico, Peter Lourie
Summit Up: Riddles About Mountains, June Swanson
The Little Red Lighthouse and the Great Gray Bridge, Hildegarde Hoyt Swift
When I Was Young in the Mountains, Cynthia Rylant
Wild Flamingos, Bruce McMillan
*The Willow Pattern Story**, Allan Drummond

Alaska and Tundra Regions†

Children tend to stereotype all of Alaska as a place where people live in igloos and watch polar bears crossing the ice. However, reading books such as *Eskimo Boy: Life in an Inupiaq Eskimo Village* challenges this stereotype. It paints the picture of a boy who lives in a white-washed wooden house with his family, dresses in a parka, and attends school as all children do. The books below also introduce students to the animals and people who live and survive the harshness of life in the tundra regions at the top or bottom of the world.

Alaska's Three Bears, Shelley Gill
Arctic Son, Jean Craighead George
Arctic Tundra (Habitats Children's Press), Michael H. Forman
Arctic Tundra: Land With No Trees (Rookie Read-About-Geography series), Allan Fowler
Arctic Winter, Arctic Summer, Susan Canizares
Bear, John Schoenherr
Eskimo Boy: Life in an Inupiaq Eskimo Village, Russ Kendall
Gray Wolf Pup, Doe Boyle
The Great Serum Race: Blazing the Iditarod Trail, Debbie Miller
Honey Paw and Lightfoot, Jonathan London
How Raven Brought Light to the People, Ann Dixon
Ice Bear and Little Fox, Jonathan London
Ka-Ha-Si and the Loon: An Eskimo Legend, Terri Cohlene
Life in the Polar Lands, Monica Byles
Little Walrus, Carol Young
Living in the Arctic (Rookie Read-About-Geography series), Allan Fowler
Long Claws, James Houston
Look to the North: A Wolf Pup Diary, Jean Craighead George
My Arctic 1, 2, 3, Michael Arvaarluk
Kusugak, Vladyana Krykorka
North Pole, South Pole: Journeys to the Ends of the Earth, Bertrand Imbert
The Magic School Bus in the Arctic: A Book About Heat, Joanna Cole
Seal Pup Grows Up: The Story of a Harbor Seal, Kathleen Weidner Zoehfeld
The Eye of the Needle, retold by Teri Sloat
The Very Last First Time, Jan Andrew

†This section of regional books about Alaska and the tundra regions was compiled by Louise Stearn, Librarian.

2.12 *continued*

Totem Pole, Diane Hoyt-Goldsmith
Polar Wildlife (Usborne World Wildlife), Kamini Khanduri
Dashing Through the Snow: The Story of the Junior Iditarod, S. Shahan
The Arctic, Alan Baker
Pole to Pole: The Arctic and Antarctic, Dr. Mary R. Dawson
Who Lives in the Arctic? (Science Emergent Readers), Susan Canizares and Pamela Chanko

U.S. HISTORY

Topics in social studies at the early elementary levels usually include the Native Peoples and the Colonial period, the American Revolution, Westward Expansion, the Civil War and Slavery as well as an introduction to American heroes who helped to build the country. The following books supplement the curriculum by adding characterization, humor, and drama to the facts children acquire.

Native Americans and Colonial Times

1621: A New Look at Thanksgiving, Catherine O'Neill Grace
The Colonial Cook (Colonial People), Bobbie Kalman
Colonial Life (Historic Communities), Bobbie Kalman
A Day in the Life of a Colonial Schoolteacher (Library of Living and Working in Colonial Times), Kathy Wilmore
The Discovery of the Americas, Betsy C. Maestro
Eating the Plates: A Pilgrim Book of Food and Manners, Lucille Recht Penner
*Giving Thanks: The 1621 Harvest Feast**, Kate Waters
If You Lived with the Cherokee (If You Lived), Peter Roop
If You Lived with the Sioux Indians (If You Lived), Ann McGovern
*If You Sailed on the Mayflower in 1621**, Ann McGovern
Kids in Colonial Times (Kids Throughout History), Lisa A. Wroble
On the Mayflower: Voyage of the Ship's Apprentice and a Passenger Girl, Kate Waters
People of the Breaking Day, Marcia Sewall
A Picture Book of Sacagawea, David A. Adler
The Pilgrims of Plimoth, Marcia Sewall
Pocahontas: Young Peacemaker (Childhood of Famous Americans), Leslie Gourse
The Pueblos (True Book), Alice K. Flanagan
*Samuel Eaton's Day: A Day in the Life of a Pilgrim Boy**, Kate Waters
*Sarah Morton's Day: A Day in the Life of a Pilgrim Girl**, Kate Waters
Sitting Bull, Lucille Recht Penner
*Tapenum's Day: A Wampanoag Indian Boy in Pilgrim Times**, Kate Waters

American Revolution

And Then What Happened, Paul Revere?, Jean Fritz
*The Boston Coffee Party** (I Can Read Book), Doreen Rappaport
Buttons for General Washington, Peter and Connie Roop
Can't You Make Them Behave, King George?, Jean Fritz

2.12 *continued*

Daughter of Liberty: A True Story of the American Revolution, Robert Quackenbush
The 4th of July Story, Alice Dalgliesh
George Washington's Socks, Elvira Woodruff
*The Hatmaker's Sign: A Story by Benjamin Franklin**, retold by Candace Fleming
If You Lived at the Time of the American Revolution, Kay Moore
Katie's Trunk, Ann Warren Turner
Phoebe the Spy, Judith Berry Griffin
Redcoats and Petticoats, Katherine Kirkpatrick
*Sam the Minuteman** (I Can Read Book), Nathaniel Benchley
Samuel's Choice, Richard Berleth
Sleds on Boston Commons: A Story from the American Revolution, Louise Bordon
Thomas Jefferson: A Picture Book Biography, James Cross Giblin
*Toliver's Secret**, Esther Wood-Brady
Why Don't You Get a Horse, Sam Adams?, Jean Fritz
Will You Sign Here, John Hancock?, Jean Fritz
Yankee Doodle, Edward Bangs

Westward Expansion and Pioneer Life

Cassie's Journey: Going West in the 1860's, Brett Harvey
*Dakota Dugout**, Ann Morris
If You Traveled West in a Covered Wagon (If You Lived), Ellen Levine
If You Were a Pioneer on the Prairie (If You Were), Anne Kamma
The Josefina Story Quilt (An I-Can-Read Book), Eleanor Coerr
Kindle Me a Riddle: A Pioneer Story, Roberta Karim
Life on a Pioneer Homestead (Picture the Past), Sally Senzell Isaacs
*The Long Way to a New Land**, Joan Sandin
Prairie Fire, Marilynn Reynolds
*Sarah, Plain and Tall**, Patricia MacLachlan
Singing Our Way West: Songs and Stories of America's Westward Expansion, Jerry Silverman
Wagon Train, Sydelle A. Kramer
Wagons West!, Roy Gerrard
*Wagon Wheels**, Barbara Brenner

Civil War and Slavery

Big Jabe, Jerdine Nolen
Civil War for Kids: If You Lived at the Time of the Civil War, Kay Moore
F Is for Freedom, Roni Schotter
Follow the Drinking Gourd, Jeanette Winter
Frederick Douglass: The Last Day of Slavery, William Miller
Freedom River, Doreen Rappaport
Freedom's Wings: Corey's Diary, Kentucky to Ohio 1857 (My America), Sharon Dennis
Harriet Tubman: The Moses of Her People, Sarah Bradford
If You Traveled on the Underground Railroad, Ellen Levine

2.12 *continued*

*Imani's Music**, Sheron Williams
Journey to Freedom: A Story of the Underground Railroad, Courtney Wright
Many Thousand Gone: African Americans from Slavery to Freedom, Virginia Hamilton
Minty: A Story of Young Harriet Tubman, Alan Schroeder
Now Let Me Fly: The Story of a Slave Family, Dolores Johnson
Only Passing Through: The Story of Sojourner Truth, Anne F. Rockwell
*A Picture of Freedom: The Diary of Clotee: A Slave Girl** (Dear America), Patricia McKissack
The Secret to Freedom, Marcia K. Vaughan
*Sweet Clara and the Freedom Quilt**, Deborah Hopkinson
Under the Quilt at Night, Deborah Hopkinson
Underground Man, Milton Meltzer
Wanted Dead or Alive, Ann McGovern

U.S. PATRIOTIC BOOKS

Our Flag (I Know America), Eleanor Ayer
Our National Holidays (I Know America), Karen Spies
Our National Symbols (I Know America), Linda Carlson
Our National Parks (I Know America), Michael Weber
Our National Monuments, Linda Carson Johnson
Ellis Island (True Books, American Symbols), Patricia Ryon Quiri
I Was Dreaming to Come to America: Memories from the Ellis Island Oral History Project
The Bald Eagle (True Books, American Symbols), Patricia Ryon Quiri
Dreaming of America: An Ellis Island Story, Eve Bunting
The Flag We Love, Pam Muñoz Ryan
Uncle Sam and Old Glory: Symbols of America, Delno C. West
Red, White, and Blue: The Story of the American Flag, John Herman
How the U.S. Government Works, Syl Sobel
House Mouse, Senate Mouse, Peter W. Barnes
A Mice Way to Learn About Government: A Curriculum Guide, Peter W. Barnes
Marshall, the Courthouse Mouse: A Tail of the U.S. Supreme Court, Peter W. Barnes
If Your Name Was Changed at Ellis Island, Ellen Levine
The Scrambled States of America, Laurie Keller
Celebrate the 50 States, Loreen Leedy
I Pledge Allegiance: The Pledge of Allegiance, Francis Bellamy with commentary by Bill Martin Jr. and Michael Sampson
The American Flag (Symbols, Landmarks and Monuments), Tamara L. Britton
America Is, Louise Borden
Liberty, Allan Drummond
The White House (American Symbols), Lynda Sorensen
Fireworks, Picnics, and Flags: The Story of the Fourth of July, Ursula Arndt
The Statue of Liberty (True Books, American Symbols), Patricia Ryon Quiri
The Liberty Bell: Sounds of Freedom, Jon Wilson
The White House (American Symbols and Their Meanings), Hal Marcovitz

2.13 Multicultural Books

Bringing multicultural books into the second- and third-grade classroom helps children to develop an appreciation for the traditions, experiences, and values of the diverse groups of people who make up the United States. It is important to seek out books that depict the unique people and experiences within a particular cultural group. (See List 1.19 and List 2.13.)

Across Cultures

Busy Toes, C. Bowie
The Colors of Us, Karen Katz
Different Just Like Me, Lori Mitchell
Everybody Bakes Bread, Norah Dooley
Everybody Cooks Rice, Norah Dooley
Miss Tizzy, Libba Moore Gray
My Two Grandmothers, Effin Older
One Hundred Is a Family, Pam Munoz Ryan
We Are a Rainbow, Nancy Mar's Grande Tabor

African American

A Band of Angels, Deborah Hopkinson
Back Home, Gloria Jean Pinkney
The Blue and the Gray, Eve Bunting
Dinner at Aunt Connie's House, Faith Ringgold
The Face at the Window, Regina Henson
Julian (series), Ann Cameron
Everett Anderson (series), Lucille Clifton
Juneteenth Jamboree, Carole Boston Weatherford
More Than Anything Else, Marie Bradley
Stars in the Darkness, Barbara Joose
*Uncle Jed's Barbershop**, Margaret King Mitchell
The Wagon, Tony Johnston
Working Cotton, Sherley Williams
*Yo? Yes!**, Chris Raschka
Ring! Yo, Chris Raschka
Tar Beach, Faith Ringgold
Follow the Drinking Gourd, Jeanette Winter
Sweet Clara and the Freedom Quilt, Valerie Flourney
Happy Birthday, Martin Luther King, Jean Marzollo
Ma Dear's Aprons, Patricia McKissack
Black Cowboy, Wild Horses, Julius Lester
I Am Rosa Parks, Jim Haskins
Pink and Say, Patricia Polacco
I Have Heard of a Land, Joyce Carol Thomas
Poppa's New Pants, Angela Shelf Medearis
Danitra Brown Leaves Town, Nikki Grimes
A Place Called Freedom, Scott Sanders
Tree of Hope, Amy Littlesugar
One Hundred-and-One African American Read-Aloud Stories, Susan Kantor (editor)

Alternative Lifestyles

All Kinds of Families, Noima Simon
Daddy's Roommate, Michael Willhoite
Heather Has Two Mommies, Leslea Newman
My Two Uncles, Judith Vigna
Zach's Story: Growing Up With Same-Sex Parents, Keith Elliot Greenberg

Amish

Henner's Lydia, Marguerite de Angeli
The Amish Wedding, Richard Ammon
An Amish Christmas, Richard Ammon
Reuben and the Fire, P. Buckley Moss

Appalachian

Appalachia: The Voices of Sleeping Birds, Cynthia Rylant
Ashpet, Joanne Compton
Aunt Skilly and the Stranger, Kathleen Stevens
Cecil's Story, George Ella Lyon
Did You Carry the Flag Today, Charley?, Rebecca Caudill
In Coal Country, Judith Hendershot
Littlejim's Gift: An Appalachian Christmas Story, Gloria Houston
Miss Maggie, Cynthia Rylant
Rag Coat, Lauren Mills

2.13 *continued*

Regular Rolling Noah, George Ella Lyon
Silver Package, Cynthia Rylant
When the Whippoorwill Calls, Candice F. Ransome

Asian

Aekyung's Dream, Min Paek
The American Wei, Marion Hess Pomeranc
Angel Child, Dragon Child, Michele Surat
Baseball Saved Us, Ken Mochizuki
Chin Chiang and the Dragon's Dance, Ian Wallace
Coolies, Yin
Crow Boy, Taro Yashima
Dia's Story Cloth, Dia Cha
Dumpling Soup, Vol. 1, Jama Kim Rattigan
How My Parents Learned to Eat, Ina R. Friedman
How My Family Lives in America, Susan Kuklin
Lion Dance: Ernie Wan's Chinese New Year, Kate Waters
Konichiwa! I Am a Japanese-American Girl, Tricia Brown
Love as Strong as Ginger, Lenore Look
Nim and the War Effort, Milly Lee
Pink Paper Swans, Virginia Kroll
So Far from the Sea, Eve Bunting
Song Lee (series), Suzy Kline
Leaving Vietnam: The Journey of Tuan Ngo, a Boat Boy (Ready to Read), Sarah Kilborne
Tea with Milk, Allen Say
The Whispering Cloth: A Refugee's Story, Pegi Deitz Shea
Chinatown, William Low
The Name Jar, Yangsook Choi
101 Read-Aloud Asian Myths and Legends, Joan C. Veriern

Hispanic

Abuelitos' Heart, Amy Cordova
Bakery Lady, Pat Mora
A Day's Work, Eve Bunting
Family, Diane Gonzalez Bertrand
Family Pictures, Carmen Lomas Garza
Fernando's Gift, Douglas Keister
Fiesta U.S.A., George Ancona
Friends from the Other Side, Gloria Anzaldua
Hector Lives in the United States Now: The Story of a Mexican American Child, Joan Hewett
In My Family, Carmen Lomas Garza
Josefina, Jeanette M. Winter
Mama Does the Mambo, Katherine Leiner
Mayeros: A Yucatan Maya Family, George Ancona
Pablo Remembers: The Fiesta of the Day of the Dead, George Ancona
Tomas and the Library Lady, Pat Mora
Uncle Nacho's Hat, Harriet Rohmer
When the Monkeys Came Back, Kristine Franklin
I Speak English for My Mom, Pat Mora
The Tortilla Factory, Gary Paulsen
Barrio: Jose's Neighborhood, George Ancona
Going Home, Eve Bunting
On the Pampas, Marcia Brusca
The Skirt, Gary Soto
The Old Man and His Door, Gary Soto
Mama Provi and the Pot of Rice, Sylvia Rosa-Casenova
Latino Read-Aloud Stories, Maite Suarez-Rivas (editor)

Jewish

*The Always Prayer Shawl**, Sheldon Oberman
Annushka's Voyage, Elizabeth Tarbescu
The Carp in the Bathtub, Barbara Cohen
Danny Loves a Holiday, Sydney Taylor
Jalapeno Bagels, Natasha Wing
Journey to Ellis Island: How My Father Came to America, Carol Bierman
Make a Wish, Molly, Barbara Cohen
Memory Coat: An Ellis Island Story, Elvira Woodruff
Once I Was a Plum Tree, Johanna Hurwitz
Rivka's First Thanksgiving, Elsa Okon Rael
Tikvah Means Hope, Patricia Polacco

2.13 *continued*

Native American

Ahyoka and the Talking Leaves, Peter Roop
Annie and the Old One, Miska Miles
The Chief's Blanket, Michael Chanin
The Journal of Julia Singing Bear, Gay Matthaei
Maple Moon, Connie Brummel Crook
Navajo Wedding Day, Eleanor Schick
Songs from the Loom: A Navajo Girl Learns to Weave, Monty Roessel
Truth Is a Bright Star, Joan Price
Hawk, I'm Your Brother, Byrd Baylor
The Desert Is Theirs, Byrd Baylor

Quaker

Thee, Hannah, Marguerite de Angeli

2.14 Biographies

A biography introduces the reader to specific facts, events, and stories about a person's life. Some biographies are purely narrative; others are informational and illustrated with photographs that highlight important events in the person's life. Through the following books, children can dig deeper into the lives of figures they meet in their texts. One enjoyable activity is for children to role-play reporters and interview famous people.

Note: There is some overlap of titles within this list.

Athletes

Wilma Unlimited: How Wilma Rudolph Became the World's Fastest Woman, Kathleen Krull
A Picture Book of Jessie Owens, David A. Adler
Coming Home: A Story of Josh Gibson, Baseball's Greatest Home Run Hitter, Nanette Mellage
Lou Gehrig: The Luckiest Man, David A. Adler
NBA Superstar Shaquille O'Neal (NBA Reader series), Lyle Spencer
Home Run: The Story of Babe Ruth, Robert Burleigh
A Picture Book of Jackie Robinson, David A. Adler
Tiger Woods (Checkerboard Awesome Athletes), Paul Joseph

Great Americans

A Picture Book of Abraham Lincoln, David A. Adler
A Picture Book of John F. Kennedy, David A. Adler
A Picture Book of Martin Luther King Jr., David A. Adler
A Picture Book of Thomas Jefferson, David A. Adler
A Picture Book of George Washington, David A. Adler
A Weed Is a Flower: The Life of George Washington Carver, Aliki
Aunt Harriet's Underground Railroad in the Sky, Faith Ringgold
Malcolm X: A Fire Burning Brightly, Walter Dean Myers
*One Giant Leap: The Story of Neil Armstrong**, Don Brown
Rare Treasure: Mary Anning and Her Remarkable Discoveries, Don Brown
Stone Girl, Bone Girl: The Story of Mary Anning, Laurence Anholt
Mary Anning and the Sea Dragon, Jeannine Atkins
Grandpa Is a Flyer, Sanna Anderson Baker
Sakako and the Thousand Paper Cranes, Eleanor Coerr
Chocolate by Hershey: A Story About Milton S. Hershey, Betty Burford
Meet Martin Luther King Jr. (A Step-up Book), James Tertius de Kay
My Brother Martin: A Sister Remembers Growing Up with the Rev. Dr. Martin Luther King Jr., Christine King Farris
My Dream of Martin Luther King, Faith Ringgold
Booker T. Washington, Alan Schroeder
Ragtime Tumpie (Josephine Baker), Alan Schroeder
Martin Luther King Jr., Jacqueline Woodson
Johnny Appleseed, Steven Kellogg
Rocks in His Head, Carol Otis Hurst
Duke Ellington: The Piano Prince and His Orchestra, Andrea Davis Pinkney

2.14 *continued*

Five Brave Explorers (Great Black Heroes series), Wade Hudson
Helen Keller: From Tragedy to Triumph (Childhood of Famous Americans series), Katharine E. Wilkie
Young Amelia Earhart: A Dream to Fly, Sarah Alcott
Young Orville and Wilbur Wright: First to Fly, Andrew Woods
Pasteur's Fight Against Microbes, Beverly Birch
Will Rogers: An American Legend, Frank Keating
On the Frontier with Mr. Audubon, Barbara Brenner
Buffalo Bill and the Pony Express (An I-Can-Read Book), Eleanor Coerr
Mary McLeod Bethune, Eloise Greenfield
Young Frederick Douglass: Freedom Fighter, Andrew Woods
Talkin' About Bessie: The Story of Aviator Bessie Coleman, Nikki Grimes
Harvesting Hope: The Story of Cesar Chavez, Kathleen Krull

Native Americans

A Picture Book of Sitting Bull, David A. Adler
The True Story of Pocahontas, Lucille Recht Penner
Sacagawea, American Pathfinder, Flora W. Seymour
Sitting Bull, Lucille Recht Penner

People of Conviction: Activists, Dreamers, and Leaders

Abraham Lincoln, Patricia Miles Martin
Aunt Harriet's Underground Railroad in the Sky, Faith Ringgold
Elizabeth Blackwell: Girl Doctor (Childhood of Famous Americans), Joanne Landers Henry
George Washington (A Buddy Book), Christy Devillier
Harvesting Hope: The Story of Cesar Chavez, Kathleen Krull
Helen Keller, Katharine Wilkie
Malcolm X: A Fire Burning Brightly, Walter Dean Myers
Martin Luther King Jr., Jacqueline Woodson
Martin's Big Words, Dorreen Rappaport
Mary McLeod Bethune, Eloise Greenfield
Meet Martin Luther King Jr. (A Step-up Book), James T. de Kay
My Brother Martin: A Sister Remembers Growing Up with the Rev. Dr. Martin Luther King Jr., Christine King Farris
Pass the Quill, I'll Write a Draft: A Story of Thomas Jefferson, Robert Quackenbush
A Picture Book of Harriet Tubman, David A. Adler
A Picture Book of Rosa Parks, David A. Adler
A Picture Book of Sojourner Truth, David A. Adler
Sadako and the Thousand Paper Cranes, Eleanor Coerr
They Called Her Molly Pitcher, Anne F. Rockwell
Young Frederick Douglass: Freedom Fighter, Andrew Woods
Joseph, Brian Wildsmith
Patrick: Patron Saint of Ireland, Tomie dePaola

2.14 *continued*

Francis: The Poor Man of Assisi, Tomie dePaola
The Lady of Guadalupe, Tomie dePaola
Moses, Leonard Everett Fisher
Buddha, Hitz Demi
Gandhi: Peaceful Warrior, Rae Baines
The Prince Who Ran Away: The Story of Guatama Buddha, Anne F. Rockwell
Mother Teresa (First Biographies), Lola M. Schaefer
Brother Wolf of Gubbio: A Legend of Saint Francis, Colony Santangelo

People of Courage: Explorers and Adventurers

Alice Ramsey's Great Adventure, Don Brown
Amelia and Eleanor Go for a Ride, Pam Muñoz Ryan
Buffalo Bill and the Pony Express (An I-Can-Read Book), Eleanor Coerr
Ferdinand Magellan (Famous Explorers series), Claude Hurwicz
Henry Hudson (Famous Explorers series), Claude Hurwicz
Johnny Appleseed, Reeve Lindbergh
Lindbergh, Chris L. Demarest
Little Sure Shot: The Story of Annie Oakley, Stephanie Spinner
On the Frontier with Mr. Audubon, Barbara Brenner
*One Giant Leap: The Story of Neil Armstrong**, Don Brown
A Picture Book of Christopher Columbus, David A. Adler
A Picture Book of Davy Crockett, David A. Adler
Talkin' About Bessie: The Story of Aviator Bessie Coleman, Nikki Grimes
Young Amelia Earhart: A Dream to Fly, Sarah Alcott

People with Talent: Writers, Artists, and Entertainers

Action Jackson, Jan Greenberg and Sandra Jordan
Bach (Famous Children), Ann Rachlin
The Beatles (Getting to Know the World's Greatest Composers), Mike Venezia
Diego, Jeannette Winter
Duke Ellington: The Piano Prince and His Orchestra, Andrea Davis Pinkney
Frida, Jonah Winter
Her Piano Sang: A Story About Clara Schumann (Carolrhoda Creative Minds Books), Barbara Allman
Mark Twain? What Kind of a Name Is That?: A Story of Samuel Langhorne Clemens, Robert Quackenbush
My Name Is Georgia: A Portrait by Jeannette Winter, Jeannette Winter
"Nothing Is Impossible," said Nellie Bly, Judy Carlson
Oh the Places He Went: A Story About Dr. Seuss, Maryann N. Weidt
Picasso (Getting to Know the World's Greatest Artists), Mike Venezia
Ragtime Tumpie, Alan Schroeder
Walt Disney, Wendy Lynch
When Marian Sang, Pam Muñoz Ryan

2.14 *continued*

Will Rogers: An American Legend, Frank Keating
Wolfgang Amadeus Mozart (Getting to Know the World's Greatest Composers), Mike Venezia

People with Vision: Scientists and Inventors

The Adventurous Chef: Alexis Soyer, Ann Arnold
Ahoy! Ahoy! Are You There?: A Story of Alexander Graham Bell, Robert Quackenbush
Booker T. Washington, Alan Schroeder
Chocolate by Hershey: A Story About Milton S. Hershey, Betty Burford
Dear Benjamin Banneker, Andrea Davis Pinkney
George Eastman (Checkerboard Inventors), Paul Joseph
Henry Ford, (Checkerboard Inventors), Paul Joseph
Here a Plant, There a Plant, Everywhere a Plant, Plant: A Story of Luther Burbank, Robert Quackenbush
Marie Curie (What Would You Ask?), Anita Ganeri
Mary Anning and the Sea Dragon, Jeannine Atkins
Michael Faraday (What Would You Ask?), Anita Ganeri
Pasteur's Fight Against Microbes, Beverly Birch
A Picture Book of Benjamin Franklin, David A. Adler
A Picture Book of Thomas Edison, David A. Adler
Rare Treasure: Mary Anning and Her Remarkable Discoveries, Don Brown
Robert Fulton: From Submarine to Steamboat, Steven Kroll
Rocks in His Head, Carol Otis Hurst
Starry Messenger: Galileo Galilei, Peter Sis
Stone Girl, Bone Girl: The Story of Mary Anning, Laurence Anholt
Thomas Edison (What's Their Story?), Hadyn Middleton
A Weed Is a Flower: The Life of George Washington Carver, Aliki
Young Orville and Wilbur Wright: First to Fly, Andrew Woods

2.15 Books About Feelings and Conflicts

Feelings and social conflicts are central themes of many stories throughout grades 2 and 3. They are important because they mirror everyday conflicts among children, such as bullying and fighting on the playground. Encouraging positive behavior requires a variety of interventions, including classroom rules and modeling. The following books can be used effectively to discuss specific problems in grades 2 and 3.

Anger

When Sophie Gets Angry, Really, Really Angry, Molly Bang
Alexander and the Terrible, Horrible, No Good, Very Bad Day, Judith Viorst
I'm Mad, Elizabeth Crary
Zeee, Elizabeth Enright
Martha's Mad Day, Miranda Hapgood
Lilly's Purple Plastic Purse, Kevin Henkes
Dealing with Anger, Marianne Johnston
Angry, Marcia Leonard
The Little Cat and the Greedy Old Woman: Story and Pictures, Joan Rankin
When I Feel Angry, Cornelia Spelman
The Quarreling Book, Charlotte Zolotow

Bullying

Bootsie Barker Bites, Barbara Bottner
Bailey, the Big Bully, Lizi Boyd
Willy the Champ, Anthony Browne
Terrible Tyrannosaurus, Elizabeth Charlton
Big Bad Bunny, Alan Durant
Jerome Camps Out, Eileen Christelow
Push and Shove: Bully and Victim Activity Book, Jim Boulden
Hurray for Ethelyn, Babette Cole
Don't Call Me Names!, Joanna Cole
The Meanest Thing to Say (Little Bill series), Bill Cosby
Chester's Way, Kevin Henkes
The Rat and the Tiger, Keiko Kasza
Nobody Knew What to Do: A Story About Bullying, Becky R. McCain
Hey, Pipsqueak!, Kate McMullan
Flowers for Mom, Jirina Marton
The Little Girl and the Dragon, Else Holmelund Minarik
The Recess Queen, Alexis O'Neill
Surviving Brick Johnson, Laurie Myers
The Two Bullies, Junko Morimoto
Crafty Chameleon, Hadithi Mwenye
Big Bad Bruce, Bill Peet
The Berenstain Bears and the Bully, Stan and Jan Berenstain
I'll Fix Anthony, Judith Viorst
How Mr. Monkey Saw the Whole World, Walter Dean Myers

Fear

Fang, Barbara Shook Hazen
The Ankle Grabber, Rose Impey
The Flat Man, Rose Impey
The Old Woman and the Wave, Shelley Jackson
Switch on the Night, Ray Bradbury
Goodnight Orange Monster, Betty Jean Lifton
A House by the River, William Miller
Boo!, Bernard Most
Thunder Cake, Patricia Polacco
Bubba and Trixie, Lisa Campbell Ernst

Fighting

Fighting, Joy Wilt Berry
The Fight, Betty Boegehold
The Great Ball Game, Joseph Bruchac
The Sand Lot, Mary Blount Christian
Who Is the Boss?, Josse Goffin
Someone's Fighting, Nikki Grimes
Stormy Weather, Amanda Harvey
The Sorely Trying Day, Russell Hoban
It's Mine!, Leo Lionni
No Fighting, No Biting!, Else Holmelund Minarik
The Quarreling Book, Charlotte Zolotow
Monkey in the Middle, Eve Bunting

2.15 *continued*

Grief

Everett Anderson's Goodbye, Lucille Clifton
The Tenth Good Thing About Barney, Judith Viorst
Saying Good-Bye to Grandma, Jane Resh Thomas
Flamingo Dreams, Donna Jo Napoli
Sweet, Sweet Memory, Jacqueline Woodson
When Dinosaurs Die, Laurie Krasny Brown and Marc Brown
I Wish I Could Hold Your Hand: A Child's Guide to Grief and Loss, Dr. Pat Palmer
What's Heaven?, Maria Shriver
Grandma's Purple Flowers, Adjoa J. Burrowes
The Black Dog Who Went into the Woods, Edith Thatcher Hurd
I Had a Friend Named Peter: Talking to Children About the Death of a Friend, Janice Cohn
The Happy Funeral, Eve Bunting
Time for Uncle Joe, Nancy Jewell
Upside-Down Cake, Carol Carrick
Where Is Grandpa?, T. A. Barron
You Hold Me and I'll Hold You, Jo Carson

Jealousy

Julius, the Baby of the World, Kevin Henkes
Mary's Mirror, Jim Aylesworth
Country Mailman, Jerrold Beim
I Don't Like It!, Ruth Brown
Arthur's Baby, Marc Brown
Molly Gets Mad, Suzy Kline
Pinky and Rex and the School Play, James Hower
Feeling Jealous (Exploring Emotions series), Althea
It Isn't Fair: A Book About Sibling Rivalry, Barbara Shook Hazen

Lying

Annie Bananie and the People's Court, Leah Komaiko
Arthur in a Pickle, Marc Brown
The Berenstain Bears and the Truth, Stan and Jan Berenstain
The Boy Who Cried Wolf, Tony Ross
A Children's Book About Lying, Joy Berry
Don't Tell a Whopper on Friday, Adolph Moser
Fancy Feet (New Kids at Polk Street School series), Patricia Reilly Giff
The Honest-to-Goodness Truth, Patricia C. McKissack
My Big Lie (Little Bill series), Bill Cosby
The Principal's New Clothes, Stephanie Calmenson
Telling the Truth (Exploring Emotions series), Althea

Manners

Table Manners, Vladimir Radunsky and Chris Raschka
Lady Lupin's Book of Etiquette, Babette Cole
Rude Mule, Pamela Duncan Edwards
The Berenstain Bears Forget Their Manners, Stan and Jan Berenstain
Bears Always Share, Barbara Shook Hazen

Rejection

Best Friends, Steven Kellogg
Cannonball Simp, John Burningham
Horace and Morris But Mostly Dolores, James Howe

Self-Esteem

Willie the Wimp, Anthony Browne
Arthur's Eyes, Marc Tolan Brown
Cendrillon: A Caribbean Cinderella, Robert D. SanSouci
Lilly's Purple Plastic Purse, Kevin Henkes
Nappy Hair, Carolivia Herron
Harry and Willy and Carrothead, Judith Casely
A Weekend with Wendell, Keven Henkes
Practically Perfect Pajamas, Erik Brooks
Fly!, Christopher Myers
I'm Gonna Like Me: Letting Off a Little Self-Esteem, Jamie Lee Curtis

2.15 *continued*

Charlie the Caterpillar, Dom DeLuise
DeDe Takes Charge, Johanna Hurwitz
Hooway for Wodney Wat, Helen Lester

Selfishness

How to Lose All of Your Friends, Nancy L. Carlson
The Beggar's Magic: A Chinese Tale, Margaret Scrogin Chang
One Grain of Rice: A Mathematical Folktale, Demi
A Weekend with Wendell, Kevin Henkes
Rebecca Hatpin, Robert Kraus
The Little Cat and the Greedy Old Woman, Joan Rankin
The Best Friends Club: A Lizzie and Harold Story, Elizabeth Winthrop
Tiger Woman, Laurence Yep
Dealing with Someone Who Is Selfish (The Conflict Resolution Library), Don Middleton

Stealing

Hanna's Hog, Jim Aylesworth
A Cat's Tale, Rikki Cate
The Secret Box, Joanna Cole
Bill and Pete Go Down the Nile, Tomie dePaola
Gogol's Coat, Cary Fagan
Paddy to the Rescue, John S. Goodall
The Tale of Ali Baba and the Forty Thieves: A Story from the Arabian Nights, Eric A. Kimmel
Who Stole the Cookies?, Judith Moffatt
Pigasus, Pat Murphy
The Swan Maiden, Howard Pyle
Piggins, Jane Yolen

Talking to Strangers

It's OK to Say No, Amy C. Bahr
The Berenstain Bears Learn About Strangers, Stan and Jan Berenstain
Strangers, Dorothy Chlad
Mother Goose and the Fly Fox, Chris Conover
Little Red Riding Hood: A New-fangled Prairie Tale, Lisa Campbell Ernst
Who Is a Stranger, and What Should I Do?, Linda Walvoord Girard
Safety Zone: A Book Teaching Children Abduction-Prevention Skills, Linda D. Meyer
Being Careful with Strangers, Kate Petty
The Danger of Strangers, Carole Garbuny Vogel
Heckedy Peg, Audrey Wood

Tattling

Nosey Mrs. Rat, Jeffrey Allen
Tattle Tails (Barkley's School for Dogs series), Marcia Thornton Jones
Telling Isn't Tattling, Kathryn M. Hammerseng

Teasing and Getting into Trouble

Dealing with Teasing, Lisa K. Adams
Miss Nelson Is Back, Harry Allard
Revenge of the Small Small, Jean Little
Dancing in the Wings, Debbie Allen
Madeline and the Bad Hat, Ludwig Bemelmans
Being Destructive, Joy Wilt Berry
Jigsaw Jackson, David F. Birchman
A Dog Named Sam, Janice Boland
Arthur's Computer Disaster, Marc Brown
How to Lose All of Your Friends, Nancy L. Carlson
Yanni's Rubbish, Shulamith Levey Oppenheim

Tough Times

Tight Times, Barbara Shook Hazen

Unconditional Love

Even If I Did Something Awful, Barbara Shook Hazen
It Wasn't My Fault, Helen Lester

2.16 Books About Holidays and Traditions

The following books can be used to compare the various traditions and customs of people everywhere. Many of the books listed can be used to explore how these traditions came about and how holidays originated.

Birthday

Benjamin's 365 Birthdays, Judi Barrett
Cranberry Birthday, Wende and Harry Devlin
Handtalk Birthday: A Number & Story Book in Sign Language, Remy Charlip, Mary Beth, and Georg Ancona
Some Birthday!, Patricia Polacco
The Happy Birthday Book, Carolyn Ewing

Chinese New Year

Celebrating Chinese New Year, Diane Hoyt-Goldsmith
Chinese New Year, Tricia Brown
Chinese New Year's Dragon, Rachel Sing
Gung Hay Fat Choy! Happy New Year, Terry Behrens
Sam and the Lucky Money, Karen Chinn
Runaway Rice Cake, Yin Chang Compestine

Christmas

The Bells of Christmas, Virginia Hamilton
Chita's Christmas Tree, Elizabeth Fitzgerald Howard
Christmas Moon, Denys Cazet
Christmas Without a Tree, Elizabeth B. Rodger
Cranberry Christmas, Wende and Harry Devlin
Daniel's Gift, Mary-Claire Helldorfer
The "Jingle Bells" Jam (Lincoln Lions Band series), Patricia Reilly Giff
The Christmas Party, Adrienne Adams
The Night Before Christmas, Clement C. Moore
Christmas After All: The Great Depression Diary of Minnie Swift (Dear America series), Kathryn Lasky
Carlos, Light the Favolito, Jean Ciavonne
Merry Christmas: Children at Christmas Time Around the World, Robina Becklees Willson
The Favolitos of Christmas, Rudolfo A. Anaya
The Remarkable Christmas of the Cobbler's Sons, told by Ruth Sawyer

Diwali

Diwali, Christina Mia Gardeski
Here Comes Diwali: The Festival of Lights, Meena Atul Pandya

Easter

The Bunny Who Found Easter, Charlotte Zolotow
Cranberry Easter, Wende and Harry Devlin
The Easter Cat, Meindert DeJong
The Easter Egg Artist, Adrienne Adams
The Egg Tree, Katherine Milhous
The Big Bunny and the Easter Eggs, Steven Kroll
The Easter Mystery, Joan Lowery Nixon
The Easter Pig, Louise McClenathan
Easter, Gail Gibbons

Fourth of July

*Apple Pie Fourth of July**, Janet S. Wong
Celebration, Jane Resh Thomas
A Fourth of July on the Plains, Jean Van Leeuwen
The Fourth of July Story, Alice Dalgliesh
Happy Birthday, America!, Marsha Wilson Chall
How Many Days to America? A Fourth of July Story, Eve Bunting
Uncle Chente's Picnic, Diane Gonzales Bertrand

2.16 *continued*

Halloween

Cranberry Halloween, Wende and Harry Devlin
The Biggest Pumpkin Ever, Steven Kroll
Halloween Is . . ., Gail Gibbons
The Hallo-wiener, Dav Pilkey
Horrible Harry at Halloween (Horrible Harry series), Suzy Kline
Jack the Bum and the Halloween Handout, Jack Schulman
Picnic at Mudsock Meadow, Patricia Polacco
The Pumpkin Smasher, Anita Benarde
Scared Silly: A Halloween Treat, James Howe
Scary, Scary Halloween, Eve Bunting
Something Queer at the Haunted School (Something Queer series), Elizabeth Levy

Jewish Holidays and Observances

Chanukah, Frank Daniel
Dance, Sing, Remember: A Celebration of Jewish Holidays, Leslie Kimmelman
Festival of Freedom, Maida Silverman
Festival of Lights, Maida Silverman
The First Passover, Leslie Swartz
Hanukkah, Alan Benjamin
*Here Come the Purim Players**, Barbara Cohen
Holiday Tales of Sholom Aleichem, Aliza Shvrin
Malke's Secret Recipe, David A. Adler
On Hanukkah, Cathy Goldberg Fishman
On Passover, Cathy Goldberg Fishman
On Purim, Cathy Goldberg Fishman
On Rosh Hashanah and Yom Kippur, Cathy Goldberg Fishman
One Candle, Eve Bunting
Purim, Miriam Nerlove
Shabbat, Miriam Nerlove

Kwanzaa

Imani's Gift at Kwanzaa, Denise Burden-Patmon
It's Kwanzaa Time!, Linda Gross
Kwanzaa, Dana M. Rau
A Kwanzaa Miracle, Sharon Shavers Gayle
Seven Candles for Kwanzaa, Andrea Davis Pinkney
Seven Spools of Thread: A Kwanzaa Story, Angela Shelf Medearis
Together for Kwanzaa, Juwanda G. Ford
A Very Special Kwanzaa, Debi Chocolate

Ramadan

Celebrating Ramadan, Diane Hoyt-Goldsmith
Magid Fasts for Ramadan, Mary Matthews
Ramadan, Suhaib Hamid Ghazi

Thanksgiving

A Turkey for Thanksgiving, Eve Bunting
How Many Days to America? A Thanksgiving Story, Eve Bunting
Molly's Pilgrim, Barbara Cohen
Cranberry Thanksgiving, Wende and Harry Devlin
The Wampanoags (True Books, American Indians), Alice Flanagan
The First Thanksgiving, Jean Craighead George
Thanksgiving Day, Gail Gibbons
Three Young Pilgrims, Cheryl Harness
Oh, What a Thanksgiving!, Steven Kroll
An Outlaw Thanksgiving, Emily A. McCully
Eating the Plates: A Pilgrim Book of Food and Manners, Lucille Recht Penner
Twas the Night Before Thanksgiving, Dav Pilkey
It's Thanksgiving, Jack Prelutsky
Thanksgiving Treat, Catherine Stock
The Thanksgiving Story, Alice Dalgliesh
New Friends in a New Land: A Thanksgiving Story, Judith Bauer Stamper
Thank You, Sarah! The Woman Who Saved Thanksgiving, Laurie Halse Anderson
We Gather Together, Now Please Get Lost, Diane De Groat

2.16 *continued*

Valentine's Day

The Case of the Tattletale Heart, Elizabeth Levy
*Cody's Secret Admirer**, Betsy Duffey
Cranberry Valentine, Wende and Harry Devlin
*Little Mouse's Big Valentine**, Edith Thatcher Hurd
Love Bugs, David A. Carter
One Very Best Valentine's Day, Joan W. Blos
*Roses Are Pink, Your Feet Really Stink**, Diane De Groat
The Valentine Star, Patricia Reilly Giff
A Valentine for Norman Noggs, Valiska Gregory
A Village Full of Valentines, James Stevenson
Valentine's Day: Story and Pictures, Miriam Nerlove

2.17 Books About Music, Art, and Dance

The creative and performing arts add excitement and joy to the 2–3 curriculum. The following books will help children become familiar with different instruments, forms of music, craft projects, artists and their works, and songs. These books can make grades 2 and 3 come alive!

Art Books

Addy's Craft Book (The American Girls series), edited by Jodi Evert
Bird Buddies, Better Homes and Gardens
Building with Paper, E. Richard Churchill
How Artists See Animals (How Artists See series), Colleen Carroll
A Child's Book of Art: Great Pictures, First Words, Lucy Micklethwait
*A Child's Book of Art: Discover Great Paintings**, Lucy Micklethwait
*Looking at Faces in Art**, Joy Richardson
Looking at Pictures: An Introduction to Art for Young People, Joy Richardson

Great Artists

Diego Velasquez, Ernest Raboff
Claude Monet: Sunshine and Water Lilies, True Kelley
Edgar Degas: Painting the Dance, Maryann Cocca-Leffler
Henri Matisse: Drawing with Scissors, Jane O'Connor
My Name Is Georgia: A Portrait, Jeanette Winter
Vincent van Gogh: Sunflowers and Swirly Stars, Jane O'Connor
Michelangelo (Getting to Know the World's Great Artists series), Mike Venezia
Paul Klee (Art for Children series), Ernest Raboff

Dance

Folk Dancing, Lydia Anderson
Lakota Hoop Dancer, Jacqueline Left Hand Bull
Tap Dancing: Let's Dance, Tracy M. Maurer
Twins on Toes: A Ballet Debut, Joan Anderson
A Very Young Dancer, Jill Krementz
Starting Ballet, Helen Edom and Nicola Katrak
Ballet School: What It Takes to Be a Dancer, Camilla Jessel
Ballet School, Bobbie D. Kalman
Irish Step Dancing (Let's Dance series), Mark Thomas
Dance with Rosie (Ballet Slippers series), Patricia Reilly Giff
Abiyoyo: Based on a South African Lullaby and Folk Song, Pete Seeger
Swine Lake, James Marshall
I Dreamed I Was a Ballerina, Anna Pavlova
All Tutus Should Be Pink, Sheri Brownrigg
I Have Another Language: Language of Dance, Eleanor Schick
Swan Lake, Rachel Isadora

2.17 *continued*

Music

I Like Music: What Can I Be?, Muriel DuBois
The Magic of Music, Lisl Weil
The Enchanted Flute, James Mayhew
Rondo in C, Paul Fleischman
Pages of Music, Tony Johnston
*Ben's Trumpet**, Rachel Isadora
Bach's Big Adventure, Sallie Ketchum
Flute (Musical Instruments of the World series), Barrie Carson Turner
*I See the Rhythm**, Toyomi Igus
The Kids-Can-Press Jumbo Book of Music, Deborah Dunleavy
Meet the Lincoln Lion's Band, Patricia Reilly Giff
Meet the Orchestra, Ann Hayes
Peter Tchaikovsky (Getting to Know the World's Greatest Composers series), Mike Venezia
The Sound that Jazz Makes, Carole Boston Weatherford
The Story of the Incredible Orchestra, Bruce Koscielniak
*When Marian Sang: The True Recital of Marian Anderson**, Pam Muñoz Ryan
Zin! Zin! Zin!: A Violin, Lloyd Moss
Hip Cat, Jonathan London
Saxophone Sam and His Snazzy Jazz Band, Christine M. Schneider
Making Musical Things, Ann Wiseman
Musicians, Louise Conlon

Songs

Caribbean Carnival: Songs of the West Indies, Irving Burgie
Dancing, Denys Cazet
Dem Bones, Bob Barner
Glory, Glory, How Peculiar, compiled by Charles Keller
Over the River and Through the Woods, Lydia Maria Child
She'll Be Comin' Round the Mountain, Tom Birdseye
A Real Nice Clambake, Richard Rodgers
*This Land Is Your Land**, Woody Guthrie

2.18 Sports Books

Books are written on a wide variety of sports for the early elementary grades. These action and fast-read books encourage children to read about their sports heroes or help them to better understand how a certain sport is played. Many of the following books emphasize the importance of being a team player, that winning isn't everything, and that everyone should have a lot of fun.

Baseball

The Home Run Trick, Scott Corbett
The Baseball Trick, Scott Corbett
The Spy on First Base (Peach Street Mudders series), Matt Christopher
Arthur Makes the Team, Marc Brown
Something Queer at the Ball Park, Elizabeth Levy
Catch Flies!, Tristan Howard
The Dog that Pitched a No-Hitter, Matt Christopher
The Dog that Stole Home, Matt Christopher
Playing Favorites (Hit and Run Gang series), Steven Kroll
The Great McGonnigle Switches Pitches, Scott Corbett
How Georgie Radburn Saved Baseball, David Shannon

Basketball

Fast Break, Tristan Howard
Basketball, Tim Withers
Making the Team in Basketball, Clair Bee
Center Court Sting (sports series), Matt Christopher
Basketball: You Are the Coach, Nate Aaseng
Teamwork: The New York Liberty in Action (Women's Professional Basketball), Thomas S. Owens and Diana Star Helmer

Bicycling

Bicycles, Eugene H. Baker
Delphine, Molly Bang
Monster, Lady Monster and the Bike Ride, Ellen Blance
Mrs. Armitage on Wheels, Quentin Blake
My Sister's Rusty Bike, Jim Aylesworth
Summer Wheels, Eve Bunting
A Tale of Two Bicycles, Leonard Kessler

Fishing

Deep River, Elaine Moore
No, No Rosina, Miska Miles
Rosie's Fishing Trip, Any Hest
*Six Foolish Fisherman**, Robert D. SanSouci
The Biggest Fish in the Sea, Dahlov Ipcar
Tobias Catches Trout, Ole Hertz
Yann and the Whale, Hanze Frissen
A River Dream, Allen Say
Winter Rescue, W. D. Valgardson

Football

Football, Dave Raffo
The Game of Football, Jack Newcombe
The Dog that Called the Signals, Matt Christopher
The Dog that Stole Football Plays, Matt Christopher
Football Friends, Jean Marzollo
Bogeymen Don't Play Football, Debbie Dadey

Gymnastics

I Am a Gymnast, Jane Feldman
The Fantastic Book of Gymnastics, Lloyd Readhead
Gymnastics, Bobbie Kalman
First Day of Gymnastics (DK Readers), Anita Ganeri

2.18 *continued*

Ice Skating

Sam the Zamboni Man, James Stevenson
Sophie Skates, Rachel Isadora
This Is Figure Skating, Margaret Blackstone
It's Great to Skate, Alexa Witt
I Am a Skater, Jane Feldman
Sarah Hughes, Nancy E. Kralik
A Very Young Skater, Jill Krementz
The Best Ice Show Ever (Silver Blades Figure Eights series), Effin Ader

Other Sports

The Magic Hockey Stick, Peter Maloney
The Mud Flat Olympics, James Stevenson
A Very Young Rider, Jill Krementz
Call Me Gretzky!, Jim O'Connor
The Final Game, William Roy Brownridge
Bobsledding and the Luge (A True Book), Larry Dane Brimner

Skateboarding

Arnie and the Skateboard Gang, Nancy L. Carlson
Rhinos Who Skateboard, Julie Mammano
Skateboarding, Dorothy Childers Schmitz

Skiing

Downhill Megan (Magic Attic Club series), Trisha Magraw
A Very Young Skier, Jill Krementz

Sledding

Mush!: Across Alaska in the World's Longest Sled-Dog Race, Patricia Seibert
Dogsled to Dread, Robert M. Quackenbush
Aklak: A Tale from the Iditarod, Robert J. Blake

Soccer

A Good Sport, Patricia Lakin
Coach John and His Soccer Team, Alice K. Flanagan
Preston's Goal!, Colin McNaughton
Soccer Mom from Outer Space, Barney Saltzberg
Soccer Cats, Matt Christopher
Owen Foote, Soccer Star, Stephanie Greene
The Soccer Mystery, Gertrude Chandler Warner

T-Ball

Trouble on the T-Ball Team, Eve Bunting

2.19 Poetry

Poetry is to be read aloud and listened to. The rhythm of poetry encourages children to write their own poems. Teachers of grades 2 and 3 can introduce poetry sessions where children share their favorite poems: their own and those of others.

General

A Poke in the I: A Collection of Concrete Poems, selected by Paul Janeczko
Amber Was Brave, Essie Was Smart, Vera B. Williams
Ashley Bryan's ABC of African American Poetry (A Jean Karl Book), Ashley Bryan
Baby Tamer, Mark Teague
Barn Dance, Bill Martin Jr. and John Archambault
Big Talk, Poems for Four Voices, Paul Fleischman
Black Is Brown Is Tan, Arnold Adoff
Confetti: Poems for Children, Pat Mora
Custard the Dragon and the Wicked Knight, Ogden Nash
Daddy Poems, John Micklos Jr.
Dance with Me, Barbara Juster Esbensen
Daydreamers, Eloise Greenfield, illustrated by Tom Feelings
Desert Song, Tony Johnston, illustrated by Ed Young
Distant the Talking Drum: Poems from Nigeria, Isaac Olaleye
Donna O'Neeshuck Was Chased by Some Cows, Bill Grossman
The Dragons Are Singing Tonight, Jack Prelutsky, illustrated by Peter Sis
Exploding Gravy: Poems to Make You Laugh, X. J. Kennedy
Families, Dorothy Strickland
Father Fox's Penny Rhymes, Clyde Watson, illustrated by Wendy Watson
*Hailstones and Halibut Bones**, Mary O'Neill
Hairy Maclary's Rumpus at the Vet, Lynley Dodd
Home to Me: Poems Across America, selected by Lee Bennett Hopkins
I Hear America Singing, Walt Whitman, illustrated by Robert Sabuda
I Like Being Me, Judi Lalli
If You're Not Here Raise Your Hand: Poems About School, Kalli Dakos
Iguanas in the Snow and Other Winter Poems, Francisco X. Alarcon
In Daddy's Arms I Am Tall (African Americans Celebrating Fathers), Javaka Steptoe
A Hippopotamusn't and Other Animal Poems, J. Patrick Lewis
Jump Back, Honey, Laurence Dunbar
The Jungle Baseball Game, Tom Paxton
Laughing Tomatoes and Other Spring Poems, Francisco X. Alarcon
Mammalabilia: Poems and Paintings, Douglas Florian
Nathaniel Talking, Eloise Greenfield, illustrated by Jan Spivey Gilchrist
Oddhopper Opera: A Bug's Garden of Verses, Kurt Cyrus
One Day Dog, J. Patrick Lewis
Possum Come A-Knockin', Nancy Van Laan
Redbird at Rockefeller Center, Peter Maloney
Sailboat Lost, Leonald Everett Fisher

2.19 *continued*

*Saturday Night at the Dinosaur Stomp**, Carol Diggory Shields
Secret Places, selected by Charlotte Huck
The Flag of Childhood, selected by Naomi Shihab Nye
Muslim Child: Understanding Islam Through Stories and Poems, Rukhsana Khan
Some from the Moon, Some from the Sun, Margot Zemach
Something on My Mind, Tom Feelings
Soul Looks Back in Wonder, Tom Feelings
Spectacular Science: A Book of Poems, selected by Lee Bennett Hopkins
Spin a Soft Black Song, Nikki Giovanni
Stories by Firelight, Shirley Hughes
The Lesson of Moogoo-Maagooville, Karen Jensen
The Pelican Chorus and Other Nonsense, adapted by Fred Marcellino
There's a Zoo in Room 22, Judy Sierra
*This Place I Know: Poems of Comfort**, selected by Georgia Heard
Under Your Feet, Joanne Ryder
Visiting Langston, Willie Perdomo
Walking the Bridge of Your Nose: Wordplay Poems, selected by Michael J. Rosen, illustrated by Cloe Cheese
You Read to Me, I'll Read to You, John Ciardi, illustrated by Edward Gorey
The Earth Under Sky Bear's Feet: Native American Poems of the Land, Joseph Bruchac

Humorous

A Giraffe and a Half, Shel Silverstein
Poems Stew, selected by William Cole
Sing a Song of Popcorn: Every Child's Book of Poems, selected by Beatrice Schenk de Regniers, illustrated by nine Caldecott Medal Artists
Falling Up, Shel Silverstein
Where the Sidewalk Ends, Shel Silverstein
The New Kid on the Block, Jack Prelutsky
A Pizza the Size of the Sun, Jack Prelutsky, illustrated by James Stevenson
Ride a Purple Pelican, Jack Prelutsky, illustrated by Garth Williams
It's Raining Pigs and Noodles, Jack Prelutsky, illustrated by James Stevenson
The Frogs Wore Red Suspenders, Jack Prelutsky, illustrated by Petra Mathers
Bing, Bang, Boing, Douglas Florian
Kids Pick the Funniest Poems, selected by Bruce Lansky
Polkabats and Octopus Slacks: 14 Stories, Calef Brown

Insects, Animals, and Fish

Insectlopedia, Douglas Florian
Animal Trunk, Silly Poems to Read Aloud, Charles Chigna
Lizards, Frogs and Pollywogs, Douglas Florian
Little Wolf's Handy Book of Poems, Ian Whybrow
In the Swim (Poems About Fish), written and illustrated by Douglas Florian

2.19 *continued*

Play on Words

Chocolate Moose for Dinner, Fred Gwynne
A Mink, a Fink, a Skating Rink: What Is a Noun?, Fred Gwynne
Hairy Scary, Ordinary: What Is an Adjective?, Fred Gwynne
To Root, to Toot to Parachute: What Is A Verb?, Brian P. Cleary
Under Over, by the Clover: What Is a Preposition?, Brian P. Cleary

Traditional

*A Child's Calender**, John Updike, illustrated by Trina Schart Hyman
A Friend Is Someone Who Likes You, Joan Walsh Anglund
Poetry for Young People, Emily Dickinson
Noisy Poems, collected by Jill Bennett
Good Night Sleep Tight, compiled by Ivan and Mal Jones
A Child's Garden of Verses, Robert Louis Stevenson, illustrated by Gyo Fujikawa

2.20 Reference and Map Books

The following books can be used to introduce children to such important reference skills as alphabetizing; using tables of contents, indexes, glossaries; finding word meanings; and understanding maps. These resources are appropriate for grades K–3.

Atlases

A First Atlas (A Scholastic First Encyclopedia), Sue Hook and Angela Royston
National Geographic Beginner's World Atlas, National Geographic
National Geographic Our World: A Child's First Picture Atlas, National Geographic

Dictionaries

American Heritage Picture Dictionary, Maggie Swanson
A Hole Is to Dig: A First Book of First Definitions, Ruth Krauss
The Dorling Kindersley Children's Illustrated Dictionary, John McIlwain
My Big Dictionary (American Heritage), Pamela Cote
My First Dictionary (Dorling Kindersley), Betty Root
My First Incredible Amazing Dictionary CD-ROM (Dorling Kindersley)
My Very Own Big Dictionary (American Heritage), Pamela Cote
Sesame Street Dictionary: Featuring Jim Henson's Sesame Street Muppets, Linda Hayward
Scholastic First Dictionary, Judith Levey (editor)

Encyclopedias

The Dorling Kindersley Children's Illustrated Encyclopedia
Usborne First Encyclopedia of Space, Paul Dowswell

Maps

Are We There Yet, Daddy? (Puffin), Virginia Walters
Blast Off to Earth: A Look at Geography (Holiday House), Loreen Leedy
Looking at Maps and Globes (Rookie Read-About Geography), Carmen Bredeson
Mapping Penny's World (Henry Holt), Loreen Leedy
Me on the Map (Dragonfly Books), Joan Sweeney
My Map Book (HarperCollins), Sara Fanelli
There's a Map in My Lap (Cat in the Hat Learning Library), Tish Rabe
We Need Directions! (Rookie Read-About Geography), Sarah DeCapua
Which Way to the Revolution: A Book About Maps, Bob Barner

Questions and Answers

Still More Questions & Answers for Ages 4–6 (Lowell House), Kathie Sweeney
What Happens When?: You Turn on the TV, Flick on a Light, Mail a Letter, John Farndon

Space

Me and My Place in Space (Dragonfly Books), Joan Sweeney
There's No Place Like Space (Cat in the Hat Learning Library), Tish Rabe

SECTION THREE

Books for Grades 4 Through 6

3.1 Classics

In recent years, several children's classics for grades 4–6 have been reissued by publishers in a variety of formats and as spinoffs. It is best to have children become familiar with the original versions, which also work well as read-alouds. Children may enjoy comparing the movie versions of the stories with original stories. Here are some of the most popular.

Adventures of Tom Sawyer, Mark Twain
Adventures of Ulysses, Homer, translated by Bernard Evslin
Alice's Adventures in Wonderland, Lewis Carroll
All-of-a-Kind-Family, Sydney Taylor
Anne of Green Gables (series), Lucy Maud Montgomery
Around the World in Eighty Days, Jules Verne
Black Beauty, Anna Sewell
The Black Stallion (series), Walter Farley
The Call of the Wild, Jack London
Charlotte's Web, E. B. White
Stuart Little, E. B. White
A Christmas Carol, Charles Dickens
The Favorite Uncle Remus, Joel Chandler Harris
Five Little Peppers and How They Grew, Margaret Sidney
Hans Brinker, or the Silver Skates, Mary Mapes Dodge
Heidi, Johanna Spyri
The Hobbit, J. R. R. Tolkien
Johnny Tremain, Esther Forbes
The Jungle Book, Rudyard Kipling
Lad, a Dog, Albert Payson Terhune
Lassie Come Home, Eric Knight
The Lion, the Witch, and the Wardrobe (series), C. S. Lewis
Little Men, Louisa May Alcott
Little Princess, Frances Hodgson Burnett
Little Women, Louisa May Alcott
Mary Poppins, P. L. Travers
The Merry Adventures of Robin Hood of Great Renown in Nottinghamshire, Howard Pyle
Misty of Chincoteague (series), Marguerite Henry
Old Yeller, Fred Gipson
Onion John, Joseph Krumgold
Peter Pan, James Barrie
Pinocchio, Carlo Collodi
Rascal, Sterling North
Rebecca of Sunnybrook Farm, Kate Douglas Smith Wiggin
Robinson Crusoe, Daniel Defoe
The Secret Garden, Frances Hodgson Burnett
The Swiss Family Robinson, Johann David Wyss
Treasure Island, Robert Louis Stevenson
20,000 Leagues Under the Sea, Jules Verne
White Fang, Jack London
The Wind in the Willows, Kenneth Grahame
The Wizard of Oz (series), L. Frank Baum

3.2 Recent Favorites

The following list includes titles that every fourth, fifth, and sixth grader will enjoy reading not once, but many, many times. The memorable characters as well as the engaging stories and exceptional writing will endure in the reader's mind forever. Many of the titles are award winners, and all of the books received a star (*) rating from teachers.

Anastasia (series), Lois Lowry
The Borrowers, Mary Norton
Bridge to Terabithia, Katherine Paterson
Bud, Not Buddy, Christopher Paul Curtis
Charlie and the Chocolate Factory, Roald Dahl
Dear Mr. Henshaw, Beverly Cleary
From the Mixed-up Files of Mrs. Basil E. Frankweiler, E. L. Konigsburg
The Giver, Lois Lowry
Harriet the Spy, Louise Fitzhugh
Harry Potter (series), J. K. Rowling
Hatchet, Gary Paulsen
Holes, Louis Sachar
The Incredible Journey, Sheila Burnford
Island of the Blue Dolphins, Scott O'Dell
Julie of the Wolves, Jean Craighead George
M. C. Higgins the Great, Virginia Hamilton
Maniac Magee, Jerry Spinelli
Missing May, Cynthia Rylant
Mrs. Frisby and the Rats of NIMH, Robert C. O'Brien
My Brother Sam Is Dead, James Lincoln Collier and Christopher Collier
Number the Stars, Lois Lowry
Out of the Dust, Karen Hesse
The Phantom Tollbooth, Norton Juster
Rascal, Sterling North
Roll of Thunder Hear my Cry (Logan family series), Mildred D. Taylor
Sarah, Plain and Tall, Patricia MacLachlan
Sounder, William H. Armstrong
Tuck Everlasting, Natalie Babbitt
The View from Saturday, E. L. Konigsburg
Walk Two Moons, Sharon Creech
Where the Red Fern Grows, Wilson Rawls
The Whipping Boy, Sid Fleischman
A Wrinkle in Time, Madeleine L'Engle

3.3 Picture Books for Older Readers

Picture books are not solely for the youngest children. Older children can benefit from the color and vitality that illustrations bring to a story. Picture books in this category often take the reader into adventures in times past, on magical journeys, or to foreign lands; they can be used to introduce a unit of study on a specific historical period, on the environment, or on a genre of literature. Picture book retellings of the classics make ideal read-alouds in grades 4–6.

A Name on the Quilt by Jeanne Atkins (AIDS memorial quilt project)
Abuelito Eats with His Fingers by Janice Levy (intergenerational)
Adventures with Vikings by Linda Bailey (comic illustrations; notes)
Akiak: Tale from Iditarod by Robert J. Blake
An Angel for Solomon Singer by Cynthia Rylant (Westway Café, New York City)
The Apple and the Arrow by Mary and Conrad Buff (William Tell)
Bach's Big Adventure by Sallie Ketcham (an organist sets out to meet his rival)
The Bear Who Wanted to Be a Bear by Jorg Steiner (environment)
Behold the Trees by Sue Alexander (trees of Israel)
Benito's Bizcochitos by Ana Baca (Spanish Christmas cookies called Bizochitos)
The Blue and the Gray by Eve Bunting (Civil War tale of friendship)
The Bobbin Girl by Emily Arnold McCully (1830's textile mill worker)
Cocoa Ice by Diana Appelbaum (trading Santa Domingo chocolate for Maine ice)
Crazy Horse's Vision by Joseph Bruchac (famous Lakota warrior)
Don Quixote by Cervantes, translated and adapted by Magda Bogin (classic)
Eggs Mark the Spot by Mary Jane Auch (theft of Degas painting)
El Cid by Geraldine McCaughrean (classic)
El Chino by Allen Say (Bill Wong, the Chinese-American bull-fighter)
Emerald Blue by Anne Marie Linden (memories of author's childhood)
Glass Town by Michael Bedard, paintings by Michael Bedard (Brontë sisters)
Going with the Flow by Claire H. Blatchford (handicapped/friendship)
The Great Red Wall Feast by Brian Jacques (surprise feast in rhyme and pictures)
Handel Who Knew What He Liked by M. T. Anderson (stubborn boy becomes a great composer)
Gulliver in Lilliput retold by Margaret Hodges (classic)
Hey, Al by Arthur Yorinks (Al and Eddie travel from New York to "Paradise")
How the Camel Got Its Hump by Rudyard Kipling (classic)
Jigsaw Jackson by David F. Birchman (tall tale)
Joshua's Masai Mask by Dakari Hru (boy changes into others but notes his self-worth)
Juma and the Honey Guide: An African Story by Robin Bernard (the honey guide bird)
The Lady in the Box by Ann McGovern (two siblings help a homeless woman)
Lassie Come Home by Eric Knight, reissue by Rosemary Wells (classic)
The Lion and the Unicorn by Shirley Hughes (Jewish boy in England during WWII)
Lucy Dove by Janice Del Negro (spooky tale)
Mansa Musa: The Lion of Mali by Khephra Burns (one of the greatest kings of Mali)
Marianthe's Painted Words/Spoken Words by Aliki (immigrant experience)
Matthew's Meadow by Corinne Demas Bliss (ecological fable)
Melanie by Carol Carrick (a visually challenged girl)
Moonlite Kite by Helen E. Buckley (all ages)
My Great Grandmother's Gourd by Cristina Kessler (grandmother dislikes modern technology)

3.3 *continued*

The Great Houdini by Robert Burleigh (magician)
Lives of Artists by Kathleen Krull (series: Lives of Musicians, Athletes, Writers)
Nim and the War Effort by Milly Lee (a young girl enters a paper-drive contest)
Nine for California by Sonia Levitan (a family travels to California to meet their father)
Old Home Day by Donald Hall (evolution of Blackwater Pond from the Ice Age to 1999)
Only a Pigeon by Jane and Christopher Kurtz (a boy who trains pigeons)
Parallel Universe: An Interactive Time Adventure by Nicola Baxter (search for objects chronologically out of place)
*Passage to Freedom** by Ken Mochizuki (Chuine Sugihara, the Japanese "Schindler")
Pinocchio by Carlo Collodi, illustrated by Ed Young (classic)
Peacebound Trains by Haemi Balgassi (escape from Seoul during Korean War)
The Pasteboard Bandit by Anna Bontemps and Langston Hughes (meeting of two cultures)
Romeo and Juliet retold and illustrated by Margaret Early (classic)
Roses Sing on New Snow by Paul Yee (recognition)
Shoeless Joe and Black Betsy by Phil Bildner (greatest hitter ever and his bat Black Betsy)
Singing with Momma Lou by Linda Jacobs Altman (Alzheimer's)
So Far from the Sea by Eve Bunting (Manzanar war relocation)
Something Is Growing by Walter Lyon Krudop (a seed grows out of control)
Something Queer in the Cafeteria by Elizabeth Levy (two children get in trouble)
Sundiata: Lion King of Mali by David Wisniewski (13th-century West Africa)
Tchaikovsky Discovers America by Esther Kalman (11-year-old girl meets the composer)
Train to Somewhere by Eve Bunting (orphan train)
Up the River by Frank Asch (environmental river cleanup)
The Unbreakable Code by Sara Hoagland (how Navaho ways helped win WWII)
The Wagon by Tony Johnson (freed young slave is saddened by Lincoln's death)
Women of Camelot by Mary Hoffman (Arthurian legend's female characters' viewpoint)
The Worst Band in the Universe by Graeme Base (music in the Blip planetary system)

MORE PICTURE BOOKS FOR OLDER CHILDREN

The 5,000 Year-Old Puzzle: Solving a Mystery of Ancient Egypt by Claudia Logan (photos, postcards)
Across the Wide Dark Sea: The Mayflower Journey by Jean Van Leeuwen
Ali: Child of the Desert by Jonathan London (takes place in Morocco and on the Great Sahara Desert)
Around the Oak by Gerda Muller (environment–trees)
Arthur, High King of Britain by Michael Morpurgo (read-aloud)
Aunt Nancy and Cousin Lazybones by Phyllis Root (original trickster tale)
Ballad of the Pirate Queens by Jane Yolen (real-life women pirates)
Beethoven Lives Upstairs by Barbara Nichol
Big Jabe by Jerdine Nolan (original tall tale)
Black Cowboy, Wild Horses: A True Story by Julius Lester (story of Bob Lemmons, Texas cowboy)
The Boy in the Attic by Paul Yee (ghost story about a boy who moves from a Chinese village to a U.S. city)
The Bracelet by Yoshiko Uchida (author's family is being relocated to an internment camp)

3.3 *continued*

Brave as a Mountain Lion by Ann Herbert Scott (contemporary Shoshone reservation life)
The Bunyans by Audrey Wood (tall-tale retelling)
The Canterbury Tales by Geoffrey Chaucer, retold by Selina Hastings
The Canterville Ghost by Oscar Wilde ("one of the . . . funniest ghost stories of all time")
Caravan by Lawrence McKay Jr. (Kirghiz caravaneers of Afghanistan)
Castle Diary: The Journal of Tobias Burgess, Page by Richard Platt (author notes and a glossary)
Charlotte by Janet Lunn (true story of a girl caught up in the war between the Rebels and the Loyalists)
Chess-Dream in a Garden by Rosemary Sutcliff (the tale of White King and his Queen)
The Chocolate Cow by Lilian Obligado (all ages)
Coolies by Yin (harsh life of Chinese transcontinental rail laborers)
*The Dark-Thirty: Southern Tales of the Supernatural** by Patricia McKissack
*The Day Gogo Went to Vote** by Elinor Batezat Sisuleu (first time that black South Africans voted)
Day of Delight: A Jewish Sabbath in Ethiopia by Maxine Rose Schur, woodcuts by Brian Pinkney
Dear Ellen Bee: A Civil War Scrapbook of Two Union Spies by Mary E. Lyons and Muriel M. Branch
Don Quixote retold by Virginia Hamilton (classic)
The Dream Jar by Bonnie Pryor (Russian immigrant experience)
Elephant Truck: A True-Life Adventure Story by Will Travers (African Elephant Relocation Project)
Encounter by Jane Yolen (Columbus's landing in the Americas through the eyes of Taino boy)
Fireboat: The Heroic Adventures of the John J. Harvey by Maira Kalman (September 11, 2001)
Freedom's Gifts: A Juneteenth Story by Valerie Wesley (celebration of liberation day for slaves)
Garden in the City by Gerda Muller (fiction with sketches, maps, and project ideas)
Ghost Train by Paul Yee (fantasy story of Chinese workers working on the transcontinental railroad)
*The Girl With a Watering Can** by Ewa Zadrzynska (based on Renoir's *The Girl With a Watering Can*)
God in Between by Sandy Eisenberg Sasso (all ages; see other titles by this author)
*The Great Quillow** by James Thurber (read-aloud)
Hear, Hear Mr. Shakespeare: Story, Illustrations, and Selections from Shakespeare's Plays by Bruce Koscielniak
Heroes by Ken Mochizuki (author of *Baseball Saved Us*)
Hiroshima No Pika by Toshi Maruki (U.S. attack on Japan during WWII)
The House in the Mail by Rosemary and Tom Wells (Sears Roebuck house arrives ready to be assembled)
How Georgie Radbourn Saved Baseball by David Shannon (a good discussion starter)
How I Survived the Oregon Trail (part of the Time Travelers Series)
I Can Hear the Sun by Patricia Polacco (modern myth of faith and hope)
*The Island-Below-the-Star** by James Rumford (retelling of a Hawthorne tale)
Joan of Arc by Michael Morpurgo (read-aloud)
Johnny on the Spot by Edward Sorel (Johnny's radio begins to broadcast news from tomorrow)
Journey to Freedom: A Story of the Underground Railroad by Courtni C. Wright
Jumping the Broom by Courtni C. Wright (wedding day in the slave quarters)
Katie's Trunk by Ann Turner (glimpse into the beginnings of the American Revolution)

3.3 *continued*

*A Knight's Book** by Ali Mitgutsch (all ages)
Lassie Come Home by Rosemary Wells (modern retelling ideal as a read-aloud)
Leah's Pony by Elizabeth Friedrich (the Dust Bowl)
Let My People Go: Bible Stories Told by a Freeman of Color by Patricia and Frederick McKissack
Making of a Knight by Patrick O'Brien (facts about the life of a knight)
The Man Who Kept His Heart in a Bucket by Sonia Levitan (all ages)
Marguerite Makes a Book by Bruce Robertson (the making of illuminated books)
Marie in the Fourth Position by Amy Littlesugar (story of Degas's *The Little Dancer*)
Mary Celeste: An Unsolved Mystery from History by Jane Yolen (true mystery)
Meeting Trees by Scott Russell Sanders (environment—the land)
The Memory Coat by Elvira Woodruff (fleeing the Jewish shtetl in Russia)
Michaelangelo's Surprise by Tony Parillo (an introduction to the Italian Renaissance period)
Miss Alaineous: A Vocabulary Disaster by Debra Frasier (clever wordplay)
Morning on the Lake by Jan Bourdeau (Ojibway grandfather and grandson set out in a birchbark canoe)
Mountains to Climb by Richard Wainwright (Roberto, climber of mountains, comes to the U.S.)
Nettie's Trip South by Ann Turner (real-life diary of the author's great-grandmother)
New York's Bravest by Mary Pope Osbome (the first urban folk hero/firefighters)
On the Wings of Eagles: An Ethiopian Boy's Story by Jeffrey Schrier (rescue of the Ethiopian Jews)
*An Outlaw Thanksgiving** by Emily Arnold McCully (author is Caldecott winner for *Mirette on the Highwire*)
Oz: The Hundredth Anniversary Celebration (authors and illustrators pay tribute to *The Wizard of Oz*)
Pirate Diary: The Journal of Jake Carpenter by Richard Platt (includes author notes and a glossary)
Pooh Story Book by A. A. Milne (all ages)
Rebecca of Sunnybrook Farm by Kate Douglas Wiggin (read-aloud)
*A Right Fine Life: Kit Carson on the Sante Fe Trail** by Andrew Glass
Rome Antics by David Macaulay (Caldecott-winning artist's crosshatched pen-and-ink images of Rome)
Satchmo's Blues by Alan Schroeder (story of Louis Armstrong, jazz trumpeter)
The Sorcerer's Apprentice by Nancy Willard (read-aloud)
The Stone in the Sword: The Quest for a Stolen Emerald by Deri and Jim Robins (medieval picture search)
*The Storytellers** by Ted Lewin (storytellers of Morocco; beautiful illustrations of tapestries)
Stranger in the Mirror by Allen Sam (Sam transforms into an old person)
A Strawbeater's Thanksgiving by Irene Smalls (a story of strength and spirit during the days of slavery)
*The Three Golden Keys** by Peter Sis (the author celebrates his childhood in Prague)
To Find the Way by Susan Nunes (the voyage from Tahiti to Hawaii by ancient Polynesians)
Together in Pinecone Patch by Thomas Yezerski (a Polish boy and an Irish boy meet in a mining camp)
Warm as Wool by Scott Russell Sanders (true pioneer story of the first woman to own sheep)
When I Left My Village by Maxine Rose Schur, woodcuts by Brian Pinkney (plight of Ethiopian Jews)
Whispering Cloth: A Refugee Story by Pegi Deitz Shea (a young girl in a Thai refugee camp)

3.4 Favorite Author Series

Popular series for students in grades 4–6 include stories of mystery, magic, science fiction, modern realistic fiction, and historical fiction. The series below are among the most frequently sought after by children who love being "hooked-in" by a favorite author, character, or type of adventure that will take them to new places and will lead to new discoveries about themselves and the world.

Amazing Day of Abby Hayes (*Anne Mazer*) Fifth-grade Abby is stuck in the middle between her "super-sibs" (twins Isabel and Eva) and younger brother Alex. In addition to her family, there are friends and Briana, the fifth-grade boaster. Abby has a collection of calendars rather than posters so she can change the pictures monthly. Her journals, written in purple, are sprinkled with quotes from the calendars. The books are split between her first-person diaries and third-person accounts of her life. The seven books are published by Scholastic.

Amelia (*Marissa Moss*) Amelia is a delightful contemporary 9-year-old who records her life in notebooks—complete with lined paper and "handwritten" text. There are lots of clever pictures of the people, places, and mementos that are important to her. She's funny, emotional, and very real—and sure to appeal to girls. Excerpts from her books appear in *American Girl* magazine, so she has a built-in fan base. (ages 8+)

Animal Ark (*Ben M. Baglio*) Animal Ark Veterinary Clinic is where Mandy Hope helps her parents. Her love for animals extends beyond the clinic to wherever animals are mistreated or in need of help. Some of the animals Mandy helps are an abandoned lamb, twin bunnies, a stolen school hamster, and a squirrel that pest control is after. The books, published by Scholastic, are illustrated with black-and-white sketches. (grades 4–5; Animal Ark Pets, grade 3)

Animorphs (*K. A. Applegate*) In this Scholastic fantasy/science fiction series, five kids are given the power to morph into animals by a dying alien. Their mission: to save Earth. There are over 40 books in the series including books about the alien. Books are over 100 pages long.

The Babysitters Club (*Ann M. Martin*) Seven experienced babysitters, all students of Stoneybrook Middle School, form a club and meet to share babysitting jobs. The girls are good friends, and share each other's lives, problems, and joys. Although they have a lot in common, each is a very unique individual: Jessi is African American, Claudia is Japanese American, Stacey is diabetic, Mallory is from a big family, Dawn was originally from California, Mary Anne has no mother, and Kristy has a stepfamily. There are more than 120 books in the series.

Chester Cricket (*George Selden, illustrated by Garth Williams*) The series, which began with *The Cricket in Times Square*, is over 40 years old. Chester, the country cricket, lands in bustling Times Square where he meets three friends: Mario, a little boy; Tucker, a mouse; and Harry the cat. The characters are charming, and in later books Lulu Pigeon and Huppy Puppy are added. Books in the series include: *Chester Cricket's New Home*, *Harry Cat's Pet Puppy*, and *Tucker's Countryside*.

Chinatown Mysteries (*Laurence Yep*) Twelve-year-old Lily Lew and her auntie, actress Tiger Lil, solve crimes in San Francisco's Chinatown. These contemporary Chinese-American detectives are colorful characters and describe a lifestyle unfamiliar to many. The three titles are: *The Case of the Firecracker*, *The Case of the Goblin Pearls*, and *The Case of the Lion Dance*. (ages 8–12)

3.4 *continued*

Deltora Quest (*Emily Rodda*) Sixteen-year-old Leif and his companions are on a dangerous quest to save Deltora from the evil Shadow Lord. They can only do that by finding the gems of the magic belt of Deltora. This 8-book fantasy series is published by Scholastic. (reading level 4; http://www.scholastic.com/deltora quest)

Einstein Anderson (*Seymour Simon*) Continuing in the Encyclopedia Brown tradition, the whiz-kid science detective solves short cases, matching wits with the reader. Each story is followed by Einstein's solution along with his scientific reasoning. These eight books actually make science fun! HarperCollins publishes the 80-page books.

Goosebumps (*R. L. Stine*) These books caused quite a sensation when they first hit the shelves. Written as horror stories for children, many adults felt they were too intense for tender minds. However, the kids inhale these stories, many of which have a quirky, offbeat ending a la Hitchcock. The books are published by Scholastic.

Hank the Cowdog (*John R. Erickson*) Hank is the wise-cracking Head of Ranch Security. The dialogue between him and the other animals is lively and clever. He thinks quite highly of himself as he, along with hapless Deputy Drover, solve over 30 humorous cases. Titles include: *Lost in the Blinding Blizzard*, *The Mopwater Files*, *The Case of the Kidnapped Collie*, and *The Garbage Monster from Outer Space*.

Hardy Boys (*Franklin W. Dixon*) Dixon is the pseudonym of Leslie McFarlane, the original author. The series, which began in the 1920s, was the brainchild of Edward Stratemeyer. Other authors have continued and updated the series under the Dixon name. The stories (original and newer) are still very popular. Originally written for boys, these adventurous, quickly plotted mysteries attract both genders almost equally. There are hundreds of books in the series. (grades 4–8)

Harry Potter (*J. K. Rowling*) Rowling received a national grant from the British government based on her proposal for the first book of this series. Readers follow young Harry, an orphaned child with magical talent, through his adventures with his despicable relatives, eccentric friends, and the consistently, obvious evil of his protagonist (and the murderer of his parents), Voldemort (Shhh! You must never say his name.) Excellent for reading aloud. All children recognize the school setting although most American children do not go to boarding school. The ordinary occurrences of school life strike a chord with school children and former school children. Each book is greeted by a frenzy of enthusiasm that seems to grow with each volume. There are five volumes completed in a projected 7-volume set which will end with Harry graduating Hogwarts.

Help! I'm Trapped . . . (*Todd Strasser*) The Dirksen Intelligence Transfer System doesn't work properly. Instead of transferring knowledge from teachers to their students, it transfers bodies! That's how ordinary, average 12-year-old Jake Sherman becomes Santa Claus, his gym teacher, a vampire, a supermodel, and a movie star. This clever 15-book Scholastic series has short chapters and lots of wise-cracking dialogue.

A Magic Shop (*Bruce Coville*) Children don't let the scary titles in this series steer them away from these truly imaginative but engaging stories. Coville, winner of the New York State Knickerbocker Award for Quality in Children's Literature, "brings humor to serious topics without trivializing them." Children also enjoy Coville's *The Teacher Is an Alien* series.

3.4 *continued*

Nancy Drew (*Caroline Keene*) Another brainchild of Edward Stratemeyer, this series was begun by Mildred Wirt under the pseudonym Carolyn Wirt. Nancy was fresh, independent, and strong-minded. Although not the image her male creator had in mind, she was highly popular. The characters come across as real, especially after being updated in the 1970s. There are over 150 Nancy Drew books. (grades 4–8; http://www.stratemeyer.net)

Replica (*Marilyn Kaye*) Twelve-year-old Amy has superpowers—she knows all the answers to questions, is incredibly gifted athletically, and has extraordinary hearing and vision. But she can't remember her past. Amy is a clone, one of thirteen from a secret project. Will she be found out? Although these are suspenseful science fiction books, Amy and her best friend Tasha are realistic, and her relationship with her adopted mother is warm. (ages 9–12)

Rockett's World (*Lauren Day*) Rockett Movado has moved a lot in her life. Now the new girl in eighth grade, she has lots of decisions to make—about friendship, hurting feelings, cliques, who to trust, and which secrets she should keep. Her experiences in school are funny and realistic, making Rockett a very likeable character. There are six books in the series.

Saddle Club (*Bonnie Bryant*) Best friends Carole (the horse lover), Lisa (straight-A student), and Stevie (practical joker) are bound together by their love of horses. While the girls first meet at Pine Hollow Stables, their adventures take them all over New York, Washington D.C., the West. Filled with riding and adventures, the girls also solve mysteries. Bantam Skylark publishes the more than 40 books in the series. (reading level 5)

A Series of Unfortunate Events (*Lemony Snicket*) The Baudelaire orphans suffer unimaginable horrors in this 9-book soap opera. One miserable episode follows another in their wretched lives, as the plucky children barely manage to survive the constant efforts of a persistent villain. The darkly humorous tales run from 160–259 pages. (www.lemonysnicket.com)

Seventh Tower (*Garth Nix*) Scholastic publishes this 6-book fantasy series. The hero, Tal, is a "Chosen" and must undertake a quest to save his family. He is accompanied by Milla, an Ice Carl Warrior. The books are suspenseful adventures in another world. They are in the 200-page range. (ages 9–12; grades 6–8)

Thoroughbred (*Joanna Campbell*) These tales of riding and racing begin with Ashleigh Griffen and Samantha McLean and the horses they love. Later books are about the new generation, Melanie Graham and Christina Reese, and are written by other authors while keeping the "created by Joanna Campbell" label. The 185-page books are about the challenges, both personal and physical, the girls and their horses face. The more than 50 books in the series are published by Harper. (reading levels 5.1, 5.2)

Time Warp Trio (*Jon Scieszka*) There are over ten titles in this adventurous and humorous time-travel series. When the green mist appears, the boys know they will be transported in time to such places as the Wild West, King Arthur's Britain, or Blackbeard's Desert Island. A favorite title in this series is *Summer Reading Is Killing Me*.

Source: List 3.4 was compiled by Debby Kyritz, Children's Librarian, Oradell (New Jersey) Public Library with input from Linda Orvell, Librarian at Harris Stowe College, St. Louis, MO.

3.5 Favorite Publisher Series

Choose Your Own Adventures (*Bantam*) Depending on which page is chosen, a reader can end up with many variations of a story including different endings. These books can be read over and over, with never the same plot. There are over 100 books in the series written by such authors as Edward Packard, R. A. Montgomery, and Richard Brightfield. Readers can have adventures with UFOs, dragons, vampires, knights, Kung Fu masters, or in the pyramids.

Dear America (*Scholastic*) Written as journals by well-known authors, these books are fictional stories based on actual historical events. The girls who write the diaries live in all parts of the country and in different time periods. The 160-page stories include "Life in America," historical notes with maps, recipes, and photographs: a girl on board the *Mayflower*; a girl who makes the journey with her family on the Oregon Trail; a girl who witnesses the building of the transcontinental railroad; a slave girl; and a girl who takes a voyage on the *Titanic*. "My Name Is America" is the comparable boy's series; "My America" is a series for younger readers. These historical journal series from Scholastic are favorites at grades 3–5.

Eyewitness Books (*DK*) There are over 120 titles in this fantastic nonfiction series that covers almost every subject you could think of. The photography is breath-taking and incredibly detailed and well-matched to the text. Subjects range from insects, dinosaurs, and fish to dance, evolution, and explorers and on to weather, volcano and earthquake, and ocean. There are also books on artists, sports, ancient civilizations, and pretty much everything else!

Fast Forward (*Franklin Watts*) These 32-page, nonfiction books have a unique split-page layout. There are lots of detailed full-colored illustrations that are labeled. A main idea is presented; the illustrations and fact "blurbs" fill out the information. Each includes an index, glossary, and fact page. Subjects range from the space shuttle, cars, and ships and submarines, to Egyptian mummies, rain forest, and natural disasters.

Making of America (*Raintree/Steck-Vaughn*) America's history from the first migration from Northeast Asia right up to the beginning of the 21st century are covered in this 12-volume series. Each volume discusses a major era covering politics, conflicts, foreign affairs, biographies, and daily life. There are full-color illustrations, photographs, and maps in the 96-page books as well as a timeline, further reading, Web sites, index, glossary, and bibliography. (grades 5–8)

Reading Expeditions (*National Geographic*) This is a series of high-interest nonfiction science and social studies readers on twelve topics highlighting five titles per topic. Topics include American Communities Across Time, Voices from America's Past, Kids Make a Difference, and Physical Science and Science Issues Today. Each book is 32 pages. (ages 8–11)

Royal Diaries (*Scholastic*) Jam-packed with historical notes, illustrations, maps, and family trees, these action-filled personal accounts are based on lives of historical royal figures of ancient Europe and Asia. Titles include: *Jahanara: Princess of Princesses, India 1627* by Kathryn Lasky; *Elizabeth I* by Kathryn Lasky; *Mary, Queen of Scots, Queen Without a Country, France, 1553* by Kathryn Lasky; *Sondok: Princess of the Moon and Stars, Korea A.D. 595* by Sheri Holman; *Cleopatra VII: Daughter of the Nile, Egypt, 57 B.C.* by Kristiana Gregory; and *Eleanor: Crown Jewel of Aquitane* by Kristiana Gregory. (ages 9–12)

3.5 *continued*

Superguides (*DK*) The books are step-by-step instructional guides to sports and other activities. There are beautiful full-color photographs that detail the actions that readers can follow and learn from. A glossary, index, and "useful addresses" are provided. Titles include: *Ballet*, *Gymnastics*, *Soccer*, *Martial Arts*, *Tennis*, *Snowboarding*, and *Fishing*.

You Wouldn't Want to Be . . . (*Franklin Watts*) History takes on a whole new look in these blood-and-guts retellings. The books are 32 pages each and full of facts and colorful, cartoon-like illustrations. They can be violent—these are not for the squeamish. Readers can see why it wouldn't have been a good idea to be a Roman gladiator, a Polar explorer, an Aztec sacrifice, a Viking explorer, an Egyptian mummy, or to sail on the *Titanic*. Boys in particular enjoy these funny, if somewhat gruesome, books. (ages 7–10, grades 4–6)

MORE FAVORITE SERIES FOR GRADES 4–6

American Girl History Mysteries, Elizabeth McDavid Jones
The Bailey School Kids, Debbie Dadey and Marcia Thornton Jones
The Boxcar Children, Gertrude Chandler Warner
California Diaries, Ann M. Martin
Dinotopia, David F. Glut
The Friendship Ring, Rachel Vail
From the Files of Madison Finn, Laura Dowers
Genny in a Bottle, Kristen Kemp
The Magic Attic Club, Sheri Cooper Sinykin
Malcolm in the Middle, Tom Mason and Dan Danko
Replica, Marilyn Kaye
The Saddle Club, Bonnie Bryant
A Series of Unfortunate Events, Lemony Snicket
Sports Series for Kids, Matt Christopher
Thoroughbred Series, Joanna Campbell
The Three Investigators, Robert Arthur
Two of a Kind Diaries, Nancy Butcher
Wishbone Classics, Miguel de Cervantes

Source: List 3.5 was compiled by Debby Kyritz, Children's Librarian, Oradell (New Jersey) Public Library with input from Linda Orvell, Librarian at Harris Stowe College, St. Louis, MO.

3.6 Realistic Fiction

Realistic fiction depicts events in a contemporary setting that are not necessarily true but could happen. In this type of story, the characters are believable and the plots often deal with handling everyday problems such as feelings, family relationships, and friendships. Through these books children examine different ways of resolving conflicts and begin to understand that their problems are not unique.

All the Answers, Anne C. Lemieux
Anastasia Krupnik (series), Lois Lowry
A Stranger Came Ashore: A Story of Suspense, Mollie Hunter
The Adventures of Tom Sawyer, Mark Twain
The Alfred Summer, Jan Slepian
All About Sam, Lois Lowry
All Because I'm Older, Phyllis Reynolds Naylor
Almost Starring Skinny Bones, Barbara Park
Are You There God? It's Me, Margaret, Judy Blume
Arthur the Kid, Alan Coren
At the Back of the Woods, Claudia Mills
The Bathwater Gang, Jerry Spinelli
The Bathwater Gang Gets Down to Business, Jerry Spinelli
Benny, Barbara Cohen
Bingo Brown (series), Betsy Byars
The Black Pearl, Scott O'Dell
Blubber, Judy Blume
Blue Ribbon Blues Tooter Tale, Jerry Spinelli
*The Box of Delights When the Wolves Were Running**, John Masefield
Bridge to Terabithia, Katherine Paterson
Can You Sue Your Parents for Malpractice?, Paula Danziger
The Case of the Missing Cutthroats: An Ecological Mystery, Jean Craighead George
The Cat Ate My Gymsuit, Paula Danziger
Chester, Mary Francis Shura
Children of the Fox, Jill Paton Walsh
The Computer Nut, Betsy Byars
Cousins, Virginia Hamilton
Cracker Jackson, Betsy Byars
Crash, Jerry Spinelli
The Cybil War, Betsy Byars
Dear Mr. Henshaw, Beverly Cleary
Dicey's Song, Cynthia Voight
Do the Funky Pickle, Jerry Spinelli
A Dog Called Kitty, Bill Wallace
*Dog Friday**, Hilary McKay
Eating Ice Cream with a Werewolf, Phyllis Green
Emily's Runaway Imagination, Beverly Cleary
Eunice (the Egg Salad) Gottlieb, Tricia Springstubb
*The Exiles at Home**, Hilary Mckay
February Dragon, Colin Thiele
Figgs & Phantoms, Ellen Raskin
The Flying Fingers Club, Jean F. Andrews
Fourth Grade Rats, Jerry Spinelli
Fourth Grade Wizards, Barthe DeClements
The Fox Steals Home, Matt Christopher
Frindle, Andrew Clements
Ginger Pye, Eleanor Estes
Go and Catch a Flying Fish, Mary Stolz
The Great Gilly Hopkins, Katherine Paterson
The Green Ghost of Appleville, Jean Marzollo
The Half-a-Moon Inn, Paul Fleischman
Hatchet, Gary Paulsen
Here's to You, Rachel Robinson, Judy Blume
Homecoming, Cynthia Voigt
Homer Price, Robert McCloskey
The House on Hackman's Hill, Joan Lowery Nixon
How to Eat Fried Worms, Thomas Rockwell
Impy for Always, Jackie French Koller
It's Like This, Cat, Emily Neville
Jace the Ace, Joanne Rocklin
Jennifer Hecate, MacBeth, William McKinley and Elizabeth, E. L. Konigsburg
Jenny Archer (series), Ellen Conford
Joel and the Great Merlini, Eloise Jarvis McGraw
Julia and the Hand of God, Eleanor Cameron

3.6 *continued*

Just as Long as We're Together, Judy Blume
Just Ask Iris, Lucy Frank
Lily and Miss Liberty, Carla Stevens
Lizzie Logan (series), Eileen Spinelli
The Magic Moth, Virginia Lee
Make Like a Tree and Leave, Paula Danziger
Midnight Fox, Betsy Byars
The Moves Make the Man, Bruce Brooks
My Side of the Mountain, Jean Craighead George
Nutty Can't Miss, Dean Hughes
Nutty for President, Dean Hughes
On My Honor, Marion Dane Bauer
Once I Was a Plum Tree, Johanna Hurwitz
One-Eyed Cat: A Novel, Paula Fox
Otherwise Known as Sheila the Great, Judy Blume
Popcorn Days and Buttermilk Nights, Gary Paulsen
Poppy and the Outdoor Cat, Dorothy Haas
Race of the Radical, Fanny Howe
The Railway Children, Edith Nesbit
Raymond's Best Summer, Jean Rogers
Rebecca of Sunnybrook Farm, Kate Douglas Wiggin
Seedfolks, Paul Fleischman
Silver, Gloria Whelan
The Singing Hill, Meindert DeJong
Sixth Grade Secrets, Louis Sachar
Smoke Over Golan, Uriel Ofek
Some Friend!, Carol Carrick
Something Fishy at Macdonald Hall, Gordon Korman
Spider Web for Two: A Melendy Maze, Elizabeth Enright
A Stranger Came Ashore: A Story of Suspense, Mollie Hunter
Superfudge, Judy Blume
Tales of a Fourth Grade Nothing, Judy Blume
There's a Bat in Bunk Five, Paula Danziger
There's a Boy in the Girl's Bathroom, Louis Sachar
Thirteen Ways to Sink a Sub, Jamie Gilson
This Island Isn't Big Enough for the Four of Us!, Gery Greer
Too Many Murphys (series), Colleen O'Shaughnessy McKenna
Tooter Pepperday, Jerry Spinelli
Tornado, Betsy Byars
Tough Tiffany, Belinda Hurmence
Unclaimed Treasures, Patricia MacLachlan
Uncle Lemon's Spring, Jane Yolen
Uncle Mike's Boy, Jerome Brooks
The Village by the Sea, Paula Fox
Where the Lilies Bloom, Vera Cleaver
Who Ran My Underwear Up the Flagpole?, Jerry Spinelli
Woodsong, Gary Paulsen
Words of Stone, Kevin Henkes
Wringer, Jerry Spinelli

3.7 Science Fiction and Fantasy

Science fiction writers often take children on adventures to distant galaxies or into future centuries. The plots in science fiction stories involve conflict between good and evil and the dilemma of the future of humanity. The appeal of fantasy, on the other hand, not only is the pull between good and evil, but also the unusual circumstances that could be believable. Children in these creative and imaginary stories overcome problematic situations through courage and ingenuity. In this way the world of fantasy becomes relevant to young readers.

SCIENCE FICTION

A Light in Space, Wendy Orr
A Swiftly Tilting Planet, Madeleine L'Engle
A Wrinkle in Time, Madeleine L'Engle
Angela's Aliens, Janet Lisle
Anna to the Infinite Power, Mildred Ames
City of Gold and Lead, John Christopher
Enchantress from the Stars, Sylvia Engdahl
Eva, Peter Dickinson
Harry the Explorer, Dyan Sheldon
Interstellar Patrol, Christopher Anvil
Interstellar Pig, William Sleater
Lost in Cyberspace, Richard Peck
Monsters in Cyberspace, Dian C. Regan
Mushroom Planet (series), Eleanor Cameron
Norby (series), Janet Asimov and Isaac Asimov
Shape-Changer, Bill Brittain
The Computer Nut, Betsy Byars
The Forgotten Door, Alexander Key
The Golden Aquarians, Monica Hughes
The Great Interactive Dream Machine: Another Adventure in Cyberspace, Richard Peck
The Guardian of Isis, Monica Hughes
The Iron Giant (series), Ted Hughes
The Keeper of the Isis Light, Monica Hughes
The Mystery Machine, Herbie Brennan
The White Mountains, John Christopher
The Tripods Trilogy, John Christopher
Wanted: UFO, Beatrice Gormley

FANTASY

Abel's Island, William Steig
Adventures in the Middle Ages, Linda Bailey
*Afternoon of the Elves**, Janet T. Lisle
A Is for Apple, W Is for Witch, Catherine Dexter
Alice's Adventures in Wonderland, Lewis Carroll
The Amber Coat, Hilary Mckay
Amy's Eyes, Richard Kennedy
Aquamarine, Alice Hoffman
Ask Mr. Bones: Scary Stories from Around the World, Arielle North
Awfully Short for the Fourth Grade, Elvira Woodruff
Bad Dreams, Anne Fine
The Battle for the Castle, Elizabeth Winthrop
The Beasties, William Sleator
Beauty: A Retelling of Beauty and the Beast, Robin McKinley
The Black Cauldron, Lloyd Alexander
The Bookstore Mouse, Peggy Christian
The Borrowers (series), Mary Norton
The Boy with Dinosaur Hands, Albert R. Carusone
Cassie Loves Beethoven, Alan Arkin
A Cat of a Different Color, Steven Bauer
The Cat Who Wished to Be a Man, Lloyd Alexander
Charlie Muffin's Miracle Mouse, Dick King-Smith
Charlotte's Web, E. B. White
Charmed Life, Diana Wynne Jones
The Children Next Door, Jean Ure
Chitty Chitty Bang Bang, Ian Fleming
Christina's Ghost, Betty Ren Wright
Chuck and Danielle, Peter Dickinson

3.7 *continued*

*The Circle Quartet**, Tamora Pierce
The Court of the Stone Children, Eleanor Cameron
The Cricket in Times Square, George Selden
Devil's Donkey, Bill Brittain
The Devil's Other Storybook, Natalie Babbitt
The Devil's Storybook, Natalie Babbitt
The Doll People, Ann M. Martin and Laura Godwin
Dominic, William Steig
Dracula Is a Pain in the Neck, Elizabeth Levy
Ereth's Birthday: A Tale from Dimwood Forest, Avi
Eric in the Land of the Insects, Godfried Bomans
The Eye of the Stone, Tom Birdseye
Faith and the Electric Dogs, Patrick Jennings
The Field of the Dogs, Katherine Paterson
Figgs and Phantoms, Ellen Raskin
The Firework-maker's Daughter, Philip Pullman
The First Two Lives of Lukas-Kasha, Lloyd Alexander
Frankenstein Moved in on the Fourth Floor, Elizabeth Levy
Freaky Friday, Mary Rodgers
The Fresh Grave: And Other Ghostly Stories, Raymond Bial
The Genie of Sutton Place, George Selden
The Ghost by the Sea, Eileen Dunlop
The Ghost Comes Calling, Betty Ren Wright
Ghost Eye, Marion Dane Bauer
The Ghost from Beneath the Sea, Bill Brittain
Ghost of a Hanged Man, Vivian Vande Velde
The Ghost of Fossil Glen, Cynthia DeFelice
Ghost of the Southern Belle: A Sea Tale, Odds Bodkin
The Gold Dust Letters, Janet T. Lisle
Harry Potter (series), J. K. Rowling
Harry the Poisonious Centipede: A Story to Make You Squirm, Lynne Reid Banks
The Horribly Haunted School, Margaret Mahy
H.O.W.L. High, Ellen Leroe
The Hunky-Dory Dairy, Anne Lindbergh
The Indian in the Cupboard (series), Lynne Reid Banks
Islands in the Sky, Tanith Lee
I Was a Rat!, Philip Pullman
Jack Black and the Ship of Thieves, Carol Hughes
*James and the Giant Peach**, Roald Dahl
The Legend of Sleepy Hollow, Washington Irving
The Lemming Condition, Alan Arkin
The Lion, the Witch, and the Wardrobe, C. S. Lewis
The Lost Flower Children, Janet T. Lisle
The Mansion in the Mist, John Bellairs
McMummy, Betsy Byars
Mean Margaret, Tor Seidler
The Midnight Horse, Sid Fleischman
Miss Hickory, Carolyn Sherwin Bailey
The Moonlight Man, Betty Ren Wright
The Moorchild, Eloise McGraw
Morgan's Zoo, James Howe
The New Kid at School, Kate McMullan
Nightmare Hour, R. L. Stine
Nutty's Ghost, Dean Hughes
Orwell's Luck, Richard Jennings
Perloo the Bold, Avi
Peter Pan, J. M. Barrie
The Phantom Tollbooth, Norman Juster
The Pictish Child, Jane Yolen
Pigs Might Fly: A Novel, Dick King-Smith
Pinocchio, Carlo Collodi
Poppy, Avi
Poppy and Rye, Avi
Princess Nevermore, Dian Curtis Regan
Purrfectly Purrfect: Life at the Academy, Patricia Lauber
Rabbit Hill, Robert Lawson
The Red-Eared Ghosts, Vivien Alcock
Redwall (series), Brian Jacques
Red Wizard, Nancy Springer
Rewind, William Sleator
Rip Van Winkle, Washington Irving
Ronia, the Robber's Daughter, Astrid Lindgren
The Roundhill, Dick King-Smith

3.7 *continued*

*The Outlaws of Sherwood**, Robin McKinley
The School Mouse, Dick King-Smith
School Spirits, Michael O. Tunnell
The Search for Delicious, Natalie Babbitt
The Secret of Platform 13, Eva Ibbotson
Seven Spiders Spinning, Gregory Maguire
Seven Strange and Ghostly Tales, Brian Jacques
The Shadow Children, Steven Schnur
Smart Dog, Vivian Vande Velde
Storm at the Edge of Time, Pamela Service
Sugarcane House and Other Stories About Mr. Fat, Adrienne Bond
The Sword in the Stone, T. H. White
The Summer I Shrank My Grandmother, Elvira Woodruff
Summer Switch, Mary Rodgers
A Taste of Smoke, Marion Dane Bauer
The Things with Wings, Gregory Holch
The Three-Day Traffic Jam, John Keefauver
Through the Looking Glass, Lewis Carroll
Throwing Smoke, Bruce Brooks
The Time Bike, Jane Langton
Time Cat: The Remarkable Journeys of Jason and Gareth, Lloyd Alexander
The Time Warp Trio (series)*, Jon Scieszka
Tom, Babette, and Simon: Three Tales of Transformation, Avi
*Tom's Midnight Garden**, Philippa Pearce
Tournament of Time, Elaine M. Alphin
A Treasury of Witches and Wizards, David Bennitt, ed.
The Trumpet of the Swan, E. B. White
Tuck Everlasting, Natalie Babbitt
Vampire State Building, Elizabeth Levy
The Volcano Disaster, Peg Kehret
The Water Horse, Dick King-Smith
The Wayfinder, Darcy Pattison
Website of the Warped Wizard, Eric A. Kimmel
The Well of the Wind, Alan Garner
Wings: A Novel, Bill Brittain
The Wish, Gail Carson Levine
Wishes, Kisses, and Pigs, Betsy Hearne
The Wizard in the Tree, Lloyd Alexander
The Wizard of Oz (series), L. Frank Baum
Wizard's Hall, Jane Yolen
The Wizard's Map, Jane Yolen
The Word Eater, Mary Amato

Source: List 3.7 was compiled by M. Jerry Weiss, Distinguished Service Professor Emeritus, New Jersey City University, Jersey City, NJ.

3.8 Folktales, Fairy Tales, and Myths

Traditional literature portrays the beliefs, values, and cultural background of the people it represents. These stories are helpful in offering children a picture of the past. Children of all ages enjoy original tales and modern retellings. (Also see List 2.7 for grades 2 and 3.)

FOLKTALES AND FAIRY TALES

African

Mufaro's Beautiful Daughters: An African Tale, John Steptoe
Lord of the Dance: An African Retelling, Veronique Tadjo
Bringing the Rain to Kapiti Plain: A Nandi Tale, Verna Aardema
In the Beginning: Creation Stories from Around the World, Virginia Hamilton
Anansi the Spider: A Tale from the Ashanti, Gerald McDermott
Mirandy and Brother Wind, Patricia McKissack
Shaka King of the Zulus, Diane Stanley
Ashanti to Zulu: African Traditions, Margaret W. Musgrove
Why Mosquitoes Buzz in People's Ears, Verna Aardema
The Dancing Palm Tree and Other Nigerian Folktales, Barbara K. Walker
Sundiata: Lion King of Mali, David Wisniewski
Tower to Heaven, Ruby Dee
How the Guinea Fowl Got Her Spots: A Swahili Tale of Friendship, Barbara Knutson
Why the Crab Has No Head: An African Tale, Barbara Knutson
Beat the Story-Drum, Pum-Pum, Ashley Bryan
A Promise to the Sun: A Story of Africa, Tololwa M. Mollel

American

American Tall Tales, Mary Pope Osborne
The Complete Tales of Uncle Remus (read-aloud), Joel Chandler Harris
The Dark Thirty: Southern Tales of the Supernatural, Patrica McKissack
Grandfather Tales: American-English Folk Tales, Richard Chase
Haunted Bayou: And Other Cajun Ghost Stories, J. J. Reneaux
Jump! The Adventures of Brer Rabbit, Joel Harris, adapted by Van Dyke Parks
More Tales of Uncle Remus: Further Adventures of Brer Rabbit, His Friends, Enemies, and Others, Julius Lester
Ol' Paul, the Mighty Logger: Being a True Account of the Seemingly Incredible Exploits and Inventions of the Great Paul Bunyan, Glen Rounds
Paul Bunyan Swings His Axe, Dell J. McCormick
The People Could Fly: American Black Folktales, Virginia Hamilton
Railway Ghosts and Highway Horrors, Daniel Cohen
Scary Stories to Tell in the Dark, retold by Alvin Schwartz
Soap! Soap! Don't Forget the Soap!, Tom Birdseye
Southern Fried Rat and Other Gruesome Tales, Daniel Cohen
Tailypo: A Newfangled Tall Tale, Angela Medearis
The Tales of Uncle Remus: The Adventures of Brer Rabbit, Julius Lester

3.8 *continued*

Whoppers: Tall Tales and Other Lies, Alvin Schwartz (ed.)
Why Alligator Hates Dog, J. J. Reneaux
With a Whoop and a Holler: A Bushel of Lore from Way Down South, Nancy Van Laan

Asian

Two of Everything: A Chinese Folktale, Lily Toy Hong
White Tiger, Blue Serpent, Grace Tseng
Why Rat Comes First: A Story of the Chinese Zodiac, Clara Yen
A Japanese Fairy Tale, Jane Hori Ike
Fairytale Favorites in Story and Song (CD), Jim Weiss
Story of the Chinese Zodiac, Monica Chang
Monkey King Wreaks Havoc in Heaven, Debby Chen
The Magic Tapestry: A Chinese Folktale, Demi
The Making of the Monkey King, Robert Kraus
The Enchanted Tapestry: A Chinese Folk Tale, Robert SanSouci
Ghost Train, Paul Yee
The Dragon Prince: A Chinese Beauty and the Beast Tale, Laurence Yep
The Dragon New Year: A Chinese Legend, Dave Bouchard
The Mouse Bride: A Chinese Folktale, Monica Chang
Why Snails Have Shells: Minority and Han Folktales from China, Carolyn Han
The Dragon's Pearl, Julie Lawson
In the Land of Small Dragon: A Vietnamese Folk Tale, Dang Manh Kha
The Ch'i-lin Purse: A Collection of Ancient Chinese Stories, Linda Fang
The Wise Old Woman, Yoshiko Uchida

Buddhist

The Hungry Tigress: Buddhist Myths, Legends and Jataka Tales, Rafe Martin
I Once was a Monkey, Stories Buddha Told, Jeanne M. Lee
One Hand Clapping: Zen Stories for All Ages, Rafe Martin

Hispanic

The Tree That Rains: The Flood Myth of Huichol Indians of Mexico, Emery Bernhard
The Flame of Peace: A Tale of the Aztecs, Deborah Nourse Lattimore
The Monkey's Haircut: And Other Stories Told by the Maya, John Bierhorst (ed.)
Spirit Child: A Story of the Nativity, Bernardino de Sahagun, translated by John Bierhorst
Princess Florecita and the Iron Shoes: A Spanish Fairy Tale, John Warren Stewig
The Bossy Gallito/El Gallo de Bodas: A Traditional Cuban Folktale, Lucia M. Gonzalez
The Race of Toad and Deer, Pat Mora
The Golden Flower: A Taino Myth from Puerto Rico, Nina Jaffe
The Desert Is My Mother: El Desierto Es Mi Madre (poetry), Pat Mora
This Big Sky (poetry), Pat Mora

3.8 *continued*

Native American

Anpao: An American Indian Odyssey, Jamake Highwater
Echoes of the Elders: The Stories and Paintings of Chief Lelooska, Christina Normandin (ed.)
The Girl Who Lived With the Bears, Barbara Diamond Goldin
Who Speaks for Wolf: A Native American Learning Story as told to Turtle, Paula Underwood Spencer
Where the Buffaloes Begin, Olaf Baker
Buffalo Woman, Paul Goble
The Turkey Girl: A Zuni Cinderella Story, Penny Pollack
Woman Singing by Her Father, Sharp-Eyed Hawk
The Rough-Face Girl, Rafe Martin
Between Earth and Sky: Legends of Native American Sacred Places, Joseph Bruchac
Stories from the Canadian North, Muriel Whitaker
Keepers of the Earth, Native American Stories and Environmental Activities for Children, Michael J. Caduto and Joseph Bruchac
The Star Maiden: An Ojibway Tale, Barbara Esbensen
Navajo Visions and Voices Across the Mesa, Shonto Begay
Crow and Hawk: A Traditional Pueblo Indian Story, Michael Rosen
How Raven Brought Light to People, Ann Dixon
Brother Eagle, Sister Sky: A Message From Chief Seattle, Chief Seattle
Thirteen Moons on a Turtle's Back: A Native American Year of Moons, Joseph Bruchac

Russian

The Fool and the Fish: A Tale from Russia, Alexander Nikolayevich Afanasyev, retold by Lenny Hort
The Rumor of Pavel and Paali: A Ukranian Fairy Tale, Carole Kismaric
The Devils Who Learned to Be Good, Michael McCurdy
Babushka: An Old Russian Folktale, Charles Mikolaycak
The Fool of the World and the Flying Ship: A Russian Tale, Arthur Ransome
Vassilisa the Wise: A Tale of Medieval Russia, Josepha Sherman

MYTHS

Myths are stories created by ancient peoples to explain natural phenomena such as thunder and lightning as well as other mysteries and terrors of the world around them. Elements of myths include gods and goddesses of the sun, moon, earth, and sky; warrior kings and warrior women; human relationships between gods and mortals; and worship of beauty.

Arachne Speaks, Kate Hovey
Atalanta's Race: A Greek Myth, Shirley Climo
The Children's Dictionary of Mythology, David Leeming (ed.)
The Children's Homer: The Adventures of Odysseus and the Tale of Troy, Padraic Colum
Cupid and Psyche, Marie Craft

3.8 *continued*

Daedalus and the Minotaur, Priscilla Galloway
D'Aulaire's Book of Greek Myths, Ingri and Edgar D'Aulaire
Favorite Greek Myths, Mary Pope Osborne
Favorite Norse Myths, Mary Pope Osborne
Gods and Goddesses of the Ancient Maya, Leonard Everett Fisher
The Golden Fleece and the Heroes Who Lived Before Achilles, Padraic Colum
The Golden Hoard: Myths and Legends of the World, Geraldine McCaughrean
Greek Myths, Olivia Coolidge
Have a Hot Time, Hades!, Kate McMullan
Hercules, Robert Burleigh
Heroes, Gods and Emperors from Roman Mythology, Kerry Usher
Lord of the Sky: Zeus, Doris Gates
The Myths of the Norsemen, Richard L. Green
The Olympians: Great Gods and Goddesses of Ancient Greece, Leonard Everett Fisher
Pegasus, Marianna Mayer
Phone Home, Persephone, Kate McMullan
The Random House Book of Greek Myths, Joan D. Vinge
Stolen Thunder: A Norse Myth, Shirley Climo
Tales of the Greek Heroes: Retold from the Ancient Authors, Roger L. Green
Theseus and the Minotaur, Leonard Everett Fisher
The Warrior Goddess: Athena, Doris Gates

Source: The list of mythology books was compiled by M. Jerry Weiss, Distinguished Professor Emeritus, New Jersey City University, Jersey City, NJ.

3.9 Friends and Family

Children acquire their beliefs, values, and behaviors through their friends and family. By reading and discussing these stories, children learn how others deal with relationships. Regional and culturally diverse stories are included in the following list.

Friends

Alice in Rapture, Sort Of, Phyllis Reynolds Naylor
The All-New Amelia, Marissa Moss
All the Way Home, Patricia Reilly Giff
Amelia Takes Command, Marissa Moss
Bad Dreams, Anne Fine
Baseball in April and Other Stories, Gary Soto
*Because of Winn-Dixie**, Kate DiCamillo
Bluish, Virginia Hamilton
Cabin Six Plays Cupid, Marilyn Kaye
Carolina Crow Girl, Valerie Hobbs
Changing Tunes, Donna Jo Napoli
Charlie Is a Chicken, Jane D. Smith
The Hot and Cold Summer, Johanna Hurwitz
Cracker Jackson, Betsy Byars
Crazy Lady!, Jane Leslie Conly
The Cybil War, Betsy Byars
Dangling, Lillian Eige
Dork in Disguise, Carol Gorman
Ernestine and Amanda: Members of the C.L.U.B., Sandra Belton
Ernestine and Amanda: Summer Camp, Ready or Not!, Sandra Belton
Fat Fanny, Beanpole Bertha and the Boys, Barbara Ann Porte
Figuring Out Frances, Gina Willner-Pardo
A Friend Like Phoebe, Marilyn Kaye
Gaffer Samson's Luck, Jill Paton Walsh
The Gift-Giver, Joyce Hansen
Going for Great, Carolee Brockmann
The Gypsy Game, Zilpha Keatley Snyder
Holly's First Love, Beverly Lewis
*Hoot**, Carl Hiaasen
Horse Crazy, Bonnie Bryant
How Do You Spell GEEK?, Julie Anne Peters
The Invisible Enemy, Marthe Jocelyn
Jake Drake, Bully Buster, Andrew Clements
Jennifer, Hecate, MacBeth, William McKinley and Me, Elizabeth Konigsburg
Jonah, the Whale, Susan Shreve
Katie John, Mary Calhoun
Liar, Liar, Barthe DeClements
*Lily's Crossing**, Patricia Reilly Giff
Maniac Monkeys on Magnolia Street, Angela Johnson
My Name Is Brain/Brian, Jeanne Betancourt
Never Say Quit, Bill Wallace
The Noonday Friends, Mary Stolz
Odd Man Out, Gail Radley
Off and Running, Gary Soto
One Lucky Summer, Laura McGee Kvasnosky
Philip Hall Likes Me, I Reckon Maybe, Bette Greene
*Pictures of Hollis Woods**, Patricia Reilly Giff
Romance of the Snob Squad, Julie Anne Peters
The Storyteller's Beads, Jane Kurtz
Marisol and Magdalene: The Sound of Our Sisterhood, Veronica Chambers
The Secret Garden, Frances Hodgson Burnett
Shannon, Lost and Found: San Francisco, 1880, Kathleen V. Kudlinski
Sixth Grade Secrets, Louis Sachar
Starting School With an Enemy, Elisa Carbone
45 & 47 Stella Street and Everything that Happened, Elizabeth Honey
Stranger at the Window, Vivien Alcock
Tac's Island, Ruth Yaffe Radin
Tangled Fortunes, Margaret Mahy
The Tiger Rising, Kate DiCamillo
The Trouble with Zinny Weston, Amy Goldman Koss
True Friends, Bill Wallace
Uncle Shamus, James Duffy
Understanding Buddy, Marc Kornblatt
Yellow Bird and Me, Joyce Hansen

3.9 *continued*

Family

Alicia's Treasure, Diane Gonzalez Bertrand
Anastasia Again!, Lois Lowry
The Animal, the Vegetable, and John D. Jones, Betsy Byars
Baby, Patricia MacLachlan
Baseball Fever, Johanna Hurwitz
The Best Christmas Pagent Ever, Barbara Robinson
Big Trouble in Little Twinsville, Elizabeth Levy
The Birthday Room, Kevin Henkes
Breath of the Dragon, Gail Giles
By Lizzie, Mary Eccles
The Canning Season, Margaret Carlson
Can You Sue Your Parents for Malpractice?, Paula Danziger
Child of the Owl, Laurence Yep
A Corner of the Universe, Ann M. Martin
The Cook's Family, Laurence Yep
Dust of the Earth, Vera Cleaver and Bill Cleaver
Dear Lola: Or, How to Build Your Own Family: A Tale, Judie Angell
The Divorce Express, Paula Danziger
An Eritrean Family, Lois Anne Berg
Father Figure, Richard Peck
For the Love of Pete: A Novel, Jan Marino
Getting Nowhere, Constance Greene
The Great Gilly Hopkins, Katherine Paterson
Hannah in Between, Colby Rodowsky
Here We Go Round, Alice McGill
Homecoming, Cynthia Voigt
Hound Heaven, Linda Oatman High
Ida Early Comes Over the Mountain, Robert Burch
If Wishes Were Horses, Natalie Kinsey-Warnock
The In-Between Days, Eve Bunting
In Plain Sight, Carol Otis Hurst
Jacob Have I Loved, Katherine Paterson
Jason Rat-a-Tat, Colby Rodowsky
Kidnap Kids, Todd Strasser
A Kurdish Family, Karen O'Connor
A Long Way from Chicago: A Novel in Stories, Richard Peck
Looking for Red, Angela Johnson
Margo's House, Peni Griffin
Mountain Pose, Nancy Hope Wilson
My Louisiana Sky, Kimberly Willis Holt
The Nose from Jupiter, Richard Scrimger
Ola Shakes It Up, Joanne Hyppolite
Our Only May Amelia, Jennifer Holm
The Pistachio Prescription, Paula Danziger
The Polyester Grandpa, Martha Freeman
Prairie Summer, Bonnie Geisert
Queen of Hearts, Vera Cleaver and Bill Cleaver
A Question of Trust, Marion Dane Bauer
Regular Guy, Sarah Weeks
Roll of Thunder, Hear My Cry, Mildred D. Taylor
Ruby Holler, Sharon Creech
Sing for Your Father, Su Phan, Stella Pevsner and Fay Tang
Sometimes I Don't Love My Mother, Hila Colman
Sometimes I Think I Hear My Name, Avi
Sport, Louise Fitzhugh
Superfudge, Judy Blume
Thirteen Going on Seven, Marilyn Sachs
Toughboy and Sister, Kirkpatrick Hill
Under the Royal Palms: A Childhood in Cuba, Alma Flor Ada
Walking to the Bus-Rider Blues, Harriette Gillem Robinet
Walk Two Moons, Sharon Creech
West Along the Wagon Road, 1852, Laurie Lawlor
Will's Choice, Joan Lowery Nixon
Yang the Third and Her Impossible Family, Lensey Namioka
A Year Down Yonder, Richard Peck
Yolonda's Genius, Carol Fenner

Source: List 3.9 was compiled by M. Jerry Weiss, Distinguished Professor Emeritus, New Jersey City University, Jersey City, NJ.

3.10 Humorous Books

Humorous stories strongly appeal to children since humorous events happen in every child's life. A twist of words or exaggerated events characterize many of these stories. (Also see List 4.20.)

Adventures of Captain Underpants (series), Dav Pilkey
Alice (series), Phyllis Reynolds Naylor
Alien for Rent, Betsy Duffey
All About Sam, Lois Lowry
Almost Famous, David Getz
Amber Brown (series), Paula Danziger
Anastasia Krupnik (series), Lois Lowry
Annie Pitts, Burger Kid, Diane De Groat
Apple Island, or, the Truth About Teachers, Douglas Evans
Attaboy, Sam!, Lois Lowry
Beetles, Lightly Toasted, Phyllis Reynolds Naylor
The BFG, Roald Dahl
Big Bazoohley, Peter Carey
A Billion for Boris, Mary Rodgers
Boys Against Girls, Phyllis Reynolds Naylor
Burton and the Giggle Machine, Dorothy Haas
By the Great Horn Spoon!, Sid Fleischman
Charlie and the Chocolate Factory, Roald Dahl
Charlie and the Glass Elevator, Roald Dahl
Chocolate Fever, Robert Kimmel Smith
Cody Unplugged, Betsy Duffey
Dear Mrs. Ryan, You're Ruining My Life, Jennifer B. Jones
Desdemona, Twelve Going on Desperate, Beverly Keller
Don't Pat the Wombat!, Elizabeth Honey
Dork in Disguise, Carol Gorman
The Enormous Egg, Eric Butterworth
Everything on a Waffle, Polly Horvath
Fat Men from Space, Daniel Pinkwater
Freaky Friday, Mary Rodgers
Freddy (series), Walter R. Brooks
Granville Jones: Commando, Natalie Honeycutt
The Great Brain (series), John D. Fitzgerald
Guy Time, Sarah Weeks
The Happy Yellow Car, Polly Horvath
Henry Reed (series), Keith Robertson
The Hoboken Chicken Emergency, Daniel Pinkwater
Hoot, Carl Hiassen
How to Eat Fried Worms, Thomas Rockwell
Humbug Mountain, Sid Fleischman
I Can't Believe I Have to Do This, Jan Alford
Kevin Corbett Eats Flies, Patricia Hermes
The Kid in the Red Jacket, Barbara Park
Kidnap Kids, Todd Strasser
The Kid Who Ran for President, Dan Gutman
The Library Card, Jerry Spinelli
Love That Dog, Sharon Creech
The Magic Mean Machine, Beatrice Gormley
The Man in the Ceiling, Jules Feiffer
Matilda, Roald Dahl
Mr. Popper's Penguins, Richard Atwater and Florence Atwater
My Babysitter Is a Vampire, Ann Hodgman
My Brother Louis Measures Worms, Barbara Robinson
Nerd No More, Kristine Franklin
The Nose from Jupiter, Richard Scrimger
Nothing But Trouble, Trouble, Trouble, Patricia Hermes
Nutty (series), Dean Hughes
An Occasional Cow, Polly Horvath
Oliver Dibbs to the Rescue, Barbara Steiner
101 Ways to Bug Your Parents, Lee Wardlaw
Operation: Dump the Chump, Barbara Park
The Poltergoose: A Jiggy McCue Story, Michael Lawrence
The Polyester Grandpa, Martha Freeman
The Practical Joke War, Alane Ferguson
Regarding the Fountain: A Tale in Letters of Liars and Leaks, Kate Klise
Regular Guy, Sarah Weeks
Revenge of the Snob Squad, Julie Anne Peters
Romance of the Snob Squad, Julie Anne Peters
The Secret Knowledge of Grown-ups, David Wisniewski
The Secret Life of Dagmar Schultz, Lynn Hall
A Series of Unfortunate Events (series)*, Lemony Snicket

3.10 *continued*

Sideways Stories from Wayside School, Louis Sachar
45 & 47 Stella Street and Everything that Happened, Elizabeth Honey
Summer Switch, Mary Rodgers
Susanna Siegelman Grows Up, June Foley
Surviving the Applewhites, Sephanie Tolan
This Island Isn't Big Enough for the Four of Us!, Gerry Greer and Bob Ruddick
The Time Warp Trio (series), Jon Scieszka
The Trolls, Polly Horvath
Venola in Love, Cheryl Ware
Wishes, Kisses, and Pigs, Betsy Hearne

Source: List 3.10 was compiled by M. Jerry Weiss, Distinguished Professor Emeritus, New Jersey City University, Jersey City, NJ.

3.11 Ghost Stories and Mystery Stories

This genre is popular in grades 4–6. Authors of mysteries involve the reader by providing clues that lead to solving the crime. The suspense that builds motivates children to use these clues along with their own experiences, imagination, and observations to try to solve the mystery.

Baby-sitting Is a Dangerous Job, Willo Davis Roberts
Beware! R. L. Stine Picks His Favorite Scary Stories, R. L. Stine (ed.)
The Big Smith Snatch, Jane L. Curry
The Bodies in the Besseldorf Hotel, Phyllis Reynolds Naylor
The Bones in the Cliff, James Stevenson
The Brick House Burglars, Peni R. Griffin
The Case of the Invisible Dog (McGurk series), E. W. Hildick
The Case of the Haunted Health Club, Carol Farley
Cirque du Freak (series), Darren Shan
The Dark Stairs (Herculeah Jones series), Betsy Byars
Deep Doo-Doo and the Mysterious E-Mail, M. C. Delaney
Devil's Bridge, Cynthia DeFelice
Dew Drop Dead: A Sebastian Earth Mystery, James Howe
Dr. Dredd's Wagon of Wonders, Bill Brittain
Don't Call Me Toad!, Mary Francis Shura
Don't Tell Anyone, Peg Kehret
Eli's Ghost, Betsy Hearne
Escape Key, Michael Coleman
The Famous Stanley Kidnapping Case (Internet Detectives series), Zilpha Keatley Snyder
Following the Mystery Man, Mary D. Hahn
Frightmare: Don't Go Near Mrs. Tallie (Frightmares series), Peg Kehret
Ghost Horses, Gloria Skurzyrski and Alane Ferguson
The Ghost in the Third Row, Bruce Coville
Ghost Town: Seven Ghostly Stories, Joan Lowery Nixon
Ghost Trap: A Wild Willie Mystery, Barbara Joose
The Ghost Wore Gray, Bruce Coville
Goody Hall, Natalie Babbit
Great Ghosts, Daniel Cohen
The Hardy Boys Mysteries (series), Franklin W. Dixon
Have You Seen Hyacynth Macaw?, Patricia Reilly Giff
The Headless Cupid, Zilpha Keatley Snyder
Hostage, Alison Hart
How Many Miles to Babylon?: A Mystery, Paula Fox
The Kidnappers, Willo Davis Roberts
*Light on Hogback Hill**, Cynthia DeFelice
Loretta P. Sweeney, Where Are You?, Patricia Reilly Giff
Man from the Sky, Avi
Moose Tracks, Mary Casanova
The Mystery of the Missing Money, Janet Riehecky
The Nancy Drew Mysteries (series), Carolyn Keene

3.11 *continued*

A Newbery Halloween: A Dozen Scary Stories, by Newbery Award Winning Authors, Martin H. Greenberg and Charles G. Waugh (eds.)
Nutty and the Case of the Ski-Slope Spy, Dean Hughes
The Purloined Corn Popper, E. W. Hildick
The Rocking Horse Secret, Rumer Godden
Search for the Shadowman, Joan Lowery Nixon
The Secret of the Floating Phantom, Norma Lehr
Someone Is Hiding on Alcatraz Island, Eve Bunting
Something Upstairs: A Tale of Ghosts, Avi
Spell it M-U-R-D-E-R, Ivy Ruckman
The Spray Paint Mystery, Angela Shelf Medearis
Three Investigators (series)*, Robert Arthur, Alfred Hitchcock
*The Westing Game**, Ellen Raskin
What's a Daring Detective Like Me Doing in the Doghouse? (Stevie Diamond series), Linda Bailey
The Wolves of Willoughby Chase, Joan Aiken
Wrapped in a Riddle, Sharon Heisel

Source: List 3.11 was compiled by M. Jerry Weiss, Distinguished Professor Emeritus, New Jersey City University, Jersey City, NJ.

3.12 Books to Teach Math

For students who have difficulty with math or dislike traditional math activities, the books listed below stimulate math interest through "math stories and teasers," puzzles, and games. They include the introduction of statistical concepts and practice in prediction, and help develop problem-solving skills through fun activities.

Geometry

25 Super Cool Math Board Games, Lorraine H. Egan (GEOMETRY, ESTIMATION, AND LOGIC)
Area and Volume (Let's Investigate Measures), Marion Smoothey
Circles: Fun Ideas for Getting A-Round in Math, Catherine Ross
Sir Cumference and the Dragon of Pi: A Math Adventure (series), Cindy Neuschwander
The Greedy Triangle ("A Brainy Day Book"), Marilyn Burns
The Hands-on Marvelous Ball Book, Bradford Hansen-Smith (CREATING 3-D FIGURES)
Janice VanCleave's Geometry for Every Kid: Easy Activities that Make Learning Geometry Fun, Janice VanCleave
Quadrilaterals (Let's Investigate Shapes), Marion Smoothey

Numbers and Number Systems

Anno's Mysterious Multiplying Jar, Mitsumasa Anno
The Story of Numbers and Counting, Anita Ganeri
Addition, David L. Stienecker (CARTOON BOARD GAMES AND PUZZLES)
How Math Works, Carol Vorderman (PREDICTING, DECODING, ADDING, AND SUBTRACTING)
More MM's Brand Chocolate Candies Math, Barbara Barbieri McGrath (ESTIMATING, GRAPHING, FACTORING)
Roman Numerals I to M-Numberabilia Romana Uno ad Duo Mila: Liber de Difficillimo Computando Numerum, Arthur Geisert

Problems and Stories

The Adventures of Penrose the Mathematical Cat, Theoni Pappas (STORIES AND PROBLEMS)
American History Math, Jackie B. Glasthal (HISTORICAL STORIES THAT OFFER MATH CONCEPTS AND PROBLEMS)
Fractals, Googols, and Other Mathematical Tales, Theoni Pappas
Math Teasers, Mental Gymnastics, Robert Muller (STORY PROBLEMS AND PUZZLES)

Puzzles, Riddles, Cartoons, and Comic Strips

263 Brain Busters: Just How Smart Are You, Anyway?, Louis Phillips
The Book of Think: Or, How to Solve a Problem Twice Your Size, Marilyn Burns
Cartooning With Math, Bill Costello
The Colossal Book of Mathematics: Classic Puzzles, Paradoxes, and Problems, Martin Gardner
Comic-Strip Math, Dan Greenberg (CARTOONS AND STORY PROBLEMS)
Cool Math: Math Tricks, Awesome Activities, Amazing Factoids, and More!, Christy Maganzini (FUNKY GAMES, PUZZLES, AND MATH TRICKS)

3.12 *continued*

The Grapes of Math: Mind Stretchy Math Riddles, Greg Tang
Janice VanCleave's Math for Every Kid: Easy Activities That Make Learning Math Fun, Janice VanCleave (PUZZLES, GAMES AND WORD PROBLEMS INVOLVING ADDING, SUBTRACTING, AND MULTIPLYING)
Math Appeal: Mind-Stretching Riddles, Greg Tang
Math Fun with Money Puzzlers, Rose Wyler and Mary Elting
Test Your Luck (Math Fun), Rose Wyler and Mary Elting (GAMES OF CHANCE)
Perplexing Puzzles and Tantalizing Teasers, Martin Gardner
The Sneaky Square and 113 Other Math Activities for Kids, Richard M. Sharp

Statistics and Probability

Do You Wanna Bet? Your Chance to Find Out About Probability, Jean Cushman
Number Jugglers: Math Card Games, Ruth Bell Alexander
The Grapes of Math: Mind Stretching Math Riddles, Greg Tang
Math Wizardry for Kids, Margaret Kenda
The Great Book of Math Teasers, Robert Muller and Mark Weissman (eds.)
Probability Games (Mindgames series), Ivan Moscovich
Discovering Graph Secrets: Experiments, Puzzles, and Games Exploring Graphs, Sandra Markle

Time and Clocks

The Story of Time and Clocks, Anita Ganeri
This Book Is About Time, Marilyn Burns
Keeping Time: From the Beginning into the 21st Century, Franklyn M. Branley
First Morning: Poems About Time, compiled by Nikki Siegen-Smith
Time (Make it Work! science), Andrew Haslam
Time, John Farndon (SCIENCE EXPERIMENTS)
On Time: From Seasons to Split Seconds, Gloria Skurzynski

Using the Calculator

Math Fun With a Pocket Calculator, Rose Wyler
Calculator Biddles, David A. Adler

Weights and Measures

Building Toothpick Bridges (Math Project series), Jeanne Pollard
The Story of Weights and Measures, Anita Ganeri (HISTORY OF MEASUREMENT)
How Tall, How Short, How Far Away, David A. Adler
How Math Works, Carol Vorderman (RATIOS, MATH AND SCIENCE, WHAT IS ZERO?)
Measures & Space (a "Math Live" book), David Kirkby
Measuring Up! Experiments, Puzzles, and Games Exploring Measurement, Sandra Markle

3.13 Books to Teach Science

Topics such as space, space technology, and how creatures adapt to their environment are among the many themes that are part of the intermediate grade curriculum.[†] Photographs and illustrations teach as much as the text in many of the nonfiction science books listed below. Fiction and nonfiction on the topics of weather, regions, and geological formations enliven the curriculum through adventure, colorful text, and interesting, but unusual, information.

EARTH SCIENCE

The study of the Earth in the upper elementary grades becomes more complex, focusing upon the structure and composition of rock, soil, seeds, and plants. A need to preserve the environment is implied throughout the curriculum in grades 4–6 and is reflected in the fiction and nonfiction listed below. Clean air, causes for pollution, and ways of resolving such problems have grown in importance over the past ten years.

Deserts and Mountains

101 Questions About Desert Life, Alice Jablonsky
Desert Animals (Random House Tell Me About books), Michael Chinery
Eyewitness: Desert, Miranda Macquitty
One Day in the Desert (Trophy Chapter books), Jean Craighead George
Nature Unfolds Mountains and Deserts, Gerard Cheshire
America's Top 10 Mountains, Jenny E. Tesar
Great Smoky Mountains National Park (A New True Book), David Petersen
My Side of the Mountain, Jean Craighead George
Watching Desert Wild Life, Jim Arnosky
Mystery of the Desert Giant (Hardy Boys), Franklin W. Dixon (fiction)
A Walk in the Desert, Rebecca Johnson
Danger in the Desert, Terri Fields (fiction)
Mountains, Seymour Simon

Rocks, Minerals, and Gold

Earth (Eyewitness), Susanna Van Rose
Rocks and Minerals (Eyewitness), R. F. Symes
Smithsonian Handbooks: Rocks and Minerals, Chris Pelbant
The Big Rock (Aladdin Picture Books), Bruce Hiscock
Janice VanCleave's Rocks and Minerals: Mind-boggling Experiments You Can Turn into Science Fair Projects, Janice VanCleave
The California Gold Rush (Cornerstones of Freedom), Conrad Stein
Jason's Gold, Will Hobbs (fiction)
Seeds of Hope: The Gold Rush Diary of Susanna Fairchild, California Territory, 1849, Kristiana Gregory
Limestone Caves (First Books), Roy A. Gallan

[†]A list of "Outstanding Science Trade Books" is available at www.ncss.org.

3.13 *continued*

Ecology

Global Warming: The Threat of Earth's Changing Climate, Laurence Pringle
Prentice Hall Science Explorer: Environmental Science, Michael J. Padilla, Ioannis Maioulis, and Martha Cyr
Ecology (Eyewitness), Steve Pollock
The Case of the Missing Cutthroats: An Ecological Mystery, Jean Craighead George
Desert (Biomes of the World. . . . Ecobalancing), Edward R. Ricciuti
The Great Fire, Jim Murphy

Water and the Sea

What Makes an Ocean Wave?: Questions and Answers About Oceans and Ocean Life (Scholastic Question and Answer Series), Melvin Berger and Gilda Berger
Janice VanCleave's Oceans for Every Kid: Easy Activities that Make Learning Science Fun, Janice VanCleave
Exploring the Oceans: Science Activities for Kids, Anthony D. Fredericks
Lakes, Ponds and Temporary Pools (Exploring Ecosystems), David Josephs
Wings Along the Waterway, Mary Barett Brown
Dive!: My Adventures Undersea in the Deep Frontier, Sylvia Earle

LIFE SCIENCE

The composition of plants and how animals survive are central to life science study in the upper elementary grades. The introduction to zoology and how creatures function occurs at this level. Books offer adventure stories, photos, and detailed facts that hold children's interests as well as inform them.

Plants

Plants: 1000 Things You Should Know About, John Farndon
What Do We Know About the Grasslands? (Caring for Environments), Brian J. Knapp
The Tree Almanac: A Year-Round Activity Guide, Monica Russo
Plants (Nature Detective), Anita Ganeri

Animals and Reptiles

Grassland Animals, Michael Chinery
Animals in Disguise, Martine Duprez
Llama, Caroline Arnold
Zebra, Caroline Arnold
Panda, Caroline Arnold
Rhino, Caroline Arnold
Cheetah (Morrow Junior Books), Caroline Arnold
Orangutan (Morrow Junior Books), Caroline Arnold
Bat (Morrow Junior Books), Caroline Arnold

3.13 *continued*

Tule Elk (endangered California species), Caroline Arnold
Watching Desert Wildlife, Jim Arnosky
Tyrannosaurus (American Museum of Natural History), William Lindsay
Interrupted Journey: Saving Endangered Sea Turtles, Katherine Lasky
How Mammals Build Their Amazing Homes, W. Wright Robinson
Donkey Rescue, Tessa Krailing
Animal Habitats, Michael Chinery
Predators and Prey (Secrets of the Rainforest), Michael Chinery
Questions and Answers about Polar Animals, Michael Chinery
DK Pocket: Animals of the World, David Alderton

Birds, Fish, and Underwater Animals

Shark Attack Almanac, Mary Batten
How Shellmakers Build Their Amazing Homes (Animal Architects), W. Wright Robinson
How Birds Build Their Amazing Homes (Animal Architects), W. Wright Robinson
Hoot, Carl Hiaasen (fiction)
Seashore Life on Rocky Coasts (Monterey Bay Aquarium Natural History series), Judith Connor
Sea Otters (Monterey Bay Aquarium Natural History series), Marianne Riedman
Seals and Sea Lions (Monterey Bay Aquarium Natural History series), David G. Gordon
The Deep Sea (Monterey Bay Aquarium Natural History series), Bruce H. Robison
Giant Shark: Megalodon Prehistoric Super Predator, Caroline Arnold
On the Brink of Extinction: The California Condor, Caroline Arnold
Sharks (DK Pocket), Joyce Pope
Hummingbirds Can Fly Backwards and Other Facts and Curiosities, Carol Iverson

Insects and Invertebrates

Exploding Ants: Amazing Facts About How Animals Adapt, Joanne Settel
Sorting Out Worms and Other Invertebrates: Everything You Want to Know About Insects, Corals, Mollusks, Sponges, and More!, Samuel G. Woods
Invertebrate Zoology (Real Kids/Real Science Books), Ellen Doris, photographs by Len Rubenstein
True Bugs: When Is a Bug Really a Bug? (Animals in Order), Sara Swan Miller
How Spiders and Other Silkmakers Build their Amazing Homes (Animal Architects), W. Wright Robinson
Silkworms, L. Patricia Kite
Bug Boy, Carol Sonenklar (fiction)
Eyewitness: Insects, Laurence Mound
An Extraordinary Life: The Story of a Monarch Butterfly, Laurence Pringle
Caterpillers, Bugs and Butterflies (Young Naturalist Field Guide), Mel Boring
Insects (National Audubon Society First Field Guides), Christina Wilsdon
Spiders and Their Web Sites, Margery Facklam
Bugs Before Time: Prehistoric Insects and Their Relatives, Cathy Camper

3.13 *continued*

Dinosaurs

Dinosaur Mountain: Graveyard of the Past, Caroline Arnold
Dinosaurs (The Nature Company Discovers Library), Angela Milner (ed.)
DK Pocket: Dinosaurs, Neil Clark and William Lindsey
The Encyclopedia of Awesome Dinosaurs, Michael Benton
Featured Dinosaurs, Christopher Sloan
The Tiniest Giants: Discovering Dinosaur Eggs, Lowell Dingus and Luis Chiappe
Tyrannosaurus, William Lindsey
Dinosaur Sue, Fay Robinson

THE BODY

The body and how it functions is of particular interest to intermediate students as their bodies begin making significant changes. Many of the following books present rich photographic resources that teachers can use for class presentations and discussions. Activities that bring further understanding of sensory functions are fun and informative classroom projects.

It's Perfectly Normal: A Book About Changing Bodies, Growing Up, Sex and Sexual Health, Robie Harris
Smell, The Subtle Sense, Alvin, Virginia, and Robert Silverstein
Human Body, Angela Royston
The Visual Dictionary of the Human Body (Eyewitness Visual Dictionaries)
DK Guide to the Human Body: A Photographic Journey Through the Human Body, Richard Walker
DK Pockets: Body Facts, Sarah Brewer
Janice VanCleave's the Human Body for Every Kid: Easy Activities that Make Learning Science Fun, Janice VanCleave
The Care and Keeping of You: Body Book for Girls, Valorie Lee Schaefer
What's Happening to My Body? Book for Boys: A Growing Up Guide for Parents and Sons, Lynda Madaras and Area Madaras
What's Happening to My Body? Book for Girls: The New Growing Up Guide for Parents and Daughters, Lynda Madaras and Area Madaras

ENERGY

The sources of energy and how they are converted to heat or motion is important to the 4–6 curriculum, as it provides students with a basic understanding of how things work. The properties of liquids and gases, and how these elements change through heat and cold, provide a basis for the study of chemistry.

Students can find numerous experiments through the study of electricity, light, and laser. The study of the sun's energy and its conversion to solar power demonstrates one way of how the sun interrelates with Earth.

3.13 *continued*

Energy and Motion

Science Fair Projects: Energy, Bob Bonnet and Dan Keen
Alternative Energy Sources, Gary Chandler and Kevin Graham
The Cool Hot Rod and Other Electrifying Experiements on Energy and Matter, Paul Doherty
The Spinning Blackboard and Other Dynamic Experiments on Force and Motion, Paul Doherty
Projects that Explore Energy, Martin J. Gutnik and Natalie Browne Gutnik
Energy (New Energy Sources), Nigel Hawkes
Let's Investigate Force and Motion, Robin Kerrod

Light

The Magic Wand and Other Bright Experiments on Light and Color, Paul Doherty
Mirrors: Finding Out About the Properties of Light, Bernie Zubrowski
Shadow Play: Making Pictures with Light and Lenses, Bernie Zubrowski
The Science Book of Light, Neil Ardley
How Did We Find Out About Lasers?, Isaac Asimov
Sun and Light (Action Science), Neil Ardley
Sound, Heat and Light, Melvin Berger
Making Light Work: The Science of Optics, David J. Darling

Electricity and Magnetism

The Know-How Book of Batteries and Magnets, Heather Amery
Discovering Electricity (Action Science), Neil Ardley
Science Fair Projects with Electricity and Electronics, Bob Bonnet and Dan Keen
The Light Bulb, Sharon Cosner
Magnetic Magic, Paul Doherty and John Cassidy
Magnets (Young Scientist Concepts & Projects), Steve Parker

Nuclear Energy

Nuclear Accident (A Disaster! Book), Christopher Lampton
How to Split the Atom, Hazel Richardson
Nuclear Power (World Issues), Nigel Hawkes
Nuclear Energy (Inventors and Inventions), Gini Holland
Power Failure, Mary O'Neill
Powerhouse: Inside a Nuclear Power Plant, Charlotte Wilcox

Solar Energy

How Did We Find Out About Solar Power?, Isaac Asimov
Science Project Ideas About the Sun, Robert Gardner
Done in the Sun: Solar Projects for Children, Anne Hillerman
Solar Power (Energy Forever series), Ian Graham
Solar Energy (Earth at Risk), Bob Brooke

3.13 *continued*

SPACE

Poems, science fiction, and informative texts comprise the titles listed below. Space inspires young readers and the growing knowledge about our surrounding galaxies has added to the excitement of space information. Aspiring astronauts will enjoy books by Sally Ride and Elaine Scott, just as future aerospace engineers will search out books by Isaac Asimov, Sandra Markle, and others.

Aeronautics/Airplanes

Planes and Other Aircraft (How Science Works), Nigel Hawkes
Before the Wright Brothers, Don Berliner
Up, Up and Away: The Science of Flight, David Darling
Black Eagles: African Americans in Aviation, Jim Haskins
Flight (Young Scientist Concepts & Projects), Peter Mellett
Airplanes (Inventors and Inventions), Gini Holland
Planes, Gliders, Helicopters, and Other Flying Machines, Terry Jennings
Fly the Hot Ones, Steven Lindblom
Flight (Discoveries Library), Donald S. Lopez (ed.)
Flight: Great Planes of the Century, Donald S. Lopez
Sky Pioneer: A Photobiography of Amelia Earhart, Corinne Szabo
Blast Off!: Poems About Space, Lee Bennett Hopkins
1000 Facts About Space, Pam Beasant
The National Air and Space Museum ABC, Florence Cassen Mayers
Astronauts, Allison Lassieur
Moon Base, First Colony in Space, Michael D. Cole
Mission Earth: Voyage to the Home Planet, June English and Thomas Jones
Rockets (Inventors and Inventions), Mary Virginia Fox
USA from Space, Anne-Catherine Fallen
Satellites, Mary Virginia Fox
The First Men in Space (World Explorers), Gregory P. Kennedy
ETs and UFOs: Are They Real?, Larry Kettelkamp
Living in Space, Larry Kettelkamp
Pioneering Space, Sandra Markle
Unidentified Flying Objects and Extraterrestrial Life, Carole Marsh
Junk in Space, Richard Maurer
To Space and Back, Sally Ride and Susan Okie
Adventure in Space: The Flight to Fix the Hubble, Elaine Scott
Edwin Hubble: American Astronaut, Mary Virginia Fox

Planets, Moon, Sun, and Stars

The New Book of Mars, Nigel Hawkes
Sun (Our Solar System), Robin Kerrod
The Moon (Isaac Asimov's New Library of the Universe), Isaac Asimov
There Are Golf Balls on the Moon and Other Facts and Curiosities, Carol Iverson

3.13 *continued*

Discovering the Planets (Exploring the Universe), Jacqueline Mitton
Journey Into a Black Hole, Franklyn M. Branley
Look at Moons (Out of This World), Ray Spanenburg and Kit Moser
The Starry Sky, Rose Wyler
Seeing Stars: A Book and Poster About the Constellations, Barbara Seiger
See the Stars: Your First Guide to the Night Sky, Ken Croswell
Find the Constellations, H. A. Rey
Our Solar System, Seymour Simon
Done in the Sun: Solar Projects for Children, Anne Hillerman
Comets, Asteroids and Meteorites (Starting With Space), Cynthia Pratt Nicholson
The Milky Way and Other Galaxies, Gregory Vogt

WEATHER

All of us are affected by weather. The formation of storms and the work of forecasters are popular topics among intermediate students. These topics and others, including the formation of tornadoes and hurricanes, add adventure to weather stories.

General

Weather Explained: A Beginner's Guide to the Elements, Derek Elsom
Avalanche!, Howard Facklam and Margery Facklam
Science Project Ideas About Rain, Robert Gardner
Clouds: From Mare's Tails to Thunderheads, Suzanne Harper
Hazy Skies: Weather and the Environment, Jonathan D. Kahl
Weather Watch: Forecasting the Weather, Jonathan D. Kahl
Weatherwise: Learning About the Weather, Jonathan D. Kahl
Wet Weather: Rain Showers and Snowfall, Jonathan D. Kahl
Exploring the Sky by Day: The Equinox Guide to Weather and Atmosphere, Terence Dickinson
Weather (Nature Detective), Anita Ganeri
Weather: Make It Work Geography, Andrew Haslam (PROJECTS AND EXPERIMENTS)
National Audobon Society: First Field Guide of Weather, Jonathan D. Kahl

Storms

Blizzard!: The Storm that Changed America, Jim Murphy
Tornado Alert, Franklyn M. Branley
Hurricanes, Arlene Erlbach
Flash, Crash, Rumble, and Roll, Franklyn M. Branley
Storm Chasers: Tracking Twisters, Gail Herman
The Big Storm, Bruce Hiscock
Storm Warning: Tornadoes and Hurricanes, Jonathan D. Kahl
Hurricanes, Peter Murray
Lightning (Force of Nature), Peter Murray
Tornadoes (Nature Books), Peter Murray

3.13 *continued*

Lightning, Seymour Simon
Storms, Seymour Simon
Hurricane! (Nature's Disasters), Jules Archer
Tornado!, Jules Archer
Floods, Ann Armbruster
Tornadoes, Ann Armbruster and Elizabeth Taylor
Storm Chaser: Into the Eye of a Hurricane, Keith E. Greenberg
Lightning: Sheets, Streaks, Beads and Balls, Suzanne Harper
Thunderbolt: Learning About Lightning, Jonathan D. Kahl
Eye of the Storm: Chasing Storms with Warren Faidley, Stephen Kramer
Lightning, Stephen Kramer
Tornado (Nature in Action), Stephen Kramer
Blizzard (A Disaster! Book), Christopher Lampton
Hurricane, Christopher Lampton
Tornado, Christopher Lampton
Flood: Wrestling with the Mississippi, Patricia Lauber
Hurricanes: Earth's Mightiest Storms, Patricia Lauber
Hurricanes, Sally Lee
Blizzards, Steven Otfinoski
Hurricanes, Charles Rotter
Floods, Aleksandrs Rozens

INVENTIONS AND EXPERIMENTS

Books that create interest in invention at an early age are a valuable resource for teachers and parents. Listed below are books that help students in grades 4–6 understand how inventions and experiments come about, and that stimulate the students' own creative thinking.

Girls Think of Everything: Stories of Ingenious Inventions by Women, Catherine Thimmesh
Imaginative Inventions: The Who, What, Where, When and Why of Roller Skates, Potato Chips, Marbles, and Pie (and More!), Charise Harper
The Kids' Invention Book (Kids Ventures), Arlene Erlbach
Brainstorm!: The Stories of Twenty American Kid Inventors, Tom Tucker
Invention (Eyewitness Books), Lionel Bender
Mistakes that Worked, Charlotte Folz Jones
The Everything Kids Science Experiment Book, Tom Robinson
Science Experiments You Can Eat, Vicki Cobb
Simple Science Experiments With Everyday Materials, Muriel Mandell
Fifty Nifty Science Fair Projects, Carol Amato and Eric Ladizinsky
See for Yourself: More Than 100 Experiments for Science Fairs and Projects, Vicki Cobb
Janice VanCleave's Guide to More of the Best Science Fair Projects, Janice VanCleave
365 Simple Science Experiments with Everyday Materials, E. Richard Churchill
Amazing Science Experiments with Everyday Materials, E. Richard Churchill

3.13 *continued*

Janice VanCleave's 200 Gooey, Slippery, Slimy, Weird & Fun Experiments, Janice VanCleave
Sure-to-Win Science Fair Projects, Joe Rhatigan and Heather Smith
The Science Explorer Out and About: Fantastic Science Experiments Your Family Can Do Anywhere, Pat Murphy

MICROBES AND MICROSCOPES

Just about every child loves to watch life under a microscope. The following books lead to a better understanding of diseases brought about through microbes and how to track microbes through microscopes.

Hidden Worlds: Looking Through a Scientist's Microscope, Stephen Kramer
Sea Soup: Phytoplankton, Mary M. Cerullo
Pasteur's Fight Against Microbes (Science Stories series), Beverley Birch
Mysterious Microbes (Creepy Creatures), Steve Parker
The Microscope Book, Shar Levine

3.14 Books to Teach Social Studies

The books listed below can be used to supplement the social studies curriculum in grades 4 to 6. By reading informational books as well as stories that describe important historical events, children are better able to imagine the experiences of those who shaped our country and our world. Tales that are alive in historical setting provide knowledge of the past and who we are as a nation and world. (See also Lists 3.15, 4.5, and 4.12 as well as "Great Books for Teaching Content in History, Social Studies, Science, Music and Art," pp. 207–252 in *Strategies that Work* by Stephanie Harvey and Anne Goudvis [Stenhouse, 2000].

Alaska and the Tundra Regions

Woodsong, Gary Paulsen
Stone Fox, John Reynolds Gardiner
Dogsong, Gary Paulsen
Black Star, Bright Dawn, Scott O'Dell
Iditarod Dream: Dusty and His Sled Dogs Compete in Alaska's Jr. Iditarod, Ted Wood
The Igloo, Charlotte and David Yue
The Arctic, Alan Baker
Oil Spill!, Melvin Berger
Dashing Through the Snow: The Story of the Jr. Iditarod, Sherry Shahan
Iditarod: The Last Great Race to Nome, Shelley Gill et al.
The Eskimo: The Inuit and Yupik People, Alice Osinski
Welcome to the Ice House, Jane Yolen
Who Lives in the Arctic?, Susan Canizares and Pamela Chanko

The American Experience

My Brother Sam Is Dead, James Lincoln Collier and Christopher Collier
The Secret Soldier: The Story of Deborah Sampson, Ann McGovern
Boston Tea Party: Rebellion in the Colonies, James E. Knight
Now Is Your Time! The African American Struggle for Freedom, Walter Dean Myers
Many Thousand Gone: African Americans from Slavery to Freedom, Virginia Hamilton
Roll of Thunder, Hear My Cry, Mildred D. Taylor
The Story of Harriet Tubman, Conductor of the Underground Railroad, Kate McMullan
Harriet Tubman (In Their Own Words), George Sullivan
The Freedom Riddle, Angela Shelf Medearis
The Land, Mildred D. Taylor
If You Lived at the Time of the American Revolution, Kay Moore
Toliver's Secret, Esther Wood Brady
Can't You Make Them Behave, King George?, Jean Fritz
Shhh! We're Writing the Constitution, Jean Fritz
And Then What Happened, Paul Revere?, Jean Fritz
If You Traveled West in a Covered Wagon, Ellen Levine
Daily Life in a Covered Wagon, Paul Erikson
A Pioneer Sampler: The Daily Life of a Pioneer Family in 1840, Barbara Greenwood
The Way West: Journal of a Pioneer Woman, Amelia Stewart Knight, adapted by Lillian Schlissel

3.14 *continued*

Bound for America: The Story of the European Immigrants (Great Journeys), Milton Meltzer
Immigrant Kids, Russell Freedman
Land of Dreams (Ellis Island Stories), Joan Lowery Nixon
Dear America (series)
My America (series)
If Your Name Was Changed at Ellis Island, Ellen Levine
The Story of US (series), Joy Hakim
Journey to America (series)
Blue Earth Books: Coming to America (series)

Ancient History

Ancient China, Robert Nicholson
The Ancient Egyptians, Jane Shuter
The Ancient Greeks, Jane Shuter
The Buried City of Pompeii: What Was It Like When Vesuvius Exploded?, Shelley Tanaka
The Great Pyramid, Elizabeth Mann
Egyptian Mummies (Fast Forward series), Henrietta McCall
Mummies and the Secrets of Ancient Egypt, John Malam
Tut's Mummy Lost and Found, Judy Donnelly
Growing Up in Ancient Rome (Growing Up in . . . series), Mike Corbishly
Science in Ancient Rome (Science in the Past series), Jacqueline Harris
Pompeii: The Day a City Was Buried, Melanie Rice

Colonial America

People of the Breaking Day, Marcia Sewall
The Pilgrims of Plimoth, Marcia Sewall
Thunder from the Clear Sky, Marcia Sewall
On the Mayflower: Voyage of the Ship's Apprentice & A Passenger Girl, Kate Waters
Samuel Eaton's Day: A Day in the Life of a Pilgrim Boy, Kate Waters
Sarah Morton's Day: A Day in the Life of a Pilgrim Girl, Kate Waters
Tapenum's Day: A Wampanoag Indian Boy in Pilgrim Times, Kate Waters
If You Lived in Colonial Times, Ann McGovern
Landing of the Pilgrims, James Daugherty
Jamestown: New World Adventure (Adventures in Colonial America), James E. Knight
The Farm: Life in Colonial Pennsylvania, James E. Knight

Native Americans

The Ancient Cliff Dwellers of Mesa Verde, Caroline Arnold
Brother Eagle, Sister Sky: A Message from Chief Seattle, Chief Seattle
Buffalo Hunt, Russell Freedman
Children of Clay: A Family of Pueblo Potters (We Are Still Here), Rena Swentzell
Crazy Horse's Vision, Joseph Bruchac
Daily Life in a Plains Indian Village, 1868, Michael Bad Hand Terry

3.14 *continued*

The Iroquois (A First Americans Book), Virginia Driving Hawk Sneve
The Journal of Jesse Smoke, A Cherokee Boy: Trail of Tears, 1838 (My Name Is America), Joseph Bruchac
Life in a Longhouse Village, Bobbie Kalman
More than Moccasins: A Kid's Activity Guide to Traditional North American Indian Life, Laurie Carlson
Native American Rock Art: Messages from the Past, Yvette La Pierre
Pocahontas and the Strangers, Clyde Robert Bulla
Squanto, Friend of the Pilgrims, Clyde Robert Bulla
Squanto's Journey: The Story of the First Thanksgiving, Joseph Bruchac
Stories in Stone: Rock Art Pictures by Early Americans, Caroline Arnold
The Story of the Trail of Tears (Cornerstones of Freedom series), R. Conrad Stein
Who Were the First North Americans?, Phillippa Wingate

Regional and Landform Books

M. C. Higgins, the Great, Virginia Hamilton
From the Hills of Georgia: An Autobiography in Paintings, Mattie Lou O'Kelley
Rascal, Sterling North
Mist Over the Mountains: Appalachia and Its People, Raymond Bial
Growing Up in a Holler in the Mountains: An Appalachian Childhood, Karen Gravelle
When the Whippoorwill Calls, Candice F. Ransom
Arctic Memories, Normee Ekoomaik
Eskimo Boy: Life in an Inupiaq Village, Russ Kendall
How Raven Brought Light to People, Ann Dixon
Ka-ha-si and the Loon, Terri Cohlene
Life in the Polar Lands, Monica Byles
Long Claws, James A. Houston
America's Top 10 Mountains (America's Top 10), Jenny E. Tesar
As Long as There Are Mountains, Natalie Kinsey-Warnock
Great Smoky Mountains National Park (A New True Book), David Petersen
Mountains, Seymour Simon
Sierra, Diane Siebert

World Exploration

Around the World in 100 Years: From Henry the Navigator to Magellan, Jean Fritz
Explorers, Carlotta Hacker
The History News: Explorers, Michael Johnstone
Lewis and Clark: Explorers of the New American West, Steven Kroll
Locks, Crocs, and Skeeters: The Story of the Panama Canal, Nancy Winslow Parker
Lost Treasure of the Inca, Peter Loorie
Talking With Adventurers, Pat Cummings and Linda Cummings

3.14 *continued*

World History

A Day With a Noblewoman, Regine-Pernoud
England, Jean F. Blashfield
The Journey of English, Donna Brook
Black Potatoes: The Story of the Great Irish Famine 1845–1850, Susan Bartoletti
Traveling Man: The Journey of Ibn Battuta, 1325–1354, James Rumford
Viking Times (If You Were There) (series), Antony Mason
Knights in Shining Armour, Gail Gibbons
Medieval Life, Andrew C. Langley
The Great Wall of China, Leonard Everett Fisher
Mystery of the Lascaux Cave, Dorothy Hinshaw Patent
Painters of the Caves, Patricia Lauber

PATRIOTIC BOOKS

The messages of patriotism in the books below for grades 4–6 are appropriate at this time in history. Reading about the symbols of America and the struggles and hardships of the people who have helped to build this country develop the readers' sense of pride. The books about war focus upon courage, survival, and hardship; they introduce war heroes and provide readers with a realistic view of battle without being too graphic.

General

Abe Lincoln Remembers, Ann Turner
America the Beautiful, Katherine Lee Bates
By the Dawn's Early Light, Steven Kroll
Celebrations, Myra Livingston
Coming to America: The Story of Immigration, Betsy Maestro
Declaration of Independence, Sam Fink
Fireworks, Picnics, and Flags (The Story of the Fourth of July Symbols), James Giblin
From Sea to Shining Sea: A Treasury of American Folklore and Folk Songs, Amy Cohn (ed.)
Just Like Abraham Lincoln, Bernard Waber
Lady With a Torch: How the Statue of Liberty Was Born, Eleanor Coerr
Old Glory: An American Treasure, Robert Lang
Purple Mountain Majesties: The Story of Katharine Lee Bates and America the Beautiful, Barbara Younger
Puzzle Maps U.S.A., Nancy L. Clouse
So You Want to Be President, Judith St. George
Stars and Stripes and Soldiers, Richard Rosenblum
The Buck Stops Here: The Presidents of the United States, Alice Provensen
The Discovery of the Americas, Betsy and Giulio Maestro
The Flag We Love, Pam Munoz Ryan
The Gettysburg Address, Abraham Lincoln, illustrated by Michael McCurdy

3.14 *continued*

The Star Spangled Banner, Francis Scott Key, illustrated by Peter Spier
The Story of the Statue of Liberty, Betsy and Giulio Maestro
The Wall, Eve Bunting
Watch the Stars Come Out, Riki Levinson (the Reading Rainbow program for this book includes a Statue of Liberty tour)
We the People: Poems, Bobbi Katz
Yo, Millard Fillmore! (And All Those Other Presidents You Don't Know), Will Cleveland and Mark Alvarez
Yo, Sacramento! (And All Those Other State Capitals You Don't Know), Will Cleveland and Mark Alvarez
Young Abe Lincoln: The Frontier Days: 1809–1837, Cheryl Harness

The Civil War

When Johnny Went Marching: Young Americans Fight the Civil War, G. Clifton Wisler
Turn Homeward, Hannalee, Patricia Beatty
Charley Skedaddle, Patricia Beatty
Who Comes with Cannons?, Patricia Beatty
A Separate Battle—Women & the Civil War, Ina Chang
With Every Drop of Blood: A Novel of the Civil War, James and Christopher Collier
*Bull Run**, Paul Fleischman
Lincoln: A Photobiography, Russell Freedman
Brady, Jean Fritz
Thunder at Gettysburg, Patricia Lee Gauch
Sweet Clara and the Freedom Quilt, Deborah Hopkinson
*Across Five Aprils**, Irene Hunt
A Girl Called Boy, Belinda Hurmence
My Brother's Keeper: A Civil War Story, Nancy Johnson
Rifles for Watie, Harold Keith
A Light in the Storm: The Civil War Diary of Amelia Martin, Karen Hesse
True North: A Novel of the Underground Railroad, Kathryn Lasky
Three Against the Tide, Anne D. Love
The Boys' War: Confederate and Union Soldiers Talk About the Civil War, Jim Murphy
The Journal of James Edmond Pease: A Civil War Union Soldier, Jim Murphy
The Long Road to Gettysburg, Jim Murphy
A Dangerous Promise (The Orphan Train Adventure), Joan Lowery Nixon
A Soldier's Heart: A Story of the Civil War, Gary Paulsen
Silent Thunder: A Civil War Story, Andrea Davis Pinkney
Pink and Say, Patricia Polacco
The Promise Quilt, Candice F. Ransom
Shades of Gray, Carolyn Reeder
Across the Lines, Carolyn Reeder
Behind Rebel Lines: The Incredible Story of Emma Edmonds, Civil War Spy, Seymour Reit
Girl in Blue, Ann Rinaldi
Amelia's War, Ann Rinaldi

3.14 *continued*

Nettie's Trip South, Ann Turner
Mr. Lincoln's Drummer, Clifton Wisler
Thunder on the Tennessee, Clifton Wisler

World War 1

After the Dancing Days, Margaret Rostkowski
Casey Over There, Staton Rabin
Good-Bye, Billy Radish, Gloria Skurzynski
Lord of the Nutcracker Men, Iain Lawrence
Over There!: The American Soldier in World War I, Jonathan Gawne
The Night the Bells Rang, Natalie Kinsey-Warnock
The Ornament Tree, Jean Thesman
Tree by Leaf, Cynthia Voigt
When Christmas Comes Again: The World War I Diary of Simone Spencer, Beth Seidel Levine

World War 11

The Children We Remember: Photographs from the Archives of Yad Vashem, Jerusalem, Israel, Chana Byer Abells
The Night Crossing, Karen Ackerman
The Number on My Grandfather's Arm, David Adler
We Remember the Holocaust, David Adler
Hilde and Eli: Children of the Holocaust, David Adler
The Good Fight: How World War II Was Won, Stephen Ambrose
In Kindling Flame: The Story of Hannah Senesh: 1921–1944, Linda Atkinson
Tell Them We Remember: The Story of the Holocaust, Susan D. Bachrach
I Had Seen Castles, Cynthia Rylant
Rain of Fire, Marion Dane Bauer
Sheltering Rebecca, Mary Baylis-White
Along the Tracks, Tamar Bergman
Twenty and Ten, Claire Huchet Bishop
So Far from the Sea, Eve Bunting
A Nightmare in History: The Holocaust: 1933–1945, Jane Cutler
My Wartime Summers, Jane Cutler
Behind Barbed Wire: The Imprisonment of Japanese Americans During World War II, Daniel S. Davis
America Goes to War (series)
Jacob's Rescue, A Holocaust Story, Malka Drucker
True Valor, Stories of Brave Men and Women in WWII, Phyllis Raybin Emert
The Feather-Bed Journey, Paula Kurzband Feder
War Boy: A Country Childhood, Michael Foreman
The Other Victims: First Person Stories of Non-Jews Persecuted by the Nazis, Ina R. Friedman
Don't Say a Word, Barbara Gehrts
*Summer of My German Soldier**, Bette Greene

3.14 *continued*

A Special Fate: Chiune Sugihara: a Hero of the Holocaust, Alison Leslie Gold
Stepping on the Cracks, Mary Downing Hahn
The Endless Steppe: A Girl in Exile, Esther Hautzig
Love You, Soldier, Amy Hest
Rose Blanche, Roberto Innocenti and Christophe Gallaz
Sky: A True Story of Resistance during World War II, Hanneke Ippisch
When Hitler Stole Pink Rabbit, Judith Kerr
Shadow of the Wall, Christa Laird
We Survived the Holocaust, Elaine Landau (ed.)
The Big Lie: A True Story, Isabella Leitner
Tug of War, Joan Lingard
Listen for the Singing, Jean Little
Number the Stars, Lois Lowry
She Flew No Flags, Joan Manley
The Airman's War: World War II in the Sky, Albert Marrin
Hiroshima No Pika, Toshi Maruki
Daniel's Story, Carol Matas
A Boy at War: A Novel of Pearl Harbor, Harry Mazer
The Last Mission, Harry Mazer
Good Night, Maman, Norma Fox Mazer
Snow Treasure, Marie McSwigan
Rescue: The Story of How Gentiles Saved Jews in the Holocaust, Milton Meltzer
Baseball Saved Us, Ken Mochizuki
Waiting for Anya, Michael Morpurgo
Gold Star Sister, Claire Rudolf Murphy
The Lily Cupboard, Shulamith Oppenheim
The Man from the Other Side, Uri Orlev
Attack on Pearl Harbor, Shelley Tanaka
Early Sunday Morning: The Pearl Harbor Diary of Amber Billows, Hawaii, 1941 (Dear America), Barry Denenberg
Four Perfect Pebbles: A Holocaust Story, Lila Perl and Marion Blumenthal Lazan
The Butterfly, Patricia Polacco
The Other Side of the Family, Maureen Pople
David and Max, Gary Provost
*The Upstairs Room**, Johanna Reiss
Friedrich, Hans Peter Richter
Smoke and Ashes: The Story of the Holocaust, Barbara Rogasky
The Holocaust, Seymour Rossel
Touch Wood: A Girlhood in Occupied France, Renee Roth-Hano
A Pocket Full of Seeds, Marilyn Sachs
Under the Blood-Red Sun, Graham Salisbury
The Shadow Children, Steven Schnur
Escape from Warsaw, Ian Serraillier
I Am an American: A True Story of Japanese Internment, Jerry Stanley

3.14 *continued*

Behind the Secret Window. A Memoir of a Hidden Childhood During World War II, Nelly S. Toll
Hear O Israel: A Story of the Warsaw Ghetto, Terry Walton Treseder
Journey to Topaz: A Story of the Japanese-American Evacuation, Yoshiko Uchida
The Bracelet, Yoshiko Uchida
Anna Is Still Here, Ida Vos
Dancing on the Bridge of Avigon, Ida Vos
Hide and Seek, Ida Vos
My Brother, My Sister, and I, Yoko Kawashima Watkins
Let the Celebrations Begin!, Margaret Wild and Julie Vivas
Hiroshima, Laurence Yep
I Never Saw Another Butterfly: Children's Drawings and Poems from Terezin Concentration Camp 1942–1944, Hana Volavkova (ed.)

Source: List 3.14 was compiled by Louise Stearns, Department of Curriculum and Instruction, Children's Literature, Southern Illinois University, Carbondale.

3.15 The Best in Historical Fiction

Teaching history through stories is an ideal way to bring the people and events of the past to life. The details of the settings in these stories are based on fact; however, the characters may or may not have lived. It is important when reading historical fiction to help children understand the stories' events, characters, and beliefs within the social and historical context in which they take place rather than from their own modern perspective.

Across Five Aprils, Irene Hunt (CIVIL WAR)
Ajeemah and His Son, James Berry (19TH-CENTURY JAMAICA)
Amos Fortune, Free Man, Elizabeth Yates
The Ballad of Lucy Whipple, Karen Cushman (1849 CALIFORNIA)
Belle Prater's Boy, Ruth White
Benjamin West and His Cat Grimalkin, Marguerite Henry
Beyond the Divide, Kathryn Lasky
The Bite of the Gold Bug: A Story of the Alaskan Gold Rush, Barthe DeClements
Black Water, Rachel Anderson (19TH-CENTURY ENGLAND)
The Borning Room, Paul Fleischman (OHIO FRONTIER, 1851)
The Bronze Bow, Elizabeth George Speare
Bud, Not Buddy, Christopher Paul Curtis (THE DEPRESSION)
Bull Run, Paul Fleishman (CIVIL WAR)
Caddie Woodlawn, Carol Ryrie Brink
Calico Captive, Elizabeth George Speare
Cassie's Journey: Going West in the 1860's, Brett Harvey
The Courage of Sarah Noble, Alice Dagliesh
Crispin: the Cross of Lead, Avi (14TH-CENTURY ENGLAND)
Dear America (girl diary series)*, Scholastic
Encounter, Jane Yolen (TAINO VIEW OF COLUMBUS)
Fire in the Hills, Anna Myers (OKLAHOMA, 1918)
Gideon's People, Carolyn Meyer (AMISH/JEWISH FRIENDS)
A Girl Named Disaster, Nancy Farmer (AFRICA)
Hitty: Her First Hundred Years, Rachel Field
The House of Dies Drear, Virginia Hamilton
Hugh Glass, Mountain Man, Robert McClung
Johnny Tremain, Esther Forbes
Let the Circle Be Unbroken (Logan family series), Mildred D. Taylor
Letters from Rifka, Karen Hesse (1919 RUSSIAN IMMIGRANTS)
Lily's Crossing, Patricia Reilly Giff
Little House on the Prairie (series), Laura Ingalls Wilder
Lydia, Queen of Palestine, Uri Orlev
The Midwife's Apprentice, Karen Cushman
Miranda and the Movies, Janet Kendall (1914)
Mr. Tucket (series), Gary Paulsen (1840'S WEST)
My Brother Sam Is Dead, James Lincoln Collier and Christopher Collier (REVOLUTIONARY WAR)
My Name Is America (boy diary series)*, Scholastic
Nightjohn, Gary Paulsen

3.15 *continued*

No Hero for the Kaiser, Rudolf Frank
Nory Ryan's Song, Patricia Reilly Giff (IRELAND'S POTATO FAMINE)
Number the Stars, Lois Lowry (NAZI-OCCUPIED DENMARK)
On to Oregon!, Honore Morrow
Our Only May Amelia, Jennifer Holm (Finnish family)
Out of the Dust, Karen Hesse
Pedro's Journal: A Voyage with Christopher Columbus, August 1492–February 1493, Pam Conrad
*Red Scarf Girl, A Memoir of the Cultural Revolution**, Ji Li-chang
SOS. Titanic, Eve Bunting
Sarah, Plain and Tall, Patricia MacLachlan
Sign of the Chrysanthemum, Katherine Paterson
Sing Down the Moon, Scott O'Dell (NAVAJO INDIANS)
The Slave Dancer, Paula Fox
So Far from the Bamboo Grove, Yoko Kawashima Watkins (KOREA AND JAPAN AT END OF WWII)
*Sounder**, William Howard Armstrong (A POOR AFRICAN AMERICAN FAMILY IN THE SOUTH)
*Thunder Rolling in the Mountains**, Scott O'Dell and Elizabeth Hall (STORY OF A NATIVE AMERICAN GIRL)
Tituba of Salem Village, Ann Petry
Toliver's Secret, Esther Wood Brady (REVOLUTIONARY WAR)
The True Confessions of Charlotte Doyle, Avi (TRANSATLANTIC VOYAGE, 1832)
Wait for Me, Watch for Me, Eula Bee, Patricia Beatty (WEST TEXAS ADVENTURE, 1800'S)
The Watsons Go to Birmingham—1963, Christopher Paul Curtis
When Jesse Came Across the Sea, Amy Hest
When My Name Was Keoko, Linda Sue Park (WWII KOREA)
Where the Red Fern Grows: The Story of Two Dogs and a Boy, Wilson Rawls
The Whipping Boy, Sid Fleischman (PRINCE & THE PAUPER VARIATION)
White Bird, Clyde Robert Bulla (1880'S TENNESSEE)
The Wind Wagon, Celia Barker Lottridge (1860'S PRAIRIE SCHOONER)
Wingwalker, Rosemary Wells (THE DEPRESSION)
The Winter Room, Gary Paulsen (NORTHERN MINNESOTA LOGGING)
The Witch of Blackbird Pond, Elizabeth George Speare (COLONIAL CONNECTICUT)

3.16 Multicultural Books

The list below will help as you build a reading program that includes literature by and about the diverse cultures that make up our communities. Reading multicultural literature can help students in grades 4–6 build respect for the struggles, experiences, and traditions of all groups of people. (Also see List 2.13.)

African American

*Bud, Not Buddy**, Christopher Paul Curtis
Cousins, Virginia Hamilton
Willie Bea and the Time the Martians Landed, Virginia Hamilton
*M. C. Higgins, the Great**, Virginia Hamilton
*Time Pieces: The Book of Times**, Virginia Hamilton
Jennifer, Hecate, Macbeth, William McKinley, and Me, Elizabeth, E. L. Konigsburg
Letters from a Slave Girl; The Story of Harriet Jacobs, Mary E. Lyons
Let the Circle Be Unbroken, Mildred D. Taylor
Mystery of the Dark Tower, Evelyn Coleman
*Sounder**, William H. Armstrong
Tituba of Salem Village, Ann Petry
*The Watsons Go to Birmingham—1963**, Christopher Paul Curtis
The Well: David's Story, Mildred D. Taylor
Who Is Carrie? James Lincoln Collier
Zeely, Virginia Hamilton
The House of Dies Drear, Virginia Hamilton
Escape from Slavery: The Boyhood of Frederick Douglass in His Own Words, Frederick Douglass, Michael McCurdy (ed.)
Frederick Douglass in His Own Words, Frederick Douglass, Milton Meltzer (ed.)
Nightjohn, Gary Paulsen
The Land, Mildred D. Taylor
Roll of Thunder, Hear My Cry, Mildred D. Taylor
Jump Ship to Freedom, James Lincoln Collier
True North: A Novel of the Underground Railroad, Kathryn Lasky
Which Way Freedom?, Joyce Hansen
I Thought My Soul Would Rise and Fly: The Diary of Patsy, A Freed Girl, Joyce Hansen
The First Passage: Blacks in the Americas, 1502–1617, Colin A. Palmer
Through My Eyes: The Autobiography of Ruby Bridges, Ruby Bridges
A Band of Angels: A Story Inspired by the Jubilee Singers, Deborah Hopkinson
Run Away Home, Patricia McKissack
Sound the Jubilee, Sandra Forrester
Second Cousins, Virginia Hamilton
Bright Freedom's Song: A Story of the Underground Railroad, Gloria Houston
Seminole Diary: Remembrances of a Slave, Dolores Johnson
The Journal of Joshua Loper: A Black Cowboy, Walter Dean Myers
The Slave Dancer, Paula Fox
Juneteenth: A Celebration of Freedom, Charles A. Taylor
Trouble Don't Last, Shelley Pearsall
(Also see List 4.6.)

3.16 *continued*

Appalachian

After the Goat Man, Betsy Byars
Grandpa's Mountain, Carolyn Reeder
*Ida Early Comes Over the Mountain**, Robert Burch
Mountain Valor: A Novel, Gloria Houston
Return to Bitter Creek, Doris Buchanan Smith
Just Juice, Karen Hesse

Asian

Song Lee and the Hamster Hunt, Suzy Kline
Night of the Chupacabras, Marie G. Lee
Baseball Saved Us, Ken Mochizuki
Yang Family (series), Lensey Namioka
The Imp That Ate My Homework, Laurence Yep
*A Single Shard**, Linda Sue Park
Leaving Vietnam: The Journey of Tuan Ngo, A Boat Boy, Sarah S. Kilborne
The Land I Lost: Adventures of a Boy in Vietnam, Quang Nhuong Huynh
Water Buffalo Days, Growing Up in Vietnam, Quang Nhuong Huynh
The Amah, Laurence Yep
Aruna's Journeys, Jyotsna Screenivasan
The Best Bad Thing, Yoshiko Uchida
Dragonwings, Laurence Yep
Ghost Train, Paul Yee
Hello, My Name Is Scrambled Egg, Jamie Gilson
Heroes, Ken Mochizuki
If It Hadn't Been for Yoon Jun, Marie G. Lee
In the Year of the Boar and Jackie Robinson, Bette Bao Lord
Journey Home, Yoshiko Uchida
The Kite Fighters, Linda Sue Park
Little Brother, Allan Baillie
The Moon Bridge, Marcia Savin
Onion Tears, Diana Kidd
Robin Lee (series), Laurence Yep
Vatsana's Lucky New Year, Sara Gogol
(Also see List 4.13.)

Hispanic

The Children of Flight Pedro Pan, Maria Armengol Acerno
The Ice Dove and Other Stories, Diane De Anda
Josefina (series), Valerie Tripp
My Name Is Maria Isabel, Alma Flor Ada
Where the Flame Trees Bloom, Alma Flor Ada
Under the Royal Palms, Alma Flor Ada

3.16 *continued*

Calling the Doves/el Canto por Las Palomas, Juan Felipe Herrera
School Spirit, Johanna Hurwitz
The Tortilla Factory, Gary Paulsen
Baseball in April and Other Stories, Gary Soto
Going Home, Nicholasa Mohr
Felita, Nicholasa Mohr
All for the Better: A Story of El Barrio, Nicholasa Mohr
Barrio: Jose's Neighborhood, George Ancona
Hector Lives in the United States Now: The Story of a Mexican-American Child, Joan Hewett
A Library for Juana: The World of Sor Juana Ines, Pat Mora
Esperanza Rising, Pam Munoz Ryan
The Circuit: Stories from the Life of a Migrant Child, Francisco Jimenez
My Mexico, Tony Johnston
El Piñatero, the Piñata Maker, George Ancona
Look What Came from Mexico (series), Miles Harvey
Latino Rainbow: Poems About Latino Americans, Carlos Cumpian
In the Days of the Vaqueros: America's First True Cowboys, Russell Freedman
(Also see List 4.8.)

Jewish

The Devil's Arithmetic, Jane Yolen
Dreams in the Golden Country: The Diary of Zipporah Feldman: A Jewish Immigrant Girl, Kathryn Lasky
Number the Stars, Lois Lowry
The Upstairs Room, Johanna Reiss
The Journey Back, Johanna Reiss
Anne Frank: The Diary of a Young Girl, Anne Frank
About the B'nai Bagels, E. L. Konigsburg
All-of-a-Kind Family (series), Sydney Taylor
*Are You There, God? It's Me, Margaret**, Judy Blume
*Dave at Night**, Gail Carson Levine
Dear Emma, Johanna Hurwitz
Faraway Summer, Johanna Hurwitz
I Should Worry, I Should Care, Miriam Chaikin
Love You, Soldier, Amy Hest
A Papa Like Everyone Else, Sydney Taylor
Private Notebook of Katie Roberts Age 11, Amy Hest
The Rabbi's Girls, Johnna Hurwitz
A Russian Jewish Family, Jane Mersky Leder
(Also see List 4.10.)

3.16 *continued*

Muslim

Ramadan, Suhaib Hamid Ghazi
Muslim Child: Understanding Islam Through Stories and Poems, Rukhsana Khan
Caravan, Lawrence McKay Jr.
Traveling Man: The Journey of Ibn Battuta, 1325–1354, James Mumford
The Roses in My Carpet, Rukhsana Khan
Celebrating Ramadan, Diane Hoyt-Goldsmith
Eyewitness Islam, Philip Wilkinson
Mustapha's Secret: A Muslim Boy's Search to Know God, Sandra Klans

Native American

Buffalo Hunt, Russell Freedman
Indian Chiefs, Russell Freedman
Soft Rain: A Story of the Cherokee Trail of Tears, Cornelia Cornelissen
The Trail of Tears (Step Into Reading), Joseph Bruchac
Only the Names Remain: The Cherokees and the Trail of Tears, Alex W. Bealer
Lakota Hoop Dancer, Jacqueline Left Hand Bull and Suzanne Haldane
A Day With a Chumash, Georgia Lee
The Navaho, Raymond Bial
Thunder Bear and Ko: The Buffalo Nation and Nambe Pueblo, Susan Hazen-Hammond
Turtle Island: Tales of the Algonquian Nations, Jane Louise Curry
When Rain Sings: Poems by Young Native Americans, National Museum of the American Indian, Smithsonian Institution
Apache Rodeo, Diane Hoyt-Goldsmith
Arctic Hunter, Diane Hoyt-Goldsmith
Buffalo Days, Diane Hoyt-Goldsmith
Cherokee Sister, Debbie Dadey
Clambake: A Wampanoag Tradition, Russell M. Peters
Drumbeat . . . Heartbeat: A Celebration of the Powwow, Susan Braine
Earth Daughter: Alicia of Acoma Pueblo, George Ancona
Four Seasons of Corn: A Winnebago Tradition, Sally M. Hunter
The Girl Who Chased Away Sorrow: The Diary of Sarah Nita, a Navajo Girl, Ann Turner
Grandchildren of the Lakota, Lavera Rose
Ininatig's Gift of Sugar: Traditional Native Sugarmaking, Lauren Waterman Wittstock
Kaya (series), Janet Beeler Shaw
Kinaadlda: A Navajo Girl Grows Up, Monty Roessel
The Ledgerbook of Thomas Blue Eagle, Gay Matthaei
Little Herder in Autumn, Ann Nolan Clark
Minuk: Ashes in the Pathway, Kirkpatrick Hill
People of the Breaking Day, Marcia Sewall
Remember My Name, Sara H. Banks
Shannon: An Ojibway Dancer, Sandra King

3.16 *continued*

The Sketchbook of Thomas Blue Eagle, Gay Matthaei
Thunder from the Clear Sky, Marcia Sewall
Truth Is a Bright Star, Joan Price
Winter People, Joseph Bruchac
(Also see List 4.14.)

Other Multicultural Books

Bound for America, The Story of European Immigrants, Milton Meltzer
Immigrant Kids, Russell Freedman
Black Potatoes: The Story of the Great Irish Famine, 1845–1850, Susan Campbell Bartoletti
The Swedish Americans (The Immigrant Experience), Allyson McGill
The Arab Americans (The Immigrant Experience), Alixa Naff
The Italian Americans (The Immigrant Experience), J. Philip DiFranco
The Japanese Americans (The Immigrant Experience), Harry Kitano
The Mexican Americans (The Immigrant Experience), Julie Catalano

3.17 Biographies

Biography includes historical figures, famous athletes, and people from different backgrounds and eras. The appeal of biography is that it goes beyond facts to create the times and settings in which each figure lives. Although many biographies are fictionalized, good biographies are as honest and accurate as possible. They enable the reader to understand a particular era as well as learn about the character through the author's many anecdotes.

Abigail Adams, Alexandra Wallner
Babe Didrickson Zaharias: The Making of a Champion, Russell Freedman
Barbara Jordan: Voice of Democracy, Lisa Renee Rhodes
Baseball's Best Hitters: Five True Stories, Andrew Gutelle
Baseball's Greatest Players, Sydelle Kramer
Basketball's Greatest Players, Sydelle Kramer
Black Whiteness: Admiral Byrd Alone in the Antarctic, Robert Burleigh
Booker T. Washington, Thomas Amper
Bug Watching with Charles Henry Turner, Michael Elsohn Ross
Bulls-Eye: A Photobiography of Annie Oakley, Sue Macy
Colin Powell, Reggie Finlayson
Coming Home: From the Life of Langston Hughes, Floyd Cooper
Daniel Boone, James Daugherty
Eleanor Roosevelt, Mary Winget
Elephant Woman: Cynthia Moss Explores the World of Elephants, Laurence Pringle
Extraordinary People with Disabilities, Deborah Kent and Kathryn A. Quinlan
Ezra Jack Keats: A Biography with Illustration, Dean Engel and Florence B. Freedman
First in the Field: Baseball Hero Jackie Robinson, Derek Dingle
Five Brave Explorers, Wade Hudson
Frederick Douglass: A Photo-Illustrated Biography, Margo McLoone
Ludwig Van Beethoven (Getting to Know the World's Greatest Composers series), Mike Venezia
A Girl Named Helen Keller, Margo Lundell
Guion Bluford: A Space Biography, Laura S. Jeffrey
Helen Keller: Courage in the Dark, Johanna Hurwitz
Helen Keller: Rebellious Spirit, Laurie Lawlor
Hockey Stars, Sydelle Kramer
I Have a Dream, Martin Luther King Jr.
I, Tut: The Boy Who Became Pharaoh, Miriam Schlein
If I Only Had a Horn: Young Louis Armstrong, Roxane Orgill
Invincible Louisa: The Story of the Author of ***Little Women***, Cornelia Meigs
Jesse Owens, Tom Streissguth
Lives of the Musicians (Artists and Writers series), Kathleen Krull
A Long Hard Journey: The Story of the Pullman Porter, Pat McKissack
Lou Gehrig: The Luckiest Man, David A. Adler
Louis Pasteur: Disease Fighter (Great Minds of Science), Linda Wasmer Smith
Margaret, Frank and Andy: Three Writers' Stories, Cynthia Rylant (Margaret Wise Brown, L. Frank Baum, and E. B. White)
Martin Luther King, Rosemary Bray

3.17 *continued*

Martin's Big Words: The Life of Martin Luther King, Jr., Doreen Rappaport
Mary McLeod Bethune: A Photo-Illustrated Biography, Margo McLoone
Memories of Anne Frank: Reflections of a Childhood Friend, Alison Leslie Gold
The Moon and I, Betsy Byars
My Life in Dog Years, Gary Paulsen
My Name Is Georgia: A Portrait by Jeannette Winter, Jeanette Winter
On the Frontier with Mr. Audubon, Barbara Brenner
Out of Darkness: The Story of Louis Braille, Russell Freedman
Paul Revere, Gail Sakurai
Princess of the Press: The Story of Ida B. Wells-Barnett, Angela Shelf Medearis
Ralph J. Bunche: Peacemaker, Frederick and Patricia McKissack
Sacagawea, Judith St. George
She's Been Working on the Railroad, Nancy Smiler Levinson
Shipwreck at the Bottom of the World: The Extraordinary True Story of Shackleton and the Endurance, Jennifer Armstrong
Small Steps: The Year I Got Polio, Peg Kehret
Superstars of Women's Basketball, J. Kelly
Surprising Myself, Jean Fritz
The Blues Singers: Ten Who Rocked the World, Julius Lester
The Story of Two American Generals: Benjamin O. Davis, Jr., Colin L. Powell, Katherine A. Applegate
Talkin' About Bessie: The Story of Aviator Bessie Coleman, Nikki Grimes
Tiger Woods (Great Athletes), Aaron Boyd
Tiger Woods: King of the Course, Jeff Savage
Tommy Nuñez, Sue Boulais and Barbara Marvis
Vanished! The Mysterious Disappearance of Amelia Earhart, Monica Kulling
Vincent Van Gogh: Portrait of an Artist, Sandra Jordan and Jan Greenberg
We'll Never Forget You, Roberto Clemente, Trudie Engel
Wonder Women of Sports, Sydelle Kramer
Wynton Marsalis, Veronica Freeman Ellis
The Wright Brothers: How They Invented the Airplane, Russell Freedman
At Her Majesty's Request: An African Princess in Victorian England, Walter Dean Myers
Gertrude Chandler Warner and the Boxcar Children, Mary Ellen Ellsworth
Clara Schumann, Piano Virtuoso, Susanna Reich
Looking Back: A Book of Memories, Lois Lowry
Nathan Hale: Patriot and Martyr of the American Revolution, L. J. Krizner and Lisa Sita
The Revolutionary John Adams, Cheryl Harness
Year of Impossible Goodbyes, Sook Nyul Choi

3.18 Books About Feelings and Conflicts

Many children face unpleasant situations at home such as sibling rivalry, divorce, and family conflict. At school, teasing, bullying, and rejection by peers are common problems. Many students in grades 4–6 have not developed a range of responses in dealing with relationships. Reading books such as those listed below will help.

As students analyze the characters' reactions to conflicts they will begin to examine a variety of ways of dealing with specific problems.

Adoption

I, Rebekah, Take You, the Lawrences, Julia First
Dicey's Song, Cynthia Voigt
The Ocean Within, V. M. Caldwell
Saffy's Angel, Hilary McKay
The Wanderer, Sharon Creech
Nobody's Orphan, Anne Morrow Lindbergh
The Pictures of Hollis Woods, Patricia Reilly Giff
Riding the Waves, Theresa Tomlinson
A Sudden Change of Family, Mary Jane Auch

Alcoholism

Last Sunday, Robert Newton Peck
The Potlatch Family, Evelyn Sibley Lampman
The Boy Who Drank Too Much, Shepard Greene
My Daddy Is an Alcoholic, Shepard Greene
Cheat the Moon: A Novel, Patricia Hermes
Raising the Shades, Doug Wilhelm
Safe at Home!, Peggy King Anderson
The Heart of a Chief: A Novel, Joseph Bruchac
The Trouble with Perfect, Mary E. Ryan

Bullying

Dealing with Bullying, Marianne Johnston
Racing the Past, Sis Deans
Bullies Are a Pain in the Brain, Trevor Romain
Cougar, Helen V. Griffith
Find the Power!, Dean Hughes
Help, Pink Pig!, C. S. Adler
My Brother Is a Superhero, Dyan Sheldon
Radio Fifth Grade, Gordon Korman
Scrambled Eggs and Spider Legs, Gary Hogg
Stepping on the Cracks, Mary Downing Hahn
Summer Soldiers, Susan Hart Lindquist
Mr. Lincoln's Way, Patricia Polacco
Surviving Brick Johnson, Laurie Myers
Amelia Takes Command, Marisa Moss

Death

What on Earth Do You Do When Someone Dies?, Trevor Romain
Walk Two Moons, Sharon Creech
Blackwater, Eve Bunting
The Big Wave, Pearl Buck
Bridge to Terabithea, Katherine Paterson
Dicey's Song, Cynthia Voigt
Sweet By and By, Patricia Hermes

Divorce and Single-Family Homes

I Have Two Families, Doris Helmering
Just as Long as We're Together, Judy Blume
The Unmaking of Rabbit, Constance Greene
Dear Mr. Henshaw, Beverly Cleary
Where in the World Is the Perfect Family?, Amy Hest
Stand Tall, Joan Bauer
Amber Brown (series), Paula Danziger
Tuna Fish Thanksgiving, C. S. Adler
The Same Stuff as Stars, Katherine Paterson
The Comeback Challenge, Matt Christopher
P.S. Longer Letter Later, Paula Danziger and Ann M. Martin

Racial Differences

All in the Colors of the Race: Poems, Arnold Adoff
Leon's Story, Leon Walter Tillage
I, Too, Sing America: Three Centuries of African-American Poetry, Catherine Clinton (ed.)

3.18 *continued*

The Watsons Go to Birmingham—1963, Christopher Paul Curtis
The Skin I'm In, Sharon Flake
All It Takes Is Practice, Betty Miles
Iggie's House, Judy Blume
Mississippi Bridge, Mildred D. Taylor
Sounder, William Howard Armstrong
Under Our Skin: Kids Talk About Race, Debbie Holtsclaw Birdseye

Rejection

Jip: His Story, Katherine Paterson
Loser, Jerry Spinelli
The Secret Garden, Frances Hodgson Burnett
Bud, Not Buddy, Christopher Curtis
Journey to Nowhere, Mary Jane Auch
Call It Courage, Armstrong Sperry
The Blossoms Meet the Vulture Lady, Betsy Byars
Berries Goodman, Emily Neville

Relationships

Superfudge, Judy Blume
Blubber, Judy Blume
Harriet the Spy, Louise Fitzhugh
Are You There, God? It's Me, Margaret, Judy Blume
The Cat Ate My Gymsuit, Paula Danziger
Alice in Rapture, Sort Of, Phyllis Reynolds Naylor
Where the Kissing Never Stops, Ron Koertge

Self-esteem

Why Am I Different, Norma Simon
Charlotte's Web, E. B. White
Call It Courage, Armstrong Sperry
Bat Boy, Mel Cebulash
The Magic Finger, Roald Dahl
The Woman in the Wall, Patrice Kindl
The Skin I'm In, Sharon Flake

Sibling Rivalry

Eighty Eight Steps to September, Jan Marino
Tales of a Fourth Grade Nothing, Judy Blume
Who Put That Hair in My Toothbrush?, Jerry Spinelli
My Brother the Star, Alison Jackson
A Season of Comebacks, Kathy Mackel
My Brother Is a Superstar, Dyan Sheldon
Oh Brother—A Sister!: A Sister's Guide to Getting Along, Brooks Whitney

Weight Control

Dumb Old Casey Is a Fat Tree, Barbara Bottner
The Pig-Out Blues, Jan Greenberg
Blubber, Judy Blume
Ride When You're Ready (Eve Bunting Signature Library), Eve Bunting
Fat Camp Commandos, Daniel Pinkwater

3.19 Books About Holidays and Traditions

Following is a list of holiday and religious books suitable for grades 4–6. (Also see Lists 1.21 and 2.16.)

Jewish Holidays All Year Around: A Family Treasury, Mir Tamim Ansary
Lilies, Rabbits and Painted Eggs, Edna Barth
Christmas Day in the Morning, Pearl S. Buck
Alexandra's Scroll: The Story of the First Hanukkah, Miriam Chaikin
Easter, Catherine Chambers
Independence Day, Ilene Cooper
Let's Get Ready for Independence Day, Lloyd G. Douglas
The Family Treasury of Jewish Holidays, Malka Drucker
Santa Claus, Inc., Linda Ford
Ramadan, Suhaib Hamid Ghaze
Fireworks, Picnics, and Flags, James Cross Giblin
Celebrating Kwanzaa, Diane Hoyt-Goldsmith
Celebrating Ramadan, Diane Hoyt-Goldsmith
The Story of the Nutcracker Baby, Deborah Hautzig
New Year's to Kwanzaa: Original Stories of Celebration, Kendall Haven
Christmas Stories: Adapted from the Little House Books by Laura Ingalls Wilder, Heather Henson
Nutcracker (illustrated by Mauric Sendak), E. T. A. Hoffman
The Holiday Handbook, Elizabeth James
Children's Book of Kwanzaa, Dolores Johnson
A World of Holidays: Holi (Hindu), Dilip Kadodwala
Santa's Twin, Dean R. Koontz
Celebrations of Light: A Year of Holidays Around the World, Nancy Luenn
The Real Santa Claus, Marianna Mayer
Seven Spools of Thread: A Kwanzaa Story, Angela Shelf Medearis
The Seven Days of Kwanzaa, Angela Shelf Medearis
The Trees of the Dancing Goats, Patricia Polacco
Christmas Tapestry, Patricia Polacco
The Very Best Hanukkah Gift, Joanne Rocklin
Our Eight Nights of Hanukkah, Michael J. Rosen
Silver Packages: An Appalachian Christmas Story, Cynthia Rylant
Children of Christmas: Stories of the Season, Cynthia Rylant
Christmas Soul: African American Holiday Stories, Allison Samuels
Springs of Joy (Easter), Tasha Tudor
The Story of Divaali Retold, Jatinder Verma
Kwanzaa: A Family Affair, Mildred Pitts Walter
The Story of Kwanzaa, Donna L. Washington
The Bird's Christmas Carol, Kate Douglas Wiggin
Dear Santa, Please Come to the 19th floor, Chris Soentpiet Yin
Milk and Honey: A Year of Jewish Holidays, Jane Yolen

3.20 Books About Music, Dance, and Art

There are many fictional works for children in grades 4–6 focusing on the creative arts. Stories range from mysteries about stolen music and missing violins to those about secret music boxes. Biographies of musicians, dancers, and artists are also available as well as nonfiction informational books on each topic.

Art Books

Maxfield Parrish: A Treasury of Art and Children's Literature, Alma Gilbert
Maxfield Parrish: The Landscape, Alma Gilbert
The Lives of Artists (series), Kathleen Krull
How to Draw Cartoons and Caricatures (Young Artist series), Judy Tatchell
A Drawing in the Sand: A Story of African American Art, Jerry Butler
Kids' Crazy Art Concoctions: 50 Mysterious Mixtures for Art and Craft Fun, Jill Frankel Hauser
Nail Art, Designs to Paint on Fingernails, Sherrl Haab
How to Draw People, Alastair Smith

Great Artists

Marc Chagall (Getting to Know the World's Greatest Artists series), Mike Venezia
Botticelli (Getting to Know the World's Greatest Artists series), Mike Venezia
Vincent Van Gogh: Portrait of an Artist, Jan Greenberg and Sandra Jordan
A Weekend with Diego Rivera (Weekend with . . . series), Barbara Braun
Gauguin (Eyewitness Art series), Michael Howard
Dorothea Lange (Getting to Know the World's Greatest Artists series), Mike Venezia
In Praise of Our Fathers and Our Mothers: A Black Family Treasury by Outstanding Authors and Artists, Wade Hudson

Dance

The World of Dance (From Prehistoric Time to Today), Melvin Berger
The Ballet Book: The Young Performers Guide to Classical Dance, Toronto's National Ballet School
Dance: An Introduction to the World of Dance, Andree Grau
Jazz Tap: From African Drums to American Feet, Ann E. Johnson
The Random House Book of Stories from the Ballet, Geraldine McCaughrean (retells 10 full-length ballets)
Young Dreamers, I Am a Dancer, Jane Feldman
Dance, Angela Shelf Medearis and Michael Medearis (African-Americans' roles in developing dance)
Marie in the Fourth Position, Amy Littlesugar
Dancing Shoes, Noel Streatfeild
Ribbons, Laurence Yep
Aria of the Sea, Dia Calhoun

3.20 *continued*

Music

Shake, Rattle & Roll: The Founders of Rock & Roll, Holly George-Warren
Beethoven in Paradise, Barbara O'Connor
The Blues Singers: Ten Who Rocked the World, Julius Lester
Handel: Who Knew What He Liked, M. T. Anderson
Musical Instruments Around the World, Louise Tythacott
Rubber Band Banjos and a Java Jive Bass: Projects and Activities on the Science of Music and Sound, Alex Sabbeth
I Have a Song to Sing O!: An Introduction to the Songs of Gilbert and Sullivan, Arthur Sullivan
The Mystery of the Stolen Music (A Boxcar Children's Mystery), Gertrude Chandler Warner
Florence Robinson: The Story of a Jazz Age Girl, Dorothy Hoobler
Not Exactly Nashville, Betsy Kuhn
Mary Anne and the Music Box Secret, Ann M. Martin
Jellybean, Tessa Duder (dreams of being a conductor)
Tchaikovsky Discovers America, Esther Kalman
Beethoven Lives Upstairs, Barbara Nichol
The Mozart Season, Virginia Euwer Wolff
Cassie Loves Beethoven, Alan Arkin
The Facts and Fictions of Minna Pratt, Patricia MacLachlan
Yang the Youngest and His Terrible Ear, Lensey Namioka
This Land Was Made for You and Me: The Life and Songs of Woody Guthrie, Elizabeth Partridge

Theater/Performing Arts

On Stage: Theater Games and Activities for Kids, Lisa Bany-Winters (improvisation, characters, and puppetry)
The Young Actor's Book of Improvisation: Dramatic Situations Based on Literature, Sandra Caruso and Susan Kosoff
Shakespeare's Theater (the Performances), Jacqueline Morley
Great Scenes and Monologues for Children: From Fairytales to Thornton Wilder, Craig Slaight and Jack Sharrar (eds.)
On the Air, Behind the Scenes at a TV Station, Esther Hautzig
Movies: The World of Film, Deborah Hitzeroth and Sharon Heerboth (history of movie making)
Theater Shoes, Noel Streatfeild
Ernestine and Amanda: Mysteries on Monroe Street, Sandra Belton
Glass Slippers Give You Blisters, Mary Jane Auch
Break a Leg! The Kid's Guide to Acting and Stagecraft, Lise Friedman
The Skit Book: 101 Skits from Kids, Margaret Read McDonald
Fortune's Journey, Bruce Coville
Broadway Chances, Elizabeth Starr Hill
The Street Dancers, Elizabeth Starr Hill

3.21 Sports Books

Books are written on a wide variety of sports for students in grades 4–6, who are becoming more involved with after-school sports programs at this age. These action-filled, fast-paced books encourage children to read about their sports heroes or help them to better understand how a certain sport is played.

Baseball

Bobby Baseball, Robert Kimmel Smith
Double Play, Matt Christopher
The Goof That Won the Pennant, Jonah Kalb
The Kid That Only Hit Homers, Matt Christopher
Honus & Me, Dan Gutman
Mark McGwire: A Biography, Jonathan Hall
Pitchers: Twenty-seven of Baseball's Greatest, George Sullivan
Sluggers: Twenty-seven of Baseball's Greatest, George Sullivan
Southside Sluggers (series), Daniel A. Greenberg
Ruth Marini of the Dodgers (series), Mel Cebulash

Basketball

Basketball: You Are the Coach, Nate Aaseng
Michael Jordan, Sean Dolan
Charles Barkley, Sean Dolan
Meet the Chicago Bulls, Brendan Hanahan
Grant Hill: A Biography, Bill Gutman
Shery Swoopes: All-Star Basketball Player, Liza N. Burby
Scottie Pippin, Fred McMane
Shaquille O'Neal: Superhero at Center, Pohla Smith
Basketball, Tom Withers
Teammates: John Stockton and Karl Malone, Robert E. Schnackenberg
Super Sports Star Jason Kidd, Stew Thornley

Fishing

Freshwater Fish & Fishing, Jim Arnosky
Winter Rescue, W. D. Valgardson
Father Water, Mother Woods: Essays on Fishing and Hunting in the North Woods, Gary Paulsen

Football

The Game of Football, Jack Newcombe
Football, Dave Raffo
First and Goal, Dan Marino
New England Patriots, Richard Rambeck
Football Is for Me, Lowell Dickmeyer
In the Huddle with John Elway, Matt Christopher
Tackling, Running, and Kicking: Now and Again, Gary Paulsen
Fighting Tackle, Matt Christopher
Monday Night Football Club (series), Gordon Korman

Hockey

Slapshots (series), Gordon Korman
The Wolf Bay Wings (series), Bruce Brooks
Hockey (Play-by-Play series), Mike Foley
The Hockey Machine, Matt Christopher
Penalty Shot, Matt Christopher

Ice Skating

Silver Blades (series), Melissa Lowell
This Is Figure Skating, Margaret Blackstone
Hans Brinker, or the Silver Skates, Mary Mapes Dodge
DK Superguides: Ice Skating, Peter Morrissey

Soccer

Mia Hamm: Striking Superstar, Rachel Rutledge
Never Say Quit, Bill Wallace
Soccer Scoop, Matt Christopher
Top Wing, Matt Christopher
Everything Kids' Soccer Book: Rules, Techniques and More About Your Favorite Sport!, Deborah W. Crisfield

3.21 *continued*

S.O.R. Losers, Avi
Soccer Duel, Matt Christopher

Other Sports

Boardsailing, Phyllis Perry
On the Course with . . . Tiger Woods, Matt Christopher
On the Halfpipe with . . . Tony Hawk, Matt Christopher
Extreme Surfing, Edward Voeller
Broadway Ballplayers (series), Maureen Holohan (girls, all sports)
American Gold Gymnastics (series), Gabrielle Charbonnet
American Gold Swimmers (series), Sharon Dennis Wyeth

3.22 Poetry

Like songs, poems tell stories or create feelings through their lyrics. Poems evoke imagery by encouraging the reader to "hear," "see," "feel," "smell," and "taste" what is being described. Teachers use poetry to encourage writing by having students examine such elements as sound patterns, repetition, and metaphor.

All the Colors of the Race: Poems, Arnold Adoff
The Best of Michael Rosen: Poetry for Kids, Michael Rosen
Bing Bang Boing, Douglas Florian
Call Down the Moon: Poems of Music, Myra Cohn Livingston (ed.)
A Caribbean Dozen: Poems from Caribbean Poets, John Agard and Grace Nichols (eds.)
Celebrate America: In Poetry and Art, Nora Panzer (ed.)
A Cold Snap: Frosty Poems, Audrey B. Baird
Come with Me: Poems for a Journey, Naomi Shihab Nye
Cornflakes, James Stevenson
The Distant Talking Drum: Poems from Nigeria, Isaac Olaleye
Doctor Knickerbocker and Other Rhymes, David Booth (ed.)
The Dream Keeper and Other Poems, Langston Hughes
Exploding Gravy: Poems to Make You Laugh, X. J. Kennedy
Fast and Slow: Poems for Advanced Children and Beginning Parents, John Ciardi
The Flag of Childhood: Poems from the Middle East, Naomi Shihab Nye (ed.)
Food Fight: Poets Join the Fight Against Hunger with Poems to Favorite Foods, Michael J. Rosen (ed.)
Footprints on the Roof: Poems about the Earth, Marilyn Singer
Ghost Poems, Daisy Wallace (ed.)
Hand in Hand: An American History Through Poetry, Lee Bennett Hopkins (ed.)
Have You Been to the Beach Lately?, Ralph Fletcher
Hiawatha, Henry Wadsworth Longfellow
Honey, I Love, and Other Love Poems, Eloise Greenfield
The Hopeful Trout and Other Limericks, John Ciardi
If I Were in Charge of the World and Other Worries: Poems for Children and Their Parents, Judith Viorst
In the Swim: Poems and Paintings, Douglas Florian
It's Raining Pigs and Noodles: Poems, Jack Prelutsky
Joyful Noise: Poems for Two Voices, Paul Fleischman
Just Around the Corner, James Stevenson
The Kite that Braved Old Orchard Beach: Year-Round Poems for Young People, X. J. Kennedy
Awful Ogre's Awful Day, Jack Prelutsky
The Blackbirch Treasury of American Poetry, Frances Schoonmaker Bolin, Gary D. Schmidt and Brod Bagert (eds.)
Casey at the Bat, Ernest Lawrence Thayer
Cautionary Tales for Children, Hilaire Belloc, illustrated by Edward Gorey
Celebrations, Myra Cohn Livingston
A Child's Garden of Verses, Robert Louis Stevenson
Heart to Heart: New Poems Inspired by Twentieth Century American Art, Jan Greenberg (ed.)

3.22 *continued*

I Have Heard of a Land, Joyce Carol Thomas
Journey Through Heartsongs, Mattie Stepanek
My America: A Poetry Atlas of the United States, Lee Bennett Hopkins (ed.)
A Pizza the Size of the Sun: Poems, Jack Prelutsky
Poetry for Young People: Edgar Allen Poe (Poetry for Young People series), Brod Bagert (ed.)
A Poke in the I: A Collection of Concrete Poems, Paul B. Janeczko (ed.)
Sad Underwear: And Other Complications: More Poems for Children and Their Parents, Judith Viorst
The Shooting of Dan McGrew, Robert W. Service
The 20th Century Children's Poetry Treasures, Jack Prelutsky (ed.)
Walking the Bridge of Your Nose, Michael Rosen (ed.)
Laugh-Eteria: Poems & Drawings, Douglas Florian
Leaf by Leaf: Autumn Poems, Barbara Rogasky (ed.)
A Light in the Attic, Shel Silverstein
Lives: Poems About Famous Americans, Lee Bennett Hopkins (ed.)
Lots of Limericks, Myra Cohn Livingston (ed.)
Miracles: Poems by Children of the English Speaking World, Richard Lewis (ed.)
More Spice than Sugar: Poems About Feisty Females, Lillian Morrison (ed.)
My America: A Poetry Atlas of the United States, Lee Bennett Hopkins (ed.)
My Black Me: A Beginning Book of Black Poetry, Arnold Adoff (ed.)
My Own Song and Other Poems to Groove to, Michael R. Strickland (ed.)
Night Garden: Poems From the World of Dreams, Janet S. Wong
One at a Time, David McCord
Outside the Lines: Poetry at Play, Brad Burg
The Oxford Boook of Story Poems, Michael Harrison and Christopher Stuart-Clark (eds.)
Poems that Sing to You, Michael R. Strickland (ed.)
Poetry by Heart: A Child's Book of Poems to Remember, Liz Attenborough (ed.)
Rainbow in the Sky, Louis Untermeyer (ed.)
The Random House Book of Poetry for Children, Jack Prelutsky (ed.)
Runaway Opposites, Richard Wilbur
Salting the Ocean: 100 Poems by Young Poets, Naomi Shihab Nye (ed.)
A Sea Within a Sea: Secrets of the Sargasso, Ruth Heller
Snuffles and Snouts, Laura Robb (ed.)
Something New Begins: New & Selected Poems, Lilian Moore
Splash! Poems of Our Watery World, Constance Levy
Sports Pages, Arnold Adoff
Sprints and Distances: Sports in Poems and the Poetry in Sport, Lillian Morrison (ed.)
Summersaults: Poems & Paintings, Douglas Florian
Ten-Second Rainshowers: Poems by Young People, Sanford Lyne (ed.)
That Sweet Diamond: Baseball Poems, Paul Janeczko
A Thousand Cousins: Poems of Family Life, David L. Harrison
We the People: Poems, Bobbi Katz
When Riddles Come Rumbling: Poems to Ponder, Rebecca Kai Dotlich

3.22 *continued*

When the Rain Sings: Poems by Young Native Americans, National Museum of the American Indian, Smithsonian Institution
Where the Sidewalk Ends: The Poems and Drawings of Shel Silverstein, Shel Silverstein
Whisper and Shout: Poems to Memorize, Patrice Vecchione (ed.)
Wild Wings: Poems for Young People, Jane Yolen
Witch Poems, Daisy Wallace (ed.)
Words with Wings: A Treasury of African-American Poetry and Art, Belinda Rochelle (ed.)

Source: List 3.22 was compiled by M. Jerry Weiss, Distinguished Professor Emeritus, New Jersey City University, Jersey City, NJ.

3.23 Fun With Language: Idioms, Homonyms, Palindromes, Oxymorons, and Riddles

This list of books that play with words will delight children of all ages.

Best Riddle Book Ever, Charles Keller
A Cache of Jewels and Other Collective Nouns (World of Language series), Ruth Heller
Eight Ate: A Feast of Homonym Riddles, Marvin Terban
Elvis Lives: And Other Anagrams, Jon Agee (ed.)
Fantastic! Wow! and Unreal!: A Book About Interjections and Conjunctions, Ruth Heller
500 Hilarious Jokes for Kids, Jeff Rovin
Go Hang a Salami! I'm a Lasagna Hog!: And Other Palindromes, Jon Agee
Hairy, Scary, Ordinary: What Is an Adjective?, Brian P. Cleary
In a Pickle, and Other Funny Idioms, Marvin Terban
It Figures!: Fun Figures of Speech, Marvin Terban
Kites Sail High: A Book About Verbs (World of Language series), Ruth Heller
Knock, Knock! Who's There?: My First Book of Knock-Knock Jokes, Tad Hills
A Little Pigeon Toad, Fred Gwynne
Mad as a Wet Hen: And Other Funny Idioms, Marvin Terban
Many Luscious Lollipops: A Book About Adjectives (World of Language series), Ruth Heller
Merry-Go-Round: A Book About Nouns (World of Language series), Ruth Heller
Mine, All Mine: A Book About Pronouns (World of Language series), Ruth Heller
A Mink, a Fink, a Skating Rink: What Is a Noun?, Brian P. Cleary
Jon Agee's Palindromania!, Jon Agee
Sit on a Potato Pan, Otis!: More Palindromes, Jon Agee
So Many Dynamos!: And Other Palindromes, Jon Agee
The Dove Dove: Funny Homograph Riddles, Marvin Terban
The King Who Rained, Fred Gwynne
To Root to Toot to Parachute: What Is a Verb? (Words Are Categorical series), Brian P. Cleary
Too Hot to Hoot: Funny Palindrome Riddles, Marvin Terban
Up, Up and Away: A Book About Adverbs (World of Language series), Ruth Heller
Who Ordered the Jumbo Shrimp?: And Other Oxymorons, Jon Agee
Your Foot's on My Feet!: And Other Tricky Nouns, Marvin Terban
Yours Till Niagra Falls, Lillian Morrison (editor)
Awesome Jokes, Charles Keller
Creepy Crawly Critter Riddles, Joanne E. Bernstein and Paul Cohen
Kids Are Punny: Jokes Sent by Kids to the Rosie O'Donnell Show
Knock-Knock Knees and Funnybones, Riddles for Every Body, Judith Mathews and Fay Robinson
The Laugh-a-Minute Joke Book, Gene Perret
Riddle City, USA! A Book of Geography Riddles, Marco and Mario Maestro
Six Sick Sheep: 101 Tongue Twisters, Joanna Cole
Swine Lake: Music and Dance Riddles, compiled by Charles Keller
Touchdown Riddles, Joanne E. Bernstein and Paul Cohen
TV Jokes and Riddles, Martha Bolton

3.24 Dictionaries, Encyclopedias, Atlases, and Computer Books

DICTIONARIES

Scholastic Children's Dictionary (Revised and Updated Edition) (2002)
Merriam-Webster's Elementary Dictionary, Merriam-Webster's Editorial Staff (2000)
DK Merriam-Webster Children's Dictionary
The American Heritage Student Dictionary, Editors of The American Heritage Dictionaries (Editor) (1998)
The McGraw-Hill Children's Dictionary (2001)
Thorndike Barnhart Student Dictionary, Scott Foresman-Addison Wesley et al. (1998)
Scholastic Dictionary of Idioms, Marvin Terban, John Devore (Illustrator) (1998)
Merriam-Webster's School Dictionary, Merriam-Webster's Editorial Staff (1999)
The Scholastic Dictionary of Spelling: Over 15,000 Words, Marvin Terban, Harry A. Campbell (Illustrator) (2000)
Scholastic Children's Thesaurus (Scholastic Reference), John K. Bollard, Mike Reed (Illustrator) (1998)
A Writer's Notebook: Unlocking the Writer within You, Ralph Fletcher (1996)

ENCYCLOPEDIAS

General

Children's Illustrated Encyclopedia (2000)
DK Illustrated Family Encyclopedia (2002)
The Kingfisher A–Z Encyclopedia: Up-to-the-Minute Information, Ben Hoare (Editor) (2002)
The Kingfisher Encyclopedia of the Future, Clive Gifford (2001)
The World Encyclopedia of Comics (Volume 1), Maurice Horn (Editor) (1998)
The Concise History Encyclopedia, Editors of Kingfisher (2001)
Big Book of Knowledge, Sarah Phillips (Editor) (2002)
Encyclopedia of Planet Earth (Usborne Encyclopedia Series), Anna Claybourne et al. (2000)
Oxford American Children's Encyclopedia (2002)
The Encyclopedia of Explorers and Adventurers (Watts Reference), Justine Ciovacco (2003)

Animals and Nature

National Geographic Animal Encyclopedia (2000)
Dictionary of Horses and Ponies, Struan Reid (Editor) (1999)
Animal Encyclopedia, Barbara Taylor (2000)
The Natural World (The Usborne Illustrated Encyclopedia), Lisa Watts (Editor) (1995)
DK Nature Encyclopedia (1998)
Dinosaur Encyclopedia, Michael J. Benton, Wendy Barish (Editor) (1984)
The Kingfisher Illustrated Dinosaur Encyclopedia, David Burnie (2001)
The World of Wild Animals, Ton Van Eerbeek (2002)

3.24 *continued*

ATLASES

History

The Kingfisher History Encyclopedia, Editors of Kingfisher (1999)
The Children's Atlas of World History, Neil Demarco, Neil de Marchi (2001)
Geographica's Family Atlas (2001)
The Children's Atlas of Civilizations: Trace the Rise and Fall of the World's Great Civilizations (Children's Atlases), Antony Mason (1994)

Geography and Exploration

DK Pocket-Size World Atlas, Esther Labi, Deni Bown (1995)
National Geographic World Atlas for Young Explorers, NGS Cartographer (1998)
Dorling Kindersley Children's Atlas (2000)
National Geographic Student Atlas of the World, National Geographic Society (2001)
The Young People's Atlas of the United States, James Harrison (1996)
Scholastic Atlas of the World, Scholastic (2003)
Reader's Digest Children's Atlas of the World, Reader's Digest (2003)

Science and Mathematics

The Children's Atlas of Natural Wonders, Joyce Pope (1995)

Space

The Reader's Digest Children's Atlas of the Universe, Robert Burnham (2000)
The Atlas of Space Exploration (The Atlas Library), Tim Furniss (2002)
Atlas of Space, James Muirdon et al. (2002)

The Human Body

The Children's Atlas of the Human Body: Actual Size Bones, Muscles, and Organs in Full Color/Book and Chart, Richard Walker (1994)

MULTICULTURAL RESOURCES

The Atlas of World Cultures, Brunetto Chiarelli et al. (2001)
The Children's Atlas of People & Places, Jenny Wood, David Munro (1993)
The Children's Dictionary of Folklore, David A. Leeming, General Editor; Marilee Foglesong, Advisor (Watts Reference)
The Usborne Internet-Linked Encyclopedia of World Religions (Encyclopedia of World Religions), Susan Meredith et al. (2002)
Gods, Goddesses, and Monsters: An Encyclopedia of World Mythology, Sheila Keenan, Belgin Wedman (Illustrator) (2000)

3.24 *continued*

COMPUTER BOOKS

An interest in computers starts at an early age. Teaching and learning through computers is rapidly growing in all areas of the curriculum. The books listed below not only instruct students but encourage them to create their own arts, crafts, and Web pages.

The Internet for Kids, Carnan Kazunas and Tom Kazunas
Personal Computers, Carnan Kazunas and Tom Kazunas
Mousetracks: A Kid's Computer Idea Book, Peggy L. Steinhauser
You Can Surf the Net!, Marc Gascoigne
User Friendly, Lawrence Gordon
Angela's Top Secret Computer Club, Holly Keller
The On-line Spaceman and Other Cases, Seymour Simon
Online Kids: A Young Surfer's Guide to Cyberspace, Preston Gralla
The Internet, Charles A. Jortberg
Virtual Reality and Beyond, Charles A. Jortberg
Internet, Lora Koehler
Home Page: An Introduction to Web Page Design, Christopher Lampton
The World Wide Web, Christopher Lampton
Kids' Computer Creations: Using Your Computer for Art and Craft Fun, Carol Sabbeth
Robots: Your High-Tech World, Gloria Skurzynski

SECTION FOUR

Children's Book Awards and Recommended Literature

4.1 Caldecott Award Winners and Honor Books

Randolph Caldecott was an outstanding English illustrator during the mid-1800s. The humor, action, and vitality of his drawings, along with those of Kate Greenaway and Walter Crane, ushered in the modern era of quality picture books for children. Frederic G. Melcher, editor of *Publishers Weekly*, established this award in 1937 to honor a picture-book illustrator whose book is named the most distinguished picture book published during the preceding year. Additional information on this award is available on the American Library Association Web site at www.ala.org.†

2003 Medal Winner:

My Friend Rabbit by Eric Rohmann (Roaring Brook Press/Millbrook)

Honor Books:

The Spider and the Fly by Tony DiTerlizzi (Simon & Schuster)
Hondo and Fabian by Peter McCarty (Henry Holt)
Noah's Ark by Jerry Pinkney (Sea Star/North-South Books)

2002 Medal Winner:

The Three Pigs by David Wiesner (Clarion/Houghton Mifflin)

Honor Books:

The Dinosaurs of Waterhouse Hawkins, illustrated by Brian Selznick, written by Barbara Kerley (Scholastic)
Martin's Big Words: The Life of Dr. Martin Luther King, Jr., illustrated by Bryan Collier, written by Doreen Rappaport (Jump at the Sun/Hyperion)
The Stray Dog by Marc Simont (HarperCollins)

2001 Medal Winner:

So You Want to Be President?, illustrated by David Small, written by Judith St. George (Philomel Books)

†One of the most comprehensive Web sites listing children's book awards is www.ucalgary.ca/~dkrown/usawards.html

4.1 *continued*

Honor Books:

Casey at the Bat: A Ballad of the Republic Sung in the Year 1888, illustrated by Christopher Bing, written by Ernest Lawrence Thayer (Handprint Books)

Click, Clack, Moo: Cows that Type, illustrated by Betsy Lewin, written by Doreen Cronin (Simon & Schuster Children's Publishing Division/Simon & Schuster Books for Young Readers)

Olivia by Ian Falconer (Simon & Schuster Children's Publishing Division/Atheneum Books for Young Readers)

2000 Medal Winner:

Joseph Had a Little Overcoat by Simms Taback (Viking)

Honor Books:

A Child's Calendar, illustrated by Trina Schart Hyman, written by John Updike (Holiday House)

Sector 7 by David Wiesner (Clarion Books)

When Sophie Gets Angry—Really, Really Angry by Molly Bang (Scholastic)

The Ugly Duckling, illustrated by Jerry Pinkney, written by Hans Christian Andersen, adapted by Jerry Pinkney (Morrow)

1999 Medal Winner:

Snowflake Bentley, illustrated by Mary Azarian, written by Jacqueline Briggs Martin (Houghton)

Honor Books:

Duke Ellington: The Piano Prince and the Orchestra, illustrated by Brian Pinkney, written by Andrea Davis Pinkney (Hyperion)

No, David! by David Shannon (Scholastic)

Snow by Uri Shulevitz (Farrar)

Tibet Through the Red Box by Peter Sis (Frances Foster)

1998 Medal Winner:

Rapunzel by Paul O. Zelinsky (Dutton)

Honor Books:

The Gardener, illustrated by David Small, written by Sarah Stewart (Farrar)

Harlem, illustrated by Christopher Myers, written by Walter Dean Myers (Scholastic)

There Was an Old Lady Who Swallowed a Fly by Simms Taback (Viking)

1997 Medal Winner:

Golem by David Wisniewski (Clarion)

Honor Books:

Hush! A Thai Lullaby, illustrated by Holly Meade, written by Minfong Ho (Melanie Kroupa/Orchard Books)

The Graphic Alphabet by David Pelletier (Orchard Books)

The Paperboy by Dav Pilkey (Richard Jackson/Orchard Books)

Starry Messenger by Peter Sís (Frances Foster Books/Farrar Straus Giroux)

4.1 *continued*

1996 Medal Winner:

Officer Buckle and Gloria by Peggy Rathmann (Putnam)

Honor Books:

Alphabet City by Stephen T. Johnson (Viking)

Zin! Zin! Zin! a Violin, illustrated by Marjorie Priceman, written by Lloyd Moss (Simon & Schuster)

The Faithful Friend, illustrated by Brian Pinkney, written by Robert D. SanSouci (Simon & Schuster)

Tops & Bottoms, adapted and illustrated by Janet Stevens (Harcourt)

1995 Medal Winner:

Smoky Night, illustrated by David Diaz, written by Eve Bunting (Harcourt)

Honor Books:

John Henry, illustrated by Jerry Pinkney, written by Julius Lester (Dial)

Swamp Angel, illustrated by Paul O. Zelinsky, written by Anne Issacs (Dutton)

Time Flies by Eric Rohmann (Crown)

1994 Medal Winner:

Grandfather's Journey illustrated by Allen Say, edited by Walter Lorraine (Houghton)

Honor Books:

Peppe the Lamplighter, illustrated by Ted Lewin, written by Elisa Bartone (Lothrop)

In the Small, Small Pond by Denise Fleming (Holt)

Raven: A Trickster Tale from the Pacific Northwest by Gerald McDermott (Harcourt)

Owen by Kevin Henkes (Greenwillow)

Yo! Yes?, illustrated by Chris Raschka, edited by Richard Jackson (Orchard)

1993 Medal Winner:

Mirette on the High Wire by Emily Arnold McCully (Putnam)

Honor Books:

The Stinky Cheese Man and Other Fairly Stupid Tales, illustrated by Lane Smith, written by Jon Scieszka (Viking)

Seven Blind Mice by Ed Young (Philomel Books)

Working Cotton, illustrated by Carole Byard, written by Sherley Anne Williams (Harcourt)

1992 Medal Winner:

Tuesday by David Wiesner (Clarion Books)

Honor Book:

Tar Beach by Faith Ringgold (Crown Publishers, Inc., a Random House Co.)

1991 Medal Winner:

Black and White by David Macaulay (Houghton)

4.1 *continued*

Honor Books:

Puss in Boots, illustrated by Fred Marcellino, written by Charles Perrault, trans. by Malcolm Arthur (Di Capua/Farrar)

"More More More," Said the Baby: Three Love Stories by Vera B. Williams (Greenwillow)

1990 Medal Winner:

Lon Po Po: A Red-Riding Hood Story from China by Ed Young (Philomel)

Honor Books:

Bill Peet: An Autobiography by Bill Peet (Houghton)

Color Zoo by Lois Ehlert (Lippincott)

The Talking Eggs: A Folktale from the American South, illustrated by Jerry Pinkney, written by Robert D. SanSouci (Dial)

Hershel and the Hanukkah Goblins, illustrated by Trina Schart Hyman, written by Eric Kimmel (Holiday House)

1989 Medal Winner:

Song and Dance Man, illustrated by Stephen Gammell, written by Karen Ackerman (Knopf)

Honor Books:

The Boy of the Three-Year Nap, illustrated by Allen Say, written by Diane Snyder (Houghton)

Free Fall by David Wiesner (Lothrop)

Goldilocks and the Three Bears by James Marshall (Dial)

Mirandy and Brother Wind, illustrated by Jerry Pinkney, written by Patricia C. McKissack (Knopf)

1988 Medal Winner:

Owl Moon, illustrated by John Schoenherr, written by Jane Yolen (Philomel)

Honor Book:

Mufaro's Beautiful Daughters: An African Tale by John Steptoe (Lothrop)

1987 Medal Winner:

Hey, Al, illustrated by Richard Egielski, written by Arthur Yorinks (Farrar)

Honor Books:

The Village of Round and Square Houses by Ann Grifalconi (Little, Brown)

Alphabatics by Suse MacDonald (Bradbury)

Rumpelstiltskin by Paul O. Zelinsky (Dutton)

1986 Medal Winner:

The Polar Express by Chris Van Allsburg (Houghton)

4.1 *continued*

Honor Books:

The Relatives Came, illustrated by Stephen Gammell, written by Cynthia Rylant (Bradbury)

King Bidgood's in the Bathtub, illustrated by Don Wood, written by Audrey Wood (Harcourt)

1985 Medal Winner:

Saint George and the Dragon, illustrated by Trina Schart Hyman, retold by Margaret Hodges (Little, Brown)

Honor Books:

Hansel and Gretel, illustrated by Paul O. Zelinsky, retold by Rika Lesser (Dodd)

Have You Seen My Duckling? by Nancy Tafuri (Greenwillow)

The Story of Jumping Mouse: A Native American Legend, illustrated and retold by John Steptoe (Lothrop)

1984 Medal Winner:

The Glorious Flight: Across the Channel with Louis Bleriot by Alice & Martin Provensen (Viking)

Honor Books:

Little Red Riding Hood, illustrated and retold by Trina Schart Hyman (Holiday)

Ten, Nine, Eight by Molly Bang (Greenwillow)

1983 Medal Winner:

Shadow, illustrated and translated by Marcia Brown, original text in French by Blaise Cendrars (Scribner)

Honor Books:

A Chair for My Mother by Vera B. Williams (Greenwillow)

When I Was Young in the Mountains, illustrated by Diane Goode, written by Cynthia Rylant (Dutton)

1982 Medal Winner:

Jumanji by Chris Van Allsburg (Houghton)

Honor Books:

Where the Buffaloes Begin, illustrated by Stephen Gammell, written by Olaf Baker (Warne)

On Market Street, illustrated by Anita Lobel, written by Arnold Lobel (Greenwillow)

Outside Over There by Maurice Sendak (Harper)

A Visit to William Blake's Inn: Poems for Innocent and Experienced Travelers, illustrated by Alice & Martin Provensen, written by Nancy Willard (Harcourt)

1981 Medal Winner:

Fables by Arnold Lobel (Harper)

4.1 *continued*

Honor Books:
The Brementown Musicians, retold and illustrated by Ilse Plume (Doubleday)
The Grey Lady and the Strawberry Snatcher by Molly Bang (Four Winds)
Mice Twice by Joseph Low (McElderry/Atheneum)
Truck by Donald Crews (Greenwillow)

1980 Medal Winner:

Ox-Cart Man, illustrated by Barbara Cooney, written by Donald Hall (Viking)

Honor Books:
Ben's Trumpet by Rachel Isadora (Greenwillow)
The Garden of Abdul Gasazi by Chris Van Allsburg (Houghton)
The Treasure by Uri Shulevitz (Farrar)

1979 Medal Winner:

The Girl Who Loved Wild Horses by Paul Goble (Bradbury)

Honor Books:
Freight Train by Donald Crews (Greenwillow)
The Way to Start a Day, illustrated by Peter Parnall, written by Byrd Baylor (Scribner)

1978 Medal Winner:

Noah's Ark by Peter Spier (Doubleday)

Honor Books:
Castle by David Macaulay (Houghton)
It Could Always Be Worse, retold and illustrated by Margot Zemach (Farrar)

1977 Medal Winner:

Ashanti to Zulu: African Traditions, illustrated by Leo & Diane Dillon, written by Margaret Musgrove (Dial)

Honor Books:
The Amazing Bone by William Steig (Farrar)
The Contest, illustrated and retold by Nonny Hogrogian (Greenwillow)
Fish for Supper by M. B. Goffstein (Dial)
The Golem: A Jewish Legend by Beverly Brodsky McDermott (Lippincott)
Hawk, I'm Your Brother, illustrated by Peter Parnall, written by Byrd Baylor (Scribner)

1976 Medal Winner:

Why Mosquitoes Buzz in People's Ears, illustrated by Leo & Diane Dillon, retold by Verna Aardema (Dial)

Honor Books:
The Desert Is Theirs, illustrated by Peter Parnall, written by Byrd Baylor (Scribner)
Strega Nona by Tomie dePaola (Simon & Schuster)

4.1 *continued*

1975 Medal Winner:

Arrow to the Sun by Gerald McDermott (Viking)

Honor Book:

Jambo Means Hello: A Swahili Alphabet Book, illustrated by Tom Feelings, written by Muriel Feelings (Dial)

1974 Medal Winner:

Duffy and the Devil, illustrated by Margot Zemach, retold by Harve Zemach (Farrar)

Honor Books:

Three Jovial Huntsmen by Susan Jeffers (Bradbury)
Cathedral by David Macaulay (Houghton)

1973 Medal Winner:

The Funny Little Woman, illustrated by Blair Lent, retold by Arlene Mosel (Dutton)

Honor Books:

Anansi the Spider: A Tale from the Ashanti, illustrated and adapted by Gerald McDermott (Holt)
Hosie's Alphabet, illustrated by Leonard Baskin, written by Hosea, Tobias & Lisa Baskin (Viking)
Snow-White and the Seven Dwarfs, illustrated by Nancy Ekholm Burkert, translated by Randall Jarrell, retold from the Brothers Grimm (Farrar)
When Clay Sings, illustrated by Tom Bahti, written by Byrd Baylor (Scribner)

1972 Medal Winner:

One Fine Day, illustrated and retold by Nonny Hogrogian (Macmillan)

Honor Books:

Hildilid's Night, illustrated by Arnold Lobel, written by Cheli Durán Ryan (Macmillan)
If All the Seas Were One Sea by Janina Domanska (Macmillan)
Moja Means One: Swahili Counting Book, illustrated by Tom Feelings, written by Muriel Feelings (Dial)

1971 Medal Winner:

A Story A Story, illustrated and retold by Gail E. Haley (Atheneum)

Honor Books:

The Angry Moon, illustrated by Blair Lent, retold by William Sleator (Atlantic)
Frog and Toad Are Friends by Arnold Lobel (Harper)
In the Night Kitchen by Maurice Sendak (Harper)

1970 Medal Winner:

Sylvester and the Magic Pebble by William Steig (Windmill Books)

4.1 ***continued***

Honor Books:

Goggles! by Ezra Jack Keats (Macmillan)

Alexander and the Wind-up Mouse by Leo Lionni (Pantheon)

Pop Corn & Ma Goodness, illustrated by Robert Andrew Parker, written by Edna Mitchell Preston (Viking)

Thy Friend, Obadiah by Brinton Turkle (Viking)

The Judge: An Untrue Tale, illustrated by Margot Zemach, written by Harve Zemach (Farrar)

1969 **Medal Winner:**

The Fool of the World and the Flying Ship, illustrated by Uri Shulevitz, retold by Arthur Ransome (Farrar)

Honor Book:

Why the Sun and the Moon Live in the Sky, illustrated by Blair Lent, written by Elphinstone Dayrell (Houghton)

1968 **Medal Winner:**

Drummer Hoff, illustrated by Ed Emberley, adapted by Barbara Emberley (Prentice-Hall)

Honor Books:

Frederick by Leo Lionni (Pantheon)

Seashore Story by Taro Yashima (Viking)

The Emperor and the Kite, illustrated by Ed Young, written by Jane Yolen (World)

1967 **Medal Winner:**

Sam, Bangs & Moonshine by Evaline Ness (Holt)

Honor Book:

One Wide River to Cross, illustrated by Ed Emberley, adapted by Barbara Emberley (Prentice-Hall)

1966 **Medal Winner:**

Always Room for One More, illustrated by Nonny Hogrogian, written by Sorche Nic Leodhas, pseud. [Leclaire Alger] (Holt)

Honor Books:

Hide and Seek Fog, illustrated by Roger Duvoisin, written by Alvin Tresselt (Lothrop)

Just Me by Marie Hall Ets (Viking)

Tom Tit Tot, illustrated and retold by Evaline Ness (Scribner)

1965 **Medal Winner:**

May I Bring a Friend?, illustrated by Beni Montresor, written by Beatrice Schenk de Regniers (Atheneum)

4.1 *continued*

Honor Books:

Rain Makes Applesauce, illustrated by Marvin Bileck, written by Julian Scheer (Holiday)
The Wave, illustrated by Blair Lent, written by Margaret Hodges (Houghton)
A Pocketful of Cricket, illustrated by Evaline Ness, written by Rebecca Caudill (Holt)

1964 Medal Winner:

Where the Wild Things Are by Maurice Sendak (Harper)

Honor Books:

Swimmy by Leo Lionni (Pantheon)
All in the Morning Early, illustrated by Evaline Ness, written by Sorche Nic Leodhas, pseud. [Leclaire Alger] (Holt)
Mother Goose and Nursery Rhymes, illustrated by Philip Reed (Atheneum)

1963 Medal Winner:

The Snowy Day by Ezra Jack Keats (Viking)

Honor Books:

The Sun Is a Golden Earring, illustrated by Bernarda Bryson, written by Natalia M. Belting (Holt)
Mr. Rabbit and the Lovely Present, illustrated by Maurice Sendak, written by Charlotte Zolotow (Harper)

1962 Medal Winner:

Once a Mouse, illustrated and retold by Marcia Brown (Scribner)

Honor Books:

Fox Went Out on a Chilly Night: An Old Song by Peter Spier (Doubleday)
Little Bear's Visit, illustrated by Maurice Sendak, written by Else H. Minarik (Harper)
The Day We Saw the Sun Come Up, illustrated by Adrienne Adams, written by Alice E. Goudey (Scribner)

1961 Medal Winner:

Baboushka and the Three Kings, illustrated by Nicolas Sidjakov, written by Ruth Robbins (Parnassus)

Honor Book:

Inch by Inch by Leo Lionni (Obolensky)

1960 Medal Winner:

Nine Days to Christmas, illustrated by Marie Hall Ets, written by Marie Hall Ets & Aurora Labastida (Viking)

Honor Books:

Houses from the Sea, illustrated by Adrienne Adams, written by Alice E. Goudey (Scribner)
The Moon Jumpers, illustrated by Maurice Sendak, written by Janice May Udry (Harper)

4.1 *continued*

1959 **Medal Winner:**

Chanticleer and the Fox, illustrated by Barbara Cooney, adapted from Chaucer's *Canterbury Tales* by Barbara Cooney (Crowell)

Honor Books:

The House that Jack Built: La Maison Que Jacques A Batie by Antonio Frasconi (Harcourt)

What Do You Say, Dear?, illustrated by Maurice Sendak, written by Sesyle Joslin (W. R. Scott)

Umbrella by Taro Yashima (Viking)

1958 **Medal Winner:**

Time of Wonder by Robert McCloskey (Viking)

Honor Books:

Fly High, Fly Low by Don Freeman (Viking)

Anatole and the Cat, illustrated by Paul Galdone, written by Eve Titus (McGraw-Hill)

1957 **Medal Winner:**

A Tree Is Nice, illustrated by Marc Simont, written by Janice May Udry (Harper)

Honor Books:

Mr. Penny's Race Horse by Marie Hall Ets (Viking)

1 Is One by Tasha Tudor (Walck)

Anatole, illustrated by Paul Galdone, written by Eve Titus (McGraw-Hill)

Gillespie and the Guards, illustrated by James Daugherty, written by Benjamin Elkin (Viking)

Lion by William Pène du Bois (Viking)

1956 **Medal Winner:**

Frog Went A-Courtin', illustrated by Feodor Rojankovsky, retold by John Langstaff (Harcourt)

Honor Books:

Play With Me by Marie Hall Ets (Viking)

Crow Boy by Taro Yashima (Viking)

1955 **Medal Winner:**

Cinderella, or the Little Glass Slipper, illustrated by Marcia Brown, translated from Charles Perrault by Marcia Brown (Scribner)

Honor Books:

Book of Nursery and Mother Goose Rhymes, illustrated by Marguerite de Angeli (Doubleday)

Wheel on the Chimney, illustrated by Tibor Gergely, written by Margaret Wise Brown (Lippincott)

The Thanksgiving Story, illustrated by Helen Sewell, written by Alice Dalgliesh (Scribner)

4.1 *continued*

1954 Medal Winner:

Madeline's Rescue by Ludwig Bemelmans (Viking)

Honor Books:

Journey Cake, Ho!, illustrated by Robert McCloskey, written by Ruth Sawyer (Viking)
When Will the World Be Mine?, illustrated by Jean Charlot, written by Miriam Schlein (W. R. Scott)
The Steadfast Tin Soldier, illustrated by Marcia Brown, written by Hans Christian Andersen, translated by M. R. James (Scribner)
A Very Special House, illustrated by Maurice Sendak, written by Ruth Krauss (Harper)
Green Eyes by A. Birnbaum (Capitol)

1953 Medal Winner:

The Biggest Bear by Lynd Ward (Houghton)

Honor Books:

Puss in Boots, illustrated by Marcia Brown, translated from Charles Perrault by Marcia Brown (Scribner)
One Morning in Maine by Robert McCloskey (Viking)
Ape in a Cape: An Alphabet of Odd Animals by Fritz Eichenberg (Harcourt)
The Storm Book, illustrated by Margaret Bloy Graham, written by Charlotte Zolotow (Harper)
Five Little Monkeys by Juliet Kepes (Houghton)

1952 Medal Winner:

Finders Keepers, illustrated by Nicolas, pseud. [Nicholas Mordvinoff], written by Will, pseud. [William Lipkind] (Harcourt)

Honor Books:

Mr. T. W. Anthony Woo by Marie Hall Ets (Viking)
Skipper John's Cook by Marcia Brown (Scribner)
All Falling Down, illustrated by Margaret Bloy Graham, written by Gene Zion (Harper)
Bear Party by William Pène du Bois (Viking)
Feather Mountain by Elizabeth Olds (Houghton)

1951 Medal Winner:

The Egg Tree by Katherine Milhous (Scribner)

Honor Books:

Dick Whittington and His Cat by Marcia Brown (Scribner)
The Two Reds, illustrated by Nicolas, pseud. [Nicholas Mordvinoff], written by Will, pseud. [William Lipkind] (Harcourt)
If I Ran the Zoo by Dr. Seuss (Random House)
The Most Wonderful Doll in the World, illustrated by Helen Stone, written by Phyllis McGinley (Lippincott)
T-Bone, the Baby Sitter by Clare Turlay Newberry (Harper)

4.1 ***continued***

1950 Medal Winner:

Song of the Swallows by Leo Politi (Scribner)

Honor Books:

America's Ethan Allen, illustrated by Lynd Ward, written by Stewart Holbrook (Houghton)
The Wild Birthday Cake, illustrated by Hildegard Woodward, written by Lavinia R. Davis (Doubleday)
The Happy Day, illustrated by Marc Simont, written by Ruth Krauss (Harper)
Bartholomew and the Oobleck by Dr. Seuss (Random House)
Henry Fisherman by Marcia Brown

1949 Medal Winner:

The Big Snow by Berta & Elmer Hader (Macmillan)

Honor Books:

Blueberries for Sal by Robert McCloskey (Viking)
All Around the Town, illustrated by Helen Stone, written by Phyllis McGinley (Lippincott)
Juanita by Leo Politi (Scribner)
Fish in the Air by Kurt Wiese (Viking)

1948 Medal Winner:

White Snow, Bright Snow, illustrated by Roger Duvoisin, written by Alvin Tresselt (Lothrop)

Honor Books:

Stone Soup by Marcia Brown (Scribner)
McElligot's Pool by Dr. Seuss (Random House)
Bambino the Clown by Georges Schreiber (Viking)
Roger and the Fox, illustrated by Hildegard Woodward, written by Lavinia R. Davis (Doubleday)
Song of Robin Hood, illustrated by Virginia Lee Burton, edited by Anne Malcolmson (Houghton)

1947 Medal Winner:

The Little Island, illustrated by Leonard Weisgard, written by Golden MacDonald, pseud. [Margaret Wise Brown] (Doubleday)

Honor Books:

Rain Drop Splash, illustrated by Leonard Weisgard, written by Alvin Tresselt (Lothrop)
Boats on the River, illustrated by Jay Hyde Barnum, written by Marjorie Flack (Viking)
Timothy Turtle, illustrated by Tony Palazzo, written by Al Graham (Welch)
Pedro, the Angel of Olvera Street by Leo Politi (Scribner)
Sing in Praise: A Collection of the Best Loved Hymns, illustrated by Marjorie Torrey, selected by Opal Wheeler (Dutton)

4.1 *continued*

1946 Medal Winner:

The Rooster Crows by Maude & Miska Petersham (Macmillan)

Honor Books:

Little Lost Lamb, illustrated by Leonard Weisgard, written by Golden MacDonald, pseud. [Margaret Wise Brown] (Doubleday)

Sing Mother Goose, illustrated by Marjorie Torrey, music by Opal Wheeler (Dutton)

My Mother Is the Most Beautiful Woman in the World, illustrated by Ruth Gannett, written by Becky Reyher (Lothrop)

You Can Write Chinese by Kurt Wiese (Viking)

1945 Medal Winner:

Prayer for a Child, illustrated by Elizabeth Orton Jones, written by Rachel Field (Macmillan)

Honor Books:

Mother Goose, illustrated by Tasha Tudor (Oxford University Press)

In the Forest by Marie Hall Ets (Viking)

Yonie Wondernose by Marguerite de Angeli (Doubleday)

The Christmas Anna Angel, illustrated by Kate Seredy, written by Ruth Sawyer (Viking)

1944 Medal Winner:

Many Moons, illustrated by Louis Slobodkin, written by James Thurber (Harcourt)

Honor Books:

Small Rain: Verses from the Bible, illustrated by Elizabeth Orton Jones, selected by Jessie Orton Jones (Viking)

Pierre Pigeon, illustrated by Arnold E. Bare, written by Lee Kingman (Houghton)

The Mighty Hunter by Berta & Elmer Hader (Macmillan)

A Child's Good Night Book, illustrated by Jean Charlot, written by Margaret Wise Brown (W. R. Scott)

Good-Luck Horse, illustrated by Plato Chan, written by Chih-Yi Chan (Whittlesey)

1943 Medal Winner:

The Little House by Virginia Lee Burton (Houghton)

Honor Books:

Dash and Dart by Mary & Conrad Buff (Viking)

Marshmallow by Clare Turlay Newberry (Harper)

1942 Medal Winner:

Make Way for Ducklings by Robert McCloskey (Viking)

Honor Books:

An American ABC by Maud & Miska Petersham (Macmillan)

In My Mother's House, illustrated by Velino Herrera, written by Ann Nolan Clark (Viking)

Paddle-to-the-Sea by Holling C. Holling (Houghton)

Nothing at All by Wanda Gag (Coward)

4.1 *continued*

1941 **Medal Winner:**

They Were Strong and Good by Robert Lawson (Viking)

Honor Book:
April's Kittens by Clare Turlay Newberry (Harper)

1940 **Medal Winner:**

Abraham Lincoln by Ingri & Edgar Parin d'Aulaire (Doubleday)

Honor Books:
Cock-a-Doodle Doo by Berta & Elmer Hader (Macmillan)
Madeline by Ludwig Bemelmans (Viking)
The Ageless Story by Lauren Ford (Dodd)

1939 **Medal Winner:**

Mei Li by Thomas Handforth (Doubleday)

Honor Books:
Andy and the Lion by James Daugherty (Viking)
Barkis by Clare Turlay Newberry (Harper)
The Forest Pool by Laura Adams Armer (Longmans)
Snow White and the Seven Dwarfs by Wanda Gag (Coward)
Wee Gillis, illustrated by Robert Lawson, written by Munro Leaf (Viking)

1938 **Medal Winner:**

Animals of the Bible, A Picture Book, illustrated by Dorothy P. Lathrop, selected by Helen Dean Fish (Lippincott)

Honor Books:
Four and Twenty Blackbirds, illustrated by Robert Lawson, compiled by Helen Dean Fish (Stokes)
Seven Simeons: A Russian Tale, illustrated and retold by Boris Artzybasheff (Viking)

Source: List 4.1 is used with the permission of the American Library Association.

4.2 Newbery Medal Winners and Honor Books

The Newbery medal is the oldest and most prestigious of all children's book awards given in the United States. This award is given annually by the American Library Association to honor an American author who has made a distinguished contribution to children's literature during the previous year. The Newbery award was established by Frederick G. Melcher, editor of *Publishers Weekly*, to pay tribute to John Newbery (1713–1767), the first publisher of children's books in England. During the mid-1870's, most of John Newbery's books, including *Gulliver's Travels* and *Robinson Crusoe*, were reprinted in America by a Massachusetts publisher Isaiah Thomas. Announcement of the medal winner and honor books is made each January. For more information go to the American Library Association Web site at www.ala.org.†

2003 Medal Winner:

Crispin: The Cross of Lead by Avi (Hyperion)

Honor Books:

The House of Scorpion by Nancy Farmer (Atheneum)
Pictures of Hollis Woods by Patricia Reilly Giff (Random House)
Hoot by Carl Hiaasen (Knopf)
Corner of the Universe by Anne M. Martin (Scholastic)
Surviving the Applewhites by Stephanie S. Tolan (HarperCollins)

2002 Medal Winner:

A Single Shard by Linda Sue Park (Clarion Books/Houghton Mifflin)

Honor Books:

Everything on a Waffle by Polly Horvath (Farrar, Straus & Giroux)
Carver: A Life in Poems by Marilyn Nelson (Front Street)

2001 Medal Winner:

A Year Down Yonder by Richard Peck (Dial)

Honor Books:

Hope Was Here by Joan Bauer (Putnam)
Because of Winn-Dixie by Kate DiCamillo (Candlewick Press)
Joey Pigza Loses Control by Jack Gantos (Farrar, Straus & Giroux)
The Wanderer by Sharon Creech (Joanna Cotler Books/HarperCollins)

2000 Medal Winner:

Bud, Not Buddy by Christopher Paul Curtis (Delacorte)

Honor Books:

Getting Near to Baby by Audrey Couloumbis (Putnam)
Our Only May Amelia by Jennifer L. Holm (HarperCollins)
26 Fairmount Avenue by Tomie dePaola (Putnam)

†One of the most comprehensive Web sites listing children's book awards is www.ucalgary.ca/dkbrown/usawards.html.

4.2 *continued*

1999 **Medal Winner:**

Holes by Louis Sachar (Frances Foster)

Honor Book:
A Long Way from Chicago by Richard Peck (Dial)

1998 **Medal Winner:**

Out of the Dust by Karen Hesse (Scholastic)

Honor Books:
Ella Enchanted by Gail Carson Levine (HarperCollins)
Lily's Crossing by Patricia Reilly Giff (Delacorte)
Wringer by Jerry Spinelli (HarperCollins)

1997 **Medal Winner:**

The View from Saturday by E. L. Konigsburg (Jean Karl/Atheneum)

Honor Books:
A Girl Named Disaster by Nancy Farmer (Richard Jackson/Orchard Books)
Moorchild by Eloise McGraw (Margaret McElderry/Simon & Schuster)
The Thief by Megan Whalen Turner (Greenwillow/Morrow)
Belle Prater's Boy by Ruth White (Farrar, Straus & Giroux)

1996 **Medal Winner:**

The Midwife's Apprentice by Karen Cushman (Clarion)

Honor Books:
What Jamie Saw by Carolyn Coman (Front Street)
The Watsons Go to Birmingham: 1963 by Christopher Paul Curtis (Delacorte)
Yolonda's Genius by Carol Fenner (Margaret McElderry/Simon & Schuster)
The Great Fire by Jim Murphy (Scholastic)

1995 **Medal Winner:**

Walk Two Moons by Sharon Creech (HarperCollins)

Honor Books:
Catherine, Called Birdy by Karen Cushman (Clarion)
The Ear, the Eye and the Arm by Nancy Farmer (Jackson/Orchard)

1994 **Medal Winner:**

The Giver by Lois Lowry (Houghton)

Honor Books:
Crazy Lady by Jane Leslie Conly (HarperCollins)
Dragon's Gate by Laurence Yep (HarperCollins)
Eleanor Roosevelt: A Life of Discovery by Russell Freedman (Clarion Books)

1993 **Medal Winner:**

Missing May by Cynthia Rylant (Jackson/Orchard)

4.2 *continued*

Honor Books:
What Hearts by Bruce Brooks (A Laura Geringer Book/HarperCollins)
The Dark-thirty: Southern Tales of the Supernatural by Patricia McKissack (Knopf)
Somewhere in the Darkness by Walter Dean Myers (Scholastic Hardcover)

1992 Medal Winner:

Shiloh by Phyllis Reynolds Naylor (Atheneum)

Honor Books:
Nothing But the Truth: A Documentary Novel by Avi (Jackson/Orchard)
The Wright Brothers: How They Invented the Airplane by Russell Freedman (Holiday House)

1991 Medal Winner:

Maniac Magee by Jerry Spinelli (Little, Brown)

Honor Book:
The True Confessions of Charlotte Doyle by Avi (Jackson/Orchard)

1990 Medal Winner:

Number the Stars by Lois Lowry (Houghton)

Honor Books:
Afternoon of the Elves by Janet Taylor Lisle (Jackson/Orchard)
Shabanu, Daughter of the Wind by Suzanne Fisher Staples (Knopf)
The Winter Room by Gary Paulsen (Jackson/Orchard)

1989 Medal Winner:

Joyful Noise: Poems for Two Voices by Paul Fleischman (Harper)

Honor Books:
In the Beginning: Creation Stories from Around the World by Virginia Hamilton (Harcourt)
Scorpions by Walter Dean Myers (Harper)

1988 Medal Winner:

Lincoln: A Photobiography by Russell Freedman (Clarion)

Honor Books:
After the Rain by Norma Fox Mazer (Morrow)
Hatchet by Gary Paulsen (Bradbury)

1987 Medal Winner:

The Whipping Boy by Sid Fleischman (Greenwillow)

Honor Books:
A Fine White Dust by Cynthia Rylant (Bradbury)
On My Honor by Marion Dane Bauer (Clarion)
Volcano: The Eruption and Healing of Mount St. Helens by Patricia Lauber (Bradbury)

4.2 *continued*

1986 **Medal Winner:**

Sarah, Plain and Tall by Patricia MacLachlan (Harper)

Honor Books:
Commodore Perry in the Land of the Shogun by Rhoda Blumberg (Lothrop)
Dogsong by Gary Paulsen (Bradbury)

1985 **Medal Winner:**

The Hero and the Crown by Robin McKinley (Greenwillow)

Honor Books:
Like Jake and Me by Mavis Jukes (Knopf)
The Moves Make the Man by Bruce Brooks (Harper)
One-Eyed Cat by Paula Fox (Bradbury)

1984 **Medal Winner:**

Dear Mr. Henshaw by Beverly Cleary (Morrow)

Honor Books:
The Sign of the Beaver by Elizabeth George Speare (Houghton)
A Solitary Blue by Cynthia Voigt (Atheneum)
Sugaring Time by Kathryn Lasky (Macmillan)
The Wish Giver: Three Tales of Coven Tree by Bill Brittain (Harper)

1983 **Medal Winner:**

Dicey's Song by Cynthia Voigt (Atheneum)

Honor Books:
The Blue Sword by Robin McKinley (Greenwillow)
Doctor DeSoto by William Steig (Farrar, Straus & Giroux)
Graven Images by Paul Fleischman (Harper)
Homesick: My Own Story by Jean Fritz (Putnam)
Sweet Whispers, Brother Rush by Virginia Hamilton (Philomel)

1982 **Medal Winner:**

A Visit to William Blake's Inn: Poems for Innocent and Experienced Travelers by Nancy Willard (Harcourt)

Honor Books:
Ramona Quimby, Age 8 by Beverly Cleary (Morrow)
Upon the Head of the Goat: A Childhood in Hungary 1939–1944 by Aranka Siegal (Farrar, Straus & Giroux)

1981 **Medal Winner:**

Jacob Have I Loved by Katherine Paterson (Crowell)

Honor Books:
The Fledgling by Jane Langton (Harper)
A Ring of Endless Light by Madeleine L'Engle (Farrar)

4.2 *continued*

1980 Medal Winner:

A Gathering of Days: A New England Girl's Journal, 1830–1832 by Joan W. Blos (Scribner)

Honor Book:
The Road from Home: The Story of an Armenian Girl by David Kherdian (Greenwillow)

1979 Medal Winner:

The Westing Game by Ellen Raskin (Dutton)

Honor Book:
The Great Gilly Hopkins by Katherine Paterson (Crowell)

1978 Medal Winner:

Bridge to Terabithia by Katherine Paterson (Crowell)

Honor Books:
Ramona and Her Father by Beverly Cleary (Morrow)
Anpao: An American Indian Odyssey by Jamake Highwater (Lippincott)

1977 Medal Winner:

Roll of Thunder, Hear My Cry by Mildred D. Taylor (Dial)

Honor Books:
Abel's Island by William Steig (Farrar, Straus & Giroux)
A String in the Harp by Nancy Bond (Atheneum)

1976 Medal Winner:

The Grey King by Susan Cooper (McElderry/Atheneum)

Honor Books:
The Hundred Penny Box by Sharon Bell Mathis (Viking)
Dragonwings by Laurence Yep (Harper)

1975 Medal Winner:

M. C. Higgins, the Great by Virginia Hamilton (Macmillan)

Honor Books:
Figgs & Phantoms by Ellen Raskin (Dutton)
My Brother Sam Is Dead by James Lincoln Collier & Christopher Collier (Four Winds)
The Perilous Gard by Elizabeth Marie Pope (Houghton)
Philip Hall Likes Me, I Reckon Maybe by Bette Greene (Dial)

1974 Medal Winner:

The Slave Dancer by Paula Fox (Bradbury)

Honor Book:
The Dark Is Rising by Susan Cooper (McElderry/Atheneum)

4.2 *continued*

1973 Medal Winner:

Julie of the Wolves by Jean Craighead George (Harper)

Honor Books:
Frog and Toad Together by Arnold Lobel (Harper)
The Upstairs Room by Johanna Reiss (Crowell)
The Witches of Worm by Zilpha Keatley Snyder (Atheneum)

1972 Medal Winner:

Mrs. Frisby and the Rats of NIMH by Robert C. O'Brien (Atheneum)

Honor Books:
Incident at Hawk's Hill by Allan W. Eckert (Little, Brown)
The Planet of Junior Brown by Virginia Hamilton (Macmillan)
The Tombs of Atuan by Ursula K. LeGuin (Atheneum)
Annie and the Old One by Miska Miles (Little, Brown)
The Headless Cupid by Zilpha Keatley Snyder (Atheneum)

1971 Medal Winner:

Summer of the Swans by Betsy Byars (Viking)

Honor Books:
Knee Knock Rise by Natalie Babbitt (Farrar, Straus & Giroux)
Enchantress from the Stars by Sylvia Louise Engdahl (Atheneum)
Sing Down the Moon by Scott O'Dell (Houghton)

1970 Medal Winner:

Sounder by William H. Armstrong (Harper)

Honor Books:
Our Eddie by Sulamith Ish-Kishor (Pantheon)
The Many Ways of Seeing: An Introduction to the Pleasures of Art by Janet Gaylord Moore (World)
Journey Outside by Mary Q. Steele (Viking)

1969 Medal Winner:

The High King by Lloyd Alexander (Holt)

Honor Books:
To Be a Slave by Julius Lester (Dial)
When Shlemiel Went to Warsaw and Other Stories by Isaac Bashevis Singer (Farrar, Straus & Giroux)

1968 Medal Winner:

From the Mixed-Up Files of Mrs. Basil E. Frankweiler by E. L. Konigsburg (Atheneum)

4.2 *continued*

Honor Books:
Jennifer, Hecate, Macbeth, William McKinley, and Me, Elizabeth by E. L. Konigsburg (Atheneum)
The Black Pearl by Scott O'Dell (Houghton)
The Fearsome Inn by Isaac Bashevis Singer (Scribner)
The Egypt Game by Zilpha Keatley Snyder (Atheneum)

1967 Medal Winner:

Up a Road Slowly by Irene Hunt (Follett)

Honor Books:
The King's Fifth by Scott O'Dell (Houghton)
Zlateh the Goat and Other Stories by Isaac Bashevis Singer (Harper)
The Jazz Man by Mary Hays Weik (Atheneum)

1966 Medal Winner:

I, Juan de Pareja by Elizabeth Borton de Treviño (Farrar, Straus & Giroux)

Honor Books:
The Black Cauldron by Lloyd Alexander (Holt)
The Animal Family by Randall Jarrell (Pantheon)
The Noonday Friends by Mary Stolz (Harper)

1965 Medal Winner:

Shadow of a Bull by Maia Wojciechowska (Atheneum)

Honor Book:
Across Five Aprils by Irene Hunt (Follett)

1964 Medal Winner:

It's Like This, Cat by Emily Neville (Harper)

Honor Books:
Rascal: A Memoir of a Better Era by Sterling North (Dutton)
The Loner by Ester Wier (McKay)

1963 Medal Winner:

A Wrinkle in Time by Madeleine L'Engle (Farrar, Straus & Giroux)

Honor Books:
Thistle and Thyme: Tales and Legends from Scotland by Sorche Nic Leodhas, pseud. [Leclaire Alger] (Holt)
Men of Athens by Olivia Coolidge (Houghton)

1962 Medal Winner:

The Bronze Bow by Elizabeth George Speare (Houghton)

4.2 *continued*

Honor Books:
Frontier Living by Edwin Tunis (World)
The Golden Goblet by Eloise Jarvis McGraw (Coward)
Belling the Tiger by Mary Stolz (Harper)

1961 Medal Winner:
Island of the Blue Dolphins by Scott O'Dell (Houghton)

Honor Books:
America Moves Forward: A History for Peter by Gerald W. Johnson (Morrow)
Old Ramon by Jack Schaefer (Houghton)
The Cricket in Times Square by George Selden, pseud. [George Thompson] (Farrar, Straus & Giroux)

1960 Medal Winner:
Onion John by Joseph Krumgold (Crowell)

Honor Books:
My Side of the Mountain by Jean Craighead George (Dutton)
America Is Born: A History for Peter by Gerald W. Johnson (Morrow)
The Gammage Cup by Carol Kendall (Harcourt)

1959 Medal Winner:
The Witch of Blackbird Pond by Elizabeth George Speare (Houghton)

Honor Books:
The Family Under the Bridge by Natalie Savage Carlson (Harper)
Along Came a Dog by Meindert DeJong (Harper)
Chucaro: Wild Pony of the Pampa by Francis Kalnay (Harcourt)
The Perilous Road by William O. Steele (Harcourt)

1958 Medal Winner:
Rifles for Watie by Harold Keith (Crowell)

Honor Books:
The Horsecatcher by Mari Sandoz (Westminster)
Gone-Away Lake by Elizabeth Enright (Harcourt)
The Great Wheel by Robert Lawson (Viking)
Tom Paine, Freedom's Apostle by Leo Gurko (Crowell)

1957 Medal Winner:
Miracles on Maple Hill by Virginia Sorenson (Harcourt)

Honor Books:
Old Yeller by Fred Gipson (Harper)
The House of Sixty Fathers by Meindert DeJong (Harper)
Mr. Justice Holmes by Clara Ingram Judson (Follett)
The Corn Grows Ripe by Dorothy Rhoads (Viking)
Black Fox of Lorne by Marguerite de Angeli (Doubleday)

4.2 *continued*

1956 Medal Winner:

Carry on, Mr. Bowditch by Jean Lee Latham (Houghton)

Honor Books:

The Secret River by Marjorie Kinnan Rawlings (Scribner)
The Golden Name Day by Jennie Lindquist (Harper)
Men, Microscopes, and Living Things by Katherine Shippen (Viking)

1955 Medal Winner:

The Wheel on the School by Meindert DeJong (Harper)

Honor Books:

Courage of Sarah Noble by Alice Dalgliesh (Scribner)
Banner in the Sky by James Ullman (Lippincott)

1954 Medal Winner:

. . . *And Now Miguel* by Joseph Krumgold (Crowell)

Honor Books:

All Alone by Claire Huchet Bishop (Viking)
Shadrach by Meindert DeJong (Harper)
Hurry Home, Candy by Meindert DeJong (Harper)
Theodore Roosevelt, Fighting Patriot by Clara Ingram Judson (Follett)
Magic Maize by Mary & Conrad Buff (Houghton)

1953 Medal Winner:

Secret of the Andes by Ann Nolan Clark (Viking)

Honor Books:

Charlotte's Web by E. B. White (Harper)
Moccasin Trail by Eloise Jarvis McGraw (Coward)
Red Sails to Capri by Ann Weil (Viking)
The Bears on Hemlock Mountain by Alice Dalgliesh (Scribner)
Birthdays of Freedom, Vol. 1 by Genevieve Foster (Scribner)

1952 Medal Winner:

Ginger Pye by Eleanor Estes (Harcourt)

Honor Books:

Americans Before Columbus by Elizabeth Baity (Viking)
Minn of the Mississippi by Holling C. Holling (Houghton)
The Defender by Nicholas Kalashnikoff (Scribner)
The Light at Tern Rock by Julia Sauer (Viking)
The Apple and the Arrow by Mary & Conrad Buff (Houghton)

1951 Medal Winner:

Amos Fortune, Free Man by Elizabeth Yates (Dutton)

4.2 *continued*

Honor Books:
Better Known as Johnny Appleseed by Mabel Leigh Hunt (Lippincott)
Gandhi, Fighter Without a Sword by Jeanette Eaton (Morrow)
Abraham Lincoln, Friend of the People by Clara Ingram Judson (Follett)
The Story of Appleby Capple by Anne Parrish (Harper)

1950 Medal Winner:
The Door in the Wall by Marguerite de Angeli (Doubleday)

Honor Books:
Tree of Freedom by Rebecca Caudill (Viking)
The Blue Cat of Castle Town by Catherine Coblentz (Longmans)
Kildee House by Rutherford Montgomery (Doubleday)
George Washington by Genevieve Foster (Scribner)
Song of the Pines: A Story of Norwegian Lumbering in Wisconsin by Walter & Marion Havighurst (Winston)

1949 Medal Winner:
King of the Wind by Marguerite Henry (Rand McNally)

Honor Books:
Seabird by Holling C. Holling (Houghton)
Daughter of the Mountain by Louise Rankin (Viking)
My Father's Dragon by Ruth S. Gannett (Random House)
Story of the Negro by Arna Bontemps (Knopf)

1948 Medal Winner:
The Twenty-one Balloons by William Pène du Bois (Viking)

Honor Books:
Pancakes-Paris by Claire Huchet Bishop (Viking)
Li Lun, Lad of Courage by Carolyn Treffinger (Abingdon)
The Quaint and Curious Quest of Johnny Longfoot by Catherine Besterman (Bobbs-Merrill)
The Cow-Tail Switch, and Other West African Stories by Harold Courlander (Holt)
Misty of Chincoteague by Marguerite Henry (Rand McNally)

1947 Medal Winner:
Miss Hickory by Carolyn Sherwin Bailey (Viking)

Honor Books:
Wonderful Year by Nancy Barnes (Messner)
Big Tree by Mary & Conrad Buff (Viking)
The Heavenly Tenants by William Maxwell (Harper)
The Avion My Uncle Flew by Cyrus Fisher, pseud. [Darwin L. Teilhet] (Appleton)
The Hidden Treasure of Glaston by Eleanor Jewett (Viking)

4.2 *continued*

1946 Medal Winner:

Strawberry Girl by Lois Lenski (Lippincott)

Honor Books:

Justin Morgan Had a Horse by Marguerite Henry (Rand McNally)
The Moved-Outers by Florence Crannell Means (Houghton)
Bhimsa, the Dancing Bear by Christine Weston (Scribner)
New Found World by Katherine Shippen (Viking)

1945 Medal Winner:

Rabbit Hill by Robert Lawson (Viking)

Honor Books:

The Hundred Dresses by Eleanor Estes (Harcourt)
The Silver Pencil by Alice Dalgliesh (Scribner)
Abraham Lincoln's World by Genevieve Foster (Scribner)
Lone Journey: The Life of Roger Williams by Jeanetter Eaton (Harcourt)

1944 Medal Winner:

Johnny Tremain by Esther Forbes (Houghton)

Honor Books:

These Happy Golden Years by Laura Ingalls Wilder (Harper)
Fog Magic by Julia Sauer (Viking)
Rufus M. by Eleanor Estes (Harcourt)
Mountain Born by Elizabeth Yates (Coward)

1943 Medal Winner:

Adam of the Road by Elizabeth Janet Gray (Viking)

Honor Books:

The Middle Moffat by Eleanor Estes (Harcourt)
Have You Seen Tom Thumb? by Mabel Leigh Hunt (Lippincott)

1942 Medal Winner:

The Matchlock Gun by Walter Edmonds (Dodd)

Honor Books:

Little Town on the Prairie by Laura Ingalls Wilder (Harper)
George Washington's World by Genevieve Foster (Scribner)
Indian Captive: The Story of Mary Jemison by Lois Lenski (Lippincott)
Down Ryton Water by Eva Roe Gaggin (Viking)

1941 Medal Winner:

Call It Courage by Armstrong Sperry (Macmillan)

Honor Books:

Blue Willow by Doris Gates (Viking)
Young Mac of Fort Vancouver by Mary Jane Carr (Crowell)

4.2 *continued*

The Long Winter by Laura Ingalls Wilder (Harper)
Nansen by Anna Gertrude Hall (Viking)

1940 Medal Winner:

Daniel Boone by James Daugherty (Viking)

Honor Books:
The Singing Tree by Kate Seredy (Viking)
Runner of the Mountain Tops: The Life of Louis Agassiz by Mabel Robinson (Random House)
By the Shores of Silver Lake by Laura Ingalls Wilder (Harper)
Boy with a Pack by Stephen W. Meader (Harcourt)

1939 Medal Winner:

Thimble Summer by Elizabeth Enright (Rinehart)

Honor Books:
Nino by Valenti Angelo (Viking)
Mr. Popper's Penguins by Richard & Florence Atwater (Little, Brown)
Hello the Boat! by Phyllis Crawford (Holt)
Leader by Destiny: George Washington, Man and Patriot by Jeanette Eaton (Harcourt)
Penn by Elizabeth Janet Gray (Viking)

1938 Medal Winner:

The White Stag by Kate Seredy (Viking)

Honor Books:
Pecos Bill by James Cloyd Bowman (Little, Brown)
Bright Island by Mabel Robinson (Random House)
On the Banks of Plum Creek by Laura Ingalls Wilder (Harper)

1937 Medal Winner:

Roller Skates by Ruth Sawyer (Viking)

Honor Books:
Phoebe Fairchild: Her Book by Lois Lenski (Stokes)
Whistler's Van by Idwal Jones (Viking)
The Golden Basket by Ludwig Bemelmans (Viking)
Winterbound by Margery Bianco (Viking)
The Codfish Musket by Agnes Hewes (Doubleday)
Audubon by Constance Rourke (Harcourt)

1936 Medal Winner:

Caddie Woodlawn by Carol Ryrie Brink (Macmillan)

Honor Books:
Honk, the Moose by Phil Stong (Dodd)
The Good Master by Kate Seredy (Viking)

4.2 *continued*

Young Walter Scott by Elizabeth Janet Gray (Viking)
All Sail Set: A Romance of the Flying Cloud by Armstrong Sperry (Winston)

1935 Medal Winner:

Dobry by Monica Shannon (Viking)

Honor Books:
Pageant of Chinese History by Elizabeth Seeger (Longmans)
Davy Crockett by Constance Rourke (Harcourt)
Day on Skates: The Story of a Dutch Picnic by Hilda Von Stockum (Harper)

1934 Medal Winner:

Invincible Louisa: The Story of the Author of ***Little Women*** by Cornelia Meigs (Little, Brown)

Honor Books:
The Forgotten Daughter by Caroline Snedeker (Doubleday)
Swords of Steel by Elsie Singmaster (Houghton)
ABC Bunny by Wanda Gag (Coward)
Winged Girl of Knossos by Erik Berry, pseud. [Allena Best] (Appleton)
New Land by Sarah Schmidt (McBride)
Big Tree of Bunlahy: Stories of My Own Countryside by Padraic Colum (Macmillan)
Glory of the Seas by Agnes Hewes (Knopf)
Apprentice of Florence by Ann Kyle (Houghton)

1933 Medal Winner:

Young Fu of the Upper Yangtze by Elizabeth Lewis (Winston)

Honor Books:
Swift Rivers by Cornelia Meigs (Little, Brown)
The Railroad to Freedom: A Story of the Civil War by Hildegarde Swift (Harcourt)
Children of the Soil: A Story of Scandinavia by Nora Burglon (Doubleday)

1932 Medal Winner:

Waterless Mountain by Laura Adams Armer (Longmans)

Honor Books:
The Fairy Circus by Dorothy P. Lathrop (Macmillan)
Calico Bush by Rachel Field (Macmillan)
Boy of the South Seas by Eunice Tietjens (Coward-McCann)
Out of the Flame by Eloise Lownsbery (Longmans)
Jane's Island by Marjorie Allee (Houghton)
Truce of the Wolf and Other Tales of Old Italy by Mary Gould Davis (Harcourt)

1931 Medal Winner:

The Cat Who Went to Heaven by Elizabeth Coatsworth (Macmillan)

4.2 *continued*

Honor Books:
Floating Island by Anne Parrish (Harper)
The Dark Star of Itza: The Story of a Pagan Princess by Alida Malkus (Harcourt)
Queer Person by Ralph Hubbard (Doubleday)
Mountains Are Free by Julie Davis Adams (Dutton)
Spice and the Devil's Cave by Agnes Hewes (Knopf)
Meggy MacIntosh by Elizabeth Janet Gray (Doubleday)
Garram the Hunter: A Boy of the Hill Tribes by Herbert Best (Doubleday)
Ood-Le-Uk the Wanderer by Alice Lide & Margaret Johansen (Little, Brown)

1930 Medal Winner:

Hitty, Her First Hundred Years by Rachel Field (Macmillan)

Honor Books:
A Daughter of the Seine: The Life of Madame Roland by Jeanette Eaton (Harper)
Pran of Albania by Elizabeth Miller (Doubleday)
Jumping-off Place by Marion Hurd McNeely (Longmans)
The Tangle-Coated Horse and Other Tales by Ella Young (Longmans)
Vaino by Julia Davis Adams (Dutton)
Little Blacknose by Hildegarde Swift (Harcourt)

1929 Medal Winner:

The Trumpeter of Krakow by Eric P. Kelly (Macmillan)

Honor Books:
Pigtail of Ah Lee Ben Loo by John Bennett (Longmans)
Millions of Cats by Wanda Gag (Coward)
The Boy Who Was by Grace Hallock (Dutton)
Clearing Weather by Cornelia Meigs (Little, Brown)
Runaway Papoose by Grace Moon (Doubleday)
Tod of the Fens by Elinor Whitney (Macmillan)

1928 Medal Winner:

Gay Neck, the Story of a Pigeon by Dhan Gopal Mukerji (Dutton)

Honor Books:
The Wonder Smith and His Son by Ella Young (Longmans)
Downright Dencey by Caroline Snedeker (Doubleday)

1927 Medal Winner:

Smoky, the Cowhorse by Will James (Scribner)

Honor Books:
[None recorded]

1926 Medal Winner:

Shen of the Sea by Arthur Bowie Chrisman (Dutton)

4.2 *continued*

Honor Book:
The Voyagers: Being Legends and Romances of Atlantic Discovery by Padraic Colum (Macmillan)

1925 Medal Winner:

Tales from Silver Lands by Charles Finger (Doubleday)

Honor Books:
Nicholas: A Manhattan Christmas Story by Annie Carroll Moore (Putnam)
The Dream Coach by Anne Parrish (Macmillan)

1924 Medal Winner:

The Dark Frigate by Charles Hawes (Little, Brown)

Honor Books:
[None recorded]

1923 Medal Winner:

The Voyages of Doctor Dolittle by Hugh Lofting (Lippincott)

Honor Books:
[None recorded]

1922 Medal Winner:

The Story of Mankind by Hendrik Willem van Loon (Liveright)

Honor Books:
The Great Quest by Charles Hawes (Little, Brown)
Cedric the Forester by Bernard Marshall (Appleton)
The Old Tobacco Shop: A True Account of What Befell a Little Boy in Search of Adventure by William Bowen (Macmillan)
The Golden Fleece and the Heroes Who Lived Before Achilles by Padraic Colum (Macmillan)
The Windy Hill by Cornelia Meigs (Macmillan)

Source: List 4.2 is used with the permission of the American Library Association.

4.3 Caldecott and Newbery Winners

CALDECOTT MEDAL WINNERS 1938-2003

2003: *My Friend Rabbit* by David Rohmann (Roaring Brook Press/Millbrook)
2002: *The Three Pigs* by David Wiesner (Clarion/Houghton Mifflin)
2001: *So You Want to Be President?* illustrated by David Small; written by Judith St. George (Philomel Books)
2000: *Joseph Had a Little Overcoat* by Simms Taback (Viking)
1999: *Snowflake Bentley*, illustrated by Mary Azarian; written by Jacqueline Briggs Martin (Houghton)
1998: *Rapunzel* by Paul O. Zelinsky (Dutton)
1997: *Golem* by David Wisniewski (Clarion)
1996: *Officer Buckle and Gloria* by Peggy Rathmann (Putnam)
1995: *Smoky Night*, illustrated by David Diaz; written by Eve Bunting (Harcourt)
1994: *Grandfather's Journey* by Allen Say; edited by Walter Lorraine (Houghton)
1993: *Mirette on the High Wire* by Emily Arnold McCully (Putnam)
1992: *Tuesday* by David Wiesner (Clarion Books)
1991: *Black and White* by David Macaulay (Houghton)
1990: *Lon Po Po: A Red-Riding Hood Story from China* retold by Ed Young (Philomel)
1989: *Song and Dance Man*, illustrated by Stephen Gammell; written by Karen Ackerman (Knopf)
1988: *Owl Moon*, illustrated by John Schoenherr; written by Jane Yolen (Philomel)
1987: *Hey, Al*, illustrated by Richard Egielski; written by Arthur Yorinks (Farrar)
1986: *The Polar Express* by Chris Van Allsburg (Houghton)
1985: *Saint George and the Dragon*, illustrated by Trina Schart Hyman; retold by Margaret Hodges (Little, Brown)
1984: *The Glorious Flight: Across the Channel with Louis Bleriot* by Alice & Martin Provensen (Viking)
1983: *Shadow*, translated and illustrated by Marcia Brown; original text in French: Blaise Cendrars (Scribner)
1982: *Jumanji* by Chris Van Allsburg (Houghton)
1981: *Fables* by Arnold Lobel (Harper)
1980: *Ox-Cart Man*, illustrated by Barbara Cooney; written by Donald Hall (Viking)
1979: *The Girl Who Loved Wild Horses* by Paul Goble (Bradbury)
1978: *Noah's Ark* by Peter Spier (Doubleday)
1977: *Ashanti to Zulu: African Traditions*, illustrated by Leo & Diane Dillon; written by Margaret Musgrove (Dial)
1976: *Why Mosquitoes Buzz in People's Ears*, illustrated by Leo & Diane Dillon; retold by Verna Aardema (Dial)
1975: *Arrow to the Sun* by Gerald McDermott (Viking)
1974: *Duffy and the Devil*, illustrated by Margot Zemach; retold by Harve Zemach (Farrar)
1973: *The Funny Little Woman*, illustrated by Blair Lent; retold by Arlene Mosel (Dutton)
1972: *One Fine Day*, illustrated and retold by Nonny Hogrogian (Macmillan)
1971: *A Story A Story*, illustrated and retold by by Gail E. Haley (Atheneum)
1970: *Sylvester and the Magic Pebble* by William Steig (Windmill Books)
1969: *The Fool of the World and the Flying Ship*, illustrated by Uri Shulevitz; retold by Arthur Ransome (Farrar)

4.3 *continued*

1968: *Drummer Hoff*, illustrated by Ed Emberley; adapted by Barbara Emberley (Prentice-Hall)
1967: *Sam, Bangs & Moonshine* by Evaline Ness (Holt)
1966: *Always Room for One More*, illustrated by Nonny Hogrogian; written by Sorche Nic Leodhas, pseud. [Leclaire Alger] (Holt)
1965: *May I Bring a Friend?* illustrated by Beni Montresor; written by Beatrice Schenk de Regniers (Atheneum)
1964: *Where the Wild Things Are* by Maurice Sendak (Harper)
1963: *The Snowy Day* by Ezra Jack Keats (Viking)
1962: *Once a Mouse*, illustrated and retold by Marcia Brown (Scribner)
1961: *Baboushka and the Three Kings*, illustrated by Nicolas Sidjakov; written by Ruth Robbins (Parnassus)
1960: *Nine Days to Christmas*, illustrated by Marie Hall Ets; written by Marie Hall Ets and Aurora Labastida (Viking)
1959: *Chanticleer and the Fox*, illustrated by Barbara Cooney; adapted from Chaucer's *Canterbury Tales* by Barbara Cooney (Crowell)
1958: *Time of Wonder* by Robert McCloskey (Viking)
1957: *A Tree Is Nice*, illustrated by Marc Simont; written by Janice May Udry (Harper)
1956: *Frog Went A-Courtin'*, illustrated by Feodor Rojankovsky; retold by John Langstaff (Harcourt)
1955: *Cinderella, or the Little Glass Slipper*, illustrated by Marcia Brown; translated from Charles Perrault by Marcia Brown (Scribner)
1954: *Madeline's Rescue* by Ludwig Bemelmans (Viking)
1953: *The Biggest Bear* by Lynd Ward (Houghton)
1952: *Finders Keepers*, illustrated by Nicolas, pseud. (Nicholas Mordvinoff); written by Will, pseud. [William Lipkind] (Harcourt)
1951: *The Egg Tree* by Katherine Milhous (Scribner)
1950: *Song of the Swallows* by Leo Politi (Scribner)
1949: *The Big Snow* by Berta & Elmer Hader (Macmillan)
1948: *White Snow, Bright Snow*, illustrated by Roger Duvoisin; written by Alvin Tresselt (Lothrop)
1947: *The Little Island*, illustrated by Leonard Weisgard; written by Golden MacDonald, pseud. [Margaret Wise Brown] (Doubleday)
1946: *The Rooster Crows* by Maude & Miska Petersham (Macmillan)
1945: *Prayer for a Child*, illustrated by Elizabeth Orton Jones; written by Rachel Field (Macmillan)
1944: *Many Moons*, illustrated by Louis Slobodkin; written by James Thurber (Harcourt)
1943: *The Little House* by Virginia Lee Burton (Houghton)
1942: *Make Way for Ducklings* by Robert McCloskey (Viking)
1941: *They Were Strong and Good* by Robert Lawson (Viking)
1940: *Abraham Lincoln* by Ingri & Edgar Parin d'Aulaire (Doubleday)
1939: *Mei Li* by Thomas Handforth (Doubleday)
1938: *Animals of the Bible, A Picture Book*, illustrated by Dorothy P. Lathrop; selected by Helen Dean Fish (Lippincott)

4.3 ***continued***

NEWBERY MEDAL WINNERS, 1922–2003

2003: *The Cross of Lead* by Avi (Hyperion)
2002: *A Single Shard* by Linda Sue Park (Clarion Books/Houghton Mifflin)
2001: *A Year Down Yonder* by Richard Peck (Dial)
2000: *Bud, Not Buddy* by Christopher Paul Curtis (Delacorte)
1999: *Holes* by Louis Sachar (Frances Foster)
1998: *Out of the Dust* by Karen Hesse (Scholastic)
1997: *The View from Saturday* by E. L. Konigsburg (Jean Karl/Atheneum)
1996: *The Midwife's Apprentice* by Karen Cushman (Clarion)
1995: *Walk Two Moons* by Sharon Creech (HarperCollins)
1994: *The Giver* by Lois Lowry (Houghton)
1993: *Missing May* by Cynthia Rylant (Jackson/Orchard)
1992: *Shiloh* by Phyllis Reynolds Naylor (Atheneum)
1991: *Maniac Magee* by Jerry Spinelli (Little, Brown)
1990: *Number the Stars* by Lois Lowry (Houghton)
1989: *Joyful Noise: Poems for Two Voices* by Paul Fleischman (Harper)
1988: *Lincoln: A Photobiography* by Russell Freedman (Clarion)
1987: *The Whipping Boy* by Sid Fleischman (Greenwillow)
1986: *Sarah, Plain and Tall* by Patricia MacLachlan (Harper)
1985: *The Hero and the Crown* by Robin McKinley (Greenwillow)
1984: *Dear Mr. Henshaw* by Beverly Cleary (Morrow)
1983: *Dicey's Song* by Cynthia Voigt (Atheneum)
1982: *A Visit to William Blake's Inn: Poems for Innocent and Experienced Travelers* by Nancy Willard (Harcourt)
1981: *Jacob Have I Loved* by Katherine Paterson (Crowell)
1980: *A Gathering of Days: A New England Girl's Journal, 1830–1832* by Joan W. Blos (Scribner)
1979: *The Westing Game* by Ellen Raskin (Dutton)
1978: *Bridge to Terabithia* by Katherine Paterson (Crowell)
1977: *Roll of Thunder, Hear My Cry* by Mildred D. Taylor (Dial)
1976: *The Grey King* by Susan Cooper (McElderry/Atheneum)
1975: *M. C. Higgins, the Great* by Virginia Hamilton (Macmillan)
1974: *The Slave Dancer* by Paula Fox (Bradbury)
1973: *Julie of the Wolves* by Jean Craighead George (Harper)
1972: *Mrs. Frisby and the Rats of NIMH* by Robert C. O'Brien (Atheneum)
1971: *Summer of the Swans* by Betsy Byars (Viking)
1970: *Sounder* by William H. Armstrong (Harper)
1969: *The High King* by Lloyd Alexander (Holt)
1968: *From the Mixed-Up Files of Mrs. Basil E. Frankweiler* by E. L. Konigsburg (Atheneum)
1967: *Up a Road Slowly* by Irene Hunt (Follett)
1966: *I, Juan de Pareja* by Elizabeth Borton de Trevino (Farrar)
1965: *Shadow of a Bull* by Maia Wojciechowska (Atheneum)
1964: *It's Like This, Cat* by Emily Neville (Harper)

4.3 *continued*

1963: *A Wrinkle in Time* by Madeleine L'Engle (Farrar)
1962: *The Bronze Bow* by Elizabeth George Speare (Houghton)
1961: *Island of the Blue Dolphins* by Scott O'Dell (Houghton)
1960: *Onion John* by Joseph Krumgold (Crowell)
1959: *The Witch of Blackbird Pond* by Elizabeth George Speare (Houghton)
1958: *Rifles for Watie* by Harold Keith (Crowell)
1957: *Miracles on Maple Hill* by Virginia Sorenson (Harcourt)
1956: *Carry On, Mr. Bowditch* by Jean Lee Latham (Houghton)
1955: *The Wheel on the School* by Meindert DeJong (Harper)
1954: *. . . And Now Miguel* by Joseph Krumgold (Crowell)
1953: *Secret of the Andes* by Ann Nolan Clark (Viking)
1952: *Ginger Pye* by Eleanor Estes (Harcourt)
1951: *Amos Fortune, Free Man* by Elizabeth Yates (Dutton)
1950: *The Door in the Wall* by Marguerite de Angeli (Doubleday)
1949: *King of the Wind* by Marguerite Henry (Rand McNally)
1948: *The Twenty-One Balloons* by William Pène du Bois (Viking)
1947: *Miss Hickory* by Carolyn Sherwin Bailey (Viking)
1946: *Strawberry Girl* by Lois Lenski (Lippincott)
1945: *Rabbit Hill* by Robert Lawson (Viking)
1944: *Johnny Tremain* by Esther Forbes (Houghton)
1943: *Adam of the Road* by Elizabeth Janet Gray (Viking)
1942: *The Matchlock Gun* by Walter Edmonds (Dodd)
1941: *Call It Courage* by Armstrong Sperry (Macmillan)
1940: *Daniel Boone* by James Daugherty (Viking)
1939: *Thimble Summer* by Elizabeth Enright (Rinehart)
1938: *The White Stag* by Kate Seredy (Viking)
1937: *Roller Skates* by Ruth Sawyer (Viking)
1936: *Caddie Woodlawn* by Carol Ryrie Brink (Macmillan)
1935: *Dobry* by Monica Shannon (Viking)
1934: *Invincible Louisa: The Story of the Author of* ***Little Women*** by Cornelia Meigs (Little, Brown)
1933: *Young Fu of the Upper Yangtze* by Elizabeth Lewis (Winston)
1932: *Waterless Mountain* by Laura Adams Armer (Longmans)
1931: *The Cat Who Went to Heaven* by Elizabeth Coatsworth (Macmillan)
1930: *Hitty, Her First Hundred Years* by Rachel Field (Macmillan)
1929: *The Trumpeter of Krakow* by Eric P. Kelly (Macmillan)
1928: *Gay Neck, the Story of a Pigeon* by Dhan Gopal Mukerji (Dutton)
1927: *Smoky, the Cowhorse* by Will James (Scribner)
1926: *Shen of the Sea* by Arthur Bowie Chrisman (Dutton)
1925: *Tales from Silver Lands* by Charles Finger (Doubleday)
1924: *The Dark Frigate* by Charles Hawes (Little, Brown)
1923: *The Voyages of Doctor Dolittle* by Hugh Lofting (Lippincott)
1922: *The Story of Mankind* by Hendrik Willem van Loon (Liveright)

4.4 Boston Globe Horn Book Award Winners and Honor Books

This prestigious award has been presented annually in the fall since 1967 by the *Boston Globe* and the *Horn Book* magazine. Today the award is given in three categories: picture book, fiction and poetry, and nonfiction. Several honor books may also be named in each category. This partial list of award-winning books represents the best in children's literature from 1985–2002. For more information, contact The Horn Book, Inc., 56 Roland Street, Boston, MA 02129; (617) 628-0225. Go to www.hbook.com for a complete listing of winners and honor books.

2002

Fiction and Poetry

Lord of the Deep by Graham Salisbury (Delacorte)

Honors:

Saffy's Angel by Hilary McKay (McElderry)

Amber Was Brave, Essie Was Smart, written and illustrated by Vera B. Williams (Greenwillow)

Nonfiction

This Land Was Made for You and Me: The Life and Songs of Woody Guthrie by Elizabeth Partridge (Viking)

Honors:

Handel, Who Knew What He Liked, written by M. T. Anderson, illustrated by Kevin Hawkes (Candlewick)

Woody Guthrie: Poet of the People, written and illustrated by Bonnie Christensen (Knopf)

Picture Book

"Let's Get a Pup!" Said Kate, written and illustrated by Bob Graham (Candlewick)

Honors:

I Stink!, written by Kate McMullan, illustrated by Jim McMullan (Cotler/Harper)

Little Rat Sets Sail, written by Monika Bang-Campbell, illustrated by Molly Bang (Harcourt)

2001

Fiction and Poetry

Carver: A Life in Poems by Marilyn Nelson (Front Street)

Honors:

Everything on a Waffle by Polly Horvath (Farrar)

Troy by Adèle Geras (Harcourt)

Nonfiction

The Longitude Prize by Joan Dash, illustrated by Dusan Petricic (Foster/Farrar)

Honors:

Rocks in His Head by Carol Otis Hurst, illustrated by James Stevenson (Greenwillow)

Uncommon Traveler: Mary Kingsley in Africa, written and illustrated by Don Brown (Houghton)

4.4 *continued*

Picture Book

Cold Feet by Cynthia DeFelice, illustrated by Robert Andrew Parker (DK Ink)

Honors:

Five Creatures by Emily Jenkins, illustrated by Tomek Bogacki (Foster/Farrar)
The Stray Dog retold and illustrated by Marc Simont (HarperCollins)

2000 **Fiction and Poetry**

The Folk Keeper by Franny Billingsley (Atheneum)

Honors:

King of Shadows by Susan Cooper (McElderry)
145th Street: Short Stories by Walter Dean Myers (Delacorte)

Nonfiction

Sir Walter Ralegh and the Quest for El Dorado by Marc Aronson (Clarion)

Honors:

Osceola: Memories of a Sharecropper's Daughter, collected and edited by Alan Govenar, illustrated by Shane W. Evans (Jump at the Sun/Hyperion)
Sitting Bull and His World by Albert Marrin (Dutton)

Picture Book

Henry Hikes to Fitchburg, written and illustrated by D. B. Johnson (Houghton)

Honors:

Buttons, written and illustrated by Brock Cole (Farrar)
a day, a dog, illustrated by Gabrielle Vincent (Front Street)

1999 **Fiction and Poetry**

Holes by Louis Sachar (Foster/Farrar)

Honors:

The Trolls by Polly Horvath (Farrar)
Monster, written by Walter Dean Myers, illustrations by Christopher Myers (HarperCollins)

Nonfiction

The Top of the World: Climbing Mount Everest, written and illustrated by Steve Jenkins (Houghton)

Honors:

Shipwreck at the Bottom of the World: The Extraordinary True Story of Shackleton and the ***Endurance*** by Jennifer Armstrong (Crown)
William Shakespeare & the Globe, written and illustrated by Aliki (HarperCollins)

Picture Book

Red-Eyed Tree Frog, written by Joy Cowley, illustrated with photographs by Nic Bishop (Scholastic Press)

4.4 *continued*

Honors:

Dance, written by Bill T. Jones and Susan Kuklin, illustrated with photographs by Susan Kuklin (Hyperion)

The Owl and the Pussycat, written by Edward Lear, illustrated by James Marshall (di Capua/HarperCollins)

Special Citation

Tibet: Through the Red Box, written and illustrated by Peter Sís (Foster/Farrar)

1998 Fiction and Poetry

The Circuit: Stories from the Life of a Migrant, written by Francisco Jiménez Child (University of New Mexico Press)

Honors:

While No One Was Watching, written by Jane Leslie Conly (Holt)

My Louisiana Sky, written by Kimberly Willis Holt (Holt)

Nonfiction

Leon's Story, written by Leon Walter Tillage, illustrated with collage art by Susan L. Roth (Farrar)

Honors:

Martha Graham: A Dancer's Life, written by Russell Freedman (Clarion)

Chuck Close Up Close, written by Jan Greenberg and Sandra Jordan (DK Ink)

Picture Book

And If the Moon Could Talk, written by Kate Banks, illustrated by Georg Hallensleben (Foster/Farrar)

Honors:

Seven Brave Women, written by Betsy Hearne, illustrated by Bethanne Andersen (Greenwillow)

Popcorn: Poems, written and illustrated by James Stevenson (Greenwillow)

1997 Fiction and Poetry

The Friends, written by Kazumi Yumoto, translated by Cathy Hirano (Farrar)

Honors:

Lily's Crossing, written by Patricia Reilly Giff (Delacourt)

Harlem, written by Walter Dean Myers, illustrated by Christopher Myers (Scholastic Press)

Nonfiction

A Drop of Water: A Book of Science and Wonder, written and illustrated with photographs by Walter Wick (Scholastic)

4.4 *continued*

Honors:

Lou Gehrig: The Luckiest Man, written by David A. Adler, illustrated by Terry Widener (Gulliver/Harcourt)
Leonardo da Vinci, written and illustrated by Diane Stanley (Morrow)

Picture Book

The Adventures of Sparrowboy, written and illustrated by Brian Pinkney (Simon)

Honors:

Home on the Bayou: A Cowboy's Story, written and illustrated by G. Brian Karas (Simon)
Potato: A Tale from the Great Depression, written by Kate Lied, illustrated by Lisa Campbell Ernst (National Geographic)

1996 Fiction and Poetry

Poppy, written by Avi, illustrated by Brian Floca (Jackson/Orchard)

Honors:

The Moorchild by Eloise McGraw (McElderry)
Belle Prater's Boy by Ruth White (Farrar)

Nonfiction

Orphan Train Rider: One Boy's True Story by Andrea Warren (Houghton)

Honors:

The Boy Who Lived with the Bears: And Other Iroquois Stories, written by Joseph Bruchac, illustrated by Murv Jacob (Harper)
Haystack, written by Bonnie and Arthur Geisert, illustrated by Arthur Geisert (Houghton)

Picture Book

In the Rain with Baby Duck, written by Amy Hest, illustrated by Jill Barton (Candlewick)

Honors:

Fanny's Dream, written by Caralyn Buehner, illustrated by Mark Buehner (Dial)
Home Lovely by Lynne Rae Perkins (Greenwillow)

1995 Fiction and Poetry

Some of the Kinder Planets by Tim Wynne-Jones (Kroupa/Orchard)

Honors:

Jericho by Janet Hickman (Greenwillow)
Earthshine by Theresa Nelson (Jackson/Orchard)

Nonfiction

Abigail Adams: Witness to a Revolution by Natalie S. Bober (Atheneum)

Honors:

It's Perfectly Normal: Changing Bodies, Growing Up, Sex, and Sexual Health, written by Robie H. Harris, illustrated by Michael Emberley (Candlewick)
The Great Fire by Jim Murphy (Scholastic)

4.4 ***continued***

Picture Book

John Henry, retold by Julius Lester, illustrated by Jerry Pinkney (Dial)

Honor:
Swamp Angel, written by Anne Isaacs, illustrated by Paul O. Zelinsky (Dutton)

1994

Fiction and Poetry

Scooter by Vera Williams (Greenwillow)

Honors:
Flour Babies by Anne Fine (Little)
Western Wind by Paula Fox (Orchard)

Nonfiction

Eleanor Roosevelt: A Life of Discovery by Russell Freedman (Clarion)

Honors:
Unconditional Surrender: U.S. Grant and the Civil War by Albert Marrin (Atheneum)
A Tree Place and Other Poems, written by Constance Levy, illustrated by Robert Sabuda (McElderry)

Picture Book

Grandfather's Journey by Allen Say (Houghton)

Honors:
Owen by Kevin Henkes (Greenwillow)
A Small Tall Tale from the Far Far North by Peter Sis (Knopf)

1993

Fiction and Poetry

Ajeemah and His Son by James Berry (Harper)

Honor:
The Giver by Lois Lowry (Houghton)

Nonfiction

Sojourner Truth: Ain't I a Woman? by Patricia C. and Frederick McKissack (Scholastic)

Honor:
Lives of the Musicians: Good Times, Bad Times (And What the Neighbors Thought), written by Kathleen Krull, illustrated by Kathryn Hewitt (Harcourt)

Picture Book

The Fortune Tellers, written by Lloyd Alexander, illustrated by Trina Schart Hyman (Dutton)

Honors:
Komodo! by Peter Sis (Greenwillow)
Raven: A Trickster Tale from the Pacific Northwest by Gerald McDermott (Harcourt)

4.4 *continued*

1992 **Fiction and Poetry**

Missing May by Cynthia Rylant (Jackson/Orchard)

Honors:

Nothing but the Truth by Avi (Jackson/Orchard)
Somewhere in the Darkness by Walter Dean Myers (Scholastic)

Nonfiction

Talking with Artists, compiled and edited by Pat Cummings (Bradbury)

Honors:

Red Leaf, Yellow Leaf by Lois Ehlert (Harcourt)
The Handmade Alphabet by Laura Rankin (Dial)

Picture Book

Seven Blind Mice by Ed Young (Philomel)

Honor:

In the Tall, Tall Grass by Denise Fleming (Holt)

1991 **Fiction and Poetry**

The True Confessions of Charlotte Doyle by Avi (Orchard)

Honors:

Paradise Cafe and Other Stories by Martha Brooks (Joy Street)
Judy Scuppernong by Brenda Seabrooke (Cobblehill)

Nonfiction

Appalachia: The Voices of Sleeping Birds, written by Cynthia Rylant, illustrated by Barry Moser (Harcourt)

Honors:

The Wright Brothers: How They Invented the Airplane by Russell Freedman (Holiday House)

Good Queen Bess: The Story of Elizabeth I of England, written by Diane Stanley and Peter Vennema, illustrated by Diane Stanley (Four Winds)

Picture Book

The Tale of the Mandarin Ducks, written by Katherine Paterson, illustrated by Leo and Diane Dillon (Lodestar)

Honors:

Aardvarks, Disembark! by Ann Jonas (Greenwillow)
Sophie and Lou by Petra Mathers (Harper)

1990 **Fiction and Poetry**

Maniac Magee by Jerry Spinelli (Little, Brown)

Honors:

Saturnalia by Paul Fleischman (Harper)
Stonewords by Pam Conrad (Harper)

4.4 ***continued***

Nonfiction

The Great Little Madison by Jean Fritz (Putnam)

Honor:

Insect Metamorphosis: From Egg to Adult, written by Ron and Nancy Goor, illustrated with photographs by Ron Goor (Atheneum)

Picture Book

Lon Po Po: A Red-Riding Hood Story from China, translated and illustrated by Ed Young (Philomel)

Honor:

Chicka Chicka Boom Boom, written by Bill Martin Jr. and John Archambault, illustrated by Lois Ehlert (Simon)

Special Citation

Valentine and Orson by Nancy Ekholm Burkert (Farrar)

1989

Fiction and Poetry

The Village by the Sea by Paula Fox (Orchard)

Honors:

Eva by Peter Dickinson (Delacorte)
Gideon Ahoy! by William Mayne (Delacorte)

Nonfiction

The Way Things Work by David Macaulay (Houghton)

Honors:

The Rainbow People by Laurence Yep (Harper)
Round Buildings, Square Buildings, & Buildings That Wiggle Like a Fish, written and illustrated with photographs by Philip M. Isaacson (Knopf)

Picture Book

Shy Charles by Rosemary Wells (Dial)

Honors:

Island Boy by Barbara Cooney (Viking)
The Nativity, illustrated by Julie Vivas (Gulliver/Harcourt)

1988

Fiction and Poetry

The Friendship, written by Mildred D. Taylor, illustrated by Max Ginsburg (Dial)

Honors:

Granny Was a Buffer Girl by Berlie Doherty (Orchard)
Joyful Noise: Poems for Two Voices, written by Paul Fleischman, illustrated by Eric Beddows (Harper/Zolotow)
Memory by Margaret Mahy (McElderry)

4.4 *continued*

Nonfiction

Anthony Burns: The Defeat and Triumph of a Fugitive Slave by Virginia Hamilton (Knopf)

Honors:

African Journey, written and illustrated with photographs by John Chiasson (Bradbury)

Little by Little: A Writer's Education by Jean Little (Viking)

Picture Book

The Boy of the Three-Year Nap, written by Dianne Snyder, illustrated by Allen Say (Houghton)

Honors:

Where the Forest Meets the Sea by Jeannie Baker (Greenwillow)

Stringbean's Trip to the Shining Sea, written by Vera B. Williams, illustrated by Jennifer Williams and Vera B. Williams (Greenwillow)

1987 Fiction and Poetry

Rabble Starkey by Lois Lowry (Houghton)

Honors:

Georgia Music, written by Helen V. Griffith, illustrated by James Stevenson (Greenwillow)

Isaac Campion by Janni Howker (Greenwillow)

Nonfiction

The Pilgrims of Plimoth by Marcia Sewall (Atheneum)

Honors:

Being Born, written by Sheila Kitzinger, illustrated with photographs by Lennart Nilsson (Grosset and Dunlap)

The Magic Schoolbus at the Waterworks, written by Joanna Cole, illustrated by Bruce Degen (Scholastic)

Steamboat in a Cornfield by John Hartford (Crown)

Picture Book

Mufaro's Beautiful Daughters by John Steptoe (Lothrop)

Honors:

In Coal Country, written by Judith Hendershot, illustrated by Thomas B. Allen (Knopf)

Cherries and Cherry Pits by Vera B. Williams (Greenwillow)

Old Henry, written by Joan W. Blos, illustrated by Stephen Gammell (Morrow)

1986 Fiction and Poetry

In Summer Light by Zibby Oneal (Viking)

4.4 *continued*

Honors:

Prairie Songs by Pam Conrad (Harper)
Howl's Moving Castle by Diana Wynne Jones (Greenwillow)

Nonfiction

Auks, Rocks, and the Odd Dinosaur: Inside Stories from the Smithsonian's Museum of Natural History by Peggy Thomson (Crowell)

Honors:

Dark Harvest: Migrant Farmworkers in America, written by Brent Ashabranner, illustrated with photographs by Paul Conklin (Dodd)
The Truth about Santa Claus by James C. Giblin (Crowell)

Picture Book

The Paper Crane by Molly Bang (Greenwillow)

Honors:

Gorilla by Anthony Browne (Knopf)
The Trek by Ann Jonas (Greenwillow)
The Polar Express by Chris Van Allsburg (Houghton)

1985 Fiction and Poetry

The Moves Make the Man by Bruce Brooks (Harper)

Honors:

Babe: The Gallant Pig, written by Dick King-Smith, illustrated by Mary Rayner (Crown)
The Changeover: A Supernatural Romance by Margaret Mahy (McElderry/Atheneum)

Nonfiction

Commodore Perry in the Land of the Shogun by Rhoda Blumberg (Lothrop)

Honors:

Boy by Roald Dahl (Farrar)
1812: The War Nobody Won by Albert Marrin (Atheneum)

Picture Book

Mama Don't Allow by Thacher Hurd (Harper)

Honors:

Like Jake and Me, written by Mavis Jukes, illustrated by Lloyd Bloom (Knopf)
How Much Is a Million?, written by David M. Schwartz, illustrated by Stephen Kellogg (Lothrop)
The Mysteries of Harris Burdick by Chris Van Allsburg (Houghton)

Special Citation

1,2,3, written and illustrated with photographs by Tana Hoban (Greenwillow)

4.5 Orbis Pictus Award for Outstanding Nonfiction for Children

The Orbis Pictus Award for Outstanding Nonfiction for Children, established in 1989, promotes and recognizes excellence in nonfiction children's books. The award is named for *Orbis Pictus (The World in Pictures)*, written by Johannes Amos Comenius in 1657, which is considered to be the first book truly intended for children. Each year, the award committee in conjunction with the National Council of Teachers of English (NCTE) chooses one award book, up to five honor books, as well as other books it considers to be outstanding.†

2002 Orbis Pictus Award

Black Potatoes: The Story of the Great Irish Famine, 1845–1850 by Susan Campbell Bartoletti, 2001.

Honor Books

The Cod's Tale by Mark Kurlansky. Illustrated by S. D. Schindler, 2001.

The Dinosaurs of Waterhouse Hawkins: An Illuminating History of Mr. Waterhouse Hawkins, Artist and Lecturer by Barbara Kerley. Illustrated by Brian Selznick, 2001.

Martin's Big Words: The Life of Dr. Martin Luther King, Jr. by Doreen Rappaport. Illustrated by Bryan Collier, 2001.

Recommended Titles

Animals in Flight by Steve Jenkins and Robin Page, 2001.

B. Franklin, Printer by David A. Adler, 2001.

Brooklyn Bridge by Lynn Curlee, 2001.

Gandhi by Demi, 2001.

Hatshepsut: His Majesty, Herself by Catherine M. Andronik & Joseph Daniel Fiedler, 2001.

Hidden Worlds: Looking Through a Scientist's Microscope by Stephen P. Kramer & Dennis Kunkel, 2001.

Leonardo's Horse by Jean Fritz & Hudson Talbott, 2001.

Vincent van Gogh: Portrait of an Artist by Jan Greenberg & Sandra Jordan, 2001.

Yellow House: Vincent van Gogh and Paul Gauguin Side by Side by Susan Goldman Rubin & Joseph A. Smith, 2001.

2001 Orbis Pictus Award

Hurry Freedom: African Americans in Gold Rush California by Jerry Stanley. Crown Publishers, 2000.

Honor Books

The Amazing Life of Benjamin Franklin by James Cross Giblin. Illustrated by Michael Dooling. Scholastic Press, 2000.

America's Champion Swimmer: Gertrude Ederle by David Adler. Illustrated by Terry Widener. Gulliver Books, 2000.

Michaelangelo by Diane Stanley. HarperCollins, 2000.

Wild and Swampy by Jim Arnosky. HarperCollins, 2000.

†See the November issue of *Language Arts* magazine, published by the National Council of Teachers of English, for an article about the Orbis Pictus winning books for that year.

4.5 *continued*

Recommended Titles

Asteroid Impact by Douglas Henderson. Dial Books for Young Readers, 2000.

Author Talk: Conversations with Judy Blume, Bruce Brooks, Karen Cushman, Russell Freedman, Lee Bennett Hopkins, James Howe, Johanna Hurwitz, E. L. Konigsburg, Lois Lowry, Ann M. Martin, Nicolasa Mohr, Gary Paulsen, Jon Scieszka, Seymour Simon, and Laurence Yep by Leonard S. Marcus. Simon & Schuster, 2000.

Darkness over Denmark: The Danish Resistance and the Rescue of the Jews by Ellen Levine. Holiday House, 2000.

Dragon Bones and Dinosaur Eggs: A Photobiography of Explorer Roy Chapman Andrews by Ann Bausum & George Borup Andrews. National Geographic Society, 2000.

Feathered Dinosaurs by Christopher Sloan. National Geographic Society, 2000.

Frank O. Gehry: Outside In by Sandra Jordan & Jan Greenberg. DK Publishing, 2000.

A Handfull of Dirt by Raymond Bial. Walker & Company, 2000.

Liberty by Lynn Curlee. Atheneum, 2000.

Nazi Germany: The Face of Tyranny by Ted Gottfried. Illustrated by Stephen Alcorn. Twenty-First Century Books, Inc., 2000.

Norman Rockwell: Storyteller With a Brush by Beverly Gherman. Illustrated by Norman Rockwell. Atheneum, 2000.

Only Passing Through: The Story of Sojourner Truth by Anne F. Rockwell. Illustrated by Gregory Christie. Alfred A. Knopf, 2000.

Pick and Shovel Poet: The Journeys of Pascal D'Angelo by Jim Murphy. Clarion Books, 2000.

Voices of the Alamo by Sherry Garland. Illustrated by Ronald Himler. Scholastic Press, 2000.

You Forgot Your Skirt, Amelia Bloomer!: A Very Improper Story by Shana Corey. Illustrated by Chesley McLaren. Scholastic Press, 2000.

2000 Orbis Pictus Award

Through My Eyes by Ruby Bridges. Illustrated with photographs. Scholastic, 1999. Ages 8 and up.

Honor Books

The Top of the World by Steve Jenkins. Houghton Mifflin, 1999. Ages 8 and up.

Mapping the World by Sylvia Johnson. Atheneum, 1999. Ages 9 and up.

The Snake Scientist by Sy Montgomery. Illustrated with photographs by Nic Bishop. Houghton Mifflin, 1999. Ages 9 and up.

At Her Majesty's Request: An African Princess in Victorian England by Walter Dean Myers. Scholastic, 1999. Ages 11 and up.

Recommended Titles

William Shakespeare & the Globe by Aliki. HarperCollins, 1999.

Kids on Strike! by Susan Campbell Bartoletti. Illustrated with photographs. Houghton Mifflin, 1999.

Fire in Their Eyes: Wildfires and the People Who Fight Them by Karen Magnuson Beil. Illustrated with photographs. Harcourt Brace, 1999.

4.5 *continued*

Rushmore by Lynn Curlee. Scholastic, 1999.

The Mystery of the Hieroglyphs: The Story of the Rosetta Stone and the Race to Decipher Egyptian Hieroglyphics by Carol Donoughue. Oxford University Press, 1999.

Babe Didrikson Zaharias: The Making of a Champion by Russell Freedman. Illustrated with photographs. Clarion Books, 1999.

In Search of the Spirit: The Living National Treasures of Japan by Sheila Hamanaka & Ayano Ohmi. Photographs by Sheila Hamanaka. Morrow Junior Books, 1999.

Bound for America: The Forced Migration of Africans to the New World by James Haskins & Kathleen Benson. Paintings by Floyd Cooper. Lothrop, Lee and Shepard, 1999.

Building the Book ***Cathedral*** by David Macaulay. Houghton Mifflin, 1999.

A Child's Book of Art: Discover Great Paintings by Lucy Micklethwait. Dorling Kindersley, 1999.

A Nest of Dinosaurs: The Story of Oviraptor by Mark A. Norell & Lowell Dingus. Doubleday Books for Young Readers, 1999.

Einstein: Visionary Scientist by John B. Severance. Illustrated with photographs. Clarion Books, 1999.

About Reptiles: A Guide for Children by Cathryn Sill. Illustrated by John Sill. Peachtree, 1999.

Tallchief: America's Prima Ballerina by Maria Tallchief with Rosemary Wells. Illustrated by Gary Kelley. Viking, 1999.

1999 Orbis Pictus Award

Shipwreck at the Bottom of the World: The Extraordinary True Story of Shackleton and the ***Endurance*** by Jennifer Armstrong. Crown, 1998. Ages 10 and up.

Honor Books

Black Whiteness: Admiral Byrd Alone in the Antarctic by Robert Burleigh. Illustrated by Walter Lyon Krudop. Atheneum, 1998. Ages 7 and up.

The Fossil Feud: The Rivalry of the First American Dinosaur Hunters written and illustrated by Thom Holmes. Messner, 1998. Ages 8 and up.

Hottest, Coldest, Highest, Deepest by Steve Jenkins. Houghton Mifflin, 1998. Ages 8 and up.

No Pretty Pictures: A Child of War by Anita Lobel. Greenwillow Press. Ages 12 and up.

Recommended Titles

Safari by Robert Bateman. Little, Brown, 1998.

What's the Deal? Jefferson, Napoleon, and the Louisiana Purchase by Rhoda Blumberg. National Geographic Society, 1998.

Samuel Adams: The Father of American Independence by Dennis Brindle Fradin. Clarion Books, 1998.

Martha Graham: A Dancer's Life by Russell Freedman. Clarion Books, 1998.

Looking Back: A Book of Memories by Lois Lowry. Houghton Mifflin, 1998.

Snowflake Bentley by Jacqueline Briggs Martin. Illustrated by Mary Azarian. Houghton Mifflin, 1998.

Light Shining Through the Mist: A Photobiography of Dian Fossey by Tom L. Matthews. National Geographic Society, 1998.

4.5 *continued*

Restless Spirit: The Life and Work of Dorothea Lange by Elizabeth Partridge. Viking, 1998.

Duke Ellington by Andrea Davis Pinkney. Illustrated by Brian Pinkney. Hyperion, 1998.

Discovering the Inca Ice Maiden: My Adventures on Ampato by Johan Reinhard. National Geographic Society, 1998.

On the Home Front: Growing Up in Wartime England by Ann Stalcup. Linnet/Shoestring Press, 1998.

Joan of Arc by Diane Stanley. Morrow Junior Books, 1998.

Frontier Merchants: Lionel and Barron Jacobs and the Jewish Pioneers Who Settled the West by Jerry Stanley. Crown, 1998.

Behind the Mask: The Life of Queen Elizabeth I by Jane Resh Thomas. Clarion Books, 1998.

Pioneer Girl: Growing Up on the Prairie by Andrea Warren. Morrow Junior Books, 1998.

1998 Orbis Pictus Award

An Extraordinary Life: The Story of a Monarch Butterfly by Laurence Pringle. Illustrated with paintings by Bob Marstall. Orchard Books, 1997. Ages 9 and up.

Honor Books

A Tree Is Growing by Arthur Dorros. Illustrated by S. D. Schindler. Scholastic, 1997. Ages 7 and up.

Charles Lindbergh: A Human Hero by James Cross Giblin. Clarion Books, 1997. Ages 10 and up.

Kennedy Assassinated! The World Mourns: A Reporter's Story by Wilborn Hampton. Candlewick, 1997. Ages 10 and up.

Digger: The Tragic Fate of the California Indians from the Missions to the Gold Rush by Jerry Stanley. Crown, 1997. Ages 12 and up.

A Drop of Water: A Book of Science and Wonder by Walter Wick. Illustrated with photographs. Scholastic, 1997. Ages 8 and up.

Recommended Titles

Animal Dads by Sneed B. Collar III. Illustrated by Steve Jenkins. Houghton Mifflin, 1997.

The Dead Sea Scrolls by Ilene Cooper. Illustrated by John Thompson. Morrow Junior Books, 1997.

Fiery Vision: The Life and Death of John Brown by Clinton Cox. Scholastic, 1997.

The Planet Hunters: The Search for Other Worlds by Dennis Brindle Fradin. McElderry/Simon & Schuster, 1997.

Dinosaur Ghosts: The Mystery of Coelophysis by J. Lynett Gillette. Illustrated by Douglas Henderson. Dial Books, 1997.

The Snake Book by Mary Ling & Mary Atkinson. Dorling Kindersley, 1997.

Catching the Fire: Philip Simmons, Blacksmith by Mary E. Lyons. Photographs by Mannie Garcia. Houghton Mifflin, 1997.

The Great Wall by Elizabeth Mann. Illustrated by Alan Witschonke. Mikaya, 1997.

4.5 *continued*

Passage to Freedom: The Sugihara Story by Ken Mochizuki. Illustrated by Dom Lee. Lee & Low, 1997.

A Log's Life by Wendy Pfeffer. Illustrated by Robin Brickman. Simon & Schuster, 1997.

The Brain: Our Nervous System by Seymour Simon. Morrow Junior Books, 1997.

Leon's Story by Leon Walter Tillage. Collage art by Susan L. Roth. Farrar, Straus and Giroux, 1997.

1997 Orbis Pictus Award

Leonardo da Vinci by Diane Stanley. Morrow Junior Books, 1996. Ages 8 and up.

Honor Books

Full Steam Ahead: The Race to Build a Transcontinental Railroad by Rhoda Blumberg. National Geographic Society, 1996. Ages 9 and up.

The Life and Death of Crazy Horse by Russell Freedman. Illustrated with pictographs by Amos Bad Heart Bull. Holiday House, 1996. Ages 10 and up.

One World, Many Religions: The Ways We Worship by Mary Pope Osborne. Knopf, 1996. Ages 10 and up.

Recommended Titles

Nearer Nature by Jim Arnosky. Lothrop, 1996.

A Strange and Distant Shore: Indians of the Great Plains in Exile by Brent Ashabranner. Cobblehill Books, 1996.

Growing Up in Coal Country by Susan Campbell Bartoletti. Houghton Mifflin, 1996.

With Needle and Thread: A Book About Quilts by Raymond Bial. Houghton Mifflin, 1996.

Dia's Story Cloth: The Hmong People's Journey of Freedom by Dia Cha. Stitched by Chue and Nhia Thao Cha. Lee and Low/Denver Museum of Natural History, 1996.

Mandela: From the Life of the South African Statesman by Floyd Cooper. Philomel, 1996.

The Abracadabra Kid: A Writer's Life by Sid Fleischman. Greenwillow Press, 1996.

"We Have Conquered Pain": The Discovery of Anesthesia by Dennis Brindell Fradin. McElderry/Simon & Schuster, 1996.

Who Were the Founding Fathers? Two Hundred Years of Reinventing American History by Steven H. Jaffe. Henry Holt, 1996.

Hurricanes: Earth's Mightiest Storms by Patricia Lauber. Scholastic, 1996.

Free to Dream: The Making of a Poet: Langston Hughes by Audrey Osofsky. Lothrop, Lee and Shepard, 1996.

John Steinbeck by Catherine Reef. Clarion Books, 1996.

Starry Messenger: A Book Depicting the Life of a Famous Scientist, Mathematician, Astronomer, Philosopher, Physician, Galileo Galilei by Peter Sis. Farrar, Straus and Giroux, 1996.

A Desert Scrapbook: Dawn to Dusk in the Sonoran Desert by Virginia Wright-Frierson. Simon & Schuster, 1996.

4.5 *continued*

1996 Orbis Pictus Award

The Great Fire by Jim Murphy. Scholastic, 1995. Ages 10 and up.

Honor Books

Rosie the Riveter: Women Working on the Home Front in World War II by Penny Colman. Crown, 1995. Ages 10 and up.

Dolphin Man: Exploring the World of Dolphins by Laurence Pringle. Photographs by Randall S. Wells and the Dolphin Biology Research Institute. Atheneum, 1995. Ages 9–13.

Recommended Titles

The Underground Railroad by Raymond Bial. Houghton Mifflin, 1995.

In Search of the Grand Canyon by Mary Ann Fraser. Henry Holt, 1995.

Everglades by Jean Craighead George. Paintings by Wendell Minor. HarperCollins, 1995.

When Plague Strikes by James Cross Giblin. HarperCollins, 1995.

Raptor Rescue! by Sylvia Johnson. Photographs by Ron Winch. Dutton, 1995.

Unraveling Fibers by Patricia A. Keeler & Francis X. McCall Jr. Atheneum, 1995.

Listen for the Bus by Patricia McMahon. Photographs by John Godt. Boyds Mill Press, 1995.

Summer Ice: Life Along the Antarctic Peninsula by Bruce McMillan. Houghton Mifflin, 1995.

The Life and Times of the Honeybee by Charles Micucci. Houghton Mifflin, 1995.

Learning from the Dalai Lama by Karen Pandell with Barry Bryant. Photographs by John B. Taylor. Dutton, 1995.

Fire in the Forest by Laurence Pringle. Paintings by Bob Marstall. Atheneum, 1995.

Air by Ken Robbins. Henry Holt, 1995.

The Book of North American Owls by Helen Roney Sattler. Illustrated by Jean Day Zallinger. Clarion Books, 1995.

The Magic of Mozart by Ellen Switzer. Photographs by Costas. Atheneum, 1995.

The Golden City by Neil Waldman. Atheneum, 1995.

1995 Orbis Pictus Award

Safari Beneath the Sea: The Wonder World of the North Pacific Coast by Diane Swanson. Photographs by the Royal British Columbia Museum. Sierra Club Books for Children, 1994. Ages 8–12.

Honor Books

Wildlife Rescue: The Work of Dr. Kathleen Ramsay by Jennifer Owings Dewey. Photographs by Don MacCarter. Boyds Mills Press, 1994. Ages 7 and up.

Kid at Work: Lewis Hine and the Crusade Against Child Labor by Russell Freedman. Illustrated with photographs by Lewis Hine. Clarion Books, 1994. Ages 8–12.

Christmas in the Big House, Christmas in the Quarters by Patricia C. & Frederick L. McKissack. Illustrated by John Thompson. Scholastic, 1994. Ages 8 and up.

4.5 *continued*

Recommended Titles

Ancient Ones: The World of the Old-Growth Douglas Fir by Barbara Bash. Sierra Club Books, 1994.

Vanilla, Chocolate, & Strawberry: The Story of Your Favorite Flavors by Bonnie Busenberg. Lerner, 1994.

Rosie, a Visiting Dog's Story by Stephanie Calmenson. Photographs by Justin Sutcliffe. Clarion Books, 1994.

Take a Look: An Introduction to the Experience of Art by Rosemary Davidson. Viking, 1994.

Animals Who Have Won Our Hearts by Jean Craighead George. Illustrated by Christine Herman Merrill. HarperCollins, 1994.

Lives of Writers: Comedies, Tragedies (and What the Neighbors Thought) by Kathleen Krull. Illustrated by Kathryn Hewitt. Harcourt Brace, 1994.

Fur, Feathers, and Flippers: How Animals Live Where They Do by Patricia Lauber. Scholastic, 1994.

Squish! A Wetland Walk by Nancy Luenn. Atheneum, 1994.

Science to the Rescue by Sandra Markle. Atheneum, 1994.

Unconditional Surrender: U. S. Grant and the Civil War by Albert Marrin. Atheneum, 1994.

Cheap Raw Material by Milton Meltzer. Viking, 1994.

Jazz: My Music, My People by Morgan Monceaux. Knopf, 1994.

Cleopatra by Diane Stanley & Peter Vennema. Morrow, 1994.

I Am an American by Jerry Stanley. Crown, 1994.

1994 Orbis Pictus Award

Across America on an Emigrant Train by Jim Murphy. Illustrated with photographs and prints. Clarion Books, 1992. Ages 10 and up.

Honor Books

To the Top of the World: Adventures with Arctic Wolves by Jim Brandenburg. Edited by Joann Bren Guernsey. Illustrated with photographs. Walker, 1993. All ages.

Making Sense: Animal Perception and Communication by Bruce Brooks. Farrar, Straus and Giroux, 1993. Ages 8–13.

Recommended Titles

Shadows of Night: The Hidden World of the Little Brown Bat by Barbara Bash. Sierra Club Books, 1993.

Whaling Days by Carol Carrick. Woodcuts by David Frampton. Clarion Books, 1993.

Eleanor Roosevelt: A Life of Discovery by Russell Freedman. Clarion Books, 1993.

Be Seated: A Book About Chairs by James Cross Giblin. HarperCollins, 1993.

Many Thousand Gone: African Americans from Slavery to Freedom by Virginia Hamilton. Illustrated by Leo & Diane Dillon. Knopf, 1993.

The Way West: Journal of a Pioneer Woman by Amelia Stewart Knight. Pictures by Michael McCurdy. Simon & Schuster, 1993.

The Great Migration: An American Story by Jacob Lawrence. HarperCollins, 1993.

4.5 *continued*

Lincoln: In His Own Words by Milton Meltzer. Illustrated by Stephen Alcorn. Harcourt Brace, 1993.
Fly! A Brief History of Flight Illustrated by Barry Moser. HarperCollins, 1993.
Seven Candles for Kwanzaa by Andrea Davis Pinkney. Pictures by Brian Pinkney. Dial Books, 1993.
Behind the Secret Window: A Memoir of a Hidden Childhood During World War Two by Nelly S. Toll. Dial Books, 1993.
Anne Frank: Beyond the Diary by Ruud van der Rol & Rian Verhoeven. Viking Press, 1993.

1993 Orbis Pictus Award

Children of the Dust Bowl: The True Story of the School at Weedpatch Camp by Jerry Stanley. Illustrated with photographs. Crown, 1992. Ages 10 and up.

Honor Books

Come Back, Salmon: How a Group of Dedicated Kids Adopted Pigeon Creek and Brought It Back to Life by Molly Cone. Photographs by Sidnee Wheelwright. Sierra Club Books, 1992. All ages.
Talking with Artists by Pat Cummings. Bradbury Press, 1992. All ages.

Recommended Titles

Wings Along the Waterway by Mary Barrett Brown. Orchard Books, 1992.
An Indian Winter by Russell Freedman. Paintings and drawings by Karl Bodmer. Holiday House, 1992.
The Great St. Lawrence Seaway by Gail Gibbons. Morrow Junior Books, 1992.
A Twilight Struggle: The Life of John Fitzgerald Kennedy by Barbara Harrison & Daniel Terris. Lothrop, Lee and Shepard, 1992.
The Tainos: The People Who Welcomed Columbus by Francine Jacobs. Putnam, 1992.
Hopscotch Around the World by Mary D. Lankford. Illustrated by Karen Milone. Morrow Junior Books, 1992.
Surtsey: The Newest Place on Earth by Kathryn Lasky. Photographs by Christopher Knight. Hyperion, 1992.
The Amazing Potato by Milton Meltzer. HarperCollins, 1992.
The Long Road to Gettysburg by Jim Murphy. Clarion Books, 1992.
Antarctica by Laurence Pringle. Simon & Schuster, 1992.
Bard of Avon: The Story of William Shakespeare by Diane Stanley & Peter Vennema. Morrow Junior Books, 1992.

1992 Orbis Pictus Award

Flight: The Journey of Charles Lindberg by Robert Burleigh. Illustrated by Mike Wimmer. Philomel Books, 1991. Ages 5 and up.

Honor Books

Prairie Visions: The Life and Times of Solomon Butcher by Pam Conrad. Period photographs by Solomon Butcher. HarperCollins, 1991. Ages 10 and up.
Now Is Your Time! The African-American Struggle for Freedom by Walter Dean Myers. Illustrated with period photographs. Harper Trophy, 1991. Ages 10 and up.

4.5 *continued*

Recommended Titles

Voyager to the Planets by Necia H. Apfel. Clarion Books, 1991.

The Remarkable Voyages of Captain Cook by Rhoda Blumberg. Bradbury Press, 1991.

The Wright Brothers: How They Invented the Airplane by Russell Freedman. Original photographs by Wilbur and Orville Wright. Holiday House, 1991.

Bully for You, Teddy Roosevelt! by Jean Fritz. Illustrated by Mike Wimmer. G. P. Putnam's, 1991.

Dawn to Dusk in the Galápagos by Rita Goldman Gelman. Photographs by Tui De Roy. Little, Brown, 1991.

The Painter's Eye: Learning to Look at Contemporary American Art by Jan Greenberg & Sandra Jordan. Delacorte Press, 1991.

Pueblo Storyteller by Diane Hoyt-Goldsmith. Holiday House, 1991.

Pueblo Boy: Growing Up in Two Worlds by Marcia Keegan. Cobblehill Books, 1991.

Summer of Fire: Yellowstone 1988 by Patricia Lauber. Orchard Books, 1991.

The Discovery of the Americas by Betsy Maestro & Giulio Maestro. Lothrop, Lee and Shepard, 1991.

Batman: Exploring the World of Bats by Laurence Pringle. Photographs by Merlin Tuttle. Charles Scribner's Sons, 1991.

Appalachia: The Voices of Sleeping Birds by Cynthia Rylant. Illustrated by Barry Moser. Harcourt, Brace, Jovanovich, 1991.

N. C. Wyeth's Pilgrims by Robert SanSouci. Chronicle Books, 1991.

Earthquakes by Seymour Simon. Morrow Junior Books, 1991.

A Young Painter: The Life and Paintings of Wang Yani—China's Extraordinary Young Artist by Zhensun Zheng & Alice Low. Scholastic, 1991.

1991 Orbis Pictus Award

Franklin Delano Roosevelt by Russell Freedman. Clarion Books, 1990. Ages 8 and up.

Honor Book

Arctic Memories written and illustrated by Normee Ekoomiak. Henry Holt, 1990. Ages 9–12.

Recommended Titles

Mom Can't See Me by Sally Hobart Alexander. Photographs by George Ancona. Macmillan, 1990.

The Magic School Bus Lost in the Solar System by Joanna Cole. Illustrated by Bruce Degen. Scholastic, 1990.

The Clover and the Bee by Anne Ophelia Dowden. Crowell, 1990.

The Oregon Trail by Leonard Everett Fisher. Holiday House, 1990.

The Riddle of the Rosetta Stone by James Cross Giblin. Crowell, 1990.

Totem Pole by Diane Hoyt-Goldsmith. Photographs by Lawrence Migdale. Holiday House, 1990.

Dinosaur Dig by Kathryn Lasky. Photographs by Christopher G. Knight. Morrow Junior Books, 1990.

Wolves by R. D. Lawrence. Sierra Club/Little, Brown, 1990.

Christopher Columbus by Nancy Smiler Levinson. Lodestar/Dutton, 1990.

4.5 *continued*

Columbus and the World Around Him by Milton Meltzer. Franklin Watts, 1990.
My Hiroshima by Junko Morimoto. Viking, 1990.
The Many Lives of Benjamin Franklin by Mary Pope Osborne. Dial Books for Young Readers, 1990.
Wood-Song by Gary Paulsen. Bradbury, 1990.
Giraffes by Helen Roney Sattler. Illustrated by Christopher Santoro. Lothrop, Lee and Shepard, 1990.
Oceans by Seymour Simon. Morrow Junior Books, 1990.
Good Queen Bess by Diane Stanley & Peter Vennema. Illustrated by Diane Stanley. Four Winds Press, 1990.

1990 Orbis Pictus Award

The Great Little Madison by Jean Fritz. Illustrated with prints and engravings. G. P. Putnam's Sons, 1989. Ages 10 and up.

Honor Books

The Great American Gold Rush by Rhoda Blumberg. Illustrated with period photographs. Bradbury Press, 1989. Ages 10 and up.
The News About Dinosaurs by Patricia Lauber. Illustrated by various artists. Bradbury Press, 1989. Ages 8–12.

Recommended Titles

We Remember the Holocaust by David Adler. Henry Holt, 1989.
The King's Day: Louis XIV of France by Aliki. Crowell, 1989.
The American Family Farm by George Ancona (Text by Joan Anderson). Harcourt, Brace, Jovanovich, 1989.
Operation Grizzly Bear by Marian Calabro. Four Winds Press, 1989.
Illuminations by Jonathan Hunt. Bradbury, 1989.
Once Upon a Horse: A History of Horses and How They Shaped History by Suzanne Jurmain. Lothrop, 1989.
Polar Bear Cubs by Downs Matthews. Photographs by Dan Guravich. Simon & Schuster, 1989.
Voices from the Civil War: A Documentary History of the Great American Conflict by Milton Meltzer. Crowell, 1989.
Wild Turkey, Tame Turkey by Dorothy Hinshaw Patent. Photographs by William Muñoz. Clarion, 1989.
Bill Peet: An Autobiography by Bill Peet. Houghton Mifflin, 1989.
Inspirations: Stories about Women Artists by Leslie Sill. Albert Whitman, 1989.
Whales by Seymour Simon. Crowell, 1989.
Panama Canal: Gateway to the World by Judith St. George. Putnam, 1989.

Source: Adapted from *The Best in Children's Nonfiction Reading, Writing, & Teaching Orbis Pictus Award Books*, edited by Myra Zarnowski, Richard M. Kerper, and Julie M. Jensen, published in 2001 by the National Council of Teachers of English in Urbana, Illinois.

4.6 Coretta Scott King Award and Honor Books

The Coretta Scott King Award was established in 1969 by two librarians, Mabel McKissick and Glyndon Greer, and a publisher, John Carroll. It was first presented in 1970 to commemorate the work of Martin Luther King Jr., and honor his wife, Coretta. It is given annually to an African-American author whose books are inspirational and pay tribute to an understanding of the African-American culture. In 1974, a separate award was added for illustrators. For additional information, go to www.ala.org/srrt/csking/.

2003 **Author Award:**

Bronx Masquerade by Nikki Grimes (Dial Books for Young Readers)

Honor Books:

The Red Rose Box by Brenda Woods (G. P. Putnam & Sons)

Talkin' About Bessie: The Story of Aviator Elizabeth Coleman by Nikki Grimes (Orchard Books/Scholastic)

Illustrator Award:

Talkin' About Bessie: The Story of Aviator Elizabeth Coleman, E. B. Lewis; written by Nikki Grimes (Orchard Books/Scholastic)

Honor Books:

Rap a Tap Tap: Here's Bojangles—Think of That by Leo and Diane Dillon (Blue Sky Press/Scholastic)

Visiting Langston by Bryan Collier (Henry Holt)

2002 **Author Award:**

The Land by Mildred D. Taylor (Phyllis Fogelman/Penguin Putnam)

Honor Books:

Money Hungry by Sharon G. Flake (Jump at the Sun/Hyperion)

Carver: A Life in Poems by Marilyn Nelson (Front Street)

Illustrator Award:

Goin' Someplace Special, Jerry Pinkney; written by Patricia McKissack (Anne Schwartz Book/Atheneum)

Honor Book:

Martin's Big Words, Bryan Collier; written by Doreen Rappoport (Jump at the Sun/Hyperion)

2001 **Author Award:**

Miracle's Boys by Jacqueline Woodson (G. P. Putnam's Sons)

Honor Book:

Let It Shine! Stories of Black Women Freedom Fighters by Andrea Davis Pinkney, illustrated by Stephen Alcorn (Gulliver Books, Harcourt)

Illustrator Award:

Uptown by Bryan Collier (Henry Holt)

4.6 ***continued***

Honor Books

Freedom River by Bryan Collier (Jump at the Sun/Hyperion)
Only Passing Through: The Story of Sojourner Truth, R. Gregory Christie; text by Anne Rockwell (Random House)
Virgie Goes to School with Us Boys, E. B. Lewis; text by Elizabeth Fitzgerald Howard (Simon & Schuster)

2000 Author Award:

Bud, Not Buddy by Christopher Paul Curtis (Delacorte)

Honor Books:

Francie by Karen English (Farrar, Straus and Giroux)
Black Hands, White Sails: The Story of African-American Whalers by Patricia C. and Frederick L. McKissack (Scholastic Press)
Monster by Walter Dean Myers (HarperCollins)

Illustrator Award:

In the Time of the Drums, Brian Pinkney; text by Kim L. Siegelson (Jump at the Sun/Hyperion Books for Children)

Honor Books:

My Rows and Piles of Coins, E. B. Lewis; text by Tololwa M. Mollel (Clarion Books)
Black Cat by Christopher Myers (Scholastic)

1999 Author Award:

Heaven by Angela Johnson (Simon & Schuster)

Honor Books:

Jazmin's Notebook by Nikki Grimes (Dial Books)
Breaking Ground, Breaking Silence: The Story of New York's African Burial Ground by Joyce Hansen and Gary McGowan (Henry Holt and Company)
The Other Side: Shorter Poems by Angela Johnson (Orchard Books)

Illustrator Award:

I see the rhythm, Michele Wood; text by Toyomi Igus (Children's Book Press)

Honor Books:

I Have Heard of a Land, Floyd Cooper; text by Joyce Carol Thomas (Joanna Cotler Books/HarperCollins)
The Bat Boy and His Violin, E. B. Lewis; text by Gavin Curtis (Simon & Schuster)
Duke Ellington: The Piano Prince and His Orchestra, Brian Pinkney; text by Andrea Davis Pinkney (Hyperion Books for Children)

1998 Author Award:

Forged by Fire by Sharon M. Draper (Atheneum)

4.6 *continued*

Honor Books:

Bayard Rustin: Behind the Scenes of the Civil Rights Movement by James Haskins (Hyperion)

I Thought My Soul Would Rise and Fly: The Diary of Patsy, a Freed Girl by Joyce Hansen (Scholastic)

Illustrator Award:

In Daddy's Arms I Am Tall: African Americans Celebrating Fathers, Javaka Steptoe; text by Alan Schroeder (Lee & Low)

Honor Books:

Ashley Bryan's ABC of African American Poetry by Ashley Bryan (Jean Karl/Atheneum)

Harlem, Christopher Myers; text by Walter Dean Myers (Scholastic)

The Hunterman and the Crocodile by Baba Wagué Diakité (Scholastic)

1997

Author Award:

Slam by Walter Dean Myers (Scholastic)

Honor Book:

Rebels Against Slavery: American Slave Revolts by Patricia C. & Frederick L. McKissack (Scholastic)

Illustrator Award:

Minty: A Story of Young Harriet Tubman, Jerry Pinkney; text by Alan Schroeder (Dial Books for Young Readers)

Honor Books:

The Palm of My Heart: Poetry by African American Children, Gregorie Christie; edited by Davida Adedjouma (Lee & Low)

Running the Road to ABC, Reynold Ruffins; text by Denize Lauture (Simon & Schuster Books for Young Readers)

Neeny Coming, Neeny Going, Synthia Saint James; text by Karen English (Bridgewater Books)

1996

Author Award:

Her Stories by Virginia Hamilton (Scholastic/Blue Sky Press)

Honor Books:

The Watsons Go to Birmingham—1963 by Christopher Paul Curtis (Delacorte)

Like Sisters on the Homefront by Rita Williams-Garcia (Delacorte)

From the Notebooks of Melanin Sun by Jacqueline Woodson (Scholastic/Blue Sky Press)

Illustrator Award:

The Middle Passage: White Ships Black Cargo by Tom Feelings (Dial Books for Young Readers)

4.6 ***continued***

Honor Books:

Her Stories, Leo & Diane Dillon; text by Virginia Hamilton (Scholastic/Blue Sky Press)
The Faithful Friend, Brian Pinkney; text by Robert SanSouci (Simon & Schuster Books for Young Readers)

1995 Author Award:

Christmas in the Big House, Christmas in the Quarters by Patricia C. & Frederick L. McKissack (Scholastic)

Honor Books:

The Captive by Joyce Hansen (Scholastic)
I Hadn't Meant to Tell You This by Jacqueline Woodson (Delacorte)
Black Diamond: Story of the Negro Baseball League by Patricia C. & Frederick L. McKissack (Scholastic)

Illustrator Award:

The Creation, James Ransome; text by James Weldon Johnson (Holiday House)

Honor Books:

The Singing Man, Terea Shaffer; text by Angela Shelf Medearis (Holiday House)
Meet Danitra Brown, Floyd Cooper; text by Nikki Grimes (Lothrop, Lee and Shepard)

1994 Author Award:

Toning the Sweep by Angela Johnson (Orchard)

Honor Books:

Brown Honey in Broom Wheat Tea by Joyce Carol Thomas; illustrated by Floyd Cooper (HarperCollins)
Malcolm X: By Any Means Necessary by Walter Dean Myers (Scholastic)

Illustrator Award:

Soul Looks Back in Wonder, Tom Feelings; text edited by Phyllis Fogelman (Dial Books for Young Readers)

Honor Books:

Brown Honey in Broom Wheat Tea, Floyd Cooper; text by Joyce Carol Thomas (HarperCollins)
Uncle Jed's Barbershop, James Ransome; text by Margaree King Mitchell (Simon & Schuster)

1993 Author Award:

Dark Thirty: Southern Tales of the Supernatural by Patricia C. McKissack (Knopf)

Honor Books:

Mississippi Challenge by Mildred Pitts Walter (Bradbury)
Sojourner Truth: Ain't I a Woman? by Patricia C. & Frederick L. McKissack (Scholastic)
Somewhere in the Darkness by Walter Dean Myers (Scholastic)

4.6 *continued*

Illustrator Award:

The Origin of Life on Earth: An African Creation Myth, Kathleen Atkins Wilson; retold by David A. Anderson (Sights)

Honor Books:

Little Eight John, Wil Clay; text by Jan Wahl (Lodestar)
Sukey and the Mermaid, Brian Pinkney; text by Robert SanSouci (Four Winds)
Working Cotton, Carole Byard; text by Sherley Anne Williams (Harcourt)

1992 Author Award:

Now Is Your Time: The African American Struggle for Freedom by Walter Dean Myers (HarperCollins)

Honor Book:

Night on Neighborhood Street by Eloise Greenfield; illustrated by Jan Spivey Gilchrist (Dial)

Illustrator Award:

Tar Beach by Faith Ringgold (Crown)

Honor Books:

All Night, All Day: A Child's First Book of African American Spirituals, illustrated and selected by Ashley Bryan (Atheneum)
Night on Neighborhood Street, Jan Spivey Gilchrist; text by Eloise Greenfield (Dial)

1991 Author Award:

The Road to Memphis by Mildred D. Taylor (Dial)

Honor Books:

Black Dance in America by James Haskins (Crowell)
When I Am Old With You by Angela Johnson (Orchard)

Illustrator Award:

Aida, Leo & Diane Dillon; text by Leontyne Price (Harcourt)

1990 Author Award:

A Long Hard Journey: The Story of the Pullman Porter by Patricia C. & Frederick L. McKissack (Walker)

Honor Books:

Nathaniel Talking by Eloise Greenfield; illustrated by Jan Spivey Gilchrist (Black Butterfly)
The Bells of Christmas by Virginia Hamilton (Harcourt)
Martin Luther King, Jr., and the Freedom Movement by Lillie Patterson (Facts on File)

Illustrator Award:

Nathaniel Talking, Jan Spivey Gilchrist; text by Eloise Greenfield (Black Butterfly)

4.6 *continued*

Honor Book:
The Talking Eggs, Jerry Pinkney; text by Robert SanSouci (Dial)

1989 Author Award:

Fallen Angels by Walter Dean Myers (Scholastic)

Honor Books:
A Thief in the Village and Other Stories by James Berry (Orchard)
Anthony Burns: The Defeat and Triumph of a Fugitive Slave by Virginia Hamilton (Knopf)

Illustrator Award:

Mirandy and Brother Wind, Jerry Pinkney; text by Patricia C. McKissack (Knopf)

Honor Books:
Under the Sunday Tree, Amos Ferguson; text by Eloise Greenfield (Harper)
Storm in the Night, Pat Cummings; text by Mary Stolz (Harper)

1988 Author Award:

The Friendship by Mildred L. Taylor (Dial)

Honor Books:
An Enchanted Hair Tale by Alexis De Veaux (Harper)
The Tales of Uncle Remus: The Adventures of Brer Rabbit by Julius Lester (Dial)

Illustrator Award:

Mufaro's Beautiful Daughters: An African Tale by John Steptoe (Lothrop)

Honor Books:
What a Morning! The Christmas Story in Black Spirituals, Ashley Bryan; selected by John Langstaff (Macmillan)
The Invisible Hunters: A Legend from the Miskito Indians of Nicaragua, Joe Sam; compiled by Harriet Rohmer et al. (Children's Press)

1987 Author Award:

Justin and the Best Biscuits in the World by Mildred Pitts Walter (Lothrop)

Honor Books:
Lion and the Ostrich Chicks and Other African Folk Tales by Ashley Bryan (Atheneum)
Which Way Freedom by Joyce Hansen (Walker)

Illustrator Award:

Half a Moon and One Whole Star, Jerry Pinkney; text by Crescent Dragonwagon (Macmillan)

Honor Books
Lion and the Ostrich Chicks and Other African Folk Tales by Ashley Bryan (Atheneum)
C.L.O.U.D.S. by Pat Cummings (Lothrop)

4.6 *continued*

1986 Author Award:

The People Could Fly: American Black Folktales by Virginia Hamilton; illustrated by Leo & Diane Dillon (Knopf)

Honor Books:
Junius Over Far by Virginia Hamilton (Harper)
Trouble's Child by Mildred Pitts Walter (Lothrop)

Illustrator Award:

The Patchwork Quilt, Jerry Pinkney; text by Valerie Flournoy (Dial)

Honor Book:
The People Could Fly: American Black Folktales, Leo & Diane Dillon; text by Virginia Hamilton (Knopf)

1985 Author Award:

Motown and Didi by Walter Dean Myers (Viking)

Honor Books:
Circle of Gold by Candy Dawson Boyd (Apple/Scholastic)
A Little Love by Virginia Hamilton (Philomel)

Illustrator Award:

No award

1984 Author Award:

Everett Anderson's Good-bye by Lucille Clifton (Holt)

Special Citation:

The Words of Martin Luther King, Jr., compiled by Coretta Scott King (Newmarket Press)

Honor Books:
The Magical Adventures of Pretty Pearl by Virginia Hamilton (Harper)
Lena Horne by James Haskins (Coward-McCann)
Bright Shadow by Joyce Carol Thomas (Avon)
Because We Are by Mildred Pitts Walter (William Morrow)

Illustrator Award:

My Mama Needs Me, Pat Cummings; text by Mildred Pitts Walter (Lothrop)

1983 Author Award:

Sweet Whispers, Brother Rush by Virginia Hamilton (Philomel)

Honor Book:
This Strange New Feeling by Julius Lester (Dial)

4.6 *continued*

Illustrator Award

Black Child by Peter Mugabane (Knopf)

Honor Books:
All the Colors of the Race, John Steptoe; text by Arnold Adoff (Lothrop)
I'm Going to Sing: Black American Spirituals, Ashley Bryan (Atheneum)
Just Us Women, Pat Cummings; text by Jeanette Caines (Harper)

1982 Author Award:

Let the Circle Be Unbroken by Mildred D. Taylor (Dial)

Honor Books:
Rainbow Jordan by Alice Childress (Coward-McCann)
Lou in the Limelight by Kristin Hunter (Scribner)
Mary: An Autobiography by Mary E. Mebane (Viking)

Illustrator Award:

Mother Crocodile; an Uncle Amadou Tale from Senegal, John Steptoe; text by Rosa Guy (Delacorte)

Honor Book:
Daydreamers, Tom Feelings; text by Eloise Greenfield (Dial)

1981 Author Award:

This Life by Sidney Poitier (Knopf)

Honor Book:
Don't Explain: A Song of Billie Holiday by Alexis De Veaux (Harper)

Illustrator Award:

Beat the Story Drum, Pum-Pum by Ashley Bryan (Atheneum)

Honor Books:
Grandmama's Joy, Carole Byard; text by Eloise Greenfield (Collins)
Count on Your Fingers African Style, Jerry Pinkney; text by Claudia Zaslavsky (Crowell)

1980 Author Award:

The Young Landlords by Walter Dean Myers (Viking)

Honor Books:
Movin' Up by Berry Gordy (Harper)
Childtimes: A Three-Generation Memoir by Eloise Greenfield and Lessie Jones Little (Harper)
Andrew Young: Young Man With a Mission by James Haskins (Lothrop)
James Van Der Zee: The Picture Takin' Man by James Haskins (Dodd)
Let the Lion Eat Straw by Ellease Southerland (Scribner)

Illustrator Award:

Cornrows, Carole Byard; text by Camille Yarborough (Coward-McCann)

4.6 *continued*

1979 **Author Award:**

Escape to Freedom by Ossie Davis (Viking)

Honor Books:

Benjamin Banneker by Lillie Patterson (Abingdon)
I Have a Sister, My Sister Is Deaf by Jeanne W. Peterson (Harper)
Justice and Her Brothers by Virginia Hamilton (Greenwillow)
Skates of Uncle Richard by Carol Fenner (Random)

Illustrator Award:

Something on My Mind, Tom Feelings; text by Nikki Grimes (Dial)

1978 **Author Award:**

Africa Dream by Eloise Greenfield; illustrated by Carole Byard (Crowell)

Honor Books:

The Days When the Animals Talked: Black Folk Tales and How They Came to Be by William J. Faulkner (Follett)
Marvin and Tige by Frankcina Glass (St. Martin's)
Mary McCleod Bethune by Eloise Greenfield (Crowell)
Barbara Jordan by James Haskins (Dial)
Coretta Scott King by Lillie Patterson (Garrard)
Portia: The Life of Portia Washington Pittman, the Daughter of Booker T. Washington by Ruth Ann Stewart (Doubleday)

Illustrator Award:

Africa Dream, Carole Byard; text by Eloise Greenfield (Crowell)

1977 **Author Award:**

The Story of Stevie Wonder by James Haskins (Lothrop)

Illustrator Award:

No award

1976 **Author Award:**

Duey's Tale by Pearl Bailey (Harcourt)

Illustrator Award:

No award

1975 **Author Award:**

The Legend of Africana by Dorothy Robinson (Johnson Publishing)

Illustrator Award:

No award

4.6 *continued*

1974 Author Award:

Ray Charles by Sharon Bell Mathis; illustrated by George Ford (Crowell)

Illustrator Award:

Ray Charles, George Ford; text by Sharon Bell Mathis (Crowell)

1973 Author Award:

I Never Had It Made: The Autobiography of Jackie Robinson, as told to Alfred Duckett (Putnam)

1972 Author Award:

17 Black Artists by Elton C. Fax (Dodd)

1971 Author Award:

Black Troubador: Langston Hughes by Charlemae Rollins (Rand McNally)

1970 Author Award

Martin Luther King, Jr.: Man of Peace by Lillie Patterson (Garrard)

Source: List 4.6 is used with the permission of the American Library Association.

4.7 Christopher Awards

Established in 1949, the Christophers' Books for Young People Awards are presented each February. To be eligible for a Christopher Award during their year of release, books "must affirm the highest values of the human spirit." For a complete list of winners, go to www.christophers.org. The list below gives award winners in recent years, along with age levels.

2002

Kiss Good Night, Amy Hest (preschool)
Beatrice's Goat, Page McBrier (6–8)
Love That Dog, Sharon Creech (8–10)
Uncle Daddy, Ralph Fletcher (10–12)
Soldier X, Don Wulffson (Young Adult)
Witness, Karen Hesse (Young Adult)

2001

How Do Dinosaurs Say Good-Night?, Jane Yolen (6–8)
The Mousery, Charlotte Pomerantz (9–10)
The Yellow Star, Carmen Agra Deedy (11–12)
Hope Was Here, Joan Bauer (12+)
The Wanderer, Sharon Creech (Young Adult)

2000

I Love You, Blue Kangaroo!, Emma Chichester Clark (4–6)
Good Luck, Mrs. K!, Louise Borden (7–9)
A Symphony of Whales, Steve Schuch (10–12)
Stop Pretending: What Happened When My Big Sister Went Crazy, Sonya Sones (12+)
Grandad's Prayers of the Earth, Douglas Wood (all ages)

1999

Raising Dragons, Jerdine Nolen (6–8)
The Summer My Father Was Ten, Pat Brisson (8–10)
Mary on Horseback: Three Mountain Stories, Rosemary Wells (10–12)
Shipwreck Season, Donna Hill (12+)
Holes, Louis Sachar (Young Adult)

1998

Milo and the Magical Stones, Marcus Pfister (5–8)
The Gardener, Sarah Stewart (5–8)
When Jessie Came Across the Sea, Amy Hest (8–10)
The Silver Balloon, Susan Bonners (10–12)
I Have Lived a Thousand Years: Growing Up in the Holocaust, Livia Bitton-Jackson (Young Adult)

1997

The Log Cabin Quilt, Ellen Howard (4–6)
Minty: A Story of Young Harriet Tubman, Alan Schroeder, pictures by Jerry Pinkney (6–9)

4.7 *continued*

Frindle, Andrew Clements, pictures by Brian Selznick (10–12)
Glennis, Before and After, Patricia Calvert (12+)
Irrepressible Spirit: Conversations with Human Rights Activitsts, Susan Kuklin (12+)

1996

The Christmas Miracle of Jonathan Toomey, Susan Wojciechowski, illustrated by P. J. Lynch (6–9)
Been to Yesterdays: Poems of a Life, Lee Bennett Hopkins, illustrated by Charlene Rendeiro (10–12)
Parallel Journeys, Eleanor Ayer, with Helen Waterford and Alfons Heck (Young Adult)

1995

I'll See You When the Moon Is Full, Susi Gregg Fowler, pictures by Jim Fowler (4–6)
Prize in the Snow, Bill Easterling, illustrations by Mary Beth Owens (6–8)
The Ledgerbook of Thomas Blue Eagle, Jewel H. Grutman & Gay Matthaei, illustrations by Adam Cvijanovic (8–12)
Taking Hold: My Journey Into Blindness, Sally Hobart Alexander (12+)

1994

The Crystal Ball, Gerda Marie Scheidl, illustrated by Nathalie Duroussy, translated by Rosemary Lanning (5–8)
It's Our World, Too! Stories of Young People Whe Are Making a Difference, Phillip Hoose (10+)
Anne Frank: Beyond the Diary, Ruud van der Rol & Rian Verhoeven, translated by Tony Langham & Plym Peters (Young Adult)

1993

The Rainbow Fish, Marcus Pfister, translated by J. Alison James (5–8)
Rosie & the Yellow Ribbon, Paula DePaolo, pictures by Janet Wolf (6–8)
Letters from Rifka, Karen Hesse (8–12)
Mississippi Challenge, Mildred Pitts Walter (12+)

1992

Somebody Loves You, Mr. Hatch, Eileen Spinelli, pictures by Paul Yalowitz (4–6)
Stephen's Feast, Jean Richardson, illustrated by Alice Englander (6–8)
The Gold Coin, Alma Flor Ada, illustrated by Neil Waldman, translated by Bernice Randall (8–10)
The Star Fisher, Laurence Yep (10+)
Where Does God Live? Questions and Answers for Parents and Children, Rabbi Marc Gellman & Monsignor Thomas Hartman, illustrated by William Zdinak (all ages)

1991

Mississippi Bridge, Mildred D. Taylor, illustrated by Max Ginsburg (9–12)
Paul Revere's Ride, Henry Wadsworth Longfellow's poem, illustrated by Ted Rand (all ages)

4.8 The Pura Belpré Award

Established in 1996, this award commemorates the work of Pura Belpré, a children's librarian, storyteller, and author who enriched the lives of children everywhere by preserving and disseminating Puerto Rican folklore. The award is given every two years to the Latino/Latina writer and illustrator whose outstanding work of children's literature best celebrates and affirms the Latino cultural experience.

2002 Author:

Pam Munoz Ryan, *Esperanza Rising* (Scholastic Press, 2000)

Illustrator:

Susan Guevara, *Chato and the Party Animals*, written by Gary Soto (Putnam, 2000)

Honor Books:

Authors:
Francisco Jiménez, *Breaking Through* (Houghton Mifflin, 2001)
Francisco X. Alarcón, *Iguanas in the Snow* (Children's Book Press, 2000)

Illustrator:
Joe Cepeda, *Juan Bobo Goes to Work*, retold by Marisa Montes (HarperCollins, 2000)

2000 Author:

Alma Flor Ada, *Under the Royal Palms: A Childhood in Cuba* (Atheneum, 1998)

Illustrator:

Carmen Lomas Garza, *Magic Windows* (Children's Book Press, 1999)

Honor Books:

Authors:
Francisco X. Alarcón, *From the Bellybutton of the Moon and Other Summer Poems/Del Ombligo de la Luna y Otro Poemas de Verano*, illustrated by Maya Christina Gonzalez (Children's Book Press, 1998)
Juan Felipe Herrera, *Laughing Out Loud, I Fly: Poems in English and Spanish*, illustrated by Karen Barbour (HarperCollins, 1998)

Illustrators:
George Ancona, *Barrio: José's Neighborhood* (Harcourt Brace, 1998)
Felipe Davalos, *The Secret Stars*, written by Joseph Slate (Marshall Cavendish, 1998)
Amelia Lau Carling, *Mama & Papa Have a Store* (Dial Books, 1998)

1998 Author:

Victor Martinez, *Parrot in the Oven: mi vida* (HarperCollins, 1996)

Illustrator:

Stephanie Garcia, *Snapshots from the Wedding*, written by Gary Soto (Putnam, 1997)

4.8 *continued*

Honor Books:

Authors:

Francisco Alarcón, *Laughing Tomatoes and Other Spring Poems/Jitomates Risuenos y otros poemas de primavera*, illustrated by Maya Christina Gonzalez (Children's Book Press, 1997)

Floyd Martinez, *Spirits of the High Mesa* (Arte Público Press, 1997)

Illustrators:

Carmen Lomas Garza, *In My Family/En mi familia* (Children's Book Press, 1996)

Enrique O. Sánchez, *The Golden Flower: a Taino Myth from Puerto Rico*, retold by Nina Jaffe (Simon & Schuster, 1996)

Simón Silva, *Gathering the Sun: an Alphabet in Spanish and English*, text by Alma Flor Ada; English translation by Rosa Zubizaretta (Lothrop, 1997)

1996 **Author:**

Judith Ortiz Cofer, *An Island Like You: Stories of the Barrio* (Orchard, 1995)

Illustrator:

Susan Guevara, *Chato's Kitchen*, written by Gary Soto (Putnam, 1995)

Honor Books:

Authors:

Lucía González, *The Bossy Gallito/El Gallo de Bodas: A Traditional Cuban Folktale*, illustrated by Lulu Delacre (Scholastic, 1994)

Gary Soto, *Baseball in April and Other Stories* (Harcourt, 1994)

Illustrators:

George Ancona, *Pablo Remembers: The Fiesta of the Day of the Dead* (Lothrop, 1993) Also in Spanish: *Pablo Recuerda: La Fiesta de Día de los Muertos* (Lothrop, 1993)

Lulu Delacre, *The Bossy Gallito/El Gallo de Bodas: A Traditional Cuban Folktale*, retold by Lucía González (Scholastic, 1994)

Carmen Lomas Garza, *Family Pictures/Cuadros de Familia*. Spanish language text by Rosalma Zubizaretta (Children's Book Press, 1990)

Source: List 4.8 is used with the permission of the American Library Association.

4.9 The Regina Medal

Established in 1959, the Regina Medal is awarded each year by the Catholic Library Association for an individual's continued distinguished contribution to children's literature. It is not a religiously-based award. For more information, go to the organization's Web site: www.cathla.org/regina.html.

1959 Eleanor Farjeon
1960 Anne Carroll Moore
1961 Padraic Colum
1962 Frederic G. Melcher
1963 Ann Nolan Clark
1964 May Hill Arbuthnot
1965 Ruth Sawyer Durand
1966 Leo Politi
1967 Bertha Mahony Miller
1968 Marguerite de Angeli
1969 Lois Lenski
1970 Ingri & Edgar Parin d'Aulaire
1971 Tasha Tudor
1972 Meindert DeJong
1973 Frances Clarke Sayers
1974 Robert McCloskey
1975 May McNeer & Lynd Ward
1976 Virginia Haviland
1977 Marcia Brown
1978 Scott O'Dell
1979 Morton Schindel
1980 Beverly Cleary
1981 Augusta Baker
1982 Theodor (Dr. Seuss) Geisel
1983 Thomas Anthony dePaola (Tomie dePaola)
1984 Madeleine L'Engle
1985 Jean Fritz
1986 Lloyd Alexander
1987 Betsy Byars
1988 Katherine Paterson
1989 Steven Kellogg
1990 Virginia Hamilton
1991 Leonard Everett Fisher
1992 Jane Yolen
1993 Chris Van Allsburg
1994 Lois Lowry
1995 Gary Paulsen
1996 Russell Freedman
1997 Eve Bunting
1998 Patricia C. & Frederick L. McKissack
1999 Eric Carle
2000 Milton Meltzer
2001 E. L. Konigsburg
2002 Charlotte Zolotow
2003 Jean Craighead George

4.10 The Sydney Taylor Book Awards

The Sydney Taylor Book Award was established in honor of the author of the classic *All of a Kind Family* series by her husband, Ralph Taylor, to encourage the publication of outstanding books of positive Jewish content for children.

The seal of the Association is awarded annually to the authors of the most distinguished contributions to Jewish children's literature published in the preceding year. The first Sydney Taylor Book Award was given in 1968. In most years since then, two awards have been given, one for younger readers and one for older readers. Honor books are also cited.

Sydney Taylor Body-of-Work Awards have been granted periodically since 1971. Winners include Isaac Bashevis Singer, Marilyn Hirsh, Barbara Cohen, and Barbara Diamond Goldin. For more information, go to www.nypl.org/branch/kids.

2001 Catherine Reef, *Sigmund Freud: Pioneer of the Mind* (Clarion)
Elsa Okon Rael, *Rivka's First Thanksgiving*, illustrated by Maryann Kovalski (Margaret K. McElderry/Simon & Schuster)

2000 Ida Vos, *The Key Is Lost*, translated by Therese Edelstein (HarperCollins)
Eric A. Kimmel, *Gershon's Monster: a Story for the Jewish New Year*, illustrated by Jon J. Muth (Scholastic)

1999 Sybil Rosen, *Speed of Light* (Atheneum Books for Young Readers. An Anne Schwartz Book)
Maxine Rose Schur, *The Peddler's Gift*, illustrated by Kimberly Bulcken Root (Dial Books for Young Readers)

1998 Marci Stillerman, *Nine Spoons*, illustrated by Pesach Gerber (HaChai Publishers)
Donna Jo Napoli, *Stones in Water* (Dutton)

1997 Elsa Okon Rael, *When Zaydeh Danced on Eldridge Street*, illustrated by Marjorie Priceman (Simon & Schuster)
Nina Jaffe, *The Mysterious Visitor: Stories of the Prophet Elijah*, illustrated by Elivia Savadier (Scholastic)

1996 Barbara Sofer, *Shalom, Haver: Goodbye, Friend* (Kar-Ben Copies)
Maxine Rose Schur, *When I Left My Village*, illustrated by Brian Pinkney (Dial Books)

1995 Jo Hoestlandt, *Star of Fear, Star of Hope*, illustrated by Johanna Kang (Walker and Company)
Ida Vos, *Dancing on the Bridge of Avignon* (Houghton Mifflin)

1994 Sheldon Oberman, *The Always Prayer Shawl*, illustrated by Ted Lewin (Boyds Mill Press)
Steven Schnur, *The Shadow Children*, illustrated by Herbert Tauss (Morrow Junior Books)

1993 Nina Jaffe, *The Uninvited Guest*, illustrated by Elivia Savadier (Scholastic)
Carol Matas, *Sworn Enemies* (Bantam Doubleday Dell)

4.10 *continued*

1992 Phoebe Gilman, *Something from Nothing*, illustrated by the author (North Winds Press/Scholastic Canada)
Karen Hesse, *Letters from Rifka* (Henry Holt)

1991 Barbara Diamond Goldin, *Cakes and Miracles: A Purim Tale*, illustrated by Erika Weihs (Viking)
Sandy Lanton, *Daddy's Chair*, illustrated by Shelly O. Haas (Kar-Ben Copies)
Howard Schwartz & Barbara Rush, *The Diamond Tree: Jewish Tales from Around the World*, illustrated by Uri Shulevitz (HarperCollins)

1990 Eric Kimmel, *The Chanukkah Guest*, illustrated by Giora Carmi (Holiday House)
Adèle Geras, *My Grandmother's Stories*, illustrated by Jael Jordan (Alfred A. Knopf)

1989 Esther Silverstein Blanc, *Berchick*, illustrated by Tennessee Dixon (Volcano Press)
Lois Lowry, *Number the Stars* (Houghton Mifflin)

1988 Patricia Polacco, *The Keeping Quilt*, illustrated by the author (Simon & Schuster)
Jane Yolen, *The Devil's Arithmetic* (Viking Kestrel)

1987 David Adler, *The Number on My Grandfather's Arm*, photos by Rose Eichenbaum (UAHC Press)
Sonia Levitin, *The Return* (Atheneum)

1986 Marilyn Hirsh, *Joseph Who Loved the Sabbath*, illustrated by Devis Grebu (Viking Kestrel)
Nancy Pitt, *Beyond the High White Wall* (Charles Scribner's Sons)

1985 Florence B. Freedman, *Brothers*, illustrated by Robert Andrew Parker (Harper & Row)
Carol Snyder, *Ike and Mama and the Seven Surprises* (Lothrop, Lee and Shepard)

1984 Amy Schwartz, *Mrs. Moskowitz and the Sabbath Candlesticks*, illustrated by the author (JPS)
Uri Orlev, *The Island on Bird Street* (Houghton Mifflin)

1983 Barbara Pomerantz, *Bubby, Me, and Memories*, photos by Leon Lurie (UAHC Press)
Rose Zar, *In the Mouth of the Wolf* (JPS)

1982 Marilyn Sachs, *Call Me Ruth* (Doubleday)
Linda Heller, *The Castle on Hester Street* (JPS)

1981 Barbara Cohen, *Yussel's Prayer*, illustrated by Michael J. Deraney (Lothrop, Lee and Shepard)
Kathryn Lasky, *The Night Journey* (Frederick Warne)

1980 Leonard Everett Fisher, *A Russian Farewell* (Four Winds Press)

1979 Carol Snyder, *Ike and Mama and the Block Wedding* (Coward, McCann & Geoghegan)

4.10 *continued*

1978 Doris Orgel, *The Devil in Vienna* (Dial)

1977 Anita Heyman, *Exit From Home* (Crown)

1976 Milton Meltzer, *Never to Forget* (Harper & Row)

1975 Marietta Moskin, *Waiting for Mama* (Coward, McCann & Geoghegan)

1974 No award

1973 Yuri Suhl, *Uncle Misha's Partisans* (Four Winds)

1972 Molly Cone, for her general contributions

1971 Isaac Bashevis Singer, for his general contributions

1970 Suzanne Lange, *The Year* (S. G. Phillips)

1969 Sulamith Ish-Kishor, *Our Eddie* (Pantheon)

1968 Esther Hautzig, *The Endless Steppe* (Crowell)

Source: List 4.10 is used with the permission of the Association of Jewish Libraries.

4.11 Other Children's Book Awards

In addition to the well-known Caldecott, Newbery, and King awards, there are many other prestigious awards for excellence in children's literature. This list will help you identify sources for award winners in many categories. For a list of the winners for this and previous years, visit the Web site of the organization presenting the award.

Americas Award for Children's and Young Adult Literature was launched in 1993 by the Consortium of Latin American Studies Programs to recognize annually excellence in an English or Spanish language picture book, poetry, fiction, or folklore published in the United States. The award-winning books focus on the experience and cultural heritage of Latinos in the U.S., Latin America, or the Caribbean. www.uwm.edu/Dept/CLACS/Americas2001.htm

Award for Excellence in Poetry for Children is given every three years by the National Council of Teachers of English to a living American poet in recognition of a body of work. It was first given in 1977. www.ncte.org/elem/poetry/winners.shtml

Carnegie Medal was established in 1937 by the British Library Association's Youth Libraries Group and is awarded annually for an outstanding book published in the United Kingdom. www.carnegiegreenaway.org.uk/carnegie

Edgar Allen Poe Award has been given each year since 1945 by the Mystery Writers of America to recognize excellence in the field of mystery writing. It was named for Edgar Allan Poe, the "Father of the Mystery Story." Of the 13 categories, there is one for the best mystery book for children and one for the best mystery for young adults. www.mysterywriters.org

Golden Kite Award is made by the members of the Society of Children's Book Writers and Illustrators to fellow members for excellence in the field of children's fiction, nonfiction, picture book, and picture illustration. It began in 1974. www.scbwi.org/awards.htm

Hans Christian Andersen Medals have been awarded since 1956 by the International Board on Books for Young People (IBBY) to an author and an illustrator to recognize their significant contribution of their entire body of work to children's literature. www.IBBY.org

International Reading Association Children's Book Awards were established in 1975 to encourage new talent in children's literature. They are presented for an author's first or second published fiction or nonfiction book for young (4–10) and older (10–17) readers. www.reading.org/awards/children.html

Jane Addams Children's Book Award, a presentation by the Women's International League for Peace and Freedom and the Jane Addams Peace Association since 1953, recognizes a recently published children's book that promotes peace, social justice, and world community. It is awarded on September 6 each year commemorating the birthday of Jane Addams, the first American woman to win the Nobel Peace Prize. www.janeaddamspeace.org

Kate Greenaway Medal is given each year by the British Library Association. It was established in 1956 to honor the most distinguished U.K. children's book illustrator. www.carnegiegreenaway.org/uk/green/green.html

Laura Ingalls Wilder Medal, named after its first honoree, is a tribute to a U.S. author or illustrator whose books have made a lasting contribution to children's literature. The award, estab-

4.11 *continued*

lished in 1954 by the Association for Library Service to Children (a part of the American Library Association), was given every five years from 1960 to 1980; it is now given every three years. www.ala.org

Lee Bennett Hopkins Promising Poet Award, made by the International Reading Association, is a monetary award given each three years to a promising new author of children's poetry. www.reading.org/awards/Lee.html

Margaret A. Edwards Award for Outstanding Literature for Young Adults is awarded to an author for lifetime achievement writing for teens by the Young Adult Library Services Association, a part of the American Library Association. The award was established in 1988 to honor authors who help teens better understand themselves and the world. www.ala.org

Mildred L. Batchelder Award has been presented annually since 1968 by the American Library Association for an outstanding book for children translated into English. The award goes to the U.S. publisher responsible for the English edition. www.ala.org

National Book Award for Young People's Literature was added to the National Book Awards in 1996. Before that, a Children's Book category was used by the National Book Award/American Book Award Program from 1969 to 1983. It recognizes an outstanding contribution by a U.S. author to children's literature and is based on literary merit. www.nationalbook.org

Scott O'Dell Award for Historical Fiction, established in 1981, is awarded for the best U.S. book of historical fiction written for children and set in the New World. www.readersread.com/awards/odell.htm

Young Reader's Choice Award, though made by the regional Pacific Northwest Library Association, has been respected and widely-known since 1940 for its recognition of books that children and young adults find enjoyable and therefore promote leisure reading. Books are nominated primarily by students, parents, teachers, and librarians. www.pnla.org

Source: This list is adapted from *The Reading Teacher's Book of Lists*, Fourth Edition, by Edward Fry, Jacqueline E. Kress, and Dona Lee Fountoukidis (San Francisco: Jossey-Bass, 2000).

4.12 Notable Social Studies Trade Books for Young People

Each year, the Children's Book Council (CBC) in cooperation with the National Council for Social Studies (NCSS) publishes a list of recommended children's trade books focusing on social studies topics for grades K–8. Teachers find this list invaluable when identifying quality literature to address the social studies standards. The titles are organized by subject category and recommended grade levels are given **(P = Primary, I = Intermediate, A = Advanced)**. Complete, annotated social studies lists for recent years can be found at www.ncss.org. (A comparable list of recommended science titles, "Outstanding Science Trade Books for Children," can be found at www.nsta.org, the Web site of the National Science Teachers Association.) The abbreviated social studies list below is for the year 2002.

Biography

After the Holocaust. Howard Greenfeld. Illustrated with photographs. Greenwillow Books. **(A)**

Alone Across the Arctic: One Woman's Epic Journey by Dog Team. Pam Flowers with Ann Dixon. Illustrated with photographs by Pam Flowers. Alaska Northwest Books. **(A)**

B. Franklin, Printer. David A. Adler. Illustrated with prints and photographs. Holiday House. **(A)**

Bad Boy: A Memoir. Walter Dean Myers. Amistad/HarperCollins Children's Books. **(A)**

Born in the Breezes: The Seafaring Life of Joshua Slocum. Kathryn Lasky. Illustrated by Walter Lyon Krudop. Orchard Books (Scholastic). **(I)**

Brave Harriet. Marissa Moss. Illustrated by C. F. Payne. Silver Whistle. **(P, I)**

Breaking Through. Francisco Jiménez. Illustrated with photographs. Houghton Mifflin. **(A)**

Bull's Eye: A Photobiography of Annie Oakley. Sue Macy. Illustrated with photographs. National Geographic Society. **(A)**

Carver: A Life in Poems. Marilyn Nelson. Illustrated with photographs. Front Street Books. **(A)**

Columbus Day: Celebrating a Famous Explorer (Finding Out About Holidays series). Elaine Landau. Illustrated with prints. Enslow Publishers. **(I, A)**

Countdown to Independence: A Revolution of Ideas in England and Her American Colonies: 1760–1776. Natalie S. Bober. Illustrated with prints and photographs. Atheneum Books for Young Readers. **(A)**

Despite All Obstacles: La Salle and the Conquest of the Mississippi (Great Explorers series). Joan Elizabeth Goodman. Illustrated by Tom McNeely. Mikaya Press. **(I)**

The Dinosaurs of Waterhouse Hawkins. Barbara Kerley. Illustrated by Brian Selznick. Scholastic Press. **(I)**

Elizabeth Cady Stanton: The Right Is Ours (Oxford Portraits series). Harriet Sigerman. Illustrated with prints and photographs. Oxford University Press. **(A)**

First Ladies. Amy Pastan. Illustrated with prints and photographs. DK Publishing. **(I)**

Fly High! The Story of Bessie Coleman. Louise Borden and Mary Kay Kroeger. Illustrated by Teresa Flavin. Margaret K. McElderry Books (Aladdin). **(P)**

The Great Unknown. Taylor Morrison. Illustrated by the author. Walter Lorraine Books/Houghton Mifflin. **(I)**

Handel, Who Knew What He Liked. M. T. Anderson. Illustrated by Kevin Hawkes. Candlewick Press. **(I, A)**

Hatshepsut, His Majesty, Herself. Catherine M. Andronik. Illustrated by Joseph Daniel Fiedler. Atheneum Books for Young Readers. **(A)**

4.12 *continued*

Helen Keller (In Their Own Words series). George Sullivan. Illustrated with photographs. Scholastic, Inc. **(I)**

Helen Keller: Rebellious Spirit. Laurie Lawlor. Illustrated with prints and photographs. Holiday House. **(I, A)**

Heroine of the Titanic: *The Real Unsinkable Molly Brown*. Elaine Landau. Illustrated with photographs. Clarion Books. **(A)**

Hokusai: The Man Who Painted a Mountain. Deborah Kogan Ray. Illustrated by the author. Frances Foster Books/Farrar, Straus & Giroux. **(I)**

The Holy Twins: Benedict and Scholastica. Kathleen Norris. Illustrated by Tomie dePaola. G. P. Putnam's Sons (Puffin Books). **(I)**

How I Became an American. Karin Gündisch. Translated by James Skofield. Cricket Books. **(I, A)**

John and Abigail Adams: An American Love Story. Judith St. George. Illustrated with prints. Holiday House. **(A)**

Louis XVI, Marie-Antoinette, and the French Revolution (Rulers and Their Times series). Nancy Plain. Illustrated with prints. Benchmark Books/Marshall Cavendish. **(I)**

Margaret Knight: Girl Inventor. Marlene Targ Brill. Illustrated by Joanne Friar. Millbrook Press. **(P, I)**

Martin's Big Words: The Life of Dr. Martin Luther King, Jr. Doreen Rappaport. Illustrated by Bryan Collier. Jump at the Sun/Hyperion Books for Children. **(I)**

On My Way. Tomie dePaola. Illustrated by the author. G. P. Putnam's Sons (Puffin Books). **(I)**

Our Country's Presidents. Ann Bausum. Illustrated with prints and photographs. National Geographic Society. **(A)**

Rescued Images: Memories of a Childhood in Hiding. Ruth Jacobsen. Illustrated by the author. Mikaya Press. **(A)**

Robert E. Peary: To the Top of the World (Great Explorations series). Patricia Calvert. Illustrated with photographs. Benchmark Books/Marshall Cavendish. **(I, A)**

Shakespeare: His Work and His World. Michael Rosen. Illustrated by Robert Ingpen. Candlewick Press. **(I, A)**

Shipwrecked! The True Adventures of a Japanese Boy. Rhoda Blumberg. Illustrated with prints and photographs. HarperCollins Children's Books (HarperTrophy). **(I)**

Shooting for the Moon: The Amazing Life and Times of Annie Oakley. Stephen Krensky. Illustrated by Bernie Fuchs. Melanie Kroupa Books/Farrar, Straus & Giroux. **(P)**

Standing Like a Stone Wall. James I. Robertson Jr. Illustrated with photographs and prints. Atheneum Books for Young Readers. **(A)**

Theodore Roosevelt: Letters from a Young Coal Miner (Dear Mr. President series). Jennifer Armstrong. Illustrated with photographs. Winslow House. **(A)**

Tomboy of the Air: Daredevil Pilot Blanche Stuart Scott. Julie Cummings. Illustrated with photographs. HarperCollins. **(I, A)**

Vincent van Gogh: Portrait of an Artist. Jan Greenberg and Sandra Jordan. Illustrated with prints and photographs. Delacorte Press/Random House Children's Books. **(A)**

Woody Guthrie: Poet of the People. Bonnie Christensen. Illustrated by the author. Alfred A. Knopf/Random House Children's Books. **(P, I)**

The World at Her Fingertips: The Story of Helen Keller. Joan Dash. Illustrated with photographs. Scholastic Press. **(A)**

4.12 *continued*

Contemporary Concerns

Any Small Goodness: A Novel of the Barrio. Tony Johnston. Illustrated by Raúl Colón. Blue Sky Press/Scholastic Inc. **(A)**

A Bushel of Light. Troon Harrison. Stoddart Kids. **(A)**

Freedom Summer. Deborah Wiles. Illustrated by Jerome Lagarrigue. An Anne Schwartz Book/Atheneum Books for Young Readers. **(P, I, A)**

The Gospel According to Larry. Janet Tashjian. Henry Holt (Random House). **(A)**

Lots of Grandparents. Shelley Rotner and Sheila M. Kelly, Ed.D. Illustrated with photographs by Shelley Rotner. Millbrook Press. **(P)**

Of Sound Mind. Jean Ferris. Farrar, Straus & Giroux. **(A)**

One of the Problems of Everett Anderson. Lucille Clifton. Illustrated by Ann Grifalconi. Henry Holt. **(P, I)**

Spellbound. Janet McDonald. Frances Foster Books/Farrar, Straus & Giroux. **(A)**

There Comes a Time: The Struggle for Civil Rights. Milton Meltzer. Illustrated with photographs. Landmark Books/Random House Children's Books. **(A)**

Environment and Ecology

The Chimpanzees I Love: Saving Their World and Ours. Jane Goodall. Illustrated with photographs. Scholastic Press. **(I)**

Food Watch. Martyn Bramwell. Illustrated with photographs. DK Publishing. **(I, A)**

Hidden Under the Sea: The World Beneath the Waves. Peter Kent. Illustrated by the author. Dutton Children's Books (Puffin Books). **(I, A)**

Hoover Dam: The Story of Hard Times, Tough People, and the Taming of a Wild River (Wonders of the World series). Elizabeth Mann. Illustrated by Alan Witschonke. Mikaya Press. **(A)**

Folktales

The Black Bull of Norroway: A Scottish Tale. Retold by Charlotte Huck. Illustrated by Anita Lobel. Greenwillow Books. **(P)**

Crocodile and Hen: A Bakongo Folktale (I Can Read series). Joan M. Lexau. Illustrated by Doug Cushman. HarperCollins Children's Books. **(P)**

Fiesta Feminina: Celebrating Women in Mexican Folktale. Retold by Mary-Joan Gerson. Illustrated by Maya Christina Gonzalez. Barefoot Books. **(I)**

How Animals Saved the People: Animal Tales from the South. Retold by J. J. Reneaux. Illustrated by James Ransome. HarperCollins Children's Books. **(I)**

How Chipmunk Got His Stripes. Joseph Bruchac and James Bruchac. Illustrated by Jose Aruego and Ariane Dewey. Dial Books for Young Readers (Puffin Books). **(P)**

The Lady of Ten Thousand Names: Goddess Stories from Many Cultures. Retold by Burleigh Mutén. Illustrated by Helen Cann. Barefoot Books. **(I)**

The Master Swordsman & the Magic Doorway: Two Legends from Ancient China. Retold by Alice Provenson. Illustrated by the author. Simon & Schuster Books for Young Readers. **(P, I)**

Monkey King. Ed Young. Illustrated by the author. HarperCollins Children's Books. **(P)**

Petite Rouge: A Cajun Red Riding Hood. Mike Artell. Illustrated by Jim Harris. Dial Books for Young Readers (Puffin Books). **(P, I, A)**

The Seeing Stone. Kevin Crossley-Holland. Arthur A. Levine Books/Scholastic Press. **(I, A)**

4.12 *continued*

Storm Maker's Tipi. Paul Goble. Illustrated by the author. A Richard Jackson Book/Atheneum Books for Young Readers. **(P)**

The Story Tree: Tales to Read Aloud. Retold by Hugh Lupton. Illustrated by Sophie Fatus. Barefoot Books. **(I)**

The Wolf of Gubbio. Michael Bedard. Illustrated by Murray Kimber. Stoddart Kids. **(I)**

Geography, Peoples, and Places

Building a New Land: African Americans in Colonial America. James Haskins and Kathleen Benson. Illustrated by James Ransome. Amistad/HarperCollins Children's Books. **(I, A)**

Desert Town. Bonnie Geisert. Illustrated by Arthur Geisert. Walter Lorraine Books/Houghton Mifflin. **(P)**

Desert Trek: An Eye-Opening Journey Through the World's Driest Places. Marie-Ange Le Rochais. Translated from the French by George L. Newman. Illustrated by the author. Walker & Company. **(I)**

Exploring the Ice Age. Margaret Cooper. Illustrated with prints and photographs. Atheneum Books for Young Readers. **(I)**

Girl of Kosovo. Alice Mead. Farrar, Straus & Giroux. **(I, A)**

Gold Rush Dogs. Claire Rudolf Murphy and Jane G. Haigh. Illustrated with photographs. Alaska Northwest Books. **(I)**

I Live in Tokyo. Mari Takabayashi. Illustrated by the author. Houghton Mifflin. **(P, I)**

Katie and the Sunflowers. James Mayhew. Illustrated by the author. Orchard Books (Scholastic). **(I)**

Let's Go to the Beach: A History of Sun and Fun by the Sea. Elizabeth Van Steenwyk. Illustrated with prints and photographs. Henry Holt. **(A)**

Mississippi. Diane Siebert. Illustrated by Greg Harlin. HarperCollins Children's Books. **(I, A)**

Nutik, the Wolf Pup. Jean Craighead George. Illustrated by Ted Rand. HarperCollins Children's Books. **(P)**

Rediscovering Easter Island (How History Is Invented series). Kathy Pelta. Illustrated with photographs. Lerner Publications. **(A)**

Supermarket. Kathleen Krull. Illustrated by Melanie Hope Greenberg. Holiday House. **(P)**

Traveling Man: The Journey of Ibn Battuta, 1325–1354. James Rumford. Illustrated by the author. Houghton Mifflin. **(P, I)**

The Wolf Girls: An Unsolved Mystery from History. Jane Yolen and Heidi Elisabet Yolen Stemple. Illustrated by Roger Roth. Simon & Schuster Books for Young Readers. **(I)**

History, Life, and Culture in the Americas

Abe Lincoln Remembers. Ann Turner. Illustrated by Wendell Minor. HarperCollins Children's Books (Harper Trophy). **(I, A)**

American Indian Cooking Before 1500. (Exploring History Through Simple Recipes series). Mary Gunderson. Illustrated with photographs. Blue Earth Books/Capstone Press. **(I)**

Amish Horses. Richard Ammon. Illustrated by Pamela Patrick. Atheneum Books for Young Readers. **(P)**

Attack on Pearl Harbor: The True Story of the Day America Entered World War II. Shelley Tanaka. Illustrated by David Craig. Hyperion Books for Children. **(I)**

Belle Teal. Ann M. Martin. Scholastic Press. **(A)**

4.12 *continued*

Born to Be a Cowgirl: A Spirited Ride Through the Old West. Candace Savage. Illustrated with photographs. Tricycle Press. **(I, A)**

Bound for America: The Story of the European Immigrants (Great Journeys series). Milton Meltzer. Illustrated with prints and photographs. Benchmark Books/Marshall Cavendish. **(A)**

Brooklyn Bridge. Lynn Curlee. Illustrated by the author. Atheneum Books for Young Readers. **(P, I)**

A Bus of Our Own. Freddi Williams Evans. Illustrated by Shawn Costello. Albert Whitman & Company. **(I, A)**

Children of the Indian Boarding Schools. Holly Littlefield. Illustrated with photographs. Carolrhoda Books, Inc./Lerner. **(I, A)**

Christmas After All: The Great Depression Diary of Minnie Swift, Indianapolis, Indiana, 1932 (Dear America series). Kathryn Lasky. Illustrated with photographs. Scholastic Inc. **(I)**

The Christmas Promise. Susan Bartoletti. Illustrated by David Christiana. Blue Sky Press/Scholastic Inc. **(P, I)**

Clem's Chances. Sonia Levitin. Orchard Books (Scholastic). **(I, A)**

The Cod's Tale. Mark Kurlansky. Illustrated by S. D. Schindler. G. P. Putnam's Sons (Puffin Books). **(I)**

The Cold War: A History in Documents (Pages from History series). Allan M. Winkler. Illustrated with prints and photographs. Oxford University Press. **(A)**

Conjure Times: Black Magicians in America. Jim Haskins and Kathleen Benson. Illustrated with photographs. Walker Books. **(A)**

Earthquake. Milly Lee. Illustrated by Yangsook Choi. Frances Foster Books/Farrar, Straus & Giroux. **(P, I)**

Failure Is Impossible: The History of American Women's Rights. Martha E. Kendall. Illustrated with prints and photographs. Lerner Publications. **(A)**

Fair Weather. Richard Peck. Dial Books for Young Readers (Puffin Books). **(A)**

Freedom School, Yes! Amy Littlesugar. Illustrated by Floyd Cooper. Philomel Books (Puffin Books). **(I, A)**

Freedom's Wings: Corey's Diary, Kentucky to Ohio, 1857 (My America series). Sharon Dennis Wyeth. Illustrated with prints and photographs. Scholastic, Inc. **(P, I)**

Ghost Towns of the American West. Raymond Bial. Illustrated with photographs by the author. Houghton Mifflin. **(I, A)**

Giving Thanks: The 1621 Harvest Feast. Kate Waters. Illustrated with photographs by Russ Kendall. Scholastic Press. **(I)**

Growing Up in Slavery. Sylviane A. Diouf. Illustrated with prints and photographs. Millbrook Press. **(I)**

Harvest. George Ancona. Illustrated with photographs by the author. Marshall Cavendish. **(P, I)**

Henry's First-Moon Birthday. Lenore Look. Illustrated by Yumi Heo. An Anne Schwartz Book/Atheneum Books for Young Readers. **(P)**

A Humble Life: Plain Poems. Linda Oatman High. Illustrated by Bill Farnsworth. Eerdmans Books for Young Readers. **(P, I)**

In the Days of the Vaqueros: America's First True Cowboys. Russell Freedman. Illustrated with prints and photographs. Clarion Books. **(I)**

In the Shadow of the Alamo (Great Episodes series). Sherry Garland. Gulliver Books. **(I, A)**

James Towne: Struggle for Survival. Marcia Sewall. Illustrated by the author. Atheneum Books for Young Readers. **(I)**

4.12 *continued*

The Journey. Sarah Stewart. Illustrated by David Small. Farrar, Straus & Giroux. **(P, I)**

The Lamp, the Ice, and the Boat Called Fish. Jacqueline Briggs Martin. Illustrated by Beth Krommes. Houghton Mifflin. **(I)**

The Land. Mildred D. Taylor. Phyllis Fogelman Books/Penguin Putnam (Puffin Books). **(A)**

The Minstrel's Melody (History Mysteries series). Eleanora E. Tate. Illustrated with prints and photographs. American Girl/Pleasant Company Publications. **(I)**

Mountain Men: True Grit and Tall Tales. Andrew Glass. Illustrated by the author. Doubleday/Random House Children's Books. **(P, I)**

My Family Shall Be Free: The Life of Peter Still. Dennis Brindell Fradin. Illustrated with prints and photographs. HarperCollins. **(I, A)**

The Other Dog. Madeleine L'Engle. Illustrated by Christine Davenier. SeaStar Books. **(P, I)**

The Other Side. Jacqueline Woodson. Illustrated by E. B. Lewis. G. P. Putnam's Sons (Puffin Books). **(P, I, A)**

Pearl. Debby Atwell. Illustrated by the author. Walter Lorraine Books/Houghton Mifflin. **(P, I)**

Places in Time: A New Atlas of American History. Elspeth Leacock and Susan Buckley. Illustrated by Randy Jones. Houghton Mifflin. **(I)**

Religion in Twentieth Century America (Religion in American Life series). Randall Balmer. Illustrated with photographs. Oxford University Press. **(A)**

Remember Pearl Harbor: American and Japanese Survivors Tell Their Stories. Thomas B. Allen. Illustrated with photographs. National Geographic Society. **(I, A)**

Rent Party Jazz. William Miller. Illustrated by Charlotte Riley-Webb. Lee and Low Books. **(P, I)**

Rose's Journal: The Story of a Girl in the Great Depression (Young American Voices series). Marissa Moss. Illustrated by the author and with photographs. Silver Whistle. **(I)**

Scholastic Book of World Records. Jenifer Corr Morse. Illustrated with photographs. Scholastic, Inc. **(I, A)**

Slave Spirituals and the Jubilee Singers. Michael L. Cooper. Illustrated with prints and photographs. Clarion Books. **(A)**

Stories from Where We Live: The California Coast (Stories from Where We Live series). Edited by Sara St. Antoine. Illustrated by Trudy Nicholson. Milkweed Editions. **(I, A)**

Story of the Titanic. Eric Kentley. Illustrated by Steve Noon. DK Publishing. **(I, A)**

Tattered Sails. Verla Kay. Illustrated by Dan Andreasen. G. P. Putnam's Sons (Puffin Books). **(P)**

They Came from the Bronx: How the Buffalo Were Saved from Extinction. Neil Waldman. Illustrated by the author. Boyds Mills Press. **(I, A)**

Those Building Men. Angela Johnson. Illustrated by Barry Moser. Blue Sky Press/Scholastic, Inc. **(P, I)**

Those Extraordinary Women of World War I. Karen Zeinart. Illustrated with photographs. Millbrook Press. **(A)**

We Rode the Orphan Trains. Andrea Warren. Illustrated with photographs. Houghton Mifflin. **(I)**

We Were There, Too! Young People in History. Phillip Hoose. Illustrated with prints and photographs. Melanie Kroupa Books/Farrar, Straus & Giroux. **(I, A)**

Weave Little Stars into My Sleep: Native American Lullabies. Neil Philip. Photographs by Edward S. Curtis. Clarion Books. **(P, I, A)**

When Esther Morris Headed West: Women, Wyoming and the Right to Vote. Connie Nordhielm Wooldridge. Illustrated by Jacqueline Rogers. Holiday House. **(P)**

4.12 *continued*

When Johnny Went Marching: Young Americans Fight the Civil War. G. Clifton Wisler. Illustrated with photographs. HarperCollins. **(A)**
Who Really Discovered America? Unraveling the Mystery & Solving the Puzzle (Kaleidoscope Kids series). Avery Hart. Illustrated by Michael Kline. Williamson Publishing. **(P)**
William's House. Ginger Howard. Illustrated by Larry Day. Millbrook Press. **(P)**
Words with Wings: A Treasury of African-American Poetry and Art. Selected by Belinda Rochelle. Illustrated with reproductions of art by African-American artists. Amistad/HarperCollins. **(P, I, A)**
Wounded Knee. Neil Waldman. Illustrated by the author. Atheneum Books for Young Readers. **(I, A)**

Reference

The Civil War at Sea. George Sullivan. Illustrated with photographs. Twenty-First Century Books/Millbrook. **(I)**
Flag Lore of All Nations. Whitney Smith, Ph.D. Illustrated by Dream Maker Software. Millbrook Press. **(I)**
Journeys in Time: A New Atlas of American History. Elspeth Leacock and Susan Buckley. Illustrated by Rodica Prato. Houghton Mifflin. **(I)**
The Kid Who Invented the Trampoline: More Surprising Stories About Inventions. Don L. Wulffson. Illustrated with prints and photographs. Dutton Children's Books. **(I)**
National Geographic Student Atlas of the World. Illustrated with photographs. National Geographic Society. **(A)**
Red, White, Blue, and Uncle Who? The Stories Behind Some of America's Patriotic Symbols. Teresa Bateman. Illustrated by John O'Brien. Holiday House. **(P, I)**
Remember the Ladies: One Hundred Great American Women. Cheryl Harness. HarperCollins Publishers (HarperTrophy). **(I)**
Scholastic Atlas of the World. Philip Steele. Illustrated with maps and photographs. Scholastic. **(I)**
The Usborne Book of Peoples of the World. Gillian Doherty and Anna Claybourne. Illustrated with photographs. Usborne Publishing. **(I, A)**

Social Interactions and Relationships

Becoming Little Women: Louisa May at Fruitlands. Jeannine Atkins. G. P. Putnam's Sons (Puffin Books). **(I)**
Betty Doll. Patricia Polacco. Illustrated by the author. Philomel Books (Puffin Books). **(I)**
Bluebird Summer. Deborah Hopkinson. Illustrated by Bethanne Andersen. Greenwillow Books. **(P)**
Chipper. James Lincoln Collier. Marshall Cavendish. **(A)**
Circus Girl. Tomek Bogacki. Illustrated by the author. Frances Foster Books/Farrar, Straus & Giroux. **(P, I)**
Family. Isabell Monk. Illustrated by Janice Lee Porter. Carolrhoda Books/Lerner. **(P, I)**
Happy Birthday, Mr. Kang. Susan L. Roth. Illustrated by the author. National Geographic Society. **(P, I)**
The Harlem Nutcracker. Donald Byrd and Susan Kuklin. Illustrated with photographs by Susan Kuklin. Jump at the Sun/Hyperion Books for Children. **(I, A)**

4.12 *continued*

The Hickory Chair. Lisa Rowe Fraustino. Illustrated by Benny Andrews. Arthur A. Levine Books/Scholastic. **(I)**

Just the Two of Us. Will Smith. Illustrated by Kadir Nelson. Scholastic Press.

Love to Mamá. Edited by Pat Mora. Illustrated by Paula S. Barragán. Lee and Low Books. **(P, I, A)**

Lucy's Family Tree. Karen Halvorsen Schreck. Illustrated by Stephen Gassler III. Tilbury House. **(I, A)**

Racing the Past. Sis Deans. Henry Holt. **(A)**

Rivka's First Thanksgiving. Elsa Okon Rael. Illustrated by Maryann Kovalski. Margaret K. McElderry (Aladdin). **(P)**

Sailing Home: A Story of a Childhood at Sea. Gloria Rand. Illustrated by Ted Rand. North-South Books. **(P)**

Stepping Out with Grandma Mac. Nikki Grimes. Orchard Books (Scholastic). **(I)**

Thicker Than Water: Coming-of-age Stories by Irish and Irish-American Writers. Edited by Gordon Snell. Delacorte Press/Random House Children's Books. **(A)**

Tiger's Fall. Molly Bang. Illustrated by the author. Henry Holt. **(I)**

Trapped (Wild at Heart series). Laurie Halse Anderson. American Girl/Pleasant Company Publications. **(P)**

The War. Anaïs Vaugelade. Illustrated by the author. Carolrhoda Books/Lerner. **(P)**

World History and Culture

Angel on the Square. Gloria Whelan. HarperCollins Children's Books. **(A)**

Anne Frank in the World. Compiled by the Anne Frank House. Illustrated with photographs. Alfred A. Knopf/Random House Children's Books. **(I, A)**

The Belly Gunner. Carol Edgemon Hipperson. Illustrated with photographs. Twenty-First Century Books/Millbrook. **(I, A)**

Black Potatoes: The Story of the Great Irish Famine, 1845–1850. Susan Campbell Bartoletti. Illustrated with prints and photographs. Houghton Mifflin. **(I, A)**

Displaced Persons: The Liberation and Abuse of Holocaust Survivors (The Holocaust series). Ted Gottfried. Illustrated by Stephen Alcorn. Twenty-First Century Books/Millbrook. **(A)**

Emperors and Gladiators (All in a Day's Work series). Anita Ganeri. Illustrated with prints. Peter Bedrick Books. **(I, A)**

A Farm Through Time: The History of a Farm from Medieval Times to the Present Day. Angela Wilkes. Illustrated by Eric Thomas. Dorling Kindersley. **(I, A)**

Footnotes: Dancing the World's Best-Loved Ballets. Frank Augustyn and Shelley Tanaka. Illustrated with photographs. Millbrook Press. **(I, A)**

The Jacob Ladder. Gerald Hausman and Uton Hinds. Orchard Books (Scholastic). **(I, A)**

Leonardo's Horse. Jean Fritz. Illustrated by Hudson Talbott. G. P. Putnam's Sons (Puffin Books). **(I)**

Lord of the Nutcracker Men. Iain Lawrence. Delacorte Press/Random House Children's Books. **(I, A)**

Mansa Musa: The Lion of Mali. Khephra Burns. Illustrated by Leo and Diane Dillon. Gulliver Books. **(I)**

Mummies of the Pharoahs: Exploring the Valley of the Kings. Melvin Berger and Gilda Berger.

4.12 *continued*

Illustrated with photographs. National Geographic Society. **(I, A)**

The Orphan Singer. Emily Arnold McCully. Illustrated by the author. Arthur A. Levine Books/Scholastic. **(I)**

The Other Side of Truth. Beverley Naidoo. HarperCollins (HarperTrophy). **(A)**

Slavery: Bondage Through History. Richard Watkins. Illustrated by the author. Houghton Mifflin. **(I, A)**

Soldier X. Don Wulffson. Viking Children's Books (Puffin Books). **(A)**

Surviving Hitler: A Boy in the Nazi Death Camps. Andrea Warren. Illustrated with photographs. HarperCollins Children's Books (HarperTrophy). **(A)**

There Goes the Neighborhood: Ten Buildings People Loved to Hate. Susan Goldman Rubin. Illustrated with photographs. Holiday House. **(I, A)**

Under a War-torn Sky. L. M. Elliott. Hyperion Books for Children. **(A)**

4.13 Books to Celebrate Asian-Pacific American Heritage Month

The following list of recommended titles has been created by the staff of the New York Public Library Children's Department in conjunction with Asian-Pacific American Heritage Month, which is celebrated in May. This and other recommended lists can be found on the library's Web site "on-Lion for Kids" at www.nypl.org/branch/kids.

Folk- and Fairy Tales

Aesop's Fox by Aki Sogabe. As a fox wanders the sun-dappled countryside in this handsome picture book with Japanese paper cut art, a series of classic fables comes to life.

All the Way to Lhasa: A Tale from Tibet by Barbara Helen Berger. A young boy and his yak overcome many obstacles in this lovely picture book. Himalayan vistas and Buddhist symbols enrich the classic story about the importance of persistence.

The Boy Who Drew Cats adapted by Margaret Hodges. Pictures by Aki Sogabe. Lafcadio Hearn's unforgettable legend about the childhood of a Japanese artist, retold in a picture book with dramatic illustrations.

The Brocaded Slipper and Other Vietnamese Tales by Lynette Dyer Vuong. Illustrated by Vo-Dinh Mai. Five fairy tales from Vietnam.

Brother Rabbit: A Cambodian Tale by Minfong Ho and Saphan Ros. Illustrated by Jennifer Hewitson. A crocodile, two elephants, and an old woman are no match for a mischievous rabbit.

Children of the Dragon: Selected Tales from Vietnam by Sherry Garland. Illustrated by Trina Schart Hyman. An illustrated collection of Vietnamese folktales.

The Dancing Kettle and Other Japanese Folk Tales by Yoshiko Uchida. Illustrated by Richard C. Jones. A classic collection of Japanese tales. A companion title is *The Magic Listening Cap*.

The Empty Pot by Demi. Each child tries to grow the most beautiful flower to inherit the throne from the aging Chinese emperor.

Eyes of the Dragon by Margaret Leaf. Illustrated by Ed Young. An artist is summoned to portray the Dragon King on the wall that protects a village in this haunting Chinese legend.

Folk Stories of the Hmong: Peoples of Laos, Thailand, and Vietnam by Norma L. Livo and Dia Cha. Stories to read aloud and tell.

The Funny Little Woman by Arlene Mosel. Illustrated by Blair Lent. When the monstrous Japanese "oni" captured her, the little woman only laughed.

The Green Frogs: A Korean Folktale by Yumi Heo. A folktale about two green frogs who always disobey their mother, explaining why green frogs cry out whenever it rains.

The Hunter: A Chinese Folktale by Mary Casanova. Illustrations by Ed Young. After learning to understand the language of animals, Hai Li Bu the hunter sacrifices himself to save his village.

Jojofu by Michael P. Waite. Illustrated by Yoriko Ito. The suspenseful story of a brave and devoted dog who saves her master's life. Based on an ancient story from Japan.

Lon Po Po: A Red-Riding Hood Story from China. Illustrated by Ed Young. A wolf visits three sisters while disguised as their grandmother in this 1990 Caldecott Medal Chinese Red Riding Hood.

The Luminous Pearl: A Chinese Folktale by Betty L.Torre. Illustrated by Carol Inouye. A kindly young man and his selfish older brother try to win the hand of the beautiful Dragon Princess.

4.13 *continued*

The Magical Monkey King: Mischief in Heaven by Ji-Li Jiang. Illustrated by Hui Hui Su-Kennedy. The impudent hero of Chinese legend causes trouble, over, and over, and over, in this entertaining story of his earliest years.

The Mountains of Tibet by Mordecai Gerstein. "Choose from your heart" a voice told the woodcutter whose next life was about to begin.

Nine-In-One, Grr! Grr! A Folktale from the Hmong People of Laos told by Blia Xiong. Adapted by Cathy Spagnoli. Illustrated by Nancy Horn. When the great god Shao promises Tiger nine cubs each year, Bird comes up with a clever trick to prevent the land from being overrun by tigers.

The Rainbow People by Laurence Yep. Illustrated by David Wiesner. Evocative tales of their homeland reflect the life of Chinese immigrants in California.

The River Dragon by Darcy Pattison. Illustrated by Jean and Mou-sien Tseng. A young blacksmith outwits a fierce dragon and a disapproving future father-in-law in this tale inspired by Chinese legends.

Screen of Frogs: An Old Tale by Sheila Hamanaka. A spoiled rich man in Japan discovers a respect for nature in time to turn his life around.

The Seven Chinese Brothers by Margaret Mahy. Illustrated by Jean and Mou-sien Tseng. Although they walked and talked and looked alike, each of these tall tale heroes had one amazing power all his own.

Six Chinese Brothers: An Ancient Tale by Hou-tien Cheng. Illustrated with scissor-cuts by the author. Six look-alike Chinese brothers, each with a special talent, manage to outwit the king's executioner.

The Sun Girl and the Moon Boy by Yangsook Choi. A hungry tiger tries to trick a brother and sister into opening their door by pretending to be their absent mother.

Sweet and Sour; Tales from China by Carol Kendall and Yao-wen Li. Drawings by Shirley Felts. Parables, fables, jokes, and stories retold in a lively, engaging style.

Tales from Gold Mountain; Stories of the Chinese in the New World by Paul Yee. Paintings by Simon Ng. Haunting illustrations accompany eight original narratives about the Chinese immigrant experience in North America.

Tales from the Roof of the World: Folktales of Tibet by Gioia Timpanelli. Illustrated by Elizabeth Kelly Lockwood. Traditional tales from the remote mountain country.

Tales of a Chinese Grandmother by Frances Carpenter. Illustrated by Malthe Hasselriis. The rich treasure of Chinese folklore told against the vivid and realistic background of the Ling household. Also: *Tales of a Korean Grandmother*.

Tasty Baby Belly Buttons: A Japanese Folktale by Judy Sierra. Illustrated by Meilo So. Urikohime, a girl born from a melon, battles the monstrous oni, who steal babies to eat their tasty belly buttons.

Three Strong Women; A Tall Tale from Japan by Claus Stamm. Pictures by Jean and Mou-sien Tseng. When the famous wrestler Forever Mountain tickles a plump little girl, the consequence is that he must be trained by her, her mother, and her grandmother.

The Tongue-Cut Sparrow by Momoko Ishii. Illustrated by Suekichi Akaba, translated from the Japanese by Katherine Paterson. The favorite Japanese tale of goodness rewarded.

Two of Everything by Lily Toy Hong. Mrs. Haktak is thrilled with the magic pot that duplicates things—until she falls into it. An amusing picture book version of an old story set in China.

4.13 *continued*

Which Was Witch? Tales of Ghosts and Magic from Korea by Eleanore M. Jewett. Illustrated by Taro Yashima. There is true magic in this collection based on Korean folktales.

Yeh Shen: A Cinderella Story from China by Ai-Ling Louie. Illustrated by Ed Young. A young girl overcomes the wickedness of her stepsisters and stepmother to become the bride of a prince.

Nonfiction

American Dragons: Twenty-Five Asian American Voices edited by Laurence Yep. Short stories, poems, and excerpts from plays relate the experience of growing up Asian American.

Before the Buddha Came by Walter Ashlin Fairservis. A description of life in the ancient days of China, Korea, Japan, and Central Asia.

Chinese Kites by David F. Jue. How to make and fly them.

Chingis Khan by Demi. A visually elegant and concise account of the life of the 12th-century Mongol conqueror whose horsemen ranged across Asia.

El Chino by Allen Say. Paintings recreate the mood of old photographs in this biography of a Chinese American who became a bullfighter in Spain.

Confucius: The Golden Rule by Russell Freedman. Illustrated by Frédéric Clément. The timeless wisdom of the great Chinese philosopher retold as an inspiration for today with illustrations that capture the mystery of an unusual life.

Double Luck: Memoirs of a Chinese Orphan by Chi Fa Lu. Story of the author's struggles after being orphaned at the age of three and how he held on to his dream of coming to the United States as he passed from one relative to another and was even sold to a Communist couple.

Exploring Chinatown: A Children's Guide to Chinese Culture by Carol Stepanchuk. Illustrations by Leland Wong. Food, language, religion, holidays, family, and the arts in a colorful introduction.

Extraordinary Asian-Pacific Americans by Susan Sinnott. Biographical sketches.

Farewell to Manzanar: A True Story of Japanese American Experience During and After the World War II Internment by Jeanne Wakatsuki Houston. The true story of seven-year-old Jeanne and her family, sent in 1942 to Manzanar internment camp along with 10,000 other Japanese Americans.

Fighting for Honor: Japanese Americans and World War II by Michael L. Cooper. Examines the history of Japanese in the United States, focusing on their treatment during World War II, including the mass relocation to internment camps and the distinguished service of Japanese Americans in the American military.

The Great Wall of China by Leonard Everett Fisher. The story of the building of the structure that protected China for 2,200 years.

Himalaya: Vanishing Cultures by Jan Reynolds. A Nepalese Sherpa family and their rarely seen homeland are observed in stunning photographs.

Hiroshima No Pika by Toshi Maruki. Full-color paintings show the extent of the horror and the agony of Hiroshima in this personal account of a family's flight from the devastated city.

Homesick: My Own Story by Jean Fritz. The author's compelling story of her childhood in 1920s China. A companion title is *China Homecoming*.

The Land I Lost: Adventures of a Boy in Vietnam by Quang Huynh Nhuong. Pictures by Vo-Dinh Mai. Colorful stories based on the author's treasured memories.

4.13 *continued*

The Little Lama of Tibet: Biography of Ling Rimpochey by Lois Raimondo. An illustrated biography of Ling Rimpochey, the young Buddhist monk who will be the next leader of the Tibetan people.

Red Eggs and Dragon Boats: Celebrating Chinese Festivals by Carol Stepanchuk. Describes four major Chinese festivals and a party for a baby, with stories, customs, holiday food recipes, and illustrations by a variety of folk artists.

Sadako and the Thousand Paper Cranes by Eleanor Coerr. Paintings by Ronald Himler. The classic story of the Japanese girl, dying of leukemia from the atomic bomb blast, who tried to save her life by folding 1,000 paper cranes.

Shipwrecked! The True Adventures of a Japanese Boy by Rhoda Blumberg. The amazing life of a 14-year-old fisherman in 19th-century Japan who is brought to the United States after being shipwrecked and who ends up influencing his country to open its ports to the world.

Showa: The Age of Hirohito by Dorothy and Thomas Hoobler. The life and times of the Japanese emperor whose reign meant "Enlightened Peace."

So Far from the Bamboo Grove by Yoko Kawashima Watkins. With incredible courage and determination, Yoko and her older sister survive the hardships of refugee life in post-World War II Korea and Japan.

Voices of the Heart by Ed Young. An artistic exploration of 26 Chinese characters, each of which contains the symbol for the heart. A beautifully designed book to pore over and ponder.

Poetry and Song

Cricket Songs: Japanese Haiku translated by Harry Behn. With pictures from Japanese masters. Sensitive translations capture the unique quality of haiku. Also: *More Cricket Songs.*

In a Spring Garden by Richard Lewis. Illustrated by Ezra Jack Keats. A beautifully illustrated collection of haiku poetry.

Maples in the Mist: Children's Poems from the Tang Dynasty by Minfong Ho. Illustrated by Jean and Mou-sien Tseng. Short, traditional verse, in Chinese and English, in a handsome picture book format illustrated with full-page watercolor paintings.

My Chinatown: One Year in Poems by Kam Mak. A boy from Hong Kong vividly remembers his first experiences in New York City "where the English words taste like metal in my mouth."

Red Dragonfly on My Shoulder: Haiku translated by Sylvia Cassedy and Kunihiro Suetake. Illustrated by Molly Bang. Everyday objects are transformed into imaginative collages in this picture book collection of Japanese verse.

Stories for Older Readers

The Amah by Laurence Yep. Twelve-year-old Amy finds her family responsibilities growing and interfering with her ballet practice when her mother takes a job outside the home.

The Cat Who Went to Heaven by Elizabeth Coatsworth. Pictures by Lynn Ward. A little cat comes to the home of a poor Japanese artist and, by humility and devotion, brings him good fortune.

Dragon's Gate by Laurence Yep. When he accidentally kills a Manchu, a fifteen-year-old boy is sent to America to join some of his family who are building the transcontinental railroad.

The Friends by Kazumi Yumoto. Translated by Cathy Hirano. When an unanticipated friendship develops between an elderly man and three boys, their lives all dramatically change. Set in modern-day Japan.

4.13 *continued*

The Imp that Ate My Homework by Laurence Yep. Jim teams up with his grandfather, who is known as the meanest man in Chinatown, to defeat a powerful demon.

In the Year of the Boar and Jackie Robinson by Bette Bao Lord. Illustrated by Marc Simont. Shirley Temple Wong adjusts to life in Brooklyn in 1947.

The Journal of Wong Ming-Chung: A Chinese Miner by Laurence Yep. A young Chinese boy nicknamed Runt records his experiences in a journal as he travels from southern China to California in 1852 to join his uncle during the gold rush.

Journey Home by Yoshiko Uchida. Illustrated by Charles Robinson. At the end of World War II, twelve-year-old Yuki and her parents are released from the concentration camp in Utah and return to California to rebuild their lives. A sequel to *Journey to Topaz.*

The Kite Fighters by Linda Sue Park. Decorations by Eung Won Park. In Korea in 1473, eleven-year-old Young-sup overcomes his rivalry with his older brother Kee-sup, who as the first-born son receives special treatment from their father, and combines his kite-flying skill with Kee-sup's kite-making skill in an attempt to win the New Year kite-fighting competition.

The Kite Rider by Geraldine McCaughrean. Twelve-year-old Haoyou joins the Jade Circus and finds fame, fortune, and danger. A captivating adventure set in 13th-century China.

Little Sister by Kara Dalkey. With the help of a mischievous shape-changer, young Mitsuko searches through 12th-century Japan and the realms of the Dead for the soul of her beloved older sister.

The Magic Paintbrush by Laurence Yep. Drawings by Suling Wang. A magic paintbrush transports Steve and his elderly caretakers from their drab apartment in Chinatown to a world of adventures.

The Master Puppeteer by Katherine Paterson. Illustrated by Haru Wells. A thirteen-year-old boy, apprenticed to a Bunraku theater, meets a Robin Hood-like bandit leader in old Osaka.

Seesaw Girl by Linda Sue Park. Illustrated by Jean and Mou-Sien Tseng. Rebelling against rules that forbid aristocratic girls to leave their family's Inner Court, Jade Blossom's curiosity takes her exploring beyond the walls of her home. Set in 17th-century Korea.

A Single Shard by Linda Sue Park. Tree-ear, a thirteen-year-old orphan in medieval Korea, lives under a bridge in a potters' village and longs to learn how to throw the delicate celadon ceramics himself. 2001 Newbery Award.

Songs of Papa's Island by Barbara Kerley. Illustrated by Katherine Tillotson. A mother shares family stories with her young daughter in this poetic recreation of life on Guam.

The Star Fisher by Laurence Yep. Fifteen-year-old Joan and her Chinese family face hardships when they move from Ohio to West Virginia in the 1920s. In *Dream Soul,* in 1927 as Christmas approaches, fifteen-year-old Joan Lee hopes to get her parents' permission to celebrate the holiday, one of the problems of belonging to the only Chinese American family in her small West Virginia community.

Under the Blood-Red Sun by Graham Salisbury. The Japanese attack on Pearl Harbor disrupts Tomi's life of baseball and fishing as his family faces prejudice and imprisonment.

When My Name Was Keoko: A Novel of Korea In World War II by Linda Sue Park. The Japanese occupation of her beloved homeland brings danger to Sun-hee and her family. A powerful story told in the alternating voices of a brother and sister.

4.13 *continued*

Yang the Youngest and His Terrible Ear by Lensey Namioka. Illustrated by Kees de Kiefte. Yang's Chinese immigrant family does not understand why he would rather play baseball than practice the violin. Also: *Yang the Second and Her Secret Admirers*, *Yang the Eldest and His Odd Jobs*, and *Yang the Third and Her Impossible Family*.

The Year of Impossible Goodbyes by Sook Nyul Choi. A young Korean girl survives the oppressive Japanese and Russian occupation of North Korea, and escapes to freedom in South Korea.

Stories for Younger Readers

Angel Child, Dragon Child by Michele Maria Surat. Illustrated by Vo-Dinh Mai. Ut, a Vietnamese girl attending school in the United States and lonely for her mother, makes a new friend who presents her with a wonderful gift.

Baseball Saved Us by Ken Mochizuki. A Japanese American boy learns to play during World War II.

Big Jimmy's Kum Kau Chinese Take Out by Ted Lewin. A little boy spends a busy day at his family's Brooklyn eatery.

Blue Willow by Pam Conrad. Illustrated by S. Saelig Gallagher. Kung Shi Fair's wealthy father gives her everything she asks of him; but when she requests permission to marry, he learns too late the value of listening.

The Boy of the Three Year Nap by Diane Snyder. Illustrated by Allen Say. Lazy Taro's trick is turned back on himself when his loving and clever mother takes charge. Illustrated in the style of traditional Japanese paintings.

Chang's Paper Pony by Eleanor Coerr. Illustrated by Deborah Kogan Ray. In San Francisco during the 1850's gold rush, Chang can't afford a pony until his friend Big Pete finds a solution.

Chin Yu Min and the Ginger Cat by Jennifer Armstrong. Illustrated by Mary Grandpré. A proud Chinese widow recognizes the importance of friendship when the cat who provides her with fish disappears.

Chinatown by William Low. As the Chinese New Year approaches, a young boy and his grandmother stroll through the busy streets of their colorful New York City neighborhood.

Coolies by Yin. Illustrated by Chris K. Soentpiet. A young boy hears the story of his great-great-great-grandfather and his brother who came to the United States to make a better life for themselves helping to build the transcontinental railroad.

Crow Boy by Taro Yashima. Pictures in rich colors accompany the story of a lonely Japanese boy who travels a great distance to school.

Grandfather Counts by Andrea Cheng. Illustrations by Ange Zhang. When her maternal grandfather comes from China, Helen, who is biracial, develops a special bond with him despite their age and language differences.

Grandfather Tang's Story: A Tale Told With Tangrams by Ann Tompert. Illustrated by Robert Andrew Parker. Grandfather uses ancient Chinese puzzles to tell a story about the fox fairies who change their shapes at will.

Grandfather's Journey by Allen Say. The Japanese American author recounts his grandfather's journey to America and the feelings of being torn by a love for two different countries. 1994 Caldecott Award.

4.13 *continued*

Halmoni and the Picnic by Sook Nyul Choi. Illustrated by Karen M. Dugan. A Korean American girl's third-grade class helps her newly arrived grandmother feel more comfortable with her new life in the United States. In *Yunmi and Halmoni's Trip*, Yunmi goes to Korea with her grandmother and looks forward to visiting relatives she has never seen before, but she also worries about whether Halmoni will want to return to New York.

Halmoni's Day by Edna Coe Bercaw. Pictures by Robert Hunt. Jennifer, a Korean American, is worried that her grandmother, visiting from Korea, will embarrass her on her school's Grandparents' Day, but the event brings her understanding and acceptance.

Henry's First-Moon Birthday by Lenore Look. Illustrated by Yumi Heo. A young girl helps her grandmother with preparations for the traditional Chinese celebration for her new baby brother's one-month-old birthday.

How My Parents Learned to Eat by Ina Friedman. Illustrated by Allen Say. An American sailor courts a Japanese girl and each tries, in secret, to learn the other's way of eating.

I Hate English by Ellen Levine. Illustrated by Steve Bjorkman. Mei Mei struggles to learn English in her new school.

In the Park by Huy Voun Lee. On the first day of spring, a mother and her son go to the park where they pick up sticks and draw Chinese characters, such as the earth, the bird, and insects, that represent words relating to the season. Also: *In the Snow* and *At the Beach*.

The Last Dragon by Susan Miho Nunes. Illustrated by Chris K. Soentpiet. Peter Chang spends the summer in Chinatown with his great aunt and finds unexpected friendships as he restores an old dragon costume.

Ma Jiang and the Orange Ants by Barbara Ann Porte. Illustrated by Annie Cannon. When her family's business is threatened, Ma Jiang discovers a way to trap the fierce orange ants her family sells to earn their living. A picture book set in long-ago China.

Nim and the War Effort by Milly Lee. Pictures by Yangsook Choi. Nim is determined to win her school's World War II paper drive, even if it means missing Chinese lessons.

Oranges on Golden Mountain by Elizabeth Partridge. Illustrated by Aki Sogabe. When hard times fall on his family, Jo Lee is sent from China to San Francisco, where he helps his uncle fish and dreams of being reunited with his mother and sister.

Our Home Is the Sea by Riki Levinson. Paintings by Dennis Luzak. A boy living in Hong Kong wants to become a fisherman like all of his family.

Peacebound Trains by Haemi Balgassi. Illustrated by Chris K. Soentpiet. Sumi's grandmother tells the story of her family's escape from Seoul during the Korean War, while they watch the trains that will eventually bring her mother back from army service.

Red Is a Dragon: A Book of Colors by Roseanne Thong. Illustrated by Grace Lin. A Chinese American girl provides rhyming descriptions of the great variety of colors she sees around her, from the red of a dragon, firecrackers, and lychees to the brown of her teddy bear.

Round Is a Mooncake: A Book of Shapes by Roseanne Thong. Illustrated by Grace Lin. As a little girl discovers things round, square, and rectangular in her urban neighborhood, she is reminded of her Chinese American culture.

Ruby's Wish by Shirin Yim Bridges. Illustrated by Sophie Blackall. A little girl in China who loves the color red would rather be a scholar than follow tradition.

Silent Lotus by Jeanne M. Lee. Although she cannot speak or hear, Lotus trains as a Khmer court dancer.

4.13 *continued*

So Far from the Sea by Eve Bunting. Illustrated by Chris Soentpiet. When seven-year-old Laura and her family visit Grandfather's grave at the Manzanar War Relocation Center, the Japanese American child leaves behind a special symbol.

The Squiggle by Carole Lexa Schaefer. Illustrated by Pierr Morgan. A red ribbon becomes a dragon, a thunder cloud, and the moon to an imaginative Chinese girl.

The Trip Back Home by Janet S. Wong. Illustrated by Bo Jia. A young girl and her mother travel to Korea to visit their extended family.

Umbrella by Taro Yashima. A small Japanese child delights in her first umbrella and red rubber boots.

The Warrior and the Wise Man by David Wisniewski. Elaborate paper cuts illustrate a struggle between wisdom and strength in 12th-century Japan.

White Tiger, Blue Serpent by Grace Tseng. Illustrated by Jean and Mou-sien Tseng. When his mother's beautiful brocade is snatched away by a greedy goddess, a young Chinese boy faces many perils as he attempts to get it back.

Yoko's Paper Cranes by Rosemary Wells. A young cat who misses her grandparents in faraway Japan uses origami to send them her love. A comforting book with Asian-inspired art.

Source: Copyright © The New York Public Library, Astor, Lenox and Tilden Foundations. Used with permission.

4.14 Selected Children's Books About Native Americans in the 20th Century

The following list of recommended titles was compiled by Arlene Hirschfelder, consultant in Native American studies, author of several books about American Indians, and co-author of *Native Americans Today: Resources and Activities for Education Grades 4–8*, published by Libraries Unlimited (2000). This bibliography represents years of reading children's books about and by Native people as well as over thirty years of expertise in Indian studies.

Aaseng, Nathan. *Navajo Code Talkers*. New York: Walker and Co., 1992. Photographs. Grade 6+

Ancona, George. *Earth Daughter Alicia of Acoma Pueblo*. New York: Simon & Schuster, 1994. Photographs. Grade 3+

Ashabranner, Brent. *Morning Star, Black Sun: The Northern Cheyenne Indians and America's Energy Crisis*. New York: Dodd, 1982. Photographs. Grade 6+

Ashabranner, Brent. *To Live in Two Worlds. American Indian Youth Today*. New York: Dodd, 1984. Photographs. Grade 6+

Begay, Shonto. *Navajo. Visions and Voices Across the Mesa*. New York: Scholastic, 1994. Full-color illustrations. Grade 4+

Benton-Banai, Edward. *The Mishomis Book: The Voice of the Ojibway*. (Anishinabe/Ojibway/Chippewa). Hayward, WI: Indian Country Communications, 1988. Illustrations. Grade 4+

Blood, Charles and Martin Unk. *The Goat in the Rug*. New York: Parents' Magazine Press, 1976. Full-color illustrations. Preschool+

Braine, Susan. *Drumbeat . . . Heartbeat. A Celebration of the Powwow*. Minneapolis: Lerner Publications, 1995. Photographs. Grade 3+

Broker, Ignatia. *Night Flying Woman*. (Anishinabe/Ojibway/Chippewa). St. Paul: Minnesota Historical Society Press, 1983. Grade 6+

Bruchac, Joseph. *Eagle Song*. New York: Dial Books for Young Readers, 1997. Grade 5+

Bunting, Eve. *Cheyenne Again*. New York: Clarion Books, 1995. Full-color illustrations. Preschool+

Caduto, Michael J. and Joseph Bruchac. *Keepers of the Animals: Native American Stories and Wildlife Activities for Children*. Golden, CO: Fulcrum, Inc., 1991. Teacher's guide and audiocassette. All ages

Caduto, Michael J. and Joseph Bruchac. *Keepers of the Earth: Native American Stories and Environmental Activities for Children*. Golden, CO: Fulcrum, Inc., 1988. Teacher's guide and audiocassette. All ages

Caduto, Michael J. and Joseph Bruchac. *Keepers of Life: Discovering Plants Through Native American Stories and Earth Activities for Children*. Golden, CO: Fulcrum, Inc., 1994. Teacher's guide and audiocassette. All ages

Caduto, Michael and Joseph Bruchac. *Keepers of the Night: Native American Stories and Nocturnal Activities for Children*. Golden, CO: Fulcrum, Inc., 1994. Teacher's guide and audiocassette. All ages

4.14 *continued*

Charging Eagle, Tom and Ron Zeilinger. *Black Hills: Sacred Hills.* (Sioux/Dakota/Lakota). Chamberlain, SD: Tipi Press, c/o St. Joseph's Indian School, Chamberlain, SD 57326, 1987. Photographs. Grade 3+

Clark, Ann Nolan. *In My Mother's House.* (Pueblo peoples). New York: Viking (reprint of 1941 edition). Full-color illustrations. Preschool+

Coombs, Linda. *Powwow.* Cleveland: Modern Curriculum Press, 1992. Full-color illustrations. Grade 1

Crum, Robert. *Eagle Drum: On the Powwow Trail with a Young Grass Dancer.* New York: Four Winds/Simon & Schuster, 1994. Photographs. Grade 2+

Dennis, Yvonne Wakim and Arlene Hirschfelder. *Children of Native America Today.* Watertown, MA: Charlesbridge/Global Fund for Children, 2003. Grades 1–6

Echo-Hawk, Roger C. and Walter R. *Battlefields and Burial Grounds—The Indian Struggle to Protect Ancestral Graves in the United States.* Minneapolis: Lerner Publications, 1994. Grade 7+

Ekoomiak, Normee. *Arctic Memories.* (Inuit; English and Inuktitut text). New York: Henry Holt, 1988. Full-color illustrations. Grade 3+

Erdrich, Louise. *Grandmother's Pigeon.* New York: Hyperion, 1996. Full-color illustrations. Preschool+

Ferris, Sean. *Children of the Great Muskeg.* Windsor, Ontario: Black Moss Press, 1985. Children's art and poetry. Grade 4+

Francis, Lee, ed. *When the Rain Sings: Poems by Young Native Americans.* New York: National Museum of the American Indian/Simon & Schuster, 1999. Grade 4+

Gravelle, Karen. *Growing Up Where the Partridge Drums Its Wings.* New York: Franklin Watts, 1997. Photographs. Grade 2+

Griese, Arnold. *Anna's Athabascan Summer.* Honesdale, PA: Boyds Mill Press, 1995. Photographs. Preschool+

Griffin-Pierce, Trudy. *The Encyclopedia of Native America.* New York: Penguin, 1995. Full-color illustrations and photographs. All ages

Harjo, Joy. *The Good Luck Cat.* New York: Harcourt, 2000. Full-color illustrations. Preschool+

Hazen-Hammond, Susan. *Thunder Bear and Ko: The Buffalo Nation and Nambré Pueblo.* New York: Dutton, 1999. Photographs. Grade 2+

Heath, Kristina. *Mama's Little One.* Gresham, WI: Muh-He-Con-Neew Press, N9136 Big Lake Road, Gresham, WI, 54128-4427, 1998. Preschool

Himango, Deanna. *Boozhoo, Come Play With Us.* Fond du Lac, WI: Fond du Lac Head Start Program, 2002. Preschool

Hirschfelder, Arlene and Beverly Singer, eds. *Rising Voices: Writings of Young Native Americans.* New York: Charles Scribner's Sons, 1992. Grade 4+

4.14 *continued*

Hoig, Stan. *People of the Sacred Arrows: The Southern Cheyenne Today.* New York: Cobblehill Books, 1992. Photographs. Grade 6+

Hoyt-Goldsmith, Diane. *Apache Rodeo.* New York: Holiday House, 1995. Photographs. Grade 3+

Hoyt-Goldsmith, Diane. *Arctic Hunter.* New York: Holiday House, 1992. Photographs. Grade 3+

Hoyt-Goldsmith, Diane. *Buffalo Days.* (Crow). New York: Holiday House, 1997. Photographs. Grade 3+

Hoyt-Goldsmith, Diane. *Cherokee Summer.* New York: Holiday House, 1993. Photographs. Grade 3+

Hoyt-Goldsmith, Diane. *Lacrosse: The National Game of the Iroquois.* New York: Holiday House, 1998. Photographs. Grade 3+

Hoyt-Goldsmith, Diane. *Potlatch: A Tsimshian Celebration.* New York: Holiday House, 1997. Photographs. Grade 3+

Hoyt-Goldsmith, Diane. *Pueblo Storyteller.* (Cochiti Pueblo). New York: Holiday House, 1991. Photographs. Grade 3+

Hoyt-Goldsmith, Diane. *Totem Pole.* (Tsimshian). New York: Holiday House, 1990. Photographs. Grade 3+

Hucko, Bruce. *A Rainbow at Night: The World in Words and Pictures by Navajo Children.* San Francisco: Chronicle Books, 1997. All ages

Hucko, Bruce. *Where There Is No Name for Art: Art and Voices of the Children of Santa Clara, San Ildefonso, San Juan, Pojoaque, and Nambré Pueblos.* Santa Fe: SAR Press, 1996. All ages

Hunter, Sally. *Four Seasons of Corn: A Winnebago Tradition.* Minneapolis: Lerner Publications, 1996. Photographs. Grade 3+

Katz, William Loren and Paula A. Franklin. *Proudly Red and Black: Stories of African and Native Americans.* New York: Atheneum, 1993. Grade 4+

Keegan, Marcia. *Pueblo Boy: Growing Up in Two Worlds.* (San Ildefonso Pueblo). New York: Cobblehill Books, 1991. Photographs. Grade 3+

Keegan Marcia. *Pueblo Girls: Growing Up in Two Worlds.* Santa Fe: Clear Light, 1999. Photographs. Grade 3+

Keeshig-Tobias, Lenore. *Bird Talk.* Toronto, Ontario: Sister Vision Press, 1998. Preschool–1

Kendall, Russ. *Eskimo Boy: Life in an Inupiaq Eskimo Village.* New York: Scholastic, 1992. Photographs. Grade 1+

King, Sandra. *Shannon/An Ojibway Dancer.* Minneapolis: Lerner Publications, 1993. Photographs. Grade 3+

Krull, Kathleen. *One Nation, Many Tribes: How Kids Live in Milwaukee's Indian Community.* New York: Lodestar Books, 1994. Photographs. Grade 3+

4.14 *continued*

LaDuke, Winona and Waseyabin Kapashesit. *The Sugarbush Book.* Ponsford, MN: White Earth Land Recovery Project, Route 1, Box 291, Ponsford, MN 56575, 1999. Preschool–1

Left Hand Bull, Jacqueline and Suzanne Haldane. *Lakota Hoop Dancer.* New York: Dutton, 1999. Photographs. Grade 3+

Littlechild, George. *This Land Is My Land.* Emeryville, CA: Children's Book Press, 1994. Full-color illustrations. Preschool+

Lourie, Peter. *Everglades: Buffalo Tiger and the River of Grass.* Honesdale, PA: Boyds Mill Press, 1994. Photographs. Grade 3+

Martinson, David, compiler. *Angwamas Minosewag Anishinabeq: Time of the Indian.* (Minnesota tribes). Cass Lake, MN: Minnesota Indian Tribe, Box 217, Cass Lake, MN 56633, 1979. Writings by youngsters. Grade 4+

McMillan, Bruce. *Salmon Summer.* Boston: Houghton Mifflin, 1998. Photographs. Preschool+

Mercredi, Morningstar. *Fort Chipewyan Homecoming: A Journey to Native Canada.* Minneapolis: Lerner Publications, 1997. Photographs. Grade 5+

Montaño, Marty Kreipe de. *Coyote in Love with A. Star.* New York: Abbeville Press, Inc., 1998. Preschool–1

Monture, Joel. *Cloudwalker Contemporary Native American Stories.* Golden, CO: Fulcrum Kids, 1996. Grade 4+

Moore, Reavis. *Native Artists of North America.* Santa Fe: John Muir, 1993. Grade 4+

Ortiz, Simon. *The People Shall Continue.* (General history). Emeryville, CA: Children's Book Press, 1977. Full-color illustrations. All ages.

Peters, Russell M. *Clambake: A Wampanoag Tradition.* Minneapolis: Lerner Publications, 1992. Photographs. Grade 3+

Rappaport, Doreen. *We Are the Many.* New York: HarperCollins, 2002. Grade 2+

Regguinti, Gordon. *The Sacred Harvest: Ojibway Wild Rice Gathering.* Minneapolis: Lerner Publications, 1992. Photographs. Grade 3+

Rendon, Marcie R. *Powwow Summer: A Family Celebrates the Circle of Life.* Minneapolis: Carolrhoda Books, 1996. Photographs. Grades 1–6

Roessel, Monty. *Kinaalda: A Navajo Girl Grows Up.* Minneapolis: Lerner Publications, 1993. Photographs. Grade 3+

Roessel, Monty. *Songs from the Loom: A Navajo Girl Learns to Weave.* Minneapolis: Lerner Publications, 1995. Photographs. Grade 3+

Rose, LaVera. *Grandchildren of the Lakota.* Minneapolis: Carolrhoda Books, 1998. Grade 1+

Santiago, Chiori. *Home to Medicine Mountain.* San Francisco: Children's Book Press, 1998. Full-color illustrations. Grade 3+

4.14 *continued*

Schick, Eleanor. *Navajo Wedding Day, A Diné Marriage Ceremony*. Tarrytown, NY: Marshall Cavendish, 1999. Full-color illustrations. Grade 2+

Seymour, Tryntje Van Ness. *The Gift of Changing Woman*. New York: Henry Holt, 1993. Full-color illustrations. Grade 6+

Shemie, Bonnie. *Houses of Adobe: Native Dwellings of the Southwest; Houses of Bark: Native Dwellings of the Woodland Indians; Houses of Hide and Earth: Native Dwellings of the Plains Indians; Houses of Snow, Skin, and Bones: Native Dwellings of the Far North; Houses of Wood: Native Dwellings of the Northwest Coast*. Plattsburgh, NY: Tundra Books. Full-color illustrations. Grade 3+

Smith, Cynthia Leitich. *Indian Shoes*. New York: HarperCollins, 2002. Grade 3+

Smith, Cynthia Leitich. *Jingle Dancer*. New York: Morrow, 2000. Full-color illustrations. Preschool+

Smith, Cynthia Leitich. *Rain Is Not My Indian Name*. New York: HarperCollins, 2001. Novel. Grade 7+

Sneve, Virginia Driving Hawk. *High Elk's Treasure*. New York: Holiday House, 1995. (Reprint of 1972 book). Illustrations. Grade 3+

Steltzer, Ulli. *A Haida Potlatch*. Seattle: University of Washington Press, 1984. Photographs. All ages

Swamp, Jake. *Giving Thanks. A Native American Good Morning Message*. New York: Lee and Low Books, 1995. Full-color illustrations. All ages

Swentzell, Rina. *Children of Clay: A Family of Potters*. Minneapolis: Lerner Publications, 1992. Photographs. Grade 3+

Tapahonso, Luci. *Songs of Shiprock Fair*. Walnut, CA: Kiva Publishing, 1999. Preschool–1

Tapahonso, Luci and Eleanor Schick. *Navajo ABC: A Diné Alphabet Book*. New York: Simon & Schuster, 1994. Full-color illustrations. Grade 1+

Thomson, Peggy. *Katie Henio, Navajo Sheepherder*. New York: Cobblehill, 1995. Photographs. Grade 4+

Waboose, Jan B. *Morning on the Lake*. (Ojibway). Toronto, Ontario: Kids Can Press, 1998. Full-color illustrations. Preschool+

Waboose, Jan B. *Sky Sisters*. (Ojibway). Toronto, Ontario: Kids Can Press, 2000. Full-color illustrations. Preschool+

Williams, Neva. *Patrick DesJarlait. Conversations with a Native American Artist*. Minneapolis: Runestone Press, 1995. Grade 5+

Wittstock, Laura Waterman. *Ininatig's Gift of Sugar: Traditional Native Sugarmaking*. Minneapolis: Lerner Publications, 1993. Photographs. Grade 3+

Wood, Ted with Wanbli Numpa Afraid of Hawk. *A Boy Becomes a Man at Wounded Knee*. (Sioux/Dakota/Lakota). New York: Walker and Co., 1992. Photographs. All ages

4.14 *continued*

Yue, Charlotte and David. *The Igloo*. Boston: Houghton Mifflin, 1988. Illustrations. Grade 4+

Yue, Charlotte and David. *The Pueblo*. Boston: Houghton Mifflin, 1986. Illustrations. Grade 4+

Yue, Charlotte and David. *The Tipi*. New York: Knopf, 1984. Illustrations. Grade 4+

Yue, Charlotte and David. *The Wigwam and the Longhouse*. Boston: Houghton Mifflin, 2000. Illustrations. Grade 4+

Yumane, Linda. *Weaving a California Tradition: A Native American Basketmaker*. Minneapolis: Lerner Publications, 1997. Photographs. Grade 4+

4.15 The New York Public Library's List of 100 Favorite Children's Books

Biography and History

Bully for You, Teddy Roosevelt! by Jean Fritz. The dynamic life of the 26th president who hunted big game animals and fought for conservation.

Charles A. Lindbergh: A Human Hero by James Cross Giblin. A fascinating portrait that explores the accomplishments and shortcomings of the adventurous American aviator.

Eleanor Roosevelt: A Life of Discovery by Russell Freedman. Photographs and insight portray a dynamic first lady devoted to public service and humanitarian causes.

Ezra Jack Keats by Dean Engel. Fans and young readers alike will be delighted with this insightful story of the beloved picture book author and illustrator.

Homesick: My Own Story by Jean Fritz. The author's memoir of her childhood in China in the 1920s.

Leonardo da Vinci by Diane Stanley. A re-creation of the life of the Renaissance painter and inventor through handsomely detailed illustrations.

Lincoln: A Photobiography by Russell Freedman. The life of the 16th president movingly portrayed in words and pictures. The 1988 Newbery Award.

Little: A Writer's Education by Jean Little. Recollections of the author's childhood in Taiwan and Canada and what it was like to be almost blind reveal the source for the strength and feelings in her books.

Lives of the Musicians by Kathleen Krull. Good times, bad times (and what the neighbors thought)—a witty collection. First in a series.

The Diary of a Young Girl by Anne Frank. The secret journal of a Dutch Jewish girl written during the time her family went into hiding from the Nazis during World War II.

Fantasy

Charlotte's Web by E. B. White. The story of a little girl named Fern who loves a little pig named Wilbur and of Wilbur's dear friend, Charlotte A. Cavatica, a beautiful, large grey spider who lives with Wilbur in the barn.

Falcon's Egg by Luli Gray. A girl finds a large, hot, red egg in Central Park and cares for the remarkable creature that hatches from it.

The Boggart by Susan Cooper. When an ancient and mischievous spirit is accidently transported from Scotland to Toronto, it wreaks havoc for Emily and her brother Jessup.

The Book of Three by Lloyd Alexander. Taran, would-be hero and assistant pig-keeper, assembles a group of companions to rescue the oracular pig Hen Wen from the forces of evil. One book in five of the "Prydain Chronicles."

4.15 *continued*

The Dark Is Rising by Susan Cooper. Will Stanton's 11th birthday is the beginning of a frightening yet wonderful discovery of a special gift—immortality and power against the forces of evil.

The Haunting by Margaret Mahy. After a shy and rather withdrawn 8-year-old begins receiving frightening supernatural images and messages, he learns about a family legacy that could be considered a curse or a rare gift.

The Lion, the Witch, and the Wardrobe by C. S. Lewis. Four English children go through a wardrobe door to Narnia where Aslan, the noble lion, fights the spell of the white witch. The first in the "Chronicles of Narnia" series.

The Moorchild by Eloise McGraw. Feeling that she is neither fully human nor "Folk," a changeling learns her true identity and attempts to find the human child whose place she had been given.

The Return of the Twelves by Pauline Clarke. In his new home, a young boy finds twelve old wooden soldiers (all alive) that once belonged to the famous Brontë children.

Tuck Everlasting by Natalie Babbitt. The Tuck family is confronted with an agonizing situation when they discover that a 10-year-old girl and a malicious stranger now share their secret about a spring whose water prevents one from ever growing any older.

Favorite Animal Stories

Abel's Island by William Steig. Castaway on an uninhabited island, Abel, a very civilized mouse, finds his resourcefulness and endurance tested to the limit as he struggles to survive and return home.

Babe, the Gallant Pig by Dick King-Smith. A piglet destined to be butchered arrives at the farmyard, is adopted by an old sheep dog, and discovers a special secret to success.

Bunnicula by Deborah Howe. Though scoffed at by Harold the dog, Chester the cat tries to warn his human family that their foundling baby bunny is a vampire.

Mrs. Frisby and the Rats of NIMH by Robert C. O'Brien. In need of help for her children, a widowed mouse visits the rats whose former imprisonment in a laboratory has given them wisdom. The 1972 Newbery Award.

Poppy by Avi. A courageous girl mouse embarks on a journey to save her family and defeat the tyrannical horned owl who rules the forest.

Shiloh by Phyllis Reynolds Naylor. When he finds a lost beagle in the hills behind his West Virginia home, Marty tries to hide it from his family and the dog's real owner, a mean-spirited man who shoots deer out of season and mistreats his dogs. The 1992 Newbery Award.

Sounder by William Armstrong. Angry and humiliated when his sharecropper father is jailed for stealing food for his family, a young black boy grows in courage and understanding with the help of his devoted dog Sounder. The 1970 Newbery Award.

4.15 *continued*

The Cricket in Times Square by George Selden. A fast-talking mouse and a city-wise cat welcome a country cricket to a new home in a New York City subway station.

The Incredible Journey by Sheila Burnford. Two dogs and a cat support each other through hardships, hunger, and danger as they travel 250 miles across Canada to reach home.

The Wainscott Weasel by Tor Seidler. A sensitive but heroic young weasel finds a way to save his seaside community on Long Island. Beautifully illustrated.

Historical Fiction

All-of-a-Kind Family by Sydney Taylor. A Jewish family finds life in New York City in the early 20th century a joyous and adventurous experience. The first in a series.

Bull Run by Paul Fleischman. Northerners, Southerners, generals, couriers, dreaming boys, and worried sisters describe the glory, the horror, the thrill, and the disillusionment of the first battle of the Civil War.

I, Juan de Pareja by Elizabeth Borton de Treviño. A fictionalized biography of the African slave of the great Spanish painter Velazquez.

Letters from Rifka by Karen Hesse. In letters to her cousin, a young Jewish girl chronicles her family's perilous 1919 flight from Russia to America, and her own experiences when she has to be left behind in Belgium.

Little House in the Big Woods by Laura Ingalls Wilder. Laura and her pioneer family share a home in the wilderness of Wisconsin in this first of a beloved series.

Morning Girl by Michael Dorris. Morning Girl, who loves the day, and her younger brother, Star Boy, who loves the night, take turns describing their life on a Caribbean island just before Columbus lands.

Roll of Thunder, Hear My Cry by Mildred Taylor. A black family living in Mississippi in 1933 is faced with prejudice. The 1977 Newbery Award.

The Master Puppeteer by Katherine Paterson. In 18th-century Osaka, the 13-year-old son of a poor puppet-maker becomes a theater apprentice and discovers the identity of the mysterious bandit who robs the rich and helps the starving poor in famine-struck Japan.

The Midwife's Apprentice by Karen Cushman. In medieval England, a nameless, homeless girl is taken in by a sharp-tempered midwife, and in spite of obstacles and hardship, eventually gains the three things she wants most: a full belly, a contented heart, and a place in this world. The 1996 Newbery Award.

The Witch of Blackbird Pond by Elizabeth George Speare. A 16-year-old girl from Barbados moves to a Puritan colony in Connecticut and is accused of being a witch.

Humor

Freaky Friday by Mary Rodgers. A 13-year-old girl gains a much more sympathetic understanding of her relationship with her mother when the two switch bodies.

4.15 *continued*

Harris and Me: A Summer Remembered by Gary Paulsen. Pig wrestling and mouse hunting are just two of a young boy's raucous escapades the summer he lived on his cousin's farm.

How to Eat Fried Worms by Thomas Rockwell. Two boys set out to prove that worms can make a delicious meal.

Knights of the Kitchen Table by Jon Scieszka. A magic book transports three boys back to the days of King Arthur in this first book of the "The Time Warp Trio."

Lizard Music by Daniel Manus Pinkwater. When left to take care of himself, a young boy encounters a community of intelligent lizards who tell him of a little-known invasion from outer space.

Ordinary Jack by Helen Cresswell. An 11-year-old English boy, Jack, the only "ordinary" member of the talented and eccentric Bagthorpe family, concocts a scheme to distinguish himself as a modern-day prophet. The first in "The Bagthorpe Saga."

Squashed by Joan Bauer. Ellie is determined that Max, her 600-pound pumpkin, will win the big weigh-in at the County Fair.

The Phantom Tollbooth by Norton Juster. Milo, a little boy who didn't know what to do with himself, goes through the phantom tollbooth, behind which lies a strange land and even stranger adventures.

The Twits by Roald Dahl. The misadventures of two terrible old people who enjoy playing nasty tricks and are finally outwitted by a family of monkeys.

Unreal! by Paul Jennings. Magic underpants, a ghost that haunts an outhouse, and ice cream that can make you smart are some of the ingredients in these eight surprising stories.

Mystery

Down a Dark Hall by Lois Duncan. Suspicious and uneasy about the atmosphere at her new boarding school, 14-year-old Kit slowly realizes why she and the other three students at school were selected.

Encyclopedia Brown: Boy Detective by Donald Sobol. The first in a series of detective stories in which the reader is challenged to match wits with the 10-year-old mastermind of Idaville's war on crime.

From the Mixed-up Files of Mrs. Basil E. Frankweiler by E. L. Konigsburg. A 12-year-old girl and her brother run away to The Metropolitan Museum of Art. The 1968 Newbery Award.

The Dollhouse Murders by Betty Ren Wright. A dollhouse filled with a ghostly light in the middle of the night and dolls that have moved from where she has left them lead Amy and her sister to unravel the mystery surrounding grisly murders that took place years ago.

The Egypt Game by Zilpha Keatley Snyder. Melanie and her new friend April enjoy a common interest in ancient Egypt and develop a land of Egypt in an abandoned storage yard.

4.15 *continued*

The House of Dies Drear by Virginia Hamilton. Thirteen-year-old Thomas and his family move from North Carolina to a strange, old mansion in Ohio that was once a station on the Underground Railroad.

The House With a Clock in Its Walls by John Bellairs. A boy goes to live with his magician uncle in a mansion that has a clock hidden in the walls that is ticking off the minutes until doomsday.

The Ruby in the Smoke by Phillip Pullman. In 19th-century London, 16-year-old Sally, a recent orphan, becomes involved in a deadly search for a mysterious ruby.

The View from the Cherry Tree by Willo Davis Roberts. Rob admits to having seen a murder, but in the confusion of his older sister's wedding, no one believes him—except the murderer.

The Westing Game by Ellen Raskin. The mysterious death of an eccentric millionaire brings together an unlikely assortment of heirs who must uncover the circumstances of his death before they can claim their inheritance. The 1979 Newbery Award.

Poetry and Song

A Pizza the Size of the Sun. Jack Prelutsky. Humor, rhythm, and rhyme abound in nearly 100 poems.

And the Green Grass Grew All Around: Folk Poetry from Everyone by Alvin Schwartz. Teases and taunts, wishes and warnings—a bouyant collection of beloved childhood nonsense.

Brats by X. J. Kennedy. Forty-two poems describe a variety of particularly unpleasant children.

I Am the Darker Brother by Arnold Adoff. An anthology of African American poets.

Joyful Noise: Poems for Two Voices by Paul Fleischman. The world of insects captured in poems for two voices that are perfect for reading aloud. The 1989 Newbery Award.

Singing America: Poems that Define a Nation edited by Neil Philip. Poetic voices illuminate the character and history of the United States.

Soul Looks Back in Wonder
Compilation
Artwork by Tom Feelings and poems of such writers as Maya Angelou, Langston Hughes, and Askia Toure portray the creativity, strength, and beauty of their African American heritage.

The Dream Keeper and Other Poems by Langston Hughes. Lyrical poems, songs, and blues explore the black experience.

What to Do When a Bug Crawls in Your Mouth and Other Poems to Drive You Buggy. Roaches, bees, ants, beetles—silly verse to chuckle over in a colorfully illustrated book.

Where the Sidewalk Ends by Shel Silverstein. A boy who turns into a TV set and a girl who eats a whale are only two of the characters in a collection of humorous poetry illustrated with the author's own drawings.

4.15 *continued*

Science Fiction

A Wrinkle in Time by Madeline L'Engle. A trio of whimsical characters, intent on helping Meg find her father, take her, her brother, and a friend on an interplanetary voyage to a distant planet where an omnipotent brain has robotized everyone. The 1963 Newbery Award.

Anna to the Infinite Power by Mildred Ames. A 12-year-old math whiz accidentally learns the startling facts about her true identity and her role in an important secret experiment.

Children of the Dust by Louise Lawrence. After a nuclear war devastates the earth, a small band of people struggles for survival in a new world where children are born with mutations.

Enchantress from the Stars by Sylvia Engdahl. Three civilizations from different planets in widely varying stages of development clash in what could be either a mutually disastrous or beneficial encounter.

Eva by Peter Dickinson. After a terrible accident, a young girl wakes up to discover that she has been given the body of a chimpanzee.

Interstellar Pig by William Sleator. Barney's boring seaside vacation suddenly becomes more interesting when the cottage next door is occupied by three exotic neighbors who are addicted to a doomsday game.

Stinker from Space by Pamela Service. An agent of the Sylon Confederacy, who is fleeing from enemy ships, crash lands on Earth, transfers his mind to the body of a skunk, and enlists the aid of two children in getting back to his home planet.

The Ear, the Eye, and the Arm by Nancy Farmer. In 2194 Zimbabwe, General Matsika's three children are kidnapped and put to work in a plastic mine, while three mutant detectives use their special powers to search for them.

The Giver by Lois Lowry. At the Ceremony of the Twelves, Jonas begins to learn the horrifying truth about the perfect society in which he has grown up. The 1994 Newbery Award.

The White Mountains by John Christopher. The harrowing escape of a young boy from a futuristically mechanized tyranny is compellingly described. The first book of the author's trilogy about the Tripods, of which *The City of Gold and Lead* and *The Pool of Fire* form the second and third books, respectively.

Stories

Sarah, Plain and Tall by Patricia MacLachlan. Caleb and Anna hope that the mail-order bride who comes from Maine to their prairie home will stay.

Survival and Adventure

A Girl Named Disaster by Nancy Farmer. While journeying to Zimbabwe, 11-year-old Nhamo struggles to escape drowning and starvation and in so doing comes close to the luminous world of the African spirits.

4.15 *continued*

Hatchet by Gary Paulsen. After a plane crash, 13-year-old Brian spends fifty-four days in the wilderness, learning to survive initially with only the aid of a hatchet given by his mother, and learning also to survive his parents' divorce.

Island of the Blue Dolphins by Scott O'Dell. When her younger brother dies in 1800, Karana, an Indian girl, spends eighteen years alone on the Island of San Nicholas, far off the coast of California. The 1961 Newbery Award.

Julie of the Wolves by Jean Craighead George. While running away from home and an unwanted marriage, a 13-year-old Eskimo girl becomes lost on the North Slope of Alaska and is befriended by a wolf pack. The 1973 Newbery Award.

Save Queen of Sheba by Louise Moeri. After miraculously surviving a Sioux Indian raid on the trail to Oregon, a brother and sister set out with few provisions to find the rest of the settlers.

Slake's Limbo by Felice Holman. Thirteen-year-old Aremis Slake, hounded by his fears and misfortunes, flees them into New York City's subway tunnels, never again—he believes—to emerge.

Stone Fox by John Reynolds Gardiner. Willy tries desperately to win a sled dog race against an enigmatic Indian.

The True Confessions of Charlotte Doyle by Avi. As the lone "young lady" on a transatlantic voyage in 1832, Charlotte learns that the captain is murderous and the crew, rebellious.

The Whipping Boy by Sid Fleischman. A bratty prince and his whipping boy have many adventures when they inadvertently trade places after becoming involved with dangerous outlaws. The 1987 Newbery Award.

Z for Zachariah by Robert O'Brien. Seemingly the only person left alive after the holocaust of a war, a young girl is relieved to see a man arrive into her valley until she realizes that he is a tyrant and she must somehow escape.

Today's Kids

Are You There, God? It's Me, Margaret by Judy Blume. Faced with the difficulties of growing up and choosing a religion, a 12-year-old girl talks over her problems with her own private God.

Harriet the Spy by Louise Fitzhugh. Precocious, overprivileged Harriet darts around her Manhattan neighborhood ferreting out the "scoop" on the moving scene.

Maniac Magee by Jerry Spinelli. After his parents die, Jeffrey Lionel Magee's life becomes legendary, as he accomplishes athletic and other feats that awe his contemporaries. The 1991 Newbery Award.

Motown and Didi by Walter Dean Myers. Motown and Didi, two teenage loners in Harlem, become allies in a fight against Touchy, the drug dealer whose dope is destroying Didi's brother, and find themselves falling in love with each other.

4.15 *continued*

Shabanu: Daughter of the Wind by Suzanne Fisher Staples. When 11-year old Shabanu, the daughter of a nomad in present-day Pakistan, is pledged in marriage to an older man whose money will bring prestige to the family, she must either accept the decision, as is the custom, or risk the consequences of defying her family.

The Friends by Rosa Guy. A young West Indian girl in Harlem, New York, recognizes that her own selfish pride rather than her mother's death and her father's tyrannical behavior created the gulf between her and her best friend.

The Goats by Brock Cole. Abandoned on an island by their fellow campers, a boy and a girl learn to survive both physically and emotionally.

Toning the Sweep by Angela Johnson. On a trip to the desert to bring her dying grandmother home, Emily learns about the family's tragic past and gains pride as a third-generation black woman.

Walk Two Moons by Sharon Creech. After her mother leaves home suddenly, 13-year-old Sal and her grandparents take a car trip to Idaho to retrace her mother's route. The 1995 Newbery Award.

What Jamie Saw by Carolyn Coman. Having fled to a family friend's hillside trailer after his mother's boyfriend tried to throw his baby sister against a wall, 9-year-old Jamie finds himself living an existence full of uncertainty and fear.

Source: Copyright © The New York Public Library, Astor, Lenox and Tilden Foundations. Used with permission.

4.16 The New York Public Library's 100 Picture Books Everyone Should Know

Abuela by Arthur Dorros; Illustrated by Elisa Kleven (Dutton)
Alexander and the Terrible, Horrible, No Good, Very Bad Day by Judith Viorst; Illustrated by Ray Cruz (Atheneum)
Animals Should Definitely Not Wear Clothing by Judi Barrett; Illustrated by Ron Barrett (Atheneum)
Anansi and the Moss-Covered Rock by Eric A. Kimmel; Illustrated by Janet Stevens (Holiday House)
Andy and the Lion by James Daugherty (Viking)
Ben's Trumpet by Rachel Isadora (Greenwillow)
Blueberries for Sal by Robert McCloskey (Viking)
The Bossy Gallito: A Traditional Cuban Folk Tale retold by Lucia M. Gonzalez; Illustrated by Lulu Delacre (Scholastic)
Bread and Jam for Frances by Russell Hoban; Illustrated by Lillian Hoban (HarperCollins)
Brown Bear, Brown Bear, What Do You See? by Bill Martin Jr.; Illustrated by Eric Carle (Holt)
Caps for Sale; A Tale of a Peddler, Some Monkeys and Their Monkey Business by Esphyr Slobodkina (HarperCollins)
The Carrot Seed by Ruth Krauss; Illustrated by Crockett Johnson (HarperCollins)
A Chair for My Mother by Vera B. Williams (Greenwillow)
Chicka Chicka Boom Boom by Bill Martin Jr. and John Archambault; Illustrated by Lois Ehlert (Simon & Schuster)
Corduroy by Don Freeman (Viking)
Curious George by H. A. Rey (Houghton Mifflin)
The Day Jimmy's Boa Ate the Wash by Trinka H. Noble; Illustrated by Steven Kellogg (Dial)
Dear Zoo by Rod Campbell (Simon & Schuster)
Doctor Desoto by William Steig (Farrar, Straus & Giroux)
Farmer Duck by Martin Waddell; Illustrated by Helen Oxenbury (Candlewick Press)
The Fortune-Tellers by Lloyd Alexander; Illustrated by Trina Schart Hyman (Dutton)
Freight Train by Donald Crews (Greenwillow)
George and Martha by James Marshall (Houghton Mifflin)
Go Away, Big Green Monster! by Ed Emberley (Little, Brown)
Good Night, Gorilla by Peggy Rathmann (Putnam)
Goodnight Moon by Margaret Wise Brown; Illustrated by Clement Hurd (HarperCollins)
Grandfather's Journey by Allen Say (Houghton Mifflin)
Happy Birthday, Moon by Frank Asch (Simon & Schuster)
Harold and the Purple Crayon by Crockett Johnson (HarperCollins)
Harry the Dirty Dog by Gene Zion; Illustrated by Margaret Graham (HarperCollins)
Henny Penny illustrated by Paul Galdone (Clarion)
Horton Hatches the Egg by Dr. Seuss (Random House)
I Know an Old Lady Who Swallowed a Fly illustrated by Glen Rounds (Holiday House)
If You Give a Mouse a Cookie by Laura J. Numeroff; Illustrated by Felicia Bond (HarperCollins)
Is It Red? Is It Yellow? Is It Blue? An Adventure in Color by Tana Hoban (Greenwillow)
It Could Always Be Worse: A Yiddish Folktale retold and illustrated by Margot Zemach (Farrar, Straus & Giroux)

4.16 *continued*

John Henry by Julius Lester; Illustrated by Jerry Pinkney (Dial)
The Judge: An Untrue Tale by Harve Zemach; Illustrated by Margot Zemach (Viking)
Julius by Angela Johnson; Illustrated by Dav Pilkey (Orchard)
Komodo! by Peter Sis (Greenwillow)
Leo the Late Bloomer by Robert Kraus; Illustrated by Jose Aruego (HarperCollins)
Little Blue and Little Yellow by Leo Lionni (Astor-Honor)
The Little Dog Laughed and Other Nursery Rhymes by Lucy Cousins (Dutton)
The Little Old Lady Who Was Not Afraid of Anything by Linda Williams; Illustrated by Megan Lloyd (HarperCollins)
Little Red Riding Hood retold and illustrated by Paul Galdone (McGraw-Hill)
Lunch by Denise Fleming (Holt)
Lyle, Lyle, Crocodile by Bernard Waber (Houghton)
Madeline by Ludwig Bemelmans (Viking)
Maisie Goes Swimming by Lucy Cousins (Little, Brown)
Make Way for Ducklings by Robert McCloskey (Viking)
Martha Calling by Susan Meddaugh (Houghton)
Mike Mulligan and His Steam Shovel by Virginia L. Burton (Houghton)
Millions of Cats by Wanda Gag (Putnam)
Miss Nelson Is Missing by Harry Allard and James Marshall; Illustrated by James Marshall (Houghton)
The Monkey and the Crocodile retold and illustrated by Paul Galdone (Clarion)
Morris's Disappearing Bag by Rosemary Wells (Dial)
Mouse Paint by Ellen S. Walsh (Harcourt)
Mr. Gumpy's Outing by John Burningham (Holt)
Mufaro's Beautiful Daughters: An African Tale retold and illustrated by John Steptoe (Lothrop)
Mushroom in the Rain adapted from the Russian of V. Suteyev by Mirra Ginsburg; Illustrated by Jose Aruego and Ariane Dewey (Simon & Schuster)
The Napping House by Audrey Wood; Illustrated by Don Wood (Harcourt)
Officer Buckle and Gloria by Peggy Rathmann (Putnam)
Old Black Fly by Jim Aylesworth; Illustrated by Stephen Gammell (Holt)
Over in the Meadow by John Langstaff; Illustrated by Feodor Rojankovsky (Harcourt)
Owen by Kevin Henkes (Greenwillow)
Papa, Please Get the Moon for Me by Eric Carle (Simon & Schuster)
Perez and Martina by Pura Belpré; Illustrated by Carlos Sanchez (Viking)
Pierre: A Cautionary Tale by Maurice Sendak (HarperCollins)
The Polar Express by Chris Van Allsburg (Houghton)
The Random House Book of Mother Goose: A Treasury of 386 Timeless Nursery Rhymes selected and illustrated by Arnold Lobel (Random House)
Rosie's Walk by Pat Hutchins (Simon & Schuster)
Round Trip by Ann Jonas (Greenwillow)
Rumpelstiltskin retold and illustrated by Paul O. Zelinsky (Dutton)
Seven Blind Mice by Ed Young (Putnam)
The Snowy Day by Ezra Jack Keats (Viking)
Stone Soup retold and illustrated by Marcia Brown (Simon & Schuster)

4.16 *continued*

The Story of Babar, the Little Elephant by Jean de Brunhoff (Random House)
The Story of Ferdinand by Munro Leaf; Illustrated by Robert Lawson (Viking)
Strega Nona by Tomie dePaola (Simon & Schuster)
Swamp Angel by Anne Isaacs; Illustrated by Paul O. Zelinsky (Dutton)
Swimmy by Leo Lionni (Knopf)
Sylvester and the Magic Pebble by William Steig (Simon & Schuster)
The Tale of Peter Rabbit by Beatrix Potter (Warne)
Ten, Nine, Eight by Molly Bang (Greenwillow)
There's a Nightmare in My Closet by Mercer Mayer (Dial)
The Three Billy Goats Gruff by P. C. Asbjfmsen and J. E. Moe; Illustrated by Marcia Brown (Harcourt)
The Three Robbers by Tomi Ungerer (Atheneum)
Tikki Tikki Tembo retold by Arlene Mosel; Illustrated by Blair Lent (Holt)
The True Story of the Three Little Pigs by A. Wolf as told to Jon Scieszka; Illustrated by Lane Smith (Viking)
Tuesday by David Wiesner (Houghton)
Two of Everything: A Chinese Folktale retold and illustrated by Lily Toy Hong (Whitman)
The Very Hungry Caterpillar by Eric Carle (Philomel)
We're Going on a Bear Hunt retold by Michael Rosen; Illustrated by Helen Oxenbury (McElderry)
The Wheels on the Bus adapted and illustrated by Paul O. Zelinsky (Dutton)
When I Was Young in the Mountains by Cynthia Rylant; Illustrated by Diane Goode (Dutton)
Where the Wild Things Are by Maurice Sendak (HarperCollins)
Where's Spot? by Eric Hill (Putnam)
Whistle for Willie by Ezra Jack Keats (Viking)
Why Mosquitoes Buzz in People's Ears: A West African Tale retold by Verna Aardema; Illustrated by Leo and Diane Dillon (Dial)
Zomo the Rabbit: A Trickster Tale from West Africa retold and illustrated by Gerald McDermott (Harcourt)

Source: Copyright © The New York Public Library, Astor, Lenox and Tilden Foundations. Used with permission.

4.17 American Library Assocation Notable Books for Children

So many good children's books are published each year that it's difficult for even the most avid children's book lover to determine which titles might be of the best literary value. The American Library Association Notable Children's Books Committee does this for us, developing, each year, a list of outstanding children's books published during the previous year. These notable books are chosen for their literary quality; originality of text and illustration; clarity and style of language; excellence of illustration, design, and format; and subject matter of interest and value to children. For more information on this published list and other children's book awards, go to www.ala.org/alsc/awards.html. The list below is for the year 2002.

Younger Readers

Agee, Jon. *Milo's Hat Trick*. (Michael di Capua/Hyperion Books for Children). Milo the Magician needs a spectacular new trick and turns to a bear to rescue his failing show.

Alarcón, Francisco X. *Iguanas in the Snow*. Illustrated by Maya Christina Gonzalez. (Children's Book Press). This collection of seventeen bilingual poems depicting winter in San Francisco and nearby mountains will surprise and delight like peppermint candy on the tongue. Alarcón's rich verbal imagery peppers the pages with Latino children's experiences in a multicultural setting. *A 2002 Pura Belpré Author Award Honor Book.*

Barton, Byron. *My Car*. (Greenwillow). Brilliant colors, collage, and bold graphics are combined with a simple text to tell of Sam, his beloved car, and the bus that he drives at work.

Booth, Philip. *Crossing*. Illustrated by Bagram Ibatoulline. (Candlewick). In this celebration of a freight train with 100 cars, a rollicking poem from the 1950s is matched with retro-style gouache paintings.

Crews, Donald. *Inside Freight Train*. (William Morrow/HarperCollins). Freight train car doors slide open to reveal the train's contents in an interactive board book ideal for toddlers.

Ehlert, Lois. *Waiting for Wings*. (Harcourt). Caterpillars grow and change into beautiful butterflies and explore the colorful world of garden flowers as they perpetuate their life cycle.

Falconer, Ian. *Olivia Saves the Circus*. (An Anne Schwartz Book/Atheneum). Olivia, the spunky porcine dynamo, regales her class with her imagined triumphs when "all the circus people were out sick with ear infections," and she filled in as lion tamer, juggler, and tightrope walker.

Falwell, Cathryn. *Turtle Splash: Countdown at the Pond*. (Greenwillow/HarperCollins). Textured collages and alliterative text vividly depict the countdown of turtles from ten to one, leaving their log to rest on the bottom of the pond.

Fraustino, Lisa Rowe. *The Hickory Chair*. Illustrated by Benny Andrews. (Arthur A. Levine/Scholastic). When Gran dies, Louis, a young blind boy, finds all the notes she left for her loved ones except for one—his own.

Graham, Bob. *"Let's Get a Pup," Said Kate*. (Candlewick). Kate's pierced and tattooed parents help her select a dog from the pound, but they all yearn for an additional dog that they left behind.

4.17 *continued*

Henkes, Kevin. *Sheila Rae's Peppermint Stick.* (Greenwillow/HarperCollins). In their first board book appearance, Sheila Rae teases little sister Louise with candy, until a sweet accident inspires them to share.

Hoberman, Mary Ann. *You Read to Me, I'll Read to You: Very Short Stories to Read Together.* Illustrated by Michael Emberley. (Megan Tingley Books/Little, Brown). Vivacious illustrations combine with colorful word placement to encourage the reading aloud of these short, snappy poems intended for two voices.

Inkpen, Mick. *Kipper's A to Z: An Alphabet Adventure.* (Red Wagon Books/Harcourt). Kipper and Arnold stroll through the alphabet, finding unexpected treats and friends along the way in this charming concept book.

Jenkins, Emily. *Five Creatures.* Illustrated by Tomek Bogacki. (Frances Foster Books/Farrar, Straus & Giroux). Through simple words and pictures, a young girl explores the similarities and differences between the five members of her family.

Little, Jean. *Emma's Yucky Brother.* Illustrated by Jennifer Plecas. (HarperCollins). When Emma's family adopts a 4-year-old boy, she experiences both dismay and joy in this heartwarming, appealing easy reader.

Livingston, Star. *Harley.* Illustrated by Molly Bang. (Sea Star). Harley the llama struggles to become a pack animal, until he triumphs as a sheep-herding guard. Suspenseful, warm, and funny with Bang's expressive portrayal of animal kinship.

Look, Lenore. *Henry's First-Moon Birthday.* Illustrated by Yumi Heo. (An Anne Schwartz Book/Atheneum). Jenny takes charge of her baby brother's first-month party in this loving look at a hectic family celebration where even the childlike illustrations seem to be in motion.

Lunge-Larsen, Lise. *The Race of the Birkebeiners.* Illustrated by Mary Azarian. (Houghton Mifflin). In 1206, Norway's baby prince is saved from certain murder in this true story of the warrior skiers who risked their lives one cold winter night. Azarian's strong woodcuts convey the spirit of this Scandinavian tale.

Mills, Claudia. *Gus and Grandpa at Basketball.* Illustrated by Catherine Stock. (Farrar, Straus & Giroux). In four easy-to-read chapters, Gus, with Grandpa's help, is able to close his ears to the yelling crowds so that he can finally score in a basketball game.

McKissack, Patricia C. *Goin' Someplace Special.* Illustrated by Jerry Pinkney. (An Anne Schwartz Book/Atheneum). Pinkney's illustrations focus the eye on 'Tricia Ann, who braves the segregated buses in 1950s Nashville to visit her Special Place—the integrated public library where "All are welcome." *A 2002 Coretta Scott King Illustrator Award Winner.*

Montes, Marisa. *Juan Bobo Goes to Work.* Illustrated by Joe Cepeda. (HarperCollins). This is a retelling of traditional Puerto Rican folktales. Cepeda humorously depicts Juan Bobo's determined but disastrous antics through bold brush strokes, expert use of varied perspectives, and vibrant Caribbean colors. *A 2002 Pura Belpré Illustrator Award Honor Book.*

Palatini, Margie. *The Web Files.* Illustrated by Richard Egielski. (Hyperion). A duck-tective and his partner solve a barnyard crime in this spoof of TV's *Dragnet*, complete with wry, staccato dialogue and colorful cartoon artwork.

4.17 *continued*

Ryan, Pam Muñoz. *Mice and Beans.* Illustrated by Joe Cepeda. (Scholastic). Vivid paintings and a lively text, sprinkled with Spanish, energetically portray Rosa Maria's week-long party preparations for her granddaughter's birthday.

Simont, Marc. *The Stray Dog.* (HarperCollins). A chance encounter turns into a family love affair in this disarmingly simple, gently humorous, and emotionally satisfying tale. The soft palette and subtle touches in the distinctive watercolors perfectly capture the heroic actions of the young protagonists and convey the universal feelings of longing and belonging. *A 2002 Caldecott Honor Book.*

Steen, Sandra and Susan Steen. *Car Wash.* Illustrated by G. Brian Karas. (Putnam). Come along for an unforgettable ride in a car wash that turns into an exciting underwater sea adventure with octopi and other sea monsters.

Stevens, Janet and Susan Stevens Crummel. *And the Dish Ran Away with the Spoon.* Illustrated by Janet Stevens. (Harcourt). Energetic, fun-for-all parody of this familiar nursery rhyme that tells of the hilarious search for the run-away Dish and Spoon.

Willey, Margaret. *Clever Beatrice.* Illustrated by Heather Solomon. (Atheneum). Poor girl outwits rich but slow-thinking giant in this "conte" (hard crayon style) from the French-Canadian tradition. Illustrated with fresh, imaginative collages.

Woodson, Jacqueline. *The Other Side.* Illustrated by E. B. Lewis. (Putnam). Evocative watercolors and telling placement illustrate the story of two girls challenging the notion that sides must be drawn between black and white.

Middle Readers

Allen, Thomas B. *Remember Pearl Harbor: American and Japanese Survivors Tell Their Stories.* (National Geographic). Photographs, maps, and extensive quotations from participants tell the dramatic story of the attack on Pearl Harbor from both American and Japanese sides.

Anderson, M.T. *Handel: Who Knew What He Liked.* Illustrated by Kevin Hawkes. (Candlewick). A lighthearted, yet very informative picture book biography of the noted composer. Hawkes's illustrations extend the humor and historic details.

Blumberg, Rhoda. *Shipwrecked!: The True Adventures of a Japanese Boy.* (HarperCollins). Rescued by a whaling ship, 14-year-old Manjiro becomes the first Japanese ever to visit the United States and becomes a bridge between two cultures.

Bruchac, Joseph. *Skeleton Man.* (HarperCollins). After her parents disappear, Molly lives with a "great-uncle" whose menacing behavior suggests the Skeleton Man in a traditional Mohawk story. Bruchac's scary contemporary novel respectfully incorporates traditional Mohawk lore.

Carbone, Elisa. *Storm Warriors.* (Knopf). Nathan longs to become a surfman with the only African American life-saving crew on 1890s Pea Island. When confronted with his own personal limitations, he sees a better way to contribute.

Christensen, Bonnie. *Woody Guthrie: Poet of the People.* (Knopf). A telling portrait of folk musician Woody Guthrie, whose life and work was highly influenced by his intimate experiences with the struggling poor of the Depression.

4.17 *continued*

Creech, Sharon. *Love That Dog*. (Joanna Cotler Books/HarperCollins). Spare free-verse poems tell the moving story of a boy coming to terms with loss and grief, through his reluctant discovery of the power of poetry.

Curlee, Lynn. *Brooklyn Bridge*. (Atheneum). Elegant paintings, fascinating diagrams, and compelling prose convey the tortuous creation of New York's Brooklyn Bridge. Explaining both the drama and the engineering, *Brooklyn Bridge* captivates readers of all ages by documenting the technical challenge and human perseverance that resulted in a practical structure that serves as a metaphoric victory for civilization. *A 2002 Robert F. Sibert Honor Book.*

Freedman, Russell. *In the Days of the Vaqueros: America's First True Cowboys*. (Clarion). The eye-opening history of cow herding as invented by Mexican Americans 500 years ago and adapted later by the American cowboy.

Fritz, Jean. *Leonardo's Horse*. Illustrated by Hudson Talbott. (Putnam). The dramatically illustrated story of da Vinci's plan for a giant horse statue, and how 500 years later Charles Dent realized the dream with a statue in Milan.

Gauthier, Gail. *The Hero of Ticonderoga*. (Putnam). An unlikely hero emerges when an unenthusiastic student gets the plum assignment of reporting on local legend Ethan Allen, discovering her own talent for ribald storytelling.

Goodall, Jane. *The Chimpanzees I Love: Saving Their World and Ours*. (A Byron Preiss Book/Scholastic). Jane Goodall reviews for young people her seminal studies of chimpanzees in Gome, Tanzania, and her concerns for preserving the planet, in a work beautifully illustrated with expressive photographs.

Gündisch, Karin. *How I Became an American*. Translated by James Skofield. (Cricket Books). Ten-year-old Johann recalls the hardships and triumphs of the immigrant experience in 1902, as his German family emigrates in search of the "paradise" said to lie in America. This well-researched novel has much to tell us about what it means to leave one's homeland for another. *The 2002 Batchelder Award Winner.*

Haas, Jessie. *Runaway Radish*. Illustrated by Margot Apple. (Greenwillow). In easy, straightforward language, Haas has captured the winsome life of a pony named Radish and the little girls he trains.

Horvath, Polly. *Everything on a Waffle*. (Farrar, Straus & Giroux). When 11-year-old Primrose Squarp's parents disappear at sea, her faith in their return defies all adult logic. Set in British Columbia, *Everything on a Waffle* combines quirky characters, recipes, and amazing twists of plot in a striking combination of the barely credible and profoundly true. *A 2002 Newbery Honor Book.*

Hoyt-Goldsmith, Diane. *Celebrating Ramadan*. Illustrated by Lawrence Migdale. (Holiday House). A photo-essay introduction to Islam and the feast of Ramadan as seen through the lives of one American family and their 9-year-old son.

Huck, Charlotte. *The Black Bull of Norroway: A Scottish Tale*. Illustrated by Anita Lobel. (Greenwillow/HarperCollins). Glowing illustrations enhance this Scottish folktale about a brave girl determined to rescue her true love from two witches.

4.17 *continued*

Hurst, Carol Otis. *Rocks in His Head.* Illustrated by James Stevenson. (Greenwillow/HarperCollins). A young man pursues his love of rocks until the director of a museum discovers his passion and appoints him curator despite his lack of formal education.

Kerley, Barbara. *The Dinosaurs of Waterhouse Hawkins: An Illuminating History of Mr. Waterhouse Hawkins, Artist and Lecturer.* Illustrated by Brian Selznick. (Scholastic). With a sense of showmanship echoing the spectacle of Waterhouse Hawkins's own public presentations, this dramatic biography brings the work of the nineteenth-century dinosaur artist to life. Using a rich palette, theatrical staging, and monumental dimensions, Selznick creates an exquisite balance between illustration and design in this distinguished marriage of science and art. *A 2002 Caldecott Honor Book.*

King-Smith, Dick. *Lady Lollipop.* Illustrated by Jill Barton. (Candlewick). Spoiled Princess Penelope meets her match in Johnny, a quick-witted swine-herder and his extraordinary pig, Lollipop.

Kramer, Stephen. *Hidden Worlds: Looking Through a Scientist's Microscope.* Photographs by Dennis Kunkel. (Houghton Mifflin). Readers are introduced to dramatic new worlds hidden to the naked eye in this exploration of the scientific work of Dr. Dennis Kunkel.

Kurlansky, Mark. *The Cod's Tale.* Illustrated by S. D. Schindler. (Putnam). Whimsical, fact-filled text and appealing illustrations tell the story of the relationship between humans and the once-abundant codfish.

Macy, Sue. *Bull's Eye: A Photobiography of Annie Oakley.* (National Geographic). Macy separates the fact from the myth in this dazzling celebration of the noted female sharpshooter. Rich with photos, reproductions, quotations, and page decorations.

Martin, Jacqueline. *The Lamp, the Ice, and the Boat Called Fish.* Illustrated by Beth Krommes. (Houghton Mifflin). In a story and format that dazzles and reflects the culture of the Far North, an Inupiaq family helps the survivors when their ship is destroyed by pack ice.

McDonald, Megan. *Judy Moody Gets Famous!* Illustrated by Peter Reynolds. (Candlewick). Jealous of a classmate's renown as spelling bee champion, Judy Moody devises a series of outlandish schemes to gain attention in this handsomely designed and accessible novel.

Morgenstern, Susie. *A Book of Coupons.* Translated by Gill Rosner. Illustrated by Serge Bloch. (Penguin Putnam/Viking). Monsieur Noël welcomes his fifth-grade class with permission slips for such unlikely activities as sleeping late, forgetting homework, and making lots of noise, which gets him into trouble with a sour principal. This charming and deceptively simple school story presents valuable insights into what really matters in life. *A 2002 Batchelder Award Honor Book.*

Park, Linda Sue. *A Single Shard.* (Clarion). Tree-ear, an orphan who lives under a bridge with his wise friend Crane-man, becomes fascinated with a nearby community of potters. Drawn by their exquisite craftsmanship, the adolescent boy begins to assist the master potter Min. *The 2002 Newbery Medal winner.*

Rumford, James. *Traveling Man: The Journey of Ibn Battuta, 1325–1354.* (Houghton Mifflin). Ibn Battuta's fascinating journey is described using simple text, hand-drawn maps, Arabic calligraphy, watercolors, and quotes from Battuta and other ancient travelers.

4.17 *continued*

Ryan, Pam Muñoz. *Esperanza Rising.* (Scholastic Press). Pampered 13-year-old Esperanza and her mother are forced to flee Mexico following her father's sudden death and her uncles' takeover of their land. In a California migrant-worker camp, they encounter poverty and racism that are mitigated by the support of family and friends. Esperanza's response to the fall from privileged life into a 1930s' immigrant experience transforms her from a spoiled child into a strong adolescent. *The 2002 Pura Belpré Author Medal Winner.*

Shreve, Susan. *Blister.* (Arthur A. Levine/Scholastic). Ten-year-old Alyssa, "Blister," learns about resiliency and fighting back after the breakup of her parents' marriage in this poignant, funny novel.

Wiles, Deborah. *Love, Ruby Lavender.* (Gulliver Books/Harcourt). In Wiles's first novel, 9-year-old Ruby Lavender corresponds with her beloved grandmother and copes with a death in the family as well as her archenemy, classmate Melba Jane.

Yin. *Coolies.* Illustrated by Chris Soentpiet. (Philomel). Glowing watercolors illustrate the story of brothers who immigrated to California in the mid-1800s. Enduring prejudice and dangerous working conditions, they joined thousands of other Chinese laborers to build the Transcontinental Railroad.

Zoehfeld, Kathleen. *Dinosaur Parents, Dinosaur Young: Uncovering the Mystery of Dinosaur Families.* Illustrated by Paul Carrick and Bruce Shillinglaw. (Clarion). Though focused on dinosaur parenting, this is also an exploration of the scientific process and how theories change with new discoveries.

Older Readers

Alexander, Lloyd. *The Gawgon and the Boy.* (Dutton). In a warm memoir filled with unforgettable relatives, 11-year-old David takes a year off to be sick and is tutored by Great Aunt Annie. Her lessons inspire imagined adventures with Sherlock Holmes, Leonardo da Vinci, and a pirate gang.

Almond, David. *Heaven Eyes.* (Delacorte Press). Erin, January, and Mouse take a vacation from the orphanage and accidentally float into the dark, dilapidated world of a strange young girl named Heaven Eyes.

Bartoletti, Susan Campbell. *Black Potatoes: The Story of the Great Irish Famine, 1845–1850.* (Houghton Mifflin). Using first-hand accounts, illustrations, and documents from archival sources, Bartoletti recreates the milieu of a century and a half ago, and links the lives of ordinary people to larger social, cultural, and political issues. *The 2002 Robert F. Sibert Award Winner.*

Crossley-Holland, Kevin. *The Seeing Stone.* (Arthur A. Levine/Scholastic). Arthur, a boy who lived on an English manor in 1199, finds his life meshing magically with that of his namesake, King Arthur.

Cummings, Priscilla. *A Face First.* (Dutton). A moving story of the physical and emotional recovery of 12-year-old Kelley who was horribly burned in a car accident.

Dash, Joan. *The World at Her Fingertips: The Story of Helen Keller.* (Scholastic). Dash brings to life this complex, controversial, and accomplished woman—her childhood relationship with Annie Sullivan and John Macy, and the ideas that inspired her life.

4.17 *continued*

Dickinson, Peter. *The Ropemaker.* (Delacorte). When the magic protecting their valley begins to disappear, Tilja, her grandmother, and two others journey through the empire to seek help in this richly imagined fantasy. *A 2002 Michael L. Printz Award Honor Book.*

Fleischman, Paul. *Seek.* (Cricket Books). In this innovative coming-of-age novel told in more than 50 voices, Rob searches for his long-gone father's voice by repeatedly scanning radio broadcasts.

Greenberg, Jan (editor). *Heart to Heart: New Poems Inspired by Twentieth-Century American Art.* (Abrams). A sampler of original poems celebrate the richness of American art pieces in this handsome volume. *A 2002 Michael L. Printz Award Honor Book.*

Greenberg, Jan and Sandra Jordan. *Vincent van Gogh: Portrait of an Artist.* (Delacorte). Greenberg and Jordan detail van Gogh's life in a compelling and engaging narrative that deftly incorporates quotes from his letters, and vividly portrays the circumstances that so influenced the painter's work and tormented life. The authors adeptly use first-hand material and paintings in their thoughtful interpretation of this passionate genius. *A 2002 Robert F. Sibert Award Honor Book.*

Hesse, Karen. *Witness.* (Scholastic). In simple, evocative poems through the voices of eleven townspeople, Hesse tells the story of a small Vermont town in the 1920s dealing with the Ku Klux Klan.

Hoose, Phillip. *We Were There, Too!: Young People in U.S. History.* (Farrar, Straus & Giroux). Profound portraits of the many young people who played pivotal roles in the history of the United States are accompanied by well-chosen photographs and illustrations.

Jiménez, Francisco. *Breaking Through.* (Houghton Mifflin). Jiménez's compelling autobiographical stories in *Breaking Through*, sequel to *The Circuit*, combine dramatic social issues of poverty and prejudice in the 1950s with timeless adolescent experiences of family tension, school, and romance. *A 2002 Pura Belpré Author Award Honor Book.*

Lawlor, Laurie. *Helen Keller: Rebellious Spirit.* (Holiday House). Helen Keller, the individual, emerges from this carefully researched and comprehensive biography that will make good reading for pleasure as well as for research.

Mosher, Richard. *Zazoo.* (Clarion). After a mysterious encounter with a boy on a bicycle near her home in rural France, 13-year-old Zazoo learns about family secrets, love, and death.

Myers, Walter Dean. *The Greatest: Muhammad Ali.* (Scholastic). Myers explores the very public life of heavyweight boxer Muhammad Ali, depicting not only his fights in the ring but the ones outside as well involving racism, politics, and religion.

Na, An. *A Step from Heaven.* (Front Street). Ju, a girl who immigrates from Korea as a toddler and grows up in California, is conflicted by her attraction to the American customs and her parents' urge to keep their Korean traditions. *The 2002 Michael L. Printz Award Winner.*

Naidoo, Beverley. *The Other Side of Truth.* (HarperCollins). Smuggled out of Nigeria after their mother's murder, Sade and her brother struggle to survive as exiles in London, hoping to reunite with their father. A powerful testament to the resilience of childhood.

Nelson, Marilyn. *Carver: A Life in Poems.* (Front Street). Told from multiple perspectives, this breathtaking collection of 59 poems reveals little-known facts of the remarkable scientist who is

4.17 *continued*

too often dismissed as "the peanut man." *A 2002 Newbery Honor Book* and a *2002 Coretta Scott King Honor Book.*

Nicholson, William. *Slaves of the Mastery.* (Hyperion). In this powerful sequel to *The Wind Singer,* 15-year-old twins Kestrel and Bowman pit their wits and magic against the slave-holding mastery.

Rochelle, Belinda (editor). *Words With Wings: A Treasury of African-American Poetry and Art.* (Amistad/ HarperCollins). A range of poetry and works of art by acclaimed African Americans are paired to create an evocative and powerful exploration of images and words.

Taylor, Mildred D. *The Land.* (Phyllis Fogelman/Penguin Putnam). Paul Edward, son of a slave and slave owner, searches to find his place in the world and land to call his own in this epic prequel to *Roll of Thunder, Hear My Cry. The 2002 Coretta Scott King Author Award Winner.*

Warren, Andrea. *Surviving Hitler: A Boy in the Nazi Death Camps.* (HarperCollins). This is the powerful story of Jack Mandelbaum, who as a teenager was torn from a life of warmth and family love to spend three horrific years in a concentration camp. Vintage photographs, effective design, and engrossing narrative introduce the reader to a man who still refuses to be consumed by hate, choosing instead to live a life of tolerance and forgiveness. *A 2002 Robert F. Sibert Honor Book.*

Wolff, Virginia Euwer. *True Believer.* (Atheneum). Told in free-verse form, 15-year-old La Vaughn faces serious changes with friends, family, and school, choosing in the end to "rise to the occasion which is life." *A 2002 Michael L. Printz Award Honor Book.*

All Ages

Janeczko, Paul (editor). *A Poke in the I: A Collection of Concrete Poems.* Illustrated by Chris Raschka. (Candlewick). Thirty visually-appealing concrete poems are brought to life through stunning collage illustrations—surely just the right poke-in-the-I to appeal to readers.

Longfellow, Henry Wadsworth. *The Midnight Ride of Paul Revere.* Illustrated by Christopher Bing. (Handprint Books). Hand-rendered illustrations suggest the engravings of the colonial period and combine with historic realia to give a masterful sense of time and place in this innovative rendition of the classic poem.

Rappaport, Doreen. *Martin's Big Words: The Life of Dr. Martin Luther King Jr.* Illustrated by Bryan Collier. (Jump at the Sun/Hyperion). In this picture book biography of Martin Luther King Jr., Rappaport's spare text and carefully chosen quotes are carried to a powerful emotional level by Collier's art. *A 2002 Caldecott Honor Book* and a *2002 Coretta Scott King Illustrator Honor Book.*

Wiesner, David. *The Three Pigs.* (Clarion). The plot and form of a familiar folktale unravel as the pigs are huffed and puffed off the page and into a new world. Wiesner uses a range of artistic styles and thrilling perspectives. *The 2002 Caldecott Medal winner.*

Williams, Vera B. *Amber Was Brave, Essie Was Smart.* (Greenwillow). In this beautiful collection of poems and illustrations, two sisters, Amber and Essie, comfort and sustain each other during the difficult time while their father is in jail.

Source: List 4.17 is used with the permission of the American Library Association.

4.18 International Reading Association Teachers' Choices

Each year, as part of a joint project between the International Reading Association (IRA) and the Children's Book Council (CBC), thousands of teachers and students from various regions in the United States read and vote on the most outstanding children's books published that year. Lists of *Teachers' Choices*, *Children's Choices*, and *Young Adult Choices* can be found on the IRA Web site at www.reading.org. Below are recent Teachers' Choices for the years 2001 and 2002, divided by levels into Primary (ages 3–8), Intermediate (ages 6–11), and Advanced (ages 9–YA).

2002

Primary

Beatrice's Goat by Page McBrier, illustrated by Lori Lohstoeter (Atheneum Books/Simon & Schuster)

Freedom School, Yes! by Amy Littlesugar, illustrated by Floyd Cooper (Philomel Books/Penguin Putnam)

Freedom Summer by Deborah Wiles, illustrated by Jerome Lagarrigue (Atheneum Books/Simon & Schuster)

Giraffes Can't Dance by Giles Andreae, illustrated by Guy Parker-Rees (Orchard Books/Scholastic)

Me and Mr. Mah by Andrea Spalding, illustrated by Janet Wilson (Orca Books)

Mr. Lincoln's Way by Patricia Polacco (Philomel/Penguin Putnam)

The Name Jar by Yangsook Choi (Alfred A. Knopf/Random House)

One Tiny Turtle by Nicola Davies, illustrated by Jane Chapman (Candlewick)

The Other Side by Jacqueline Woodson, illustrated by E. B. Lewis (Putnam/Penguin Putnam)

You Read to Me, I'll Read to You by Mary Ann Hoberman, illustrated by Michael Emberley (Megan Tingley Books/Little, Brown & Company)

Intermediate

50 American Heroes Every Kid Should Meet by Dennis Denenberg & Lorraine Roscoe (Millbrook Press)

Animals Nobody Loves by Seymour Simon (SeaStar Books/North-South Books)

Fly High! The Story of Bessie Coleman by Louise Borden & Mary Kay Kroeger, illustrated by Teresa Flavin (Margaret K. McElderry Books/Simon & Schuster)

The Grapes of Math: Mind-Stretching Math Riddles by Greg Tang, illustrated by Harry Briggs (Scholastic Press)

The Hickory Chair by Lisa Rowe Fraustino, illustrated by Benny Andrews (Arthur A. Levine Books/Scholastic)

Martin's Big Words: The Life of Dr. Martin Luther King, Jr. by Doreen Rappaport, illustrated by Bryan Collier (Jump at the Sun/Hyperion Books)

Mississippi by Diane Siebert, illustrated by Greg Harlin (HarperCollins)

One Riddle, One Answer by Lauren Thompson, illustrated by Linda S. Wingerter (Scholastic Press)

The Secret to Freedom by Marcia Vaughan, illustrated by Larry Johnson (Lee & Low Books)

The Waterfall's Gift by Joanne Ryder, illustrated by Richard Jesse Watson (Sierra Club Books/Gibbs Smith)

4.18 *continued*

Advanced

Extraordinary African-Americans: From Colonial to Contemporary Times by Susan Altman (Children's Press/Grolier)
Extraordinary Explorers and Adventurers by Judy Alter (Children's Press/Grolier)
Flipped by Wendelin Van Draanen (Knopf/Random House)
Guide to the Human Body: A Photographic Journey Through the Human Body by Richard Walker (Dorling Kindersley)
The Land by Mildred D. Taylor (Phyllis Fogelman/Penguin Putnam)
The Other Side of Truth by Beverley Naidoo (HarperCollins)
The Ransom of Mercy Carter by Caroline B. Cooney (Delacorte Press/Random House)
The Secret School: A Novel by Avi (Harcourt)
We Were There, Too! Young People in U.S. History by Phillip Hoose (Melanie Kroupa Books/Farrar, Straus & Giroux)
Words With Wings: A Treasury of African-American Poetry and Art selected by Belinda Rochelle (HarperCollins)

2001

Primary

100th Day Worries by Margery Cuyler, illustrated by Arthur Howard (Simon & Schuster)
Bumblebee at Apple Tree Lane by Laura Gates Galvin, illustrated by Kristin Kest (Soundprints)
Crazy Horse's Vision by Joseph Bruchac, illustrated by S. D. Nelson (Lee & Low)
Giant Octopuses by Christine Zuchora-Walske, photographs by Fred Bavendam (Lerner)
Growing Seasons by Elsie Lee Splear, paintings by Ken Stark (Putnam/Penguin Putnam)
Moses Goes to School by Isaac Millman (Frances Foster/Farrar, Straus & Giroux)
Rabbits, Rabbits & More Rabbits! by Gail Gibbons (Holiday House)
The Raft by Jim LaMarche (HarperCollins)
Yoshi's Feast by Kimiko Kajikawa, illustrated by Yumi Heo (Dorling Kindersley)
Wemberly Worried by Kevin Henkes (Greenwillow/HarperCollins)

Intermediate

The Butterfly by Patricia Polacco (Philomel/Penguin Putnam)
Dreaming of America: An Ellis Island Story by Eve Bunting, illustrated by Ben F. Stahl (BridgeWater/Troll)
The Forest in the Clouds by Sneed B. Collard, illustrated by Michael Rothman (Charlesbridge)
It's Raining Pigs & Noodles by Jack Prelutsky, drawings by James Stevenson (Greenwillow/HarperCollins)
The Kite Fighters by Linda Sue Park (Clarion)
Miss Alaineus: A Vocabulary Disaster by Debra Frasier (Harcourt)
Tiger Math: Learning to Graph from a Baby Tiger by Ann Whitehead Nagda & Cindy Bickel (Holt)
Uncle Sam and Old Glory: Symbols of America by Delno C. West & Jean M. West, woodcuts by Christopher Manson (Atheneum/Simon & Schuster)

4.18 *continued*

Weaver's Daughter by Kimberly Brubaker Bradley (Delacorte Press/Random House)
The Yellow Star: The Legend of King Christian X of Denmark by Carmen Agra Deedy, illustrated by Henri Sorensen (Peachtree)

Advanced

Aria of the Sea by Dia Calhoun (Winslow Press)
Fever 1793 by Laurie Halse Anderson (Simon & Schuster)
Forgotten Fire by Adam Bagdasarian (Dorling Kindersley)
Girls Think of Everything: Stories of Ingenious Inventions by Women by Catherine Thimmesh, illustrated by Melissa Sweet (Houghton Mifflin)
Give Me Liberty! The Story of the Declaration of Independence by Russell Freedman (Holiday House)
Kid's Almanac of Geography by Alice Siegel & Margo McLoone (Blackbirch Press)
Lives of Extraordinary Women: Rulers, Rebels (and What the Neighbors Thought) by Kathleen Krull, illustrated by Kathryn Hewitt (Harcourt)
My America: A Poetry Atlas of the United States selected by Lee Bennett Hopkins, illustrated by Stephen Alcorn (Simon & Schuster)
Nory Ryan's Song by Patricia Reilly Giff (Delacorte/Random House)
The Truth About Great White Sharks by Mary M. Cerullo, photographs by Jeffrey L. Rotman (Chronicle Books)

Source: List 4.18 is reprinted with permission of the International Reading Association.

4.19 25 Years of International Reading Association Children's Choices

Over the past quarter century, *Children's Choices* lists have spotlighted the very best in children's literature, including many books that have gone on to become classics.† For a complete listing of recently published books included in the Children's Choice booklist, go to the International Reading Association Web site at www.reading.org. Here's a sampling of titles that children have chosen over the last 25 years.

1975 *Blubber* by Judy Blume (Bradbury)
1976 *Ramona the Brave* by Beverly Cleary, illustrated by Alan Tiegreen (Morrow)
1977 *Beat the Turtle Drum* by Constance C. Greene, illustrated by Donna Diamond (Viking)
1978 *Ghosts I Have Been* by Richard Peck (Viking)
1979 *The Pistachio Prescription* by Paula Danziger (Delacorte)
1980 *Bunnicula* by Deborah and James Howell, illustrated by Alan Daniel (Atheneum)
1981 *Superfudge* by Judy Blume (Dutton)
1982 *Fritz and the Beautiful Horses* written and illustrated by Jan Brett (Houghton)
1983 *Miss Rumphius* written and illustrated by Barbara Cooney (Viking)
1984 *The Berenstain Bears and the Truth* written and illustrated by Stan and Jan Berenstain (Random)
1985 *The Butter Battle Book* written and illustrated by Dr. Seuss (Random)
1986 *Sarah, Plain and Tall* by Patricia MacLachlan (Harper)
1987 *The Tale of Peter Rabbit* by Beatrix Potter, illustrated by David McPhail (Scholastic)
1988 *Where's Waldo?* written and illustrated by Martin Handford (Little, Brown)
1989 *Babar's Little Circus Star* written and illustrated by Laurent de Brunhoff (Random)
1990 *Lon Po Po: A Red-Riding Hood Story from China* retold and illustrated by Ed Young (Philomel)
1991 *Black and White* by David Macaulay (Houghton)
1992 *The Jungle Book* by Rudyard Kipling, illustrated by Gregory Alexander (Arcade)
1993 *The Stinky Cheese Man and Other Fairly Stupid Tales* by Jon Scieszka, illustrated by Lane Smith (Viking)
1994 *The Giver* by Lois Lowry (Houghton Mifflin)
1995 *Clifford the Firehouse Dog* written and illustrated by Norman Bridwell (Scholastic)
1996 *Kashtanka* by Anton Chekhov, illustrated by Gennady Spirin (Gulliver)
1997 *Falling Up* written and illustrated by Shel Silverstein (HarperCollins)
1998 *Birdsong* by Audrey Wood, illustrated by Flobert Florczak (Harcourt Brace)
1999 *Chicken Soup for the Kid's Soul* by Jack Canfield, Mark Victor Hansen, Patty Hansen, and Irene Dunlap (Health Communications)
2000 *Harry Potter and the Chamber of Secrets* by J. K. Rowling, illustrated by Mary Grandpré (Scholastic)

†An annotated list of Children's Choices is published each year in the October issue of *The Reading Teacher*, a journal of the International Reading Association, 800 Barksdale Road, Newark, DE 19714-8139; (302) 731-1600.

Source: List 4.19 is reprinted with permission of the International Reading Association.

4.20 Humorous Books for All Ages, Grades K–6

Humor is created through word play, exaggeration, surprise, and ridiculous situations. Humorous books are among children's favorites. Whether the stories take place long ago or today, these books allow children to understand that life can be fun and enjoyable and that it is not always serious. Through humor, authors not only encourage readers to laugh at themselves and at human foibles, but also to think about a serious problem in a new way. The following list suggests individual and series titles for grades K–6.

Grades K-1

Absolutely, Positively, Alexander, Judith Viorst
Adventures of Super Diaper Baby: The First Graphic Novel, Dav Pilkey
Alexander and the Terrible, Horrible, No Good, Very Bad Day, Judith Viorst
All in One Piece, Jill Murphy
Amelia Bedelia (series), Peggy Parish
Are You My Mother?, P. D. Eastman
A Bad Case of Stripes, David Shannon
Caps for Sale, Esphyr Slobodkina
Claris Bean (series),
Click, Clack, Moo: Cows that Type, Doreen Cronin
Company's Coming, Arthur Yorinks
Curious George (series), H. A. Rey
David Gets in Trouble, David Shannon
David Goes to School, David Shannon
Duck on a Bike, David Shannon
The 500 Hats of Bartholomew Cubbins, Dr. Seuss
Giggle, Giggle Quack, Doreen Cronin
George Washington's Cows, David Small
Green Eggs and Ham, Dr. Seuss (all Dr. Seuss titles)
How Do Dinosaurs Say Goodnight?, Jane Yolen
Horton Hatches the Egg, Dr. Seuss
If You Give a Pig a Pancake, Laura J. Numeroff
If You Take a Mouse to School, Laura J. Numeroff
If You Take a Mouse to the Movies, Laura J. Numeroff
Jamberry, Bruce Degen
Jumanji, Chris Van Allsburg
Meanwhile, Back at the Ranch, Trinka Hakes Noble
No! David, David Shannon
Olivia (series)*, Ian Falconer
Pinkerton (series), Steven Kellogg
Sheep in a Jeep, Margot Apple
Silly Sally, Audrey Wood
*Thomas' Snowsuit** (Munsch for Kids), Robert H. Munsch
Tomatoes from Mars, Arthur Yorinks
Tops and Bottoms, Janet Stevens
We're Going on a Bear Hunt, Michael J. Rosen
When Bluebell Sang, Lisa Campbell
When the Relatives Came, Cynthia Rylant
Wilfred Gordon McDonald Partridge, Mem Fox

Grades 2–3

Aldo Applesauce, Johanna Hurwitz
Alien Clones from Outer Space (series), H. B. Homzie
Anastasia (series), Lois Lowry
Captain Underpants (series), Dav Pilkey
Chocolate Fever, Robert Kimmel Smith
Cloudy With a Chance of Meatballs, Judi Barrett
Company's Going, Arthur Yorinks
Dear Mrs. La Rue: Letters from Obedience School, Mark Teague
Eloise (series), Kay Thompson
Henry Huggins (series), Beverly Cleary
Herbie Jones and the Monster Ball, Suzy Kline
I Can't Take You Anywhere, Phyllis Reynolds Naylor
I Was Born About 10,000 Years Ago, Steven Kellogg
Imogene's Antlers, David Small
Jimmy's Boa (series), Trinka Hakes Noble
Junie B. Jones (series), Barbara Peck
The Know Nothings (series), Michele Sobel Spirn

4.20 *continued*

Lilly's Purple Plastic Purse, Kevin Henkes
Marvin Redpost (series), Louis Sachar
McBroom (series), Sid Fleishman
Meteor!, Patricia Polacco
The Napping House, Audrey Wood
Officer Buckle and Gloria, Peggy Rathman
Oh, the Places You'll Go!, Dr. Seuss (all ages)
The One in the Middle Is the Green Kangaroo, Judy Blume
Pickles to Pittsburgh, Judi Barrett
Ramona (series), Beverly Cleary
Ricky Ricotta's Mighty Robot, Dav Pilkey
Spongebob Squarepants (series), Terry Collins
Wayside School (series), Louis Scahar
The Wolf Who Cried Boy, Bob Hartman

Grades 4–6†

Be a Perfect Person in Just Three Days!, Stephen Manes
Ben and Me, Robert Lowell
The Best Christmas Pageant Ever, Barbara Robinson
The Best School Year Ever, Barbara Robinson
Charlie and the Chocolate Factory, Roald Dahl
The Cybil War, Betsy Byars
Double Fudge, Judy Blume
*Fudge-a-Mania**, Judy Blume
Harry Potter (series)*, J. K. Rowling
Herbie Jones (series), Suzy Kline
How to Eat Fried Worms, Thomas Rockwell
In the Year of the Boar and Jackie Robinson, Bette Bao Lord
James and the Giant Peach, Roald Dahl
Last of the Really Great Whangdoodles, Julie Andrews Edwards
Mr. Popper's Penguins, Richard and Florence Atwater
Pippi Longstocking (series), Astrid Lindgren
The Pushcart War, Jean Merrill
The Secret Funeral of Slim Jim the Snake, Elvira Woodruff
Series of Unfortunate Events (series), Lemony Snickett
Soup (series), Robert Newton Peck
Space Brat (series), Bruce Coville
Squids Will Be Squids: Fresh Morals, Beastly Fables, Jon Scieszka
Stinky Cheeseman and Other Fairly Stupid Tales, Jon Scieszka
Superfudge, Judy Blume
Tales of a Fourth Grade Nothing, Judy Blume
True Story of the Three Little Pigs, Jon Scieszka
When the Circus Came to Town, Polly Horvath

†Also see List 3.10 created by Jerry Weiss.

4.21 Old and New Favorite Books to Read Aloud, K–6

The benefits of reading aloud to children of all ages are well documented. It instills a love of books and reading, models fluent reading and inflection, aids comprehension and understanding story patterns, develops vocabulary, and is a very enjoyable experience. Because listening levels exceed children's reading levels, particularly in the primary grades, books for reading aloud may be at students' developmental reading level or two to three years above it. It has been determined that beginning picture books are written at a third-grade reading level.

Kindergarten

Allison's Zinnia, Anita Lobel
Animals Should Definitely Not Wear Clothing, Judi and Ron Barrett
Anno's Counting House, Mitsumasa Anno
Brown Bear, Brown Bear, What Do You See?, Bill Martin Jr., illustrated by Eric Carle
Bunny Cakes, Rosemary Wells
Dinorella: A Prehistoric Fairy Tale, Pamela Duncan Edwards
Elmer, David McKee
The Enormous Crocodile, Roald Dahl
Flossie and the Fox, Patricia McKissack
Gathering the Sun: An Alphabet in Spanish and English, Alma Flor Ada
Give Me a Sign! What Pictograms Tell Us Without Words, Tiphaine Samoyault
The Great Kapok Tree, Lynne Cherry
The Grey Lady and the Strawberry Snatcher, Molly Bang
Growing Vegetable Soup, Lois Ehlert
Hattie and the Fox, Mem Fox
Horace, Holly Keller
I Do Not Want to Get Up Today, Dr. Seuss
If You Give a Moose a Muffin, Laura Numeroff
In a Cabin in a Wood, Darcy McNally
Last Tales of Uncle Remus, Julius Lester, illustrated by Jerry Pinkney
Lon Po Po, Ed Young
Madeline, Ludwig Bemelmans
The Mitten, Jan Brett
My Very First Mother Goose, Iona Opie, illustrated by Rosemary Wiles
Nana Upstairs, Nana Downstairs, Tomie dePaola
The Napping House, Don and Audrey Wood
The New Adventures of Mother Goose, Bruce Lansky
The Snowy Day, Ezra Jack Keats
The Three Little Javelinas, Susan Lowell
26 Letters and 99 Cents, Tana Hoban

Grade One

Abuela, A. Dorros
The Adventures of Taxi Dog, Debra and Sal Barracca, illustrated by Mark Buehner
Araminta's Paint Box, Karen Ackerman
Bearsie Bear and the Surprise Sleepover Party, Bernard Waber
Bunny Money, Rosemary Wells
Buz, Richard Egielski
The Chanukkah Guest, Eric Kimmel
Charlotte's Web, E. B. White
Chester's Way, Kevin Henkes
Chicken Sunday, Patricia Polacco
Elizabeth and Larry, Marilyn Sadler
Emily and the Enchanted Frog, Helen V. Griffith
Eppie M. Says, Olivier Dunrea
Everybody Needs a Rock, Byrd Baylor
Feathers for Lunch, Lois Ehlert
Good Driving, Amelia Bedelia, Peggy Parish
The Handmade Alphabet, Laura Rankin
James and the Giant Peach, Roald Dahl
Julius, the Baby of the World, Kevin Henkes
Lester's Dog, Karen Hesse
Little Red Riding Hood—A Newfangle Prairie Tale, Lisa C. Ernst
Ma Dear's Apron, Patricia McKissack, illustrated by Floyd Cooper
Millions of Cats, Wanda Gag
The Mixed-Up Chameleon, Eric Carle

4.21 *continued*

The Mud Flat Olympics, James Stevenson
My Painted House, My Friendly Chicken and Me, Maya Angelou
Once Upon a Springtime, Jean Marzollo
The Polar Express, Chris Van Allsburg
Squirrels, Brian Wildsmith
Town Mouse, Country Mouse, Jan Brett
Two of Everything, L. Hong
Unanana and the Elephant, retold by Kathleen Arnott
Why Mosquitoes Buzz in People's Ears, Verna Aardema
The World That Jack Built, Ruth Brown

Grade Two

Alexander and the Terrible, Horrible, No Good, Very Bad Day, Judith Viorst
Amazing Grace, Mary Hoffman
Amelia's Road, Linda Altman
Anno's Mysterious Multiplying Jar, Mitsumasa Anno
Arthur's TV Trouble, Marc Brown
Cecil's Story, George Ella Lyon
Chickens Aren't the Only Ones, Ruth Heller
Cricket in Times Square, George Selden
Dandelions, Eve and Greg Shed Bunting
The Disappearing Alphabet, Richard Wilbur
Ella Enchanted, Gail Carson Levine
Emma, Wendy Kesselman
Fanny's Dream, Mark and Caralyn Buehner
Freckle Juice, Beverly Cleary
Hailstones and Halibut Bones, Mary O'Neill, illustrated by John Wallner
Henry Huggins, Beverly Cleary
A House Is a House for Me, Maryann Hoberman, illustrated by Betty Fraser
In a Messy, Messy Room, J. Gorog
Jumanji, Chris Van Allsburg
Lily's Purple Plastic Purse, Kevin Henkes
Many Nations, An Alphabet of Native America, Joseph Bruchac, illustrated by Robert G. Goetzl
Miss Rumphius, Barbara Cooney
My Father's Dragon, R. Gannet
One Duck Stuck, Phyllis Root
Owl Moon, Jane Yolen
Ramona the Pest, Beverly Cleary
A River Ran Wild, Lynne Cherry
Song and Dance Man, Karen Ackerman, illustrated by Stephen Gammell
Stuart Little, E. B. White
Summer of the Monkeys, Wilson Rawls
The Table Where Rich People Sit, Byrd Baylor
There Was an Old Lady Who Swallowed a Fly, Simms Taback
Tops and Bottoms, Janet Stevens
What Do Authors Do?, Eileen Christelow
The Widow's Broom, Chris Van Allsburg

Grade Three

Babe the Gallant Pig, Dick King-Smith
Castle in the Attic, Elizabeth Winthrop
Charlie and the Chocolate Factory, Roald Dahl
The Drop in My Drink: The Story of Water on Our Planet, Meredith Hooper
Fly Away Home, Eve Bunting
Frindle, Andrew Clements
Gabriella's Song, Candace Fleming
The Ghost Belonged to Me, Richard Peck
Grasshopper Summer, Ann Turner
The Great Frog Race and Other Poems, Kristine O'Connell George
The Lion, the Witch and the Wardrobe, C. S. Lewis
The Little House on the Prairie, Laura Ingalls Wilder
Maniac Magee, Jerry Spinelli
My Great-Aunt Arizona, Gloria Houston
Old Henry, Joan W. Blos
Passage to Freedom: The Sugihara Story, Ken Mochizuki
Rebel, Allan Baillie
Sami and the Time of the Troubles, Florence Parry Heide
Sarah, Plain and Tall, Patricia MacLachlan
Twenty-one Mile Swim, Matt Christopher

4.21 *continued*

Wan Hu Is in the Stars, Jennifer Armstrong
Water Dance, Thomas Locker
Where the Red Fern Grows, Wilson Rawls
Witch Week, Dianna Wynne Jones

Grade Four

Afternoon of the Elves, Janet Taylor Lisle
Autumn Street, Lois Lowry
The Bones in the Cliff, James Stevenson
BoshBlobBerBosh: Runcible Poems for Edward Lear, J. Patrick Lewis
Coyote Dreams, Susan Nunes
Dear Mom, You're Ruining My Life, Jean Van Leeuwen
Gifted Hands: The Ben Carson Story, Ben Carson
Harry Potter and the Sorcerer's Stone, J. K. Rowling
Homecoming, Cynthia Voigt
How to Eat Fried Worms, Thomas Rockwell
Kokopelli's Flute, Will Hobbs
Lassie, Come-Home, Eric Knight
A Light in the Attic, Shel Silverstein
A Long Way from Chicago, Richard Peck
Meanwhile, Jules Feiffer
The Night Journey, Kathryn Lasky
No Mirrors in My Nana's House, Ysaye M. Barnwell
Nothing Ever Happens on 90th Street, Roni Schotter
On the Far Side of the Mountain, Jean C. George
Poems Have Roots, Lilian Moore
Redwall, Brian Jacques
Roll of Thunder, Hear My Cry, Mildred Taylor
Shades of Gray, Carolyn Reeder
Tom's Midnight Garden, Philippa Pearce

Grade Five

Cousins in the Attic, Gary Paulsen
A Crack in the Clouds and Other Poems, Constance Levy
A Dog Called Kitty, Bill Wallace
I Am Regina, Sally M. Keehn
The Indian in the Cupboard, Lynn Reid Banks
Insectlopedia, Douglas Florian
Lyddie, Katherine Paterson
Mary on Horseback: Three Mountain Stories, Rosemary Wells
The Midwife's Apprentice, Karen Cushman
Mississippi Mud: Three Prairie Journals, Ann Turner
The Night the Bells Rang, Natalie Kinsey-Warnock
Nothing But the Truth, Avi
Once Upon a Dark November, Carol Beach York
The Pinballs, Betsy Byars
Seedfolks, Paul Fleischman
The Secret Garden, Frances Hodgson Burnett
Shadow Spinner, Susan Fletcher
The Spell of the Sorcerer's Skull, John Bellairs
A Taste of Salt, Frances Temple
What Jamie Saw, Carolyn Coman
Where the Sidewalk Ends, Shel Silverstein
White Wash, Ntozake Shange
The Wreckers, Iain Lawrence
A Wrinkle in Time, Madeline L'Engle

Grade Six

Balyet, Patricia Wrightson
Beauty, Robin McKinley
Call of the Wild, Jack London
Cool Melons—Turn to Frogs! The Life and Poems of Issa, Matthew Gollub
Crossing the Delaware: A History in Many Voices, Louise Peacock
Everywhere, Bruce Brooks
The Foxman, Gary Paulsen
The Hatmaker's Sign: A Story by Benjamin Franklin, retold by Candace Fleming
Holes, Louis Sachar
The House of Dies Drear, Virginia Hamilton
I Know What You Did Last Summer, Lois Duncan
The Islander, Cynthia Rylant

4.21 *continued*

Moaning Bones: African American Ghost Stories, retold by Jim Haskins
Out of the Dust, Karen Hesse
Prairie Songs, Pam Conrad
Radiance Descending, Paula Fox
Shiloh, Phyllis Reynolds Naylor
The Shakespeare Stealer, Gary Blackwood
The Slave Dancer, Paula Fox
Treasures in the Dust, Tracey Porter
Truth to Tell, Nancy Bond
Tuck Everlasting, Natalie Babbitt
Twin in the Tavern, Gary Paulsen
The Upstairs Room, Johanna Reiss

Source: List 4.21 is from *The Reading Teacher's Book of Lists*, Fourth Edition, by Edward Fry, Jacqueline E. Kress, and Dona Lee Fountoukidis (San Francisco: Jossey-Bass, 2000).

SECTION FIVE

Children's Literature Web Sites and Teacher Resources

5.1 Web Sites for Children's Literature†

There are hundreds of excellent Web sites that are related to children's literature. Here are some of the sites used in compiling the lists in this book that you might find helpful in your search for quality books. Although each site has been visited, neither the author nor the publisher is responsible for any unrelated links or unacceptable content that appear on these sites after date of publication. They are for use by adults only, or for students under strict adult supervision.

Professional Organizations

American Library Association: www.ala.org
(awards, notable books, Web links, recommended videos)

Association for Library Service to Children: www.ala.org/alsc
(news, conference information, links)

Children's Book Council: www.cbcbooks.org
(awards, recently published titles, recommended lists)

International Board on Books for Young People (IBBY): www.ibby.org
(exchange of information about children's books and reading, support, research)

International Reading Association: www.reading.org
(awards, recommended lists)

International Reading Association Online Journal: www.readingonline.org

National Council of Social Studies: www.ncss.org/resources
(lists of recommended books K–8)

National Council of Teachers of English: www.ncte.org
(awards, recommended lists)

National Council of Teachers of Science: www.nst.org/ostbc
(lists of recommended books K–8)

†Web site addresses are subject to change.

5.1 *continued*

United States Board on Books for Young People:
www.usbby.org (U.S. section of IBBY)

Miami University of Ohio/Children's Picture Book Database:
http://www.lib.muohio.edu/pictbks/search/quick_check.php

University of Calgary, Alberta, Canada
The Children's Literature Web Guide: www.ucalgary.ca/~dkbrown/index.html
(awards, ideas, resources, reviews, organizations)

University of Illinois, Champaign
The Bulletin of the Center for Children's Books: http://alexia.lis.uiuc.edu/puboff/bccb
(reviews, awards, related articles)

University of Wisconsin School of Education, Madison
Cooperative Children's Book Center: www.soemadison.wisc.edu/ccbc/
(research, publications for those interested in children's literature)

Government and Public Libraries

Boston Public Library: Booklists for Children: www.bpl.org/www/kids/booklists/listindex.htm
(about 40 recommended book lists on a variety of topics such as city tales, time travel, and so on)

California Department of Education: www.cde.ca.gov/literaturelist
(database of outstanding children's literature titles)

Carnegie Public Library: Children's Booklists:
www.clpgh.org/kidspage/homework/booklists.html
(booklists by grade levels)

Denver Public Library's Kid's Web: http://kcweb.denver.lib.co.us/kcweb/servlet/kcBestStories

Monroe Indiana Public Library's Children's Web Site:
www.monroe.lib.in.us/childrens/children_booklists.html

New York Public Library Children's "On Lion" for Kids: www2.nypl.org/home/branch/kids
(recommended lists, summer reading, awards, adventures)

New York Public Library: Favorite Children's Books:
www.nypl.org/branch/kids/100/animal.html
(Divided into ten categories: Animal Stories; Biography; Fantasy; Historical Fiction; Humor; Mystery; Poetry; Science Fiction; Survival/Adventure; Today's Kids.)

Reading Computer Assessments and Motivational Programs

Accelerated Reader: http://hamilton.dpsk12org/AR
(computer-assisted assessment)

Metametrics, Inc.: www.lexile.com
(Lexile Framework for Reading)

5.1 *continued*

Reading Recovery: http://www.readingrecovery.org
(early literacy professional development, training, publications)

Scholastic Reading Counts: www.src.scholastic.com/ecatalog/readingcounts/tour/
(reading motivation and management)

USEFUL SITES FOR TEACHERS, LIBRARIANS, AND STUDENTS

The following selective list of children's literature sites should be of interest to teachers and librarians as well as students of children's literature.

General Children's Literature

Bibliography of Children's Literature Criticism:
http://io.uwinnipeg.ca/~nodelman/resources/allbib.htm
(Developed to accompany *Pleasures of Children's Literature*, 2nd edition, by Perry Nodelman, this site includes a bibliography of books and journal articles from the 1st edition of the same title. During publication of the 2nd edition, Nodelman revised and updated the bibliography and made it available via the Web. While not a "critical" evaluation of children's literature per se, this site may lead to print resources of interest to teachers and students of children's literature. A 3rd edition of *Pleasures of Children's Literature*, written in collaboration with Mavis Reimer, was published in 2002. At that time, the bibliography was updated to cover more recent materials.)

Canadian Learning Company: www.canlearn.com
(link to the popular PBS *Reading Rainbow* show)

Carol Hurst's Children's Literature Site: www.carolhurst.com
(book reviews, the use of children's literature in the curriculum, authors and illustrators, and professional topics)

Children's Literature Comprehensive Database: www.childrenslit.com
(on-line resource of over 150,000 reviews of children's literature)

Children's Literature Web Guide: www.acs.ucalgary.ca/~dkbrown/
(resources for teachers, parents, storytellers, writers, and illustrators; an index to books and Web sites that contain useful teaching suggestions; a lits of children's literature electronic journals, and book review sources)

History of Children's Literature: www.scils.rutgers.edu/~kvander
(These pages, developed by Kay Vandergrift, a professor of children's literature at Rutgers School of Communication, Information and Library Studies, offer a useful overview of the history of children's literature and link to extensive bibliographies and other resources that she has compiled. A useful resource for the student of children's literature, parents, and teachers.)

The Horn Book Inc: http://www.hbook.com
(Founded in 1924; publishers of *The Horn Book Magazine* and *The Horn Book Guide*)

Internet School Library Media Center: http://falcon.jmu.edu/~ramseyil/multipub.htm
(multicultural links, biographies, resources)

5.1 *continued*

Midwest Book Review: www.execpc.com/~mbr/bookwatch/cbw
(monthly reviews of children's books available in *Children's Bookwatch*)

Once Upon a Time . . . A Children's Literature Web Site:
http://bsu.edu/classes/vancamp/ouat.html
(Mary Ellen Van Camp, Ball State University, is the author and developer of this site. While originally intended for use in Van Camp's Children's Literature and English Education classes, others interested in children's literature will also find the site useful. Numerous links to children's literature sites are included, plus some links for libraries and museums. Van Camp maintains several pages with links to information about contemporary and classic children's literature authors and illustrators, genres, recommended books, censorship, literary terms, and related topics that can benefit teachers and parents as well as scholars of the genre. This site is regularly updated.)

Children's Literature Awards

Caldecott Medal Home Page: www.ala.org/alsc/caldecott.html
Coretta Scott King Award: www.ala.org/srrt/csking
Newbery Medal Home Page: www.ala.org/alsc/newbery.html

Virtual Reference Library†

Every classroom (and every teacher) is just a click or two away from a world-class reference library. These sites and their links cover every school subject and then some. To make the most of these, bookmark the sites on your Internet browser so students will not have to type in the URLs.

Dictionaries

A Web of Online Dictionaries	www.yourdictionary.com
Merriam Webster Dictionary Online	www.M-W.com
My Facts Page Dictionaries & Language Resources	www.refdesk.com/factdict.html
My Virtual Reference Desk	www.refdesk.com/
OneLook Dictionary	www.onelook.com
On-line Dictionaries	www.dict.org
On-line Dictionaries	www.dictionary.com

General Reference

Ask ERIC	http://www.askeric.org/
E-Conflict World Encyclopedia (world news)	www.emulateme.com/
The Human Languages Page	www.june29.com/HLP/

†Part of this sublist is from *The Reading Teacher's Book of Lists*, fourth edition, by Edward Fry, Jacqueline Kress, and Dona Lee Fountoukidis (San Francisco: Jossey-Bass, 2000).

5.1 *continued*

Internet Public Library Youth Division	www.ipl.org/youth
MapQuest	www.mapquest.com
Roget's Thesaurus.com	www.thesaurus.com
Kidzeen	www.online-library.org/young-writers/k
New York Public Library	www.nypl.org/
The On-Line Books Page	http://onlinebooks.library.upenn.edu/
Tales of Wonder: Folk & Fairy Tales from Around the World	www.pitt.edu/~dash/folklinks.html
Amazon.com	www.amazon.com/
Barnes and Noble	www.bn.com
Borders' Children's Page	www.borders.com/

Electronic Journals

BookLinks: www.ala.org/BookLinks/
(Published by Booklist Publications. The Web version of Booklinks provides selected articles, indexes, subscription information, and submission information.)

Bulletin of the Center for Children's Books: www.uiuc.edu/puboff/bccb/
(Founded in 1945, the Bulletin is one of the major reviewing journals devoted to current books for children.)

Cyberkids	www.cyberkids.com/
Electric Library	www.elibrary.com/
Internet Public Library	www.ipl.org

Children's Classics

100 Books that Shaped the Century: www.slj.com/articles/articles/P7068.asp
(A team of experts selects the twentieth-century's most significant books for children and young adults. See the January 2000 issue.)

Children's Classics: A Booklist for Parents: www.hbook.com/childclass1.shtml
(A fourteen-page PDF file of children's classics compiled by Mary M. Burns in 1997. A list of picture books, stories, folklore, and some nonfiction. Click on "Parents Page.")

New York Public Library: 100 Picture Books Everyone Should Know: www.nypl.org/branch/kids/gloria.html
(A classic list compiled by the children's librarians of the New York Public Library.)

Reading Aloud

Jim Trelease's Book Lists: www.trelease-on-reading.com/video_biblio.html#pagetop
(Recommended read-aloud titles for elementary students; kid-safe sites.)

5.1 *continued*

Multicultural Booklists

Celebrations—African American History Month (February):
www.nypl.org/branch/kids/february.html

Dream Keepers: www.mont.lib.md.us/kidsite/dream.html
(A selected list of children's books by African heritage writers and artists from the Montgomery County [Maryland] Department of Public Libraries.)

Celebrations—Asian-Pacific American Heritage Month (May):
www.nypl.org/branch/kids/asian/asian.html

Celebrations–Hispanic Heritage Month (September–October):
www.nypl.org/branch/kids/espanol/pura.html

Native Americans

American Indian Heritage Month: www.factmonster.com/spot/aihml.html
(origins of Heritage Month celebrations from Information Please)

Canku Ota: www.turtletrack.org
(on-line newsletter)

Council for Indian Education: www.cie-mt.org/index.htm

Cradleboard Teaching Project: www.cradleboard.org

Cynthia Leitich Smith Children's Literature Resources:
www.cynthialeitichsmith.com

Native American Recommended Books and Resources: http://ericeece.org/diversity.html
(diversity resources)

Native American Resources on the Internet: www.hanksville.org/NAresources

Native Culture: www.nativeculture.com
(recommended books for children and teachers)

Native Peoples Arts & Lifeways: www.nativepeoples.com
(print and on-line magazine)

Oyate: www.oyate.org
(evaluation of texts, resources, and fiction about Native Americans)

Kids'Zines† (Magazines)

Zines are on-line counterparts for magazines (see List 6.4). These on-line versions are accessible to many students with just a few mouse clicks. Their interactive nature is also very engag-

†Part of this sublist is from *The Reading Teacher's Book of Lists*, fourth edition, by Edward Fry, Jacqueline Kress, and Dona Lee Fountoukidis (San Francisco: Jossey-Bass, 2000).

5.1 *continued*

ing. As with magazines, zines are a great source of high-interest material for reluctant and/or developing readers.

ABC Kids Gazette	www.eint.com/abagain/
American Girl	www.americangirl.com/
ClubZ!	www.clubz.org/
CyberKids	www.cyberkids.com/
Kids World Magazine	www.kidsworld-online.com/
National Geographic Kids	www.nationalgeographic.com/kids/
Sports Illustrated for Kids	www.sikids.com/
Time for Kids	www.timeforkids.com/
WebINK Online	www.ipl.org/webink/
YES Mag	www.yesmag.bc.ca/

Annual Lists of Notable Children's Literature

Association for Library Service to Children: Notable Children's Books: www.ala.org/alsc/nbook00.html

(Announced each year at the American Library Association mid-winter meeting, this is one of the most prestigious noted children's booklists.)

Association for Library Service to Children Awards: www.ala.org/alsc/awards.html

(Links to the awards page of ALSC including the Newbery Award page; Caldecott Award page; and Notable Children's Books from 1996–2000.)

Children's Literature Choices (Annual Top Choice List): www.childrenslit.com/clc.htm

(The journal *Children's Literature* established the Children's Literature Choice List in 1996. It is a national book award list that recognizes 150 outstanding children's books from among the 3,000+ books that the newsletter's reviewers evaluate during a year. The list is divided into six categories: books for children under 3; picture books; early readers; middle readers; young adult; and poetry.)

International Reading Association: "Choices" lists: www.reading.org/choices/

(The IRA offers two "Choices" lists [Children's and Teacher's] in PDF format to download and print a single copy for personal use. These lists are selected by children and by teachers, respectively. Purchasing information for multiple copies of each list is available at this site. The children's recommendations comprise a list of around 100 titles that appears each October in *The Reading Teacher* magazine, which is co-sponsored with the Children's Book Council.)

Notable Social Studies Books for Young People: www.socialstudies.org/resources/notable/

(This recommended social studies annual booklist has been evaluated and selected by Book Review Committees appointed by the National Council for the Social Studies [NCSS] and assembled in cooperation with the Children's Book Council [CBC] since 1972. The selected books are intended for the K–8 audience and are arranged under the ten thematic strands of the social studies standards. Lists from 1998–2000 are posted.)

5.1 *continued*

Outstanding Science Trade Books for Children: www.nsta.org/ostbc

(Since 1973, these lists have been selected by book review panels appointed by the National Science Teachers Association [NSTA] and assembled in cooperation with the Children's Book Council [CBC]. The selected books are intended for the K–8 audience. Lists from 1996–2003 are posted.)

School Library Journal's Best Books: www.slj.com/

(The editors of *School Library Journal* selected the best out of the thousands of picture books, fiction, and nonfiction reviewed during the previous year. Go to the journal Web site and do a keyword search for "Best Books."

5.2 Teacher Resources

Children's Literature

Calkins, Lucy, and the Teacher's College Reading & Writing Project Community. *A Field Guide to the Classroom Library*. Portsmouth, NH: Heinemann, 2002.

Darigan, Daniel L., Michael O. Tunnell, and James S. Jacobs. *Children's Literature: Engaging Teachers and Children in Good Books*. Upper Saddle River, NJ: Pearson Education, Prentice Hall, 2002.

Flor Ada, Alma. *A Magical Encounter: Latino Children's Literature in the Classroom*, second edition. Boston: Allyn and Bacon, 2002.

Fox, Mem. *Reading Magic*. New York: Harvest Books/Harcourt, 2001.

Freeman, Judy. *More Books Kids Will Sit Still For: A Read-aloud Guide*. New Providence, NJ: R. R. Bowker, 1995.

Fry, Edward Bernard, Jacqueline E. Kress, and Dona Lee Fountoukidis. *The Reading Teacher's Book of Lists*, fourth edition. San Francisco: Jossey-Bass, 2000.

Hearne, Betsy Gould, and Deborah Stevenson (contributor). *Choosing Books for Children: A Commonsense Guide*. Urbana: University of Illinois Press, 1999.

Helbig, Althea K., and Agnes Regan Perkins. *Many Peoples, One Land: A Guide to New Multicultural Literature for Children and Young Adults*. Westport, CT: Greenwood Press, 2001.

Lima, Carolyn W., and John A. Lima. *A to Zoo: Subject Access to Children's Picture Books*, sixth edition. Westport, CT: Greenwood Publishing Group, 2001.

Littlejohn, Carol. *Talk That Book: Book Talks to Promote Reading*. Tuscon, AZ: Linworth Publishing, Inc., 1999.

Lipson, Eden Ross. *The New York Times Parent's Guide to the Best Books for Children*, third edition. New York: Random House, 2000.

McElmeel, Sharron L. *100 Most Popular Picture Book Authors and Illustrators: Biographical Sketches and Bibliographies*. Englewood, CO: Libraries Unlimited, 2000.

Norton, Donna E. *Through the Eyes of a Child*, fifth edition. Upper Saddle River, NJ: Prentice Hall, 1999.

Rogers, Linda K. *Geographic Literacy Through Children's Literature*. Englewood, CO: Teacher Ideas Press/Libraries Unlimited, 1997.

Steiner, Stanley F. *Promoting a Global Community Through Multicultural Children's Literature*. Englewood, CO: Libraries Unlimited, 2001.

Strouf, Judie L. H. *The Literature Teacher's Book of Lists*. San Francisco: Jossey-Bass, 1997.

Sutherland, Zena, and Mary Hill Arbuthnot. *Children and Books*. New York: HarperCollins, 1991.

Trelease, Jim. *The Read-Aloud Handbook*, fifth edition. New York: Penguin Books, 2001.

Zarnowski, Myra, Richard M. Kerper, and Julie M. Jensen. *The Best in Children's Nonfiction: Reading, Writing, & Teaching Orbis Pictus Award Books*. Urbana, IL: National Council of Teachers of English, 2001.

5.2 *continued*

Native American Professional Resources†

DesJarlait, Robert. *Rethinking Stereotypes: Native American Imagery in Non-Native Visual Art and Illustration*. Anoka-Hennepin Indian Education Program, 11299 Hanson Blvd., NW, Coon Rapids, MN 55433.

Hirschfelder, Arlene. *American Indian Stereotypes in the World of Children: A Reader and Bibliography*, second edition. Metuchen, NJ: Scarecrow Press, 1999.

Hirschfelder, Arlene, and Yvonne Beamer. *Native Americans Today: Resources and Activities for Educators Grades 4–8*. Golden, CO: Libraries Unlimited, 2000.

Reese, Debbie and Naomi Caldwell-Wood. "Native Americans in Children's Literature." In V. J. Harris, ed., *Using Multiethnic Literature in the K–8 Classroom*. Norwood, MA: Christopher Gordon, Inc., 1997.

Slapin, Beverly, and Doris Seale, eds. *Through Indian Eyes: The Native Experience in Books for Children*. Los Angeles: American Indian Studies Center, University of California, 1988. [Includes *"How to Tell the Difference: A Checklist for Evaluating Children's Books for Anti-Indian Bias"*]

Cinderella Reference Books

Bettelheim, Bruno. *The Uses of Enchantment: The Meaning and Importance of Fairy Tales*. New York: Alfred A. Knopf Publishing Co., 1976.

Cox, Marian Roalfe. *Cinderella: Three Hundred and Forty-Five Variants of Cinderella, Catskin, and Cap O'Rushes*. Stratford, NH: Smith and Kraus Publishers, n.d.

Dundes, Alan. *Cinderella, a Folklore Casebook*. Reprinted by University of Wisconsin Press, Madison, 1998.

Edinger, Monica R. *Fantasy Literature in the Classroom*. New York: Scholastic, 1995.

MacDonald, Margaret Read. *The Storyteller's Sourcebook: A Subject, Title, and Motif Index to Folklore Collections for Children*. New York: Neal-Schuman Publishers, 1982.

Philip, Neil. *The Cinderella Story*. New York: Penguin Books, 1989.

Polette, Nancy. *Eight Cinderellas*.

Rusting, J. D. *The Multicultural Cinderella*. Oakland, CA: Rusting Educational Services, 1994.

Sierra, Judy. *Cinderella* (The Oryx Multicultural Folktales Series). Tucson, AZ: Oryx Press/University of Arizona, 1992. (24 Cinderella stories from a wide range of cultures)

Poetry Resources

Bauer, Caroline Feller. *The Poetry Break: An Annotated Anthology with Ideas for Introducing Children to Poetry*.* New York: H. W. Wilson, 1995.

Koch, Kenneth. *Rose, Where Did You Get That Red?** New York: Random House, Inc., 1973. (This book contains examples of poetry by such authors as Black, Donne, and Stevens that can be used when helping children write their own poetry.)

Koch, Kenneth. *Wishes, Lies, and Dreams: Teaching Children to Write Poetry*.* New York: Harper and Row, 1970. (A description is given by Koch of the methods he used to teach elementary students how to write poetry.)

Tucker, Shelley. *Painting the Sky*. Glenview, IL: Good Year Books, 1995. (An excellent source for the classroom teacher to show students how to write their own poetry.)

†This part of the list was compiled by Arlene Hirschfelder, a consultant in Native American studies and the author of several books about American Indians.

5.3 Magazines for Children

The magazines listed below range in grade level and theme. History, nature, arts and crafts, and poetry and stories written by children are among the topics of those included.

Ask (ages 6–9)
Cobblestone Publishers
30 Grove Street, Suite C
Peterborough, NH 03458
603-924-7200
www.cobblestone.com
Science and discovery articles; puzzles, riddles

Biography for Beginners (grades 2–3)
Favorite Impressions
P.O. Box 69108
Pleasant Ridge, MI 48069
Biographical sketches of authors, world figures, sports stars, and TV personalities

Boy's Life
Boy Scouts of America
P.O. Box 152079
Irving, TX 75015-2079
www.boyslife.org
Fiction, sports, stories, science, hobbies, and scouting

California Chronicles (ages 9–14)
Cobblestone Publishers
30 Grove Street, Suite C
Peterborough, NH 03458
603-924-7200
www.cobblestonepub.com
Theme pack of 15 issues covers topics including "Gold!," "California Missions," "Water," and "Native Americans of Northern California."

Calliope
Cobblestone Publishers
30 Grove Street, Suite C
Peterborough, NH 03458
603-924-7209
www.cobblestonepub.com
Explores world history: publishes original short poems, essays, and artworks produced by readers

Chickadee (grades 2–3)
The Owl Group
179 John Street, Suite 500
Toronto, Ontario, Canada M5T3G5
www.owlkids.com
Nature-oriented magazine containing a single theme, a two-page poster, word games, and activities

Child Art
International Child Art Foundation
1350 Connecticut Avenue NW
Washington, DC 20036-1702
www.icaf.org
Child art projects and activities: abstract, sculpture, and drawing

Children's Playmate
Children's Better Health Institute
1100 Waterway Boulevard
Box 3657
Indianapolis, IN 46206
www.cbhi.org
Creative artwork by children, poems, jokes and riddles, stories, games, and recipes

Click Magazine (ages 3–7)
The Carus Corporation
Cricket Magazine Group
315 5th Street, Suite 300
Peru, IL 61345
603-924-7200
www.cricketmag.com
(Science and exploration)

Cobblestone (ages 9–14)
Cobblestone Publishing
30 Grove Street, Suite C
Peterborough, NH 03458
603-924-7209
www.cobblestonepub.com
American history, articles, puzzles, games, and historical recipes

5.3 *continued*

Cricket (grades 9–14)
The Carus Corporation
Cricket Magazine Group
315 5th Street, Suite 300
Peru, IL 61354
603-924-7209
www.cricketmag.com
Fiction, nonfiction, folklore, and poetry

Dig: The Archaeology Magazine for Kids (grades 4–9)
Cobblestone Publishers
30 Grove Street, Suite C
Peterborough, NH 03458
603-924-7200
www.digonsite.com
Each themed issue focuses on the cultural, scientific, and archaeological traits and beliefs of different cultures)

Face: People, Places, Cultures (grades 4–6)
Cobblestone Publishing
30 Grove Street, Suite C
Peterborough, NH 03458
www.cobblestonepub.com
Study of beliefs, lifestyles, and cultures (including maps, timelines, and folktales)

Footsteps: African-American History for Kids
Cobblestone Publishing
30 Grove Street, Suite C
Peterborough, NH 03458
603-924-7209
www.cobblestonepub.com
Black history, poetry, activities, and artwork related to specific themes

Highlights for Children
Highlights for Children Inc.
P.O. Box 269
Columbus, OH 43216-0269
www.highlights.com
Parent–child activities, quality articles, puzzles, crafts, stories, and riddles

Hopscotch for Girls (ages 6–10)
Bluffton Newsprinting and Publishing Co.
P.O. Box 227
Bluffton, OH 45817-0164
www.hopscotchmagazine.com
Fiction, nonfiction, poetry, crafts, and puzzles

Humpty-Dumpty's Magazine (ages 4–6)
Children's Better Health Institute
1100 Waterway Boulevard
Box 3657
Indianapolis, IN 46206
www.cbhi.org
Science activities, coloring, fiction, and poetry

Jack and Jill (ages 7–10)
Children's Better Health Institute
1100 Waterway Boulevard
Box 3657
Indianapolis, IN 46206
www.jackandjillmag.org
Stories, health issues, recipes, and activities

Kid City (grades 2–3)
Sesame Workshop
1 Lincoln Plaza
New York, NY 10123
www.sesameworkshop.org
Specific themes, stories, puzzles, photographs, and related activities

Kids Discover
Kids Discover
139 Fifth Avenue, 12th Floor
New York, NY 10010
www.kidsdiscover.com
Each issue focuses on a different topic, such as "Rain Forests," "The Brain," or "Incas." Spectacular full-color photos and illustrations

5.3 *continued*

Ladybug (ages 2–6)
Carus Corporation
The Cricket Magazine Group
315 5th Street, Suite 300
Peru, IL 61354
www.cricketmag.com
Stories, poetry, illustrations, parent–child activities for preschoolers and young readers

Muse (ages 10 and up)
Carus Corporation
The Cricket Magazine Group
332 South Michigan Avenue
Chicago, IL 60604
www.cricketmag.com
In-depth science articles, activities, stories, pictures, and photographs and suggested Web sites for middle and upper grades

New Moon (ages 8–14)
New Moon Publishing
P.O. Box 3537
Duluth, MN 55803-35857
www.newmoon.org
Cultural customs, ceremonies, girls from many countries, and stories

Odyssey: Adventures in Science (ages 10–16)
Cobblestone Publishers
30 Grove Street, Suite C
Peterborough, NH 03458
www.odysseymagazine.com
Earth science and space written for upper elementary grades

Owl: The Discovery Magazine for Kids
The Owl Group
179 John Street, Suite 500
Toronto, Ontario Canada M5T3G5
www.owlkids.com
Companion to *Chickadee*: contains articles, projects, activities, and pen-pal opportunities

National Geographic for Kids (ages 7 and up)
World National Geographic Society
17th and M Streets NW
Washington, DC 20036
www.nationalgeographic.org
Science, travel, wildlife, history, and anthropology

Ranger Rick (ages 6 and up)
National Wildlife Federation
11100 Wildlife Center Drive
Reston, VA 20190-5362
www.nwf.org
Nature stories, articles, and colorful illustrations.

Sesame Street (grades pre-K–1)
Time Publishing Ventures
1325 Avenue of the Americas, 27th Floor
New York, NY 10019
www.ctw.org
Activity pages for cutting, tracing, and coloring; children's artwork is featured

Skipping Stones: A Multicultural Magazine (ages 8–16)
Skipping Stones
P.O. Box 3939
Eugene, OR 97403-0939
www.skippingstones.org
Cultural and linguistic diversity within the U.S. and other countries; international pen pals, book reviews, and artwork

Spider (grades 2–3)
Carus Corporation
The Cricket Magazine Group
315 5th Street, Suite 300
Peru, IL 61354
www.cricketmag.com
Fiction, fairy tales, poetry, crafts, and puzzles

5.3 *continued*

Sports Illustrated for Kids
Sports Illustrated for Kids
135 West 50th Street
New York, NY 10020-1393
www.sikids.com
Human-interest articles, boys' and girls' sports, interviews with athletes

Stone Soup: The Magazine by Young Writers and Artists
Children's Art Foundation
P.O. Box 83
Santa Cruz, CA 95063
www.stonesoup.com
Young writers and artists submit creative works, stories, poetry, book reviews, and artwork

Turtle: Magazine for Preschool Kids (grades pre-K–1)
Children's Better Health Institute
1100 Waterway Boulevard
Box 3657
Indianapolis, IN 46206
www.cbhi.org
Crafts, cutouts, puzzles, and picture stories

Your Big Backyard (ages 3–7)
National Wildlife Federation
111000 Wildlife Center Drive
Reston, VA 20190-5362
www.nwf.org
Family activities, read-to-me stories, crafts

Wild Animal Baby (12 mos.–3 yrs.)
National Wildlife Federation
111000 Wildlife Center Drive
Reston, VA 20190-5362
www.nwf.org
Color photos and articles about baby animals; shapes, simple stories, and rhymes

5.4 Author and Illustrator Web Sites[†]

Two good children's author resource sites are:
www.childrenslit.com, *and* www.edupaperback.org/top100.html.

Arnosky, Jim: www.jimarnosky.com
Asch, Frank: www.frankasch.com
Berenstain, Stan & Jan: www.berenstainbears.com
Blume, Judy: www.judyblume.com
Brett, Jan: www.janbrett.com
Brown, Marc & Arthur: www.pbs.org/wgbh/arthur
Brown, Margaret Wise: www.margaretwisebrown.com
Bruchac, Joseph: www.josephbruchac.com
Byars, Betsy: www.betsybyars.com
Carle, Eric: www.eric-carle.com
Cleary, Beverly: (*publisher site*) www.harperchildrens.com/hch/author/author/cleary
(*author site*) www.beverlycleary.com
Cobb, Vicki: www.vickicobb.coms
Cole, Joanna: (Magic School Bus *site*) www.scholastic.com/magicschoolbus/books/authors
Creech, Sharon: www.sharoncreech.com
Dahl, Roald: (*publisher site*)
www.penguinputnam.com/catalog/yreader/authors/1048_biography.html
(*author site*) www.roalddahlfans.com
DePaola, Tomie: www.bingley.com
Fox, Mem: www.memfox.net/splash.html
Freedman, Russell: (*publisher site*) www.eduplace.com/kids/hmr/mtai/freedman.html
Fritz, Jean: (*publisher site*) www.penguinputnam.com/Author/AuthorFrame?0000008926
George, Jean Craighead: www.jeancraigheadgeorge.com
Gibbons, Gail: www.gailgibbons.com
Gurney, James: www.dinotopia.com/gurney.htm
Hamilton, Virginia: www.virginiahamilton.com
Hill, Eric: (Spot *site*) www.funwithspot.com
Hoberman, Mary Ann: (*publisher site*) www.twbookmark.com/authors/22/517
Irvine, Joan: (*pop up books*) www.joanirvine.com
Kay, Verla: www.verlakay.com
Keats, Ezra Jack: http://www.ezra-jack-keats.org
Kellogg, Steven: (*publisher site*) www.harperchildrens.com/hch/author/author/skellogg
Konigsburg, E. L.: (*fan site*) slis-two.lis.fsu.edu/~5340f
Leedy, Loreen: www.loreenleedy.com
Levitin, Sonia: www.bol.ucla.edu/~slevitin
Lionni, Leo: http://coe.west.asu.edu/students/dcorley/authors/lionni.htm
Lobel, Arnold: (*publisher site*) www.eduplace.com/kids/hmr/mtai/lobel.html

[†]For a comprehensive link to authors and illustrators on the Web, go to www.acs.ucalgary.ca/~dkbrown/authors.html. This Web guide includes brief descriptions of children's author and illustrator sites and indicates those that are particularly comprehensive and useful.

5.4 *continued*

Lowry, Lois: www.loislowry.com
MacDonald, Suse: www.create4kids.com
Martin, Bill, Jr.: www.tiill.com/bill.htm
Marzollo, Jean: www.jeanmarzollo.com
McKissack, Patricia: (*publisher site*) www.eduplace.com/kids/hmr/mtai/mckissack.html
McPhail, David: (*publisher site*) www.scottforesman.com/families/authors/mcphail.html
Meltzer, Milton: (*not official site*) www.wpi.edu/Academics/Library/Archives/Worcester%20Authors/meltzer/meltzer.html
Milne, A. A.: (*official* Pooh *site*) www.pooh-corner.com
Munsch, Robert: www.robertmunsch.com
O'Dell, Scott: www.scottodell.com
Osborne, Mary Pope: (Magic Treehouse *site*) www.randomhouse.com/kids/magictreehouse/books/books.html
Paterson, Katherine: www.terabithia.com
Paulsen, Gary: www.randomhouse.com/features/garypaulsen
Pilkey, Dav: www.pilkey.com
Pinkwater, Daniel: www.pinkwater.com/pzone
Polacco, Patricia: www.patriciapolacco.com
Quackenbush, Robert: www.rquackenbush.com
Ringgold, Faith: www.faithringgold.com
Rowling, J. K.: (Harry Potter *site*) www.scholastic.com/harrypotter/author/index.htm
Roy, Ron: www.ronroy.com
Rylant, Cynthia: www.rylant.com
SanSouci, Robert: (*publisher site*) www.eduplace.com/kids/hmr/mtai/sansouci.html
Seuss, Dr.: www.randomhouse.com/seussville
Snicket, Lemony: www.lemonysnicket.com
Soto, Gary: www.garysoto.com
Stanley, Diane: www.dianestanley.com
Steig, William: www.williamsteig.com
Taylor, Theodore: www.theodoretaylor.com
Thompson, Kay: www.EloiseWebsite.com
Van Allsburg, Chris: (*not official site, but good*) www.eduplace.com/rdg/author/cva/index.html
Waters, Kate: www.katewaters.com
Wells, Rosemary: www.rosemarywells.com
Wilder, Laura Ingalls: (*fan site*) http://vvv.com/~jenslegg
Wilhelm, Hans: www.hanswilhelm.com
Wood, Audrey: www.audreywood.com
Yolen, Jane: www.janeyolen.com
Zolotow, Charlotte: www.charlottezolotow.com